The
CATALPA
RESCUE

The gripping story of the most dramatic and successful
prison break in Australian and Irish history

Peter FitzSimons

CONSTABLE

CONSTABLE

First published in Australia and New Zealand in 2019 by Hachette Australia,
an imprint of Hachette Australia Pty Limited

First published in Great Britain in 2019 by Constable

10 9 8 7 6 5 4 3 2 1

A CIP catalogue record for this book
is available from the British Library.

ISBN 978-1-4721-3134-8

Lyric on page 104 from 'A Dreamer Forever' by Latehorse courtesy of Shane Thomas.

Cover design by Luke Causby/Blue Cork
Cover images: 'The Fenian Rescue by the Catalpa 1876' by Henry McLaughlin (top)
displayed in the Celtic Club, Perth. Image taken by Fred Rea. 'A Chain Gang' c1890
by James Backhouse (bottom). Watercolour of the Fremantle Prison Main Cell Block
by Henry Wray (back). Courtesy of the National Library of Australia.
Author photo: Peter Morris/Sydney Heads

Typeset in 11.2/15.12 pt Sabon LT Pro by Bookhouse, Sydney
Printed and bound in Great Britain by Clays Ltd, Elcograf S.p.A.

Papers used by Constable are from well-managed forests
and other responsible sources.

MIX
Paper from
responsible sources
FSC
www.fsc.org FSC® C104740

Constable
An imprint of
Little, Brown Book Group
Carmelite House
50 Victoria Embankment
London EC4Y 0DZ

An Hachette UK Company
www.hachette.co.uk

www.littlebrown.co.uk

The
CATALPA
RESCUE

Also by Peter FitzSimons

Burke and Wills
Monash's Masterpiece
Mutiny on the Bounty

To the memory of John Devoy.
Sir, you are an inspiration.

CONTENTS

List of maps   ix
Introduction   xi
Dramatis Personae   xvii
Prologue   Risings and Failings   xxiii

One   A Conspiracy of Silent Soldiers   1
Two   The Circle Closes   21
Three   Court Martial   41
Four   The *Hougoumont* Hustle   65
Five   Fremantle Prison   85
Six   The Absconder   110
Seven   A Red Letter Day   140
Eight   Bold Fenian Plot   157
Nine   On Their Way a'Whaling   180
Ten   Arrival in Fremantle   216
Eleven   Making a Break for It   252
Twelve   The Chase   273
Thirteen   Flagging Fortunes   295
Fourteen   The Aftermath   319

Epilogue   341
Bibliography   369
Endnotes   377
Index   399

LIST OF MAPS

County Dublin – Village locations 38
South Africa – Rodrigues Island and principal cities 132
North-east America – State borders and coastline 144
Route of the *Catalpa* – From New Bedford to Western Australia 206
Western Australia – Swan River to Albany 241
Area for proposed rendezvous 246
Fremantle Prison area 258
Whaleboat meets *Catalpa* – Rendezvous off Rockingham Beach 288
The route of the *Georgette* 289
The police boat route 289
Catalpa picking up the men as the police boat was in pursuit 298
Route around Rottnest Island 308

INTRODUCTION

We cherish, at the bottom of our hearts, an inveterate hatred, produced by lengthened recollections of injustices – by the murder of our fathers, brothers and nearest kindred – and which will not be extinguished in our time, nor in that of our children – so that, as long as we have life, we will fight against them, without regret, or remorse, in defence of our rights. We will not cease to fight against and annoy them, until the day when they themselves, for want of power, shall have ceased to do us harm, and the Supreme Judge shall have taken just vengeance on their crimes; which, we firmly hope, will sooner or later come to pass. Until then, we will make war upon them unto death, to recover the independence, which is our natural right; being compelled thereto by very necessity, and willing rather to brave danger like men, than to languish under insult.[1]

Donal O'Neill, Prince of Ulster,
writing to Pope John XXII in the 14th century

We're slaves my boys and slaves we'll be
Till maddened by our chains
We'll raise the flag of liberty
And muster on the plains
And sweep the Saxon from our shore
As once we did the Dane[2]

Anonymous manuscript seized from
The Irish People newspaper, Dublin, 1865

They're an odd bunch, those West Australians. They are generators of the greatest, most exotic yarns beneath the Southern Cross, yet there is still this weird, unspoken sandgroper compact they all take with their mother's milk: DON'T TELL ANY BASTARD EAST OF KALGOORLIE.

I first came across this phenomenon when I heard the story about the shipwreck of the *Batavia*, in 1629, on the Abrolhos Islands, off the coast where the town of Geraldton now lies. It was, I kid you not, the most stunning tale I'd ever heard, and yet, despite the fact I was nigh on 40 years old, and had been devouring Australian history for much of that time, I had never heard a word of it. And nor had most people from the east. Well, I am proud to say, I did my best to fix that, and have been thrilled with the response to my *Batavia* book since.

The *Catalpa* Rescue is remarkably similar – an extraordinary tale that is still little known in the eastern two-thirds of the country. A few of those east of Kalgoorlie who had heard of it started telling me about it after they'd read *Batavia*, and I was hooked, knowing that one day I wanted to bring it to life. As a yarn, it has everything, including the only thing that *Batavia* lacked – political inspiration in terms of an entire country struggling for independence. Happily, the more I began researching the basic contours of the *Catalpa* story – an extraordinary saga involving Ireland's quest for liberation, transportation to Australia of Irish republican political prisoners and the quest to liberate them – the more enthralled I became.

I mean, when two of the prime movers in the affair were Irish journalists who were also passionate republicans . . . it rang a bell with me. I have been a journalist at the *Sydney Morning Herald* for over 30 years, and am the incumbent Chair of the Australian Republic Movement.

For what it's worth, writing this book gave me great cause to reflect even more on my own Irish ancestry, and to feel ever more deeply connected to it.

It is something that had never particularly registered with me, until a few years ago when, in passing, my Uncle Alec FitzSimons mentioned to me that a man had come up to him at my grandfather's funeral and said, 'He was a very nice man, Mr FitzSimons, but I never understood a word he said. His Irish accent was so thick.'

I was stunned. I knew, of course, that Grandpa Fitz had come from Ireland at the age of 30, but little more than that. And now I find he was so strongly Irish, they couldn't understand him?

Amazing!

It made me more interested in Irish subjects, and writing books on the Irish–Australian boxer Les Darcy, the Irish–Australian bushranger Ned Kelly and the Eureka Stockade – led by Peter Lalor of a famed Irish political family – immersed me more deeply in Irish culture and history.

For a book I wrote on my family, I travelled back to the village in Ireland my people had come to Australia from in the 19th century – Donaghadee in County Down – and was stunned. It is a small village by the sea, north-east of Belfast, of exquisite beauty. How bad must things have been for my family that they would have left all of that behind, to journey to faraway Australia?

All up, over the years it has awoken the 'Irish' in me, at least in the sense in which President John F. Kennedy famously said, '*Ich bin ein Berliner.*' That is, whatever your genealogy, wherever your people come from, there really is much that is inspirational in Ireland's march to independence, to becoming a republic, their own people once more, after so many centuries of subjugation.

So writing the book for me was both a joy – I loved revisiting and expanding some of my previously covered Irish political angles in Les Darcy and Eureka – and an inspiration.

Over the years, of course, there have also been many books recounting both the story of the *Catalpa* and, more particularly, this period in Fenian history, as well as biographies and autobiographies of some of the key players. In this vein, for the key Fenians, I particularly relied on John Devoy's *Recollections of an Irish Rebel* and James Jeffrey Roche's *Life of John Boyle O'Reilly* while from both the perspective of a general appreciation of Irish history, and the specific circumstances of James Stephens, I drew heavily on *Chief Organizer of the Irish Republic*. In terms of information about Fremantle[3] Prison, John Boyle O'Reilly's book *Moondyne* proved to be a singularly rich treasure trove of clearly authentic detail.

And then there is the key man on the *Catalpa*, Captain George S. Anthony. Hero!

In 1893, long after the *Catalpa* episode was over, Captain Anthony wrote to John Devoy, 'I think I will try and get my book out and see what I can do with it; a bright smart newspaper man has taken all the notes of the voyage (of course some of it will have to be out) and if you will send me your photograph or some paper that has it in it I would thank you very much or if you have any newspaper clippings that would assist me in any way.'[4]

That journalist was Zephaniah Pease, and he in turn would write in the introduction to the book he published in 1897, *The Catalpa Rescue*: 'The facts were contributed by Captain Anthony, who placed his log-book and personal records at the disposition of the writer, and the present version is authorized by the man who was most prominent in it.'[5]

For me, that book was gold from first to last, releasing a font of fabulous dialogue, together with the mood, the *feel* of the whole exercise from the *Catalpa* itself, and I record here the debt this book owes to Anthony's notes and Pease's piecing it all together.

That said, sometimes due to details and original documents being available to me now that were not available to Pease, I have felt that the actual historical record differs from Pease's account, and have marked such occasions with author's notes. I also thank and acknowledge the contribution of Captain Anthony's great-grandson Jim Ryan and his wife, Cyndi, and thank them for receiving me so wonderfully well when I visited New Bedford in January 2019, showing me documents and artefacts concerning the *Catalpa* story that have been rarely seen – as well as sharing the family's oral history. It helped fill out enormously my modern understanding of Captain Anthony's role, beyond Pease's fine book. On the same trip to New Bedford, I also visited that city's Whaling Museum, where I was afforded the great privilege of holding the *Catalpa*'s log-book in my hand, and reading what amounted to the original account of what happened. I warmly thank that fine institution for their professional care, and their librarian Mark Procknik for his help during my stay and afterwards.

In the modern age, there was no better book to call on than Philip Fennell and Marie King's *John Devoy's Catalpa Expedition*, which relied on John Devoy's serialised version of the *Catalpa* expedition in the *Gaelic American* newspaper. Though Mr Fennell has passed away, it was a delight to talk to Ms King in upstate New York, and exchange views on matters on which she is most expert.

Out of Ireland, I warmly thank Seamus Curran and Colum Kenny for their trust in showing me the precious letters written by John Devoy late in his life – suddenly illuminating a key part of the story that has never before come fully to light. I wept.

Now, as happens so frequently with my books on Australian history, I relied heavily on the National Library's extraordinary resource, Trove. Trove, the 'online library database aggregator' – though I prefer to call it 'the glowing embers of the national story' – allows you to search news-paper stories from long ago, find stunning detail, and bring that national story to life. Time and again Trove turned up major *Catalpa* stories, arrivals and departures of key ships, official reactions, the journalist take of the time and then, later, reminiscences from, and obituaries of, many of the key players. Sometimes, even more crucially, it turned up reminiscences from the minor players who, 60 years after the event, provided key detail that revealed some of the missing pieces of the jigsaw puzzle. Time and again, as a story-teller, I felt blessed to be in an age when research that once would have involved months and years of trawling through dusty library files, can now be revealed with a few clicks of a mouse.

Others have done work in the same field, and in the modern era, I warmly acknowledge the sleuthing done by none other than Sir William Heseltine, a West Australian best known as the one-time Private Secretary of Queen Elizabeth II, but now clearly a writer and researcher of no little ability. A long-form article he had published in 2018 in, of all places, the online magazine, *Fremantle Shipping News*, proved the key to unlocking much of the warders' side of the tale, as well as the official reaction to the whole saga. I similarly found another long-form piece by one Eamon McDermott, in Volume 23 of *The Old Limerick Journal*, 1988, fabulous for revealing detailed experiences of the Fenian Six in Dublin as well as the push from America to free them.

In terms of research for this book, I was blessed to have the services of a Bunbury local, Barb Kelly, who is not only a long-time devotee of the story and knew it well, but proved to be indefatigable in finding out more. With the occasional help of her son Lachlan, and counsel from another local historian, Peter Murphy, she was a delight to work with and much of the fresh information in these pages is a direct result of her, and their, prodigious digging.

When I visited Bunbury and Rockingham Beach in the course of my research she, Lachlan and Peter proved to be fine and knowledgeable guides, and great hosts. It was a particular pleasure to tramp through the very bush where much of the John Boyle O'Reilly saga in Australia reaches its climax. On matters to do with historical weaponry – the mechanics of firing an Armstrong Gun, for example – I turned as ever to my weapons expert Gregory Blake. Historian Sarah Drummond an expert on whaling in that period, was also invaluable in vetting my passages on whaling, and contributing fine detail.

I also had key early input from my long-time researcher in Canberra, Dr Peter Williams, as well as Colonel Renfrey Pearson in London, who proved as skilled as ever in raiding the archives in the United Kingdom for historical gold nuggets. In Germany, Sonja Göernitz put typical energy into checking and rechecking quotes against original documents to ensure all, including the footnotes, were accurate.

Though Dr Libby Effeney, another of my long-time researchers, came onto this project later than usual, she proved as invaluable as ever. Working from her place in Mexico, she would clock on around midnight AEST and send back ten hours later. As ever she was wonderful in adding information, subtracting dross and tirelessly checking for accuracy while making highly valued suggestions as to how the story could be told more evocatively.

I am once more indebted to Jane Macaulay for the illustrations and maps, which you will see throughout.

Meanwhile, my long-time friend at the *Sydney Morning Herald*, Harriet Veitch, took her fine-tooth comb to the whole thing, untangling hopelessly twisted sentences, eliminating many grammatical errors and giving my work a sheen which does not properly belong to it. She has strengthened my stuff for three decades now, and I warmly thank her, as ever.

With all my books, I give a draft of the near-finished product to my eldest brother, David, who has the best red pen in the business. When his interest flags, it is a fair bet so too will most readers, and I generally slash what doesn't grab him, so long as it is not key to the story. In this case his deep and long-time love of sailing helped me understand much of the workings of a sailing ship that had previously escaped me, and I am in his debt, as ever.

My thanks also, as ever, to my highly skilled editor, Deonie Fiford, who has honoured my request that she preserve most of the sometimes odd way I write, while only occasionally insisting that something come out because it just doesn't work.

I am grateful, as ever, to my friend and publisher, Matthew Kelly of Hachette, with whom I have worked many times over the last three decades, and who was enthusiastic and supportive throughout, always giving great guidance.

If I do say so myself, I love this book, and acknowledge all the afore-mentioned, particularly, for all their work in making it strong. And my final thanks to my wife, Lisa Wilkinson, for her understanding that I was for so long, otherwise engaged.

DRAMATIS PERSONAE

Fenian leaders

James Stephens. Born in 1825, in Kilkenny, Ireland. Stephens was a courageous and fiercely intelligent revolutionary who was the first to appreciate that the only way to beat the British Army in Ireland was to convert the many thousands of Irish soldiers who were serving with them to fight for Ireland instead, once he gave the word.

John Devoy. Born in 1842 in County Kildare, this charismatic leader of men was a great Irish patriot, who first learned the art of being a soldier at the age of 19 when he served a year with the French Foreign Legion in Algeria. Returning to Ireland in 1862, he was quick to join the Irish Republican Brotherhood, and assigned the task of recruiting Irish soldiers to the cause, ready to strike at the British when the day of The Rising came.

Fenian emissaries in Fremantle

John Breslin. Born in 1833, Breslin was quiet, cultured, fearless – extraordinarily competent. Raised in Drogheda in a large family of Irish patriots, he became involved with the Fenian movement for the first time in 1865, while working as a hospital steward at Dublin's Richmond Bridewell Prison. As described by a contemporary writer, in the later part of life, Breslin was 'a tall, courtly man, whose classical features, flowing white beard, and military bearing, made him a striking personage wherever he went. His history reads like a Chapter from the days of good King Arthur.'[1]

Thomas Desmond. Irish-born, he emigrated to the United States of America at the age of 16 in 1854, going on to fight in the American Civil War on the side of the Union. Joined John Breslin as one of the Fenians' two key emissaries to Fremantle.

Denis Duggan. Born in Dublin, Denis Duggan went to high school with John Devoy. He joined the Irish Republican Brotherhood in 1861, and rose to lead one of the largest circles in Dublin. He was arrested on 14 February 1866 but a lack of evidence led to his release on the condition that he leave Ireland.

Irish Fenian convicts

John Boyle O'Reilly. Born in 1844 in County Meath, O'Reilly was a poet and journalist of great repute. After a brief stint in the British Army stationed in Ireland, he joined the Irish Rupublican Brotherhood in October 1864, going on to recruit more than 80 soldiers from his regiment. He was arrested on 14 February 1866 and sentenced to 20 years.

Sergeant Thomas Darragh. Born in County Wicklow in 1834 to a farming family, he served in the 2nd Queen's Royal Regiment of the British Army for 18 years, mostly in South African, although he was decorated for bravery in the Second Opium War in China. Married with two children, he swore his oath to the Fenians in 1860 before being arrested in 1865 on a charge of mutinous conduct. He was sentenced to life.

Robert 'Big Bob' Cranston. Born in 1840 in Stewartstown, County Tyrone, he was a farmer before joining the 61st Regiment of Foot stationed in Richmond Barracks, Dublin. He joined the Fenians in 1864, was arrested in April 1866 and court-martialled in June 1866, receiving a life sentence.

William Foley. Born in Tipperary, Ireland, in 1837, the nearly six-footer of splendid physical prowess joined the 5th Dragoon Guards in 1859. He swore his oath to the Fenians in 1864, and was arrested for his trouble in February 1866.

Michael Harrington. Born in 1826 in County Cork, the one-time labourer served with distinction with the 61st Regiment of Foot from 1844 and was decorated for bravery during the Indian Mutiny of 1857. He took his oath as a Fenian in January 1866, was very active in recruiting before being arrested on 10 March, and convicted on 7 July of that year. He was sentenced to Penal Servitude for Life and sent to Western Australia.

James Wilson. Born in 1834 in County Down, he joined the 5th Dragoon Guards in 1860, and the Fenians in 1864 – whereupon he was one of John Devoy's best recruiters. After deserting with Hogan in November

1865, he was arrested in Dublin on 10 February. He was court-martialled on 20 August 1866 and sentenced to life imprisonment.

Martin Hogan. Born in Limerick in 1839, he joined the 5th Dragoon Guards in 1857, and was sworn in as a Fenian in 1864, before deserting with Wilson in November 1865. Arrested on 10 February 1865, he was court-martialled on 21 August 1866, and sentenced to life imprisonment.

Thomas Henry Hassett. Born in 1841 in County Cork, he worked as a carpenter, and joined the 24th Regiment of Foot in 1861. He took the Fenian oath in 1864, and was said to have personally sworn in a further 270 members of his regiment before deserting in January 1866. Arrested in Dublin on 28 February 1866,[2] he was court-martialled and, after pleading guilty to treason, was sentenced to life imprisonment in Australia.

John Flood. Born in Dublin in 1841, he joined the Fenians in the 1860s, and soon rose to become a trusted deputy in the organisation. After leading the attack on Chester Castle, he was arrested upon his return to Dublin, and on 8 April 1867 was convicted on a charge of treason felony, and sentenced to 15 years.

James Kiely. Born in Clonmel, County Tipperary, in 1834, he enlisted in the 53rd Regiment of Foot in 1860, which was for some time stationed in England, then Kildare, Ireland, before eventually being transferred to Clonmel in 1865, where he became involved with the Fenians. He was shortly after arrested while undertaking to manufacture skeleton keys to break into the local armoury. He was convicted on 18 June 1866 of not informing of a mutiny.

Patrick Keating. From County Clare, Keating served in the 5th Dragoons. He happened to be in the escort that took John Mitchel to the transport ship in 1848, bound for penal servitude in Van Diemen's Land. He was also in the escort that took Fenian leader Thomas Clark Luby to prison. Keating was arrested in 1866 and sentenced to life.

Thomas Delaney. Delaney was a guardsman in the 5th Dragoons. He was arrested and sentenced on 24 August 1866 to ten years penal servitude.

Key members of the whaling community

Captain George S. Anthony. Thirty-three years old in 1876. Captain of the *Catalpa*, sailing out of New Bedford, Massachusetts.

Samuel Smith. Twenty-nine years old in 1876, First Mate, *Catalpa*.

Henry C. Hathaway. Born in 1842. Fought with the Union Army during the Civil War. Third Mate on the *Gazelle*.

Key members of the Western Australian convict establishment

Sir William Cleaver Robinson. Governor of the Colony of Western Australia. The son of an Admiral, he was born and raised in Ireland and attended the Royal Navy School in Surrey. In 1855, at 21 years of age, the tall but slight lad with a distinct intellectual bearing – his passion was for music, not sports – joined the colonial service as a private secretary, going on to serve as Governor of the Falkland Islands (1866–70), Prince Edward Island (1870–73) and Leeward Islands (1874), before taking up the Governorship of Western Australia in January 1875.

William Robert Fauntleroy. Acting Governor of Fremantle Prison. Arrived in Fremantle in 1852 with his father, before joining the convict service in 1854, first as chief clerk to the registrar, then rising through the ranks all the way to Acting Comptroller-General, essentially Acting Governor, by 1872.

Joseph Doonan. Superintendent of Fremantle Prison. Promoted up from the ranks for his 'sound judgment, industry and high principles'[3] and because his superior thought of him as 'the most trustworthy and deserving subordinate officer of this service and as to education, manners and conduct I think him well qualified to take charge of any convict prison or depot . . .'[4] After a long period as Assistant Head Warden, he took over the top job in 1875.

Francis Lindsey. The Gatekeeper, responsible for everybody who passed in or out of the gates of Fremantle Prison.

Father Patrick McCabe. The Irish-born Roman Catholic was a roving priest for the areas south of Perth, all the way to Bunbury, in the latter part of the 1860s. He kept a particular eye out for the convicts, with whom he got on well. Transferred to Fremantle Prison in 1870.

Major Charles Finnerty. While describing Finnerty as a 'Colonel Blimp' character is too harsh, he was given to extremes of emotion, and inclined to take matters into his own hands, seeking immediate justice . . . irrespective of whatever the law might have to say about it.

Superintendent John Stone. Son of the long-time Advocate-General of the Swan River Colony – the highest legal officer in the land – John Stone is himself the rising star of law enforcement in the colony as the Superintendent of Fremantle's Water Police. Honest. Proper. Courageous. Conservative.

Thomas Booler. Fifty years old in 1876. Assistant Warder at Fremantle Prison.

Warder Albert Liddelow. Thirty-six years old in 1876. A 10-year veteran of the Western Australian Convict Service, he had been with The Establishment for two years.

RISINGS AND FAILINGS

Fenianism seemed to have sprung out of the very soil of Ireland itself. Its leaders were not men of high position, or distinguished name, or proved ability. They were not of aristocratic birth; they were not orators; they were not powerful writers. It was ingeniously arranged on a system by which all authority converged towards one centre, and those farthest away from the seat of direction knew proportionately less and less about the nature of the plans. They had to obey instructions only, and it was hoped that by this means weak or doubtful men would not have it in their power prematurely to reveal, to betray, or to thwart the purposes of their leaders.[1]

Zephaniah W. Pease, *The Catalpa Expedition*, 1897

Imagine a nation the two-thirds of whose revenues are spent out of it, and who are not permitted to trade with the other third, and where the pride of the women will not suffer them to wear their own manufactures even where they excel what come from abroad: This is the true state of Ireland in a very few words. These evils operate every day, and the kingdom is absolutely undone, as I have been telling it often in print these ten years past.[2]

Jonathan Swift, Letter to Alexander Pope, 11 August 1729

There are many noble traits in the Irish character, mixed with failings which have always raised obstacles to their own well-being; but an innate love of justice, and an indomitable hatred of oppression, is like a gem upon the front of our nation, which no darkness can obscure.[3]

The Bishop of Kildare and Leighlin, Dr James Doyle, quoted in the House of Lords, 15 December 1831

Ó, daoine, mo dhaoine, in iúl dúinn

Oh people, my people, let us talk.

Now is the time to tell a remarkable tale of our ancestors long gone from this earth, Irish patriots who dared to dream dangerous dreams, who fought nobly for our country against overwhelming odds, who never gave up even when hurled into the darkest tombs long forgotten at the edge of the world.

This is a story about our own fair Ireland.

There are no strangers in this story, only family and friends we will never get to meet.[4]

Is é ár scéal é. Scéal Éireannach.

It is our story. An Irish story.

All ready? Good then . . . *tús a chur le do thoil!* Let's start . . .

•

It is 1798, and revolution is in the air.

Liberation from your oppressors, independence to run your own affairs, the sweet taste of freedom, all are possible through revolution!

Look to the American War of Independence beginning in 1775. Look to the French Revolution of 1789. Both tumults have freed their peoples from those who would do them down.

But in terms of oppression, could either America or France come close to Ireland? For we, friends, have been under the English boot for over six centuries!

As is written on our green fields in the blood of our ancestors, it was the English troops of Henry II who first came here in 1171, to steal our land, force themselves on our women, and commit outrage upon the soul of our sovereignty. Centuries of oppression followed, punctuated by regular Risings of us Irish, always looking for *The* Rising, the one that would finally throw them out for good.

It got particularly bad during the reign of Henry VIII, in the first half of the 16th century, and even worse during the horrifying reign of Queen Elizabeth I, for the last half of that same century, but still we had seen nothing yet.

For never was it worse than when the newly minted English 'Lord Protector' Oliver Cromwell unleashed his forces.

'The English people were under the iron heel of the Dictator . . .' runs one historical Irish account.

This time the work of devastation was complete; fire and sword had sway unlimited; lands were laid waste; homesteads pillaged, and, in the name of God, the followers of Cromwell possessed themselves of Irish maids, and lands and gold, and made her rich soil richer still with the blood of her slaughtered sons. This time she is not only dead but buried. Before, like the son of the widow of Nain, she had arisen from the bed of death. This time she is entombed. But even from out the grave, dug by the swords of merciless soldiery, she once more emerges; the stone is rolled away for her resurrection, and she stands again to battle for her nationality. She protests once more against England's rule and England's Lord Protector, and fights with a broken sword against William [of Orange] and his hireling soldiery. This time she is not beaten, but she capitulates, and the treaty of Limerick is signed.[5]

Under the terms of the treaty, signed in 1691, we Irish agreed to lay down our arms, in return for being free to pursue our Catholic faith. (In addition, a majority of those Irish soldiers and patriots who had fought the King's army chose to leave for France, an exodus that became known in Irish lore as *The Flight of the Wild Geese*.)

Alas, betrayal once more.

Only a few years later the newly constituted Irish Parliament passed 'penal laws', which unleashed a new terror upon the land, aimed directly at the Papists.

Catholics were excluded from every profession except the medical, and from all official stations without exception.

Catholic children could only be educated by Protestant teachers at home, and it was an offence to send them abroad for education.

Catholics were forbidden to exercise trade or commerce in any corporate town.

Catholics were legally disqualified from holding leases of land for a longer tenure than 31 years, and also disqualified from inheriting the lands of Protestant relatives.

A Catholic could not legally possess a horse of greater value than five pounds, and any true Protestant meeting a Catholic with a horse worth 50 or 60 pounds might lay down the legal price of five, unhorse the idolater, and ride away.

A Catholic child, turning Protestant, could sue his parents for maintenance, to be determined by a Protestant Court of Chancery.

A Catholic's eldest son turning Protestant reduced his father to a tenant-for-life, the reversion to the convert.

A Catholic priest could not celebrate mass under severe penalties; but he who recanted was secured a stipend by law.[6]

And it wasn't just the Catholics. The Presbyterians in Ireland were excluded, too. Only the Anglicans could sit in Parliament, and the good God above knows the Anglicans in Ireland were all English settlers or Irish snakes; you only had to chop off their head and before your very eyes two would grow back. We Irish became wary, and it would be another hundred years before next we managed a Rising. Which brings us to 1798, when, by the light of the moon, with our pikes in hand, we rise, oh, how we rise!

> Murmurs rang along the valley,
> To the banshee's lonely croon,
> And a thousand pikes were flashing,
> By the rising of the moon.[7]

We are the revolutionary United Irishmen and we have such visionaries as Wolfe Tone to lead us. As he would say, we rebels are here 'to unite Catholic, Protestant and Dissenter under the common name of Irishman',[8] and against our common foe, the English.

Our rebellion lasts from 24 May to 12 October, as thousands of us attack the British wherever we find them.

In County Wexford, in the famed battle of Vinegar Hill, on 21 June 1798, some 20,000 of us clash with the same number of heavily armed British troops and acquit ourselves superbly. True, we rebels lose the battle, but the way we wield our mere pikes against the artillery and rifles of the occupiers is impressive.

'I could never have believed,' says our chief antagonist, Lord Castlereagh, the Chief Secretary of Ireland, 'that untrained peasants could have fought so well.'[9]

In the end, however, in both that battle, and this Rising as a whole, we have no hope against so many well-trained troops, and our rebellion is quelled, with the lives of a staggering 1500 Irish patriots lost.

Our great leader Wolfe Tone, who will become known as the Father of Irish Republicanism, is captured, brought before a court martial where he pleads guilty, and is sentenced to death.

But his defiant message from the dock – the only dais allowed to us Irish – will not be forgotten by those who fought under him, particularly the Catholics, for whom he fought so hard: 'From my earliest youth I have regarded the connection between Great Britain and Ireland as the curse of the Irish nation, and felt convinced that, whilst it lasted, this country could never be free nor happy . . .'[10]

Wolfe Tone died before his hanging date – the story has two sides. One says Tone cut his own throat, the other says British soldiers tortured and mortally wounded him. Either way, our great leader, ally of Napoleon and Republican France, is gone.

Can things possibly get worse you ask?

Tá, mo ghrá. Decidedly, yes.

Two years after The Rising, our Irish Parliament, still firmly controlled by the Anglican English, passes the Acts of Union and abolishes itself. Ireland is now ruled by the English Parliament alone, albeit with Irish representatives – so long as they are Protestant. A series of laws are passed which ensure that Ireland cannot compete with England in terms of trade, which sees the wealth of the Emerald Isle flow east across the Irish Sea as never before, as our country grows ever poorer, and England ever more wealthy. Land-owning? No. Most of the Irish farmers, whose land had been in their families for generations, are now mere tenants to unscrupulous English landlords, and the only way they can meet their rent is to sell most of their produce to English markets at fixed low prices.

Though the 'Emmett Rising' in 1803 tries to put a stop to it, and seize our sovereignty once more, it is as it was in 1798, and as many Irish fear it forever will be – a complete English victory.

The years pass, and it gets worse. By the 1820s, hunger has gripped our people and simply will not let go.

We still have a skerrick of support in the English Parliament, however, and some decency.

In 1822, William Cobbett puts it well: 'Money, it seems, is wanted in Ireland . . . The food is there, but those who have it in their possession will not give it without the money. And we know that the food is there; for since this famine has been declared in Parliament, thousands of quarters of corn have been imported every week from Ireland to England.'[11]

We Irish are starving. Writers and journalists echo Jonathan Swift's 'modest proposal'[12] of a century earlier – that the English would sooner support us eating our own babies than share the spoils of Irish labour and land with the Irish people.

'It is true,' Swift had written, balancing satire with pathos, 'a child just dropt from its dam, may be supported by her milk, for a solar year, with little other nourishment: at most not above the value of two shillings, which the mother may certainly get, or the value in scraps, by her lawful occupation of begging; and it is exactly at one year old that I propose to provide for them in such a manner, as, instead of being a charge upon their parents, or the parish, or wanting food and raiment for the rest of their lives, they shall, on the contrary, contribute to the feeding, and partly to the cloathing of many thousands.'[13]

Repeal the Acts of Union then?

Of course.

But Daniel O'Connell, the leader of the National Repeal Association which arises in the 1830s, is insistent in the constant public meetings he presides over.

'No amount of human liberty,' he says, 'is worth the shedding of a single drop of human blood.'[14]

He is a pacifist, and one of the climactic moments of his stump speech is to say to the crowds at the repeal meetings:

'If I want you to meet me at such a time, will you answer my call?'

The answer is always yes. *Tá!*

But if, perchance, someone in the crowd shouts back, 'Will we bring our pikes, sir?'

The answer is always no. *Uimh.*

For, remember.

'*Gan titim fola.*' No drop of blood . . .

And so there is no repeal, no liberation, and the troubles go on.

In short, it is the best of land and the worst of times.[15]

No matter that Ireland remains one of the most beautiful, and certainly the greenest, islands in the world. No matter that our people are industrious, clever, resilient and tend to good cheer despite always being in the face of manifest tragedy.

By the mid-1840s, our impoverishment and famine starts to kill us in our thousands, then *tens* of thousands.

And it is no matter that by this time we have had no fewer than 15 failed Risings since the 1500s, all seeking a return of our sovereignty. For while the famous aphorism that 'an army marches on its stomach' still holds, in this case an army starts to form for *lack* of things to put in our stomachs.

Two years of heavy rain in the mid-1840s, almost without cessation, see a potato blight take terrible hold. Green fields that had once provided the vegetable in such quantity that the people could eat potato for breakfast, lunch and dinner – and did so – become nothing but stinking black messes of mud and mouldy spuds. Without potatoes, our people now begin to starve in the *hundreds* of thousands, even as we continue to export food to England!

It becomes so bad that just about the entire class of common labourers known as *cottiers* are wiped out, with estimates of 750,000 dead. In the late 1840s, a Dublin barrister records that while doing his rounds he frequently comes across children, who are 'almost naked, hair standing on end, eyes sunken, lips pallid, protruding bones of little joints visible'.[16]

In a village just outside of the capital, a woman has been driven mad with hunger and eaten parts of her own dead children – Dr Swift is turning in his grave, to be sure – while other people manage to just stay alive by killing and eating the dogs which had been feeding off dead bodies. An infant is found trying to suck milk from her mother, who has herself died of hunger.

In the village of Greenhills in County Kildare, a 14-year-old boy, James Devoy, lies dead in his bed, with his brother John howling over the lifeless corpse, his knees swollen and bleeding from hours spent kneeling, praying for his brother's soul. John's knees were barely healed when he refused to sing 'God Save the Queen' at his school's morning assembly. The Superintendent was called for.

'Sing, sir!'[17] he commands the boy.

John trembles in defiant silence.

Crack! The Superintendent brings a piece of slate down on young John's skull.

'I vowed,' the lad would later recount, 'that when I grew big enough I would lick him . . .'[18]

In the meantime, when he returns to school a few days later, the Superintendent is waiting once more, this time with a cane. But the young Irish lad won't have it. He rams the master's thighs, he kicks his shins, he throws him off balance and . . . is summarily expelled. It is his first taste of rebellion, certainly not his last. Remember the name of John Devoy, my friends, for he is a remarkable Irishman who we shall meet again in this tale.

On a farm in County Down, a 16-year-old lad by the name of Séamus McNally survives starvation, *in extremis*, but vows never to forget who and what has done this to him, his family and his country – the British occupiers. And of course, there are other characters in our story who lived through the great hunger . . .

Down in County Cavan, another 16-year-old by the name of James Reynolds – equally devastated by the death and starvation all around – manages to scrape together the price of a ticket and escapes to America to start again.

In County Cork a young fellow by the name of Jeremiah O'Donovan Rossa sees his idyllic childhood torn asunder, and his family, with five others, must flee to America. 'Five or six other families were going away,' he would ever after recount, 'and there were five or six cars to carry them and all they could carry with them, to the cove of Cork. The cry of the weeping and wailing of that day rings in my ears still.'[19]

They are just a handful of an estimated 1.5 million Irish who emigrate at this time, many to the New World, forming a diaspora unlike any the world has ever seen.

Those who remain must suffer as the famine goes on to kill more than one million Irish, about a third of the population.[20]

For the large Breslin family, living in the ancient town of Drogheda, it deepens their already avowed nationalism, and they become determined to do all it takes to throw off the shackles of their occupiers once and for all.

Meanwhile there appears to be no sympathy from England.

It will become part of legend that at the height of the famine, the London *Times* gloats: 'They are going! They are going! The Irish are going with a vengeance! Soon a Celt will be as rare in Ireland as a red Indian on the shores of Manhattan!'[21]

Either way, there is no doubt that the land's English rulers really do sit on their hands and do *nothing* while people die.

For while the grip of starvation has taken a grim hold, the political grip of England is stronger still. Even when violent protests break out over ongoing corn exports, the British Government sends in 2000 armed troops to quell them.

Protests are not allowed, and sympathy is officially frowned upon. For the famine, in the view of Charles Trevelyan, the head of the UK Treasury, is simply a 'mechanism for reducing surplus population'.[22]

As to the cause? There is no doubt.

'The judgement of God sent the calamity to teach the Irish a lesson,' he writes, 'and that calamity must not be too much mitigated ... The real evil with which we have to contend is not the physical evil of the Famine, but the moral evil of the selfish, perverse and turbulent character of the people.'[23]

One of our great Irish revolutionary leaders, John Mitchel, disagrees.

'The Almighty, indeed, sent the potato blight, but the English created the famine.'[24]

A master of the quill – he can make words dance, or march, as he likes – Mitchel would go on, recounting of the famine, 'I could see, in front of the cottages, little children leaning against a fence when the sun shone out for they could not stand, their limbs fleshless, their bodies half-naked, their faces bloated yet wrinkled, and of a pale, greenish hue ... I saw Trevelyan's claw in the vitals of those children: his red tape would draw them to death: in his government laboratory he had prepared for them the typhus poison.'[25]

Many of the Irish at home and abroad will never forgive Trevelyan's actions, nor other British outrages, and the momentum of a violent separatist movement committed to Ireland establishing Home Rule, free from the British, begins to gather weight ...

In the stately home of Tenakill, in the village of Raheen, Queen's County, right in the heart of fiercely Catholic Ireland, a 42-year-old man by the name of Fintan Lalor is in the thick of the struggle for the people's rights from the beginning. Like many in the newly created 'Young Ireland' movement, which he is one of the leaders of, he has a rage within him that drives him away from peaceful resolution towards bloody revolution.

To that end, he continually displays his eloquence and courage for the cause in the public domain, speaking at meetings and writing to journals, while also doing more clandestine work away from the gaze of the authorities. Inspiring passion in others is where he excels.

He publishes a thundering editorial in the *Irish Felon*, on 1 July 1848, addressed directly to the British Government:

```
We hold the present existing government of this
island, and all existing rights of property in our
soil, to be mere usurpation and tyranny, and to be
null and void as of moral effect; and our purpose is
to abolish them utterly, or lose our lives in the
attempt. The right founded on conquest and affirmed
```

```
by laws made by the conquerors themselves, we
regard as no other than the right of the robber on
a larger scale. We owe no obedience to laws enacted
by another nation without our assent; nor respect to
assumed rights of property which are starving and
exterminating our people . . .26
```

Lalor is far from alone in his outrage as our people begin to rise once more. Pikes are sharpened. What arms we can secure are oiled and hidden, ready for action. Quietly, revolutionary groups are formed across the country, ready for the next Rising.

A group of revolutionary leaders arise to support Fintan Lalor and John Mitchel – who London's *Punch* magazine now portrays as an Irish monkey challenging the Great British Lion[27] – their numbers including William Smith O'Brien, Thomas Francis Meagher and John Blake Dillon, who move around the country, from parish to parish, preaching sedition, asking the people to ready themselves.

And the English prepare in turn. Fresh troops arrive from England. Artillerymen with enormous cannon make their way from the docks down Dublin's main thoroughfare, Sackville Street.

In London, in the so-called Parliament of the United Kingdom of Great Britain and Ireland, an Act is passed, dictating 'that anyone who should levy war against the Queen, or endeavour to deprive her of her title, or by open or advised speaking, printing, or publishing, incite others to the same, should be deemed guilty of felony . . .'[28]

But, as has been always the way, we Irish are never so strong, so impassioned, so unbending, as when we have the British bayonets to our bellies and our backs to the wall. Things are building to a climax, and who better than Fintan Lalor himself to provide the literary spark?

'We have determined,' he writes in the *Irish Felon* on 1 July 1848, 'to set about creating, as speedily as possible a military organisation . . .'[29]

Yes, that's it. The way to overcome the English must be by means of an actual military unit, designed with discipline, trained to perfection. For Ireland, Lalor writes, must 'close for our final struggle with England', to ensure that she could be, 'Ireland her own, and all therein, from the sod to the sky . . . without suit or service, faith or fealty, rent or render, to any power under Heaven.'[30]

And even then, he is really only warming up.

'Remember this,' he famously wrote in another article for the *Irish Felon* three weeks later, his words strong enough to echo through the ages, 'that *somewhere, somehow*, and by *somebody, a beginning must be made . . .*'[31]

'Who strikes the first blow for Ireland? Who draws first blood for Ireland? Who wins a wreath that will be green for ever?'[32]

Less than a week after publishing that last diatribe, brave Fintan Lalor is arrested and thrown into prison. Though he dies soon afterwards, his work goes on.

For the answer to Lalor's question, as to who would strike the first blow for Ireland, is emerging at the very time he pens the words . . .

His name is James Stephens and he hails from the green hills of Kilkenny. Fire is in his blood.

In his first public speech, on 25 July 1848 – just three days after Fintan Lalor had posed the question – the 23-year-old firebrand member of the Young Ireland movement, spurred on by the revolutions taking place on the Continent this very year, promotes armed insurrection as the only solution, calling on the peasants to take up arms and confront, 'the perils and the honours of a righteous war'.[33]

With the British moving to crush the building Rising by arresting leaders and calling on all Young Ireland rebels to hand in their weapons, Stephens' instinct is Shakespearean in scope. He really does want all of the peasantry 'to take arms against a sea of troubles, and by opposing end them'.[34]

From the stage in his native Kilkenny – he knows these people as his friends and neighbours, and they know him as the remarkably intelligent son of a fine family – he urges the people to join him.

'Friends,' he thunders, his left eye curiously closing as if taking aim along some unseen rifle, 'you are called upon by a proclamation of the British Executive to surrender such arms as you may have in your possession, and you are threatened with all the pains and penalties of the law from retaining them after tomorrow's sunset. Now, my deliberate advice to you is this. Treasure your arms as you would the apples of your eyes, and bury them safely with the hope of a happy resurrection.'[35]

There is something about Stephens' passion, his glittering eyes, his confidence that not only will the battle be fought, but that it will be won, which makes his words compelling.

He is a man who may strike the first blow for Ireland . . . but not yet.

For when The Rising comes, just four days after his speech, a national-ist revolt led by William Smith O'Brien against English rule, it does not go as planned.

A clue to just how small scale the failed last stand of the Young Irelanders in the Tipperary village of Ballingarry was is provided by the name the disparaging British press gave it: 'The Battle of Widow McCormack's Cabbage Patch' – referring to the small plot of land where the clash took place.

Smith O'Brien's hopes that the Irish peasantry would rise with them prove misguided. For the Irish peasants, now in the third year of the famine, less urgent than supporting the nationalists is feeding their families.

That night, young James Stephens finds himself on the run, along with the likes of John O'Mahony, Michael Doheny and Terence Bellew MacManus – as British police and soldiers search up hill and down dale for them.

Stephens, clever as he is, hires a cart from a sympathiser and returns to his own newly established nest. For in his previous travels, Stephens 'had encountered in Tipperary a young lady whose bright eyes had made sad havoc with the heart of the youthful patriot'.[36] (Every good tale has a little romance.) Her name is Jane Hopper, and Stephens is as smitten with her as she is with him.

After spending a few delightful days in her company, being succoured, nursed and fed – such pleasant respite for a wounded outlaw at the prospective in-laws' – Stephens becomes known to a nosey local magis-trate and he is forced to move on.

Eventually, after weeks of secretive dilly-dallying about the lush Comeragh mountains, Stephens is able to make his escape in an extraordinary manner, first dressed as the maid of a well-born lady and famous poetess of the day, Mrs Downing – his gentle, youthful features are perfect for the part – he travels to London before heading to Paris.

And where better for a young revolutionary?

> Bliss was it in that dawn to be alive,
> But to be young was very heaven![37]

The world's cradle of revolutionary thought, Paris proves to be the perfect place for a rising rebel like Stephens to grow his budding ideas, to refine his craft over coming years, studying and planning, supping from the font of European republicanism, while barely feeding himself by teaching English. The fact he is joined by two other rebels from the battle at Mrs

McCormack's cabbage patch – the shrewd yet prickly barrister, Michael Doheny, and the suave Irish scholar, John O'Mahony – at least makes his exile easier to bear in the first instance.

In the early 1850s, Doheny and O'Mahony make for New York with loose promises to stay in touch about all matters revolutionary, while Stephens stays … plotting, honing his best-laid plan with a rare dedication, waiting for a time to return to his homeland and begin its execution. In his leisure hours, he enjoys the society around him.

'I became,' Stephens would recount, 'the intimate friend of three men whose names were famous throughout France: Beranger, the great French poet and ballad writer; Alexander Dumas the elder, author of *The Count of Monte Cristo*, and Colonel Miles Byrne, a retired officer of the French army.'[38]

It is no less than Dumas who introduces him to a Parisian publisher who accepts the Irishman's proposal to translate the masterpieces of Charles Dickens' – *Nicholas Nickleby*, *David Copperfield* and *Martin Chuzzlewit* – into French, for the princely sum of 5000 francs per volume, to supplement the income he earns by teaching.

But as well as teaching and translating, he learns.

Stephens no longer believes that peasants armed with pikes, no matter their numbers, would ever be a match for the trained and well-armed soldiers of the British Army. No, the Irish must *organise*, they need trained soldiers of their own, they need arms, and he is already nurturing some ideas as to how that might be accomplished.

How had the Europeans and Americans done it, in their revolutions? By secret societies? By infiltrating every level of government and the army with their own people, who could then conspire to bring that government down, and turn the army to their side? The Carbonari movement in Italy and Mazzini's Young Italy certainly thrived on secrecy.

For, yes, Stephens becomes ever more convinced: they must assemble an army of their own!

Stephens' ideas begin to germinate, to the point that he decides, after seven years in Paris, the time is right to return to Ireland.

'I was irresistibly attracted towards revolutionary politics,' he will note at the end of seven years' exile. 'I hated the sedentary life of the littérateur, and my desk appeared as an instrument of torture. I passionately longed for work – to do something for the welfare of the race in whose defence I risked my career, and for whose interests I should be proud to die ... At last, not able to resist its powers any longer, I gave it free rein, and left Paris towards the close of 1855.'[39]

So it is that in 1856, Stephens returns to his homeland, hauls a knapsack over his shoulders, takes a staff in hand and begins an odyssey of 3000 miles, going from door to door around the Emerald Isle.

Disguised variously as a beggar and priest, he talks to all who will lend him an ear – friends, countrymen, the veterans of '48, common folk, farmers, tradesmen, scholars, sailors and soldiers – planting the seeds of his grand project. In the process, he attracts the Irish nickname of *Seabhach Siulach* ('Mr Shooks'), which means the Wandering Hawk, and when the Hawk comes into land, he never misses his mark. In his mesmerising tones, his well-turned and seductive phrases, he massages their sympathy for the cause – a free Ireland, independent of British rule! – and then proposes the way forward. We need to have a secret society, a brotherhood of revolutionary republicans readying for a Rising, with our members embedded in every part of the country, threaded through all her institutions, including – most importantly of all – in Her Majesty's armed forces. But it is not enough for the people to join, they need to encourage others to join and do it in a manner where the secret will be kept.

And so he keeps going, travelling throughout the country for over a year, a wandering minstrel of mayhem to come. Yes, his feet blister, and his muscles ache, but onwards he marches in the name of fair Erin, powered by the idea that she could at last be free if only her people are properly organised. And with every mile travelled the idea actually starts to crystallise into what will become one of the largest secret military societies the world has ever known – the Irish Republican Brotherhood.

At its head, James Stephens, who gives himself the title of 'Provisional Dictator' to affirm that he has absolute authority over the enterprise. He equally insists that to take his place among the ranks of the Brotherhood, a man must take an oath. So let's get started. On this night of Saint Patrick's Day of 1858, in a home in Dublin, James Stephens has his friend and fellow firebrand patriot Thomas Clarke Luby place his hand on the Bible, and repeat after him the sacred words they have worked out.

'I, Thomas Clarke Luby, do solemnly swear, in the presence of Almighty God, that I will do my utmost, at every risk, while life lasts, to make Ireland an Independent Democratic Republic; that I will yield implicit obedience, in all things not contrary to the Law of God, to the commands of my superior officers, and that I shall preserve inviolable secrecy regarding all transactions of this Secret Society that may be confided in me. So help me God! Amen.'[40]

Others quickly follow, swearing their own oath, bursting with pride and hope, certain that they are part of a great moment in history, and all because of the leadership of one great man.

'At this time,' one of those present, the patriotic Joseph Denieffe, would later recall, 'Stephens was at the highest notch in my estimation. He was grand. I would undertake anything for him. He seemed to have me under a spell. He was the only practical man I had met in the Movement up to that time. There was earnestness in his every move. He was abstemious, frugal – in fact, in adversity his greatest qualities were shown to perfection. He was all that could be desired as a leader.'[41]

And how does Stephens plan to swear in more men, beyond his considerable charisma? Each new oath-bound member is appointed as an 'A', or a 'Centre', also known as a 'Lieutenant'. He is given permission from Stephens to recruit nine 'B's, to be known as Captains. The 'B's then are given permission from their Centre to recruit nine 'C's, or Sergeants. Each 'C' can recruit nine 'D's, to be known as Privates. To preserve secrecy, Stephens insists that his strict instructions must be ruthlessly adhered to: each recruited member can only know his superior officer and the men in their own secret cell. This cell, consisting of a Centre/Lieutenant/'A' at the top and going down through the ranks to the Privates/'D's, is called a 'circle'. According to this arrangement, every circle consisted of one 'A', nine 'B's, 81 'C's and 729 'D's, to make 820 members in all – in three dimensions, it looks a lot like a cone.

By sheer force of Stephens' energy, inspiration and powers of persuasion the IRB begins to take shape, with an expanding network of circles all in orbit around their shining sun, one man – him.

Stephens' men move through the countryside for years, swearing ever more 'Centres'. Most crucially they start the delicate work of recruiting and swearing in Irish soldiers serving in British Army regiments stationed in Ireland. In many ways it is not as difficult as they feared, as so many of the soldiers have only taken the English shilling to feed their families, but are as passionate for the cause of Ireland as they had been in their teens, when they had seen their families die of famine and suffer from eviction. A chance to strike back, right at the English heart? Yes!

Some new recruits know Stephens personally, but he is never referred to by name. He is the 'Head Centre' in Ireland, or simply 'The Captain', and merely the invocation of his name, saying 'The Captain desires . . .'

is enough to see it done. The shadowy fame of 'The Captain' grows, as does the power of the IRB.

And the most wonderful thing is that they are not alone. In America – the most obvious destination for those needing an English-speaking republic to go to, a country that had already so famously and fabulously broken free of English rule – the Irish diaspora forms its own society under the leadership of Stephens' old friends John O'Mahony and Michael Doheny. It is called the Fenian Brotherhood, with the word Fenian coming from very deep Irish roots – an ancient and fabled warrior and huntsmen clan, skilled in poetry, which flourished in the 3rd century AD, much celebrated in tales and ballads in Irish literature.

The broad plan is for the Irish–Americans to send money, men and munitions to the IRB in Ireland, in preparation for The Rising.

But even the best-laid plans have a way of going awry, and the British soon get wind of some kind of secret plot involving a secret society and a secretive personage known as 'Shooks'. They even arrest and indict 14 young men on treason felony – including a notably charismatic young patriot by the name of Jeremiah O'Donovan Rossa. The English press is soon publishing the name of this fiendish force, with a handle which becomes generic: *The Fenians*.

In America further difficulty is encountered by the outbreak of the Civil War, with many Irish–Americans joining that fight instead of going to Ireland as promised.

And yet if it might seem to the British that the Fenians are in retreat, there is no denying the significance of what occurs in the final months of 1862, when, in another grand tradition of Irish politics, there is a grand funeral. It is Terence Bellew MacManus, the incarcerated veteran of '48 who had made a remarkable escape from the island prison of Van Diemen's Land to San Francisco, where long years of imprisonment caught up in cruel fashion on his health, and had finally taken his life. This son of the shamrock, this patriot tried and true, is returning in a coffin to the land that bore him, to rest in honour for eternity, and 'the Captain' gives the word to his circles. Greet him, as he deserves. And so they do. From all over Ireland, they come. Sixty thousand roaring supporters line the streets of Cork, hats off and applauding, as the cortege passes on its way. At every station between Cork and Dublin, thousands more gather to pay their respects, and by the time the coffin gets to Dublin, there are 30,000 people in the cortege, and 150,000 along the streets, as it makes its way to Glasnevin Cemetery. As it ever has been, and as it ever will be, nothing ignites Irish passion more than gathering around the coffin of a dead patriot.

So powerful is this show of strength that many wonder: is *now* the time for The Rising? Why not take to arms immediately, harness the popular emotion, and throw the British over?

But the Captain says no.

He insists: we must have more trained men and more arms. We must wait. And we must get the people as a whole behind us more. It is with this in mind that, at Stephens' behest, by 1863, the IRB have their own weekly newspaper, *The Irish People*, to push the republican cause to those souls it is named for, while also providing a source of revenue. Operating in Parliament Street, just a stone's throw from Dublin Castle, it soon sells 15,000 copies with every issue, of which 5000 are sold in the United States.

A bonus for the movement is that the office of the newspaper also serves as a quasi administrative headquarters, with sensitive lists as to Centres, members, finances and the like kept under lock and key.

With *The Irish People* running along, James Stephens marries Jane Hopper, his fair colleen from down Tipperary way, and returns to his first love, revolution. For the Fenians are gathering momentum, their circles of civilians and Irish soldiers from within British Army regiments continue to grow.

Among Stephens' prize recruits is none other than John Devoy, the young lad who, back in the day, had watched his brother die, and afterwards refused to sing 'God Save the Queen' at school. After this childhood run-in with all matters monarchy, Devoy's fiercely patriotic parents had sent him to a specially convened school in Dublin, where the *true* story of Ireland had been taught, and the infamy of England's role in it over the centuries. And now he is a strapping 22-year-old with an unusually thick set of black whiskers so committed to the cause he has just returned from a stint with the French Foreign Legion which he had specifically joined so as to learn military tactics and toughen himself for The Rising.

On one occasion, the great Irish seer Eugene O'Curry himself had placed his hand on young John's head and said, 'This will be a leader of the Gael who will speak in the tongue of the Gael.'[42]

Speaking in fluent Gaelic – the ancient Irish language, for whom perhaps the most celebrated phrase is '*Erin go Bragh!*' Ireland forever! – is just one of Devoy's many skills.

Quietly spoken, but fearless, and with a very forceful personality, he possesses precisely the kind of initiative that Stephens wants to see, and the Captain is not long in making Devoy a Centre.

While Devoy does brilliantly from the first, swearing in dozens more in just his first couple of months in the role, even he can't compare to the 23-year-old Private Thomas Hassett of the British 24th Foot Regiment, based in Dublin, who has no sooner taken the oath, becoming a Centre, than he swears in 270 members of his regiment to the cause.

Others, like the inseparable Private Martin Hogan and Private James Wilson of the 5th Dragoons, work in tandem – first signing up their immediate circle of friends to the wider circle of Fenians, and expanding from there. Wilson is the young lad Séamus McNally, who had nearly starved to death as a 16-year-old in County Down. He'd assumed an English name to enlist and now applies himself to revolution with particular passion, eager to avenge all those of his family and friends he had seen die of starvation. His friend Martin Hogan is the unofficial swordsman supreme of the British Army, capable of cutting an iron bar hanging from a barrack-room ceiling with a single mighty blow.

Clearly, he has taken at least one mighty blow himself, as attested by the huge scar on his left cheek. Still, as deep as the scar is – courtesy of an Afghani's scimitar during his service there – Hogan never fails to point out to those who stare a little too long at its cruel contours that they should see the other fellow!

Another convert is the upright, freckly, red-headed Thomas Darragh. A 30-year-old decorated Sergeant Major from Wicklow, with the 2nd Queen's Royal Regiment, based in Cork, he is a man who has spent so long in the saddle as a cavalryman that he walks bow-legged. Now, rare for a Fenian, Darragh is not only a Protestant but even a former Orangeman – that body of Protestant Irish most passionately devoted to Ireland's membership of Great Britain – who has so heartily embraced the cause to which the Orangemen are most heartily opposed, an independent Ireland, that he was even sworn in on a Catholic prayer-book.

Yes, some things are even more important than religion. Just don't tell that to the parish priest.

But I digress. We must move on; the tale is barely begun.

Excitement among the Fenians grows. And when the American Civil War ends in April 1865, O'Mahony sends word that many trained soldiers could now join the fight at home. Some 75,000 Irish-born had served in the Union army.

The Captain feels ready.

All is falling into place for The Rising.

'The organization in Ireland,' John Devoy would recall, 'had a very busy time owing to Stephens' announcement that "next year" is the year of action. All sorts of preparations were going on, except the essential one of procuring arms. That was ignored, on account of "The Captain's" assurance that we'd get all we wanted from America. Pike-making was the only kind of arming thought of . . . Country blacksmiths made many and Stephens established a pike-making factory in Dublin.'[43]

The Irish People publishes weekly thunderous editorials which maintain the fiction that 'Fenianism' is exclusively American, but everyone understands the point. The paper is making clarion calls to the people themselves. Beyond everything else, they notice ever more Irish–Americans on the streets of Dublin, men with a pronounced military strut. There is the air of something angry building.

Again the British authorities feel they have to act. Though in a certain measure alarmed at how quickly this so-called 'Fenianism' is growing in Ireland – there are disturbing reports they have penetrated every leading town, and every regiment – the British authorities at least have great experience in suppressing insurgencies from native populations around the world and know what to do, which starts with installing spies of their own.

To keep himself and his wife safe, Stephens rents lodgings at Fairfield House, in the coastal Dublin suburb of Sandymount, under assumed names, Mr and Mrs Herbert.

Meanwhile, he sends word to the American Fenians that he has over 54,000 men.

'And besides this,' he writes to John O'Mahony, 'I answer for an additional 15,000 at least. So that we can now rely on an organised power of from 80,000 to 85,000 men.'[44]

As for military Fenians, John Devoy claims that of the 26,000 men serving in the British Army in Ireland, no fewer than 8000 are Fenians – with another 6000 members from the Irish militia well-drilled and ready to fight, while another 7000 Fenians are in regiments stationed outside Ireland.

Yes, with so much frenetic activity, the only question is how long the likes of Stephens and Luby can stay invisible, how the likes of Devoy can continue to conduct Fenian affairs in public houses unnoticed, how

Wilson, Hogan and Darragh will be able to continue converting their fellow soldiers to Fenianism without the British authorities finding out.

It is a question that doesn't seem to worry the Captain. But it worries young John Devoy.

And this is where our story truly begins.

CHAPTER ONE

A CONSPIRACY OF SILENT SOLDIERS

The Fenians are the grandchildren of the rebels of 1798, and their youth was passed amid the harangues of O'Connell and the conspiracies of Smith O'Brien. When such a population as the Irish have such memories a Government of angels would not content them . . .[1]

The Times, London, 30 September 1865

One day in the summer of 1865, John Devoy is out and about in Dublin, fomenting revolution, going from one Fenian-friendly public house to another, when he comes across eight strapping soldiers of the 5th Dragoon Guards – every single one of them over six feet tall, and all of them his men, Fenians – marching in pairs, behind each other, twirling their light canes as if they were swords, and singing in joyous unison.

As they swing into Castle Street, he recognises the song, nothing less than what has become the Fenian anthem, 'O'Donnell Abú', written by Michael Joseph McCann in 1843, in honour of the great Gaelic Irish commander, 'Red Hugh' O'Donnell, who led the Nine Years' War against English rule in the 16th century.

> *Proudly the note of the trumpet is sounding;*
> *Loudly the war cries arise on the gale;*
> *Fleetly the steed by Lough Swilly is bounding,*
> *To join the thick squadrons on Saimear's green vale.*
> *On, ev'ry mountaineer,*
> *Strangers to flight or fear,*
> *Rush to the standard of dauntless Red Hugh.*
> *Bonnaught and Gallowglass,*
> *Throng from each mountain pass.*
> *On for old Erin, 'O'Donnell Abú!'*

The soldiers are roaring the words now, clearly revelling in their petty act of sedition by singing such a song openly. But Devoy is alarmed. Again and again he has drilled into them, and all Centres he deals with, that they must value secrecy above all else! And yet, on occasions like this, their Irish joy at actually starting to *do something* to liberate the nation simply overwhelms them, and they cannot help but show it. Such open rebellion goes against everything the conspirators are trying to achieve.

> *On with O'Donnell then,*
> *Fight the old fight again,*
> *Sons of Tirconnell,*
> *All valiant and true:*
> *Make the proud Saxon feel*
> *Erin's avenging steel!*
> *Strike for your country! 'O'Donnell Abú!*[2]

Devoy hurries after them, hoping for a quiet word when they are not on public display.

Still, the problem arises again, a few weeks later, when, after The Curragh races, he and other soldiers pile into a carriage to take them back to their barracks, and the soldiers start singing the anthem from the 1798 Rising, *The Rising of the Moon* . . .

> *Out from many a mud wall cabin,*
> *Eyes were watching through the night,*
> *Many a manly heart was beating,*
> *For the blessed morning light,*
> *Murmurs rang along the valley,*
> *To the banshee's lonely croon,*
> *And a thousand pikes were flashing,*
> *By the rising of the moon,*
> *By the rising of the moon,*
> *By the rising of the moon,*
> *And a thousand pikes were flashing,*
> *By the rising of the moon.*[3]

Devoy remains alarmed. Just how long can they possibly last, when it will only take one of the men they have approached to inform their superiors, who themselves cannot have failed to notice the increasing identification of the Irish soldiers with the Irish, not the British, cause?

•

By July 1865, the American Fenians are nearly satisfied that their brothers in Ireland are ready for The Rising.

It is known that all 16 Dublin circles are well-drilled, which is a good start. To confirm that the rest is ready, two American emissaries are sent to Dublin to report back. If all is ship-shape, the Americans are prepared to send the final tranche of men, money and munitions.

Still if there is 'many a slip, 'twixt cup and lip' so too can there be other misfortunes on the way to revolution, even for those counting on the famed 'luck of the Irish' to play in their favour. On this occasion, one of the two emissaries, Patrick J. Meehan, finds himself about to disembark at Kingstown, Dublin, with such important documents that it might be wise to hide them.

Carefully, he pins the documents in his underwear – including a bank draft for 500 pounds, and a letter of introduction – and it is from there that they fall onto the platform of Dublin's Kingstown Railway Station, unnoticed by him. He strides on, oblivious, until he arrives at the secret meeting place, reaches down his trouser leg to find . . . nothing. Frantically retracing his steps, he finds the same – nothing. Still, after some wild panic, calm is restored. It has likely simply fallen into a gutter and is now lost in the sewer. They pray. The alternative is unthinkable.

The main thing is the emissaries return to New York with such positive reports that from 5 August 1865, John O'Mahony, as Head Centre of the Fenian Brotherhood in America, issues the 'final call' and begins sending officers and soldiers over to Ireland.

•

There is something about Pierce Nagle that puts other workers at *The Irish People* on edge. It might be just his appearance. 'His lips are thick, the lower lip especially, which apparently from its size hangs and exhibits more of the inner lining than looks pleasing; his eyes have a "cast" to the right side, the right eye being apparently more strained in that direction than the left one . . .'[4]

Or it could be his manner, with one contemporary noting that 'his nature was a compound of the worst vices that disgraced mankind. I never touched his hand without an instinctive shudder.'[5]

Or it might even be the lowness of his position, essentially not much more than an envelope-licker.

Against that, however, there is no doubt about his commitment to the cause. A small example is when, on the point of Dublin's old Newgate Prison being demolished, it is Nagle who suggests to some of the workers at *The Irish People* that they go to the prison as a kind of pilgrimage, to pray for the spirit of the great Irish patriot Lord Edward Fitzgerald.

A fine idea!

When they get to the cell where Fitzgerald expired, as one contemporary would recall, 'Nagle's emotion seemed to have overpowered him, for he actually burst into tears as he filled his breast pocket with the stray pieces of mortar that had fallen from the dilapidated wall.'[6]

Late summer 1865, Dublin Castle, trash or treasure?

The luck of the Irish?

It depends which way you look at it.

For Superintendent Daniel Ryan, head of the Detective branch of the Dublin Metropolitan Police, known as G Division – in charge of rooting out the Fenians on behalf of Her Majesty – it is luckier luck than the luckiest four-leaf clover could ever promise.

For a package of documents has just arrived from Kingstown. They'd been handed in at Kingstown Railway Station to Miss Charlotte Mitchell, at the Telegraph Office, who had given them to her manager, who had handed them to a police inspector, who, on this late summer day, takes them straight to Dublin Castle, the bristling high citadel of all British power in Ireland, where Superintendent Ryan now gazes upon them . . .

Goodness gracious! It is a letter introducing two men, Meehan and Dunne, as representatives of the Fenian Brotherhood, 'with full powers to treat and arrange all existing relations between organisations they represent and the I.R'.[7]

For the Fenians, it is very bad luck indeed.

Their nemesis, Superintendent Ryan, now has a name. For look who the letter is addressed to . . .

James Stephens, Central Executive of the Irish Republic.[8]

Superintendent Daniel Ryan poses the obvious question: Could this James Stephens then be the fabled leader of the Fenians, the mysterious 'Mr Shooks'?

Very possibly!

And it's not long before that possibility turns to ironclad certainty.

It all fits.

Very quietly, further investigations are conducted, deeper surveillance ordered – spies and informers, wherever they can place them – and plans are made . . .

Nevertheless the Fenian ranks continue to swell.

One star recruit down Limerick way, on the banks of the River Shannon, is John Kelly. He is the new water-bailiff in town, overseeing the fishing laws, and he swiftly becomes known and admired by the local community.

A formidable presence at nearly six feet, he has 'a decidedly handsome, manly countenance, which was rendered particularly impressive by his lofty, towering bald head'.[9]

Yes, the piercing gaze from the man's rather sunken eyes can be a tad disconcerting at first, but that is more than outweighed by his warmth. Why this is a man who can play cards with card-sharps and hold his own, dance a jig or reel with the best of them, sing, court colleens in a manner to make them swoon, and tell stories that will bring the people from near and far just to listen.

'There was scarcely one in the County Cork, who could dance or sing a song at a birth or a wedding like [John Kelly],' one account would run, 'and no one was so popular among the country people.'[10]

Best of all? He is a notably pious patriot, a devout attendee of the local Mass, who believes the *Lord* wants Ireland to be free, and it doesn't take long before he is not only invited to join the local circle of the Fenians, but is soon so prospering that he is promoted progressively from 'D' to 'C' to 'B', before becoming an 'A' – a 'Centre'.

Yes, he is brilliant at convening meetings and conducting training sessions, but he also proves to have an uncanny capacity to evade police. Whenever they organise a raid it is only to find that the said Fenian meeting had been called off. Kelly has saved them again![11]

At a meeting of other 'Centres', where they refine their plans for The Rising, Kelly is introduced to a young soldier by the name of James Kiely, who confides in him, as a Centre, that 'my two uncles have two nests of pikes concealed in Dungarvan'.[12] Come The Rising, those pikes will be placed in the hands of the peasants. And when they march on the police barracks, those police will have to surrender quickly or, Kiely assures him, their leaders will be 'disposed of'.[13]

Of course, it is a danger to talk of such plans to a man he doesn't know, but Kiely is just a bit like that – both a trusting soul, and so garrulous he will talk to anyone on anything. John Kelly nods encouragingly at his well-developed plans.

•

One day in early September, Superintendent Ryan is handed another letter. And this one . . . is written by James Stephens himself!

> This year – and let there be no mistake about it – must be the year of action. I speak with a knowledge and authority to which no other man could pretend; and I repeat, the flag of Ireland – of the Irish Republic – must this year be raised.[14]

Oh, really?

Under the circumstances, the Superintendent would be most surprised . . .

15 September 1865, Office of *The Irish People*, Dublin, the hammer comes down

Police!

It's late at night. The journalists and print-setters have gone home.

Only a startled few are there to see the Dublin police break down *The Irish People*'s door and storm inside, taking possession of its types and presses and arresting everyone still on the premises.

There will be no more revolution fomented from *The Irish People*, and after the next day's edition is sold, it ceases to exist.

Ah, but that is not all. This is only the beginning, the first of many raids designed to bring the Fenians to their knees.

For on this same night, the police also storm into the home of the editor, Thomas Clarke Luby, who – fearing this very thing – is here and now engaged in trying to destroy sensitive documents. He is being helped by another key Fenian, John O'Leary.

Seize those men!

Seize those *documents*!

It is an enormous breakthrough. But James Stephens remains the one they want. Yes, they must have the head of the snake, and chop it off. If they remove that head, the body will surely die.

•

An hour after the police raid on *The Irish People*, James Stephens is in a Dublin home with another dozen Fenians – going over plans for The

Rising, when there is a furious knocking on the door. It proves to be the breathless book-keeper from *The Irish People*.

'May you spare me a few minutes,' he mutters to the Captain, 'to deliver a message?'[15]

The Captain nods, and in hushed, hurried tones, the book-keeper tells him what has happened.

The paper has been stormed, the presses seized. They say Thomas Luby has been arrested, and further documents seized.

The Captain moves quickly. Yes, the book-keeper had wanted privacy as he fears informants, but Stephens trusts his men, and quickly returns to them to relay the news. There is a shocked reaction around the room.

The Irish People? Raided? Everyone arrested?

A man slinks up next to the book-keeper and whispers a few words of comfort.

It's Pierce Nagle, the thick-lipped, fiercely patriotic envelope-licker from *The Irish People* office, but . . .

But now Stephens has a few words for them all.

'We must prevent a premature Rising,' he orders, his left eye narrowing a little more than usual, belying his unease. 'All Dublin Centres are to keep their men under control.'[16]

Aware that he is in danger as never before, Stephens puts on the clothes of a beggar, arms himself with a couple of crutches to make himself appear an impoverished cripple, and heads off into the night, to return home to Mrs Herbert.

Next morning, he writes a letter to America with news of the arrests.

'Well, long as I am free I answer for everything. But once you hear of my arrest, only a single course remains to you. Send no more money from the States. Get all you can, though, and with it purchase all the war-material you can. Gather all the fighting men about you and then sail for Ireland. The heads here may be in the hands of the enemy and much confusion may prevail; but, with a Fenian force to rally them, be sure that overwhelming numbers will be with you. But this must be done before next Christmas, after which date I would have no man risk his life or his money.'[17]

And, after appointing three IRB leaders to take over his duties, he disappears.

•

From early September flying squads of loyalist soldiers roam the barracks to regularly descend on traitorous military Fenians, before arresting them and frog-marching them off to prison cells. Civilian Fenians, meantime, are also being roused from their beds, arrested and placed in custody by the police: by the second week of October, 187 military and civilian suspects have been arrested on charges of Fenianism, with many hundreds more in the police's sights.

Meantime, dozens of Americans now in Ireland are suspected of having come to join in a Rising, and are ordered to leave the country.

Many Fenians don't wait to be arrested, and, like the well-regarded John King – a man of such sunny disposition, he always seems to be smiling whatever the circumstances – decide to get away immediately. In King's case, he embarks on what will be a long journey to Australia and an entirely different kind of life, but already we are ahead of ourselves . . .

But the Captain? It's as if he doesn't exist. Superintendent Ryan places a 200-pound reward on Stephens' head, and his description is posted in the *Police Gazette*, known as the *Hue-and-Cry* – 'James Stephens is about 42 years of age; 5 feet 7 inches high; stout make; broad high shoulders; very tight, active appearance; fair hair; bald all round top of head . . . and he generally dresses in black.'[18]

•

The British press? The *Times* of London sets the typically disparaging tone in its editorial on 18 September 1865:

> Is there any people under the sun more unfit for a
> Republican form of Government than the Irish? Is
> there any character so deficient in those political
> values which are the life of Republics as the Celtic?
> . . . The truth is that Fenianism has not and could
> not have sprung up on Irish soil. It is entirely
> of exotic growth, an importation from America, and
> entirely out of harmony with real Irish sentiment
> . . . when Irish disaffection has dwindled to
> Fenianism, there is good reason for supposing
> that it is dying out altogether, and must be very
> near its end. [19]

To achieve that end as expeditiously as possible, the British authorities establish a Special Commission to try, convict and punish those Fenians they've caught without clogging the regular courts.

Moving quickly, by the end of October, two judges – Justices William Keogh and John Fitzgerald – have been handpicked by Dublin Castle to do the honours to the dishonourable civilian Fenians. They are to start their Special Commission in Dublin and then reconvene in Cork to work through the arrested Fenians there. But will these two justices wear the blindfold of Lady Justice and conduct an impartial trial? An editorial in the *Irishman* thinks not, noting, 'They are two names which excite suspicion in the Irish mind.'[20]

As for the military Fenians who have been rounded up, they must answer to martial law in a series of courts martial being overseen by General Sir Hugh Henry Rose, the Commander-in-Chief of British Forces in Ireland – a merciless military man sent to Ireland in July specifically to root out the 'Fenian conspiracy' from the military once and for all.

As for the government's prime target . . . still no-one comes forward with any information.

James Stephens has entirely disappeared.

•

James Stephens is content to lie low and bide his time, confident that so few trusted lieutenants know of his location that, for the moment, he will be safe. Despite the lull in activity that follows, the leadership is able to get word to the Fenian soldiers that, 'in spite of the numerous arrests, the organization is still intact and the intention to fight remains'.[21]

When a Fenian Congress is held in Philadelphia in October 1865, no fewer than 400 accredited delegates are welcomed, and it is claimed from the leadership dais that the United States boasts no fewer than 380,000 Fenians.[22] Against that, so overwhelming is the police pressure in Ireland, as they continue to scour the land for him, that it becomes obvious to even Stephens that he must devolve some of his leadership duties onto others who are more free to move around the country.

To this end, Stephens appoints Captain Thomas Kelly to be in charge. Kelly is a patriot Irish military man of vast experience – including with the famed Army of the Cumberland, which fought for the Union in the American Civil War.

Stephens also takes a moment to write to John Devoy, the extraordinarily capable fellow who he has long had his eye on, one of the most promising of The Rising:

Thursday, October 26, 1865

My Dear Friend:-
There is a lull just now on the part of the enemy, and we should make
the utmost of it. To this end I hereby appoint you Chief Organizer of the
British troops here in Ireland . . .
                    Yours faithfully,
                    J. Stephens
P. S. Be very prudent now. You owe me this, to justify the appointment of
so young a man to so responsible a post.[23]

Devoy's passion for the cause is such that even though the police are closing in as never before, and he is keenly aware that there are warrants out for his arrest, still he keeps moving, recruiting to replace the men who have been arrested, using the many Fenians who are still in place in the British Army as his means of introduction to new prospects.

At this time, late October 1865, the regiment taking most of his attention is the mighty 10th Hussars, a crack light cavalry outfit quartered at Island Bridge Barracks, in the south-western part of Dublin, well positioned to control key roads and railways nearby.

'The few men I had in the 10th,' Devoy would recount, 'were not of much account and I could make no headway.'[24]

Via a friend, however, he hears tell of a curiously charismatic, quietly spoken and reflective Irish soldier in the 10th Hussars, John Boyle O'Reilly. Devoy is off to quietly meet him, when he is told O'Reilly is serving as picket on the Royal Barracks – one of many pickets the British Army is maintaining all across Dublin at this point, ready for any Rising.

Oddly enough, the man pointing the way to where O'Reilly can be found is a bluff, jolly Englishman, who pauses to sing O'Reilly's praises.

'I shouldn't wonder,' he burbles enthusiastically to Devoy, 'if in five or six years that young fellow'd be a troop sawjent majah.'[25]

Helpfully, the sentry at the gate of the Royal Barracks is a Fenian, who gives Devoy a careful smile of acknowledgement, while one of the sentry's companions – also one of theirs – steps up and quietly asks, 'Are you looking for some of the boys?'[26]

'I want to find the picket of the 10th Hussars,' Devoy replies, and is soon given directions to the stables, where, again, those on duty prove to be nearly all Fenians. One of them, Martin Hogan – the unofficial swordsman supreme of the British Army – gives him the specific directions to a fine-looking fellow tightening the saddle girths of an equally magnificent steed as he is about to set off to Vice-Regal Lodge with a dispatch from General Sir Hugh Rose to the Lord Lieutenant, Lord John Wodehouse, the governmental chief.

'O'Reilly,' Devoy will recount, 'was then a handsome, lithely built young fellow of 20, with the down of a future black moustache on his lip. He had a pair of beautiful dark eyes that changed in expression with his varying emotions. He wore the full-dress dark blue hussar uniform, with its mass of braiding across the breast, and the busby, with its tossing plume, was set jauntily on the head and held by a linked brass strap, catching under the lower lip.'[27]

He is a splendid soldier, and in fact, so proud of his appearance that when out and about in town delivering messages for the high brass, he goes out of his way to go past as many plate-glass windows as possible. Though he has no time to talk this evening, he happily agrees to meet Devoy the following evening at a quiet establishment in the city, before he effortlessly springs into the saddle, and equally effortlessly canters away, awaaaaay.

The following evening, in the back of a public house, Devoy needs to waste no energy on the virtues of the Fenian cause.

For O'Reilly is an Irish patriot, and with them from the first. He even offers to give Devoy copies of the high brass dispatches that he delivers around Dublin. But Devoy declines. For now.

Instead, Devoy quickly promotes him to the rank of Centre, the key Fenian figure in the 10th Hussars.

•

There's a reason Devoy declines O'Reilly's offer to pass on messages. They already have someone on the inside passing on valuable information, and don't need to double the risk.

His name is Private William Foley, he hails from Tipperary and is a superb physical specimen, standing nearly six feet tall. A veteran of the Bombay Horse Artillery that had seen action in India's Sepoy Mutiny, he returned to Ireland in 1859, where he remained at home for a few months before joining one of the crack cavalry regiments of the British Army, the 5th Dragoon Guards – quietly taking the Fenian oath in 1864. But here's the thing. Right now he is an orderly with the Englishman in charge of quelling this growing insurrection, General Sir Hugh Rose.

Yes, with William Foley in that key position, right at the heart of the English command, for the moment there is no need for O'Reilly to take too many risks himself – at least not in this field.

The two other key Fenians in the 5th Dragoon Guards, however, the swordsman Martin Hogan and his partner in crime, the icy blue-eyed James Wilson, decide they can no longer operate safely, and so desert, placing themselves at the service of the Fenians full-time, ready for The Rising when it comes.

The Fenians are particularly glad to have them full-time. Hogan for his strength and Wilson for his experience serving in the Bombay Artillery through all of India, Syria and Canada, emerging as an expert in explosives. Come The Rising, he will be particularly valuable.

As the British authorities will be actively looking for them, both Hogan and Wilson do their best to change their appearance, while living quietly together in Dublin.

•

Two months after the arrests of September, and still the police feel they are no closer to the breakthrough they need.

Police pound their beats, asking questions. Detectives pursue every lead. Spies are primed, everywhere, to look for the tiniest sign of Stephens.

Where *can* he be?

•

Ah, but as consuming as the passion of John Devoy is for the cause of Irish freedom, still that passion must sing in his soul with another passion that near consumes him – his love for sweet Eliza Kenny. So it is that whenever he can get away for even just a day and a night, he takes the night train from Dublin to County Kildare, stepping off in the wee hours at a sleepy rural station to trudge through the familiar fields from his childhood. For a full seven miles – his feet sure on the dark paths he could navigate blind-folded, just as he is effectively doing now – he keeps going until he reaches a small farmhouse just outside of the town of Naas. Knocking gently on the front door of the Kenny family, he does not have to wait long, despite the fact that it is still an hour before dawn.

They know who it is. Only John comes round at this hour.

The kettle is boiled and the family rises to greet him as one, led by sweet Eliza – a notably shapely and statuesque brunette, with intelligent, warm eyes – who he cannot take his eyes off. They will spend a wonderful day together, talking, picnicking, rambling through the woods, shyly holding hands, while he divulges all the Brotherhood's latest news from Dublin, the gossip, and of course their plans for the future. Theirs is a chastity doubly preserved by the fact that that night he will bunk down with her father – who by the by had been active in The Rising of 1848 – while Mrs Kenny moves into the room of her two daughters . . .

And then, alas, he must go again, but not before giving his fair colleen some tasks of her own, taking John Devoy's messages to Fenians about Naas right under the noses of unsuspecting but ubiquitous constables. In short order, he knows, they will be waving cheerily to fair Eliza Kenny as she goes by, bearing news of revolution under her skirts.

Very occasionally, he can stay longer, as in once when Eliza's sister gets married and while one of Eliza's uncles plays the fiddle and another plays the bagpipes, they are one of 52 couples who simply dance the night away, dreaming of the day when they can themselves marry.

She is, truly, one of a kind, and John Devoy whispers as much as he holds her tight before leaving once more. He will be back, love, just as soon as he can, and one day they will be together forever.

But she can never be sure that day will come. And nor can he.

•

All present?

Good.

In these days of early November 1865 John Boyle O'Reilly has brought his best Fenian soldiers to meet John Devoy, to discuss the finer details of The Rising.

In a quiet upper room of Hoey's public house in Bridgefoot Street, the gathering is some 20 strong, and the mood joyous.

The truth is, belonging to a secret society has an allure, a congeniality far beyond the life of mere soldiering. There are assignations, passwords, secret signs, and then entrée into a world where you are with your fellow conspirators, often late at night, and often in this very back-room at Hoey's, where new members are sworn in, oaths are taken, ales washed down by more ales, and songs are sung, '*We'll drive the Sassenach from our soil . . .*'[28]

Not tonight though.

Tonight there is serious business at hand, as John Boyle O'Reilly lays out on the table a makeshift but detailed map showing the key features of Island Bridge and Richmond Barracks, and discloses his plan to capture Dublin. He is explaining to all how, once The Rising takes place, instead of their Fenian forces 'taking to the hills',[29] as some want, they will first fight right here in the city. Yes, they will have to move quickly to control the key thoroughfare of the Island Bridge while also ensuring there is no counter-attack emanating from Richmond Barracks and . . .

And now he is interrupted quite rudely by an old soldier who has come with him.

What presumption, the old fellow rasps, to think that 'these gintlemin', indicating Devoy and his closest civilian confederates, didn't have maps like this growing out of their armpits, they surely have so many.

Yes, well.

Devoy doesn't like to say anything, but the sad truth is they don't have anything of the kind.

But they do have fine men like O'Reilly.

'He had . . . a good military head,' Devoy would fondly recall. 'His ideas about the capture of Dublin, and the way to get out of the city with our forces intact, in case we failed, were all practical. Mere boy as he was . . .'[30]

The meeting goes on, and Devoy hangs on every word, absorbing O'Reilly's ideas. Over coming days and weeks, the two will talk extensively of such plans, as they take to walking together, usually on empty streets to ensure their privacy.

Of all the soldiers that Devoy has recruited, none is as impressive or as effective as O'Reilly, who, in the space of just a few weeks, recruits several dozen soldiers to the cause.

In the meantime for John Devoy, things are slowly starting to fall into place. They have Fenians in key positions in regiments across the land. They have plans. What they lack, alas, is the mass of weaponry they would need to arm the peasantry when they join The Rising. Despite the promises of Stephens, no shiploads of guns have arrived from America, and the only real rifles they have are the ones the Fenian soldiers individually possess.

A possible solution to this is suggested by one of Devoy's best men, Private Thomas Hassett, the 24-year-old carpenter from Cork who has personally sworn in no fewer than 270 members. A clear thinker, Hassett is strongly of the view that the battle against the British will be won or lost in Dublin, and we Fenians need to strike hard there. Why not, then, make our first attack on the armoury known as the Pigeon House – situated near the mouth of the River Liffey – and seize the 25,000 rifles therein. This would not only arm the people, but *deny* the British. It makes a lot of sense and Devoy, after a few thoughtful strokes of his beard, agrees. True, the British either get wind of it, or are taking simple precautions, for they soon place a guard of 90 soldiers on full-time protection of the Pigeon House, but this is no problem – for fully 60 of them are Fenians.

Still, despite Hassett imploring the Fenian leadership to launch the attack immediately, the usual decision is taken: they are not yet ready.

•

On 9 November 1865, a Sandymount man visits Superintendent Ryan's G Division Office and tells of a most fascinating coincidence about a local family, surname Herbert.

'Mr Herbert,' the man says in earnest, 'was in the habit of going to town almost every day until *The Irish People* was seized. Since then, he's rarely been seen out of doors.'[31]

Intriguing indeed. But there's more.

'I believe Mr Herbert is the same man I once saw standing at the door of *The Irish People* office. I suspect it might be Stephens, but I can't be certain and I don't want my name mentioned publicly.'[32]

Quickly, quietly, the police make inquiries around the suburb, and everything their informer had told them is confirmed, and then some – there have also been some very odd nocturnal excursions, emanating from this particular house.

It is time to move.

11 November 1865, Sandymount, Dublin, the circle closes

In the coldest earthly hours, just before the night hands sentinel duty to the day, 37 policemen bristling with weaponry, along with six inspectors and Superintendent Daniel Ryan, all under the command of Colonel Henry Lake, and all with teeth chattering and lips blue, climb over the frosty garden wall at Fairfield House. They surround the building in crouched positions, waiting for the order. Just as dawn lightens the eastern skies, an officer raps at the thick wooden back door.

From inside, heavy footsteps approach. The bolt is pulled back, the door momentarily opens and here is 'Mr Herbert' in his underwear, expecting one of the gardeners. As quick as the police are, Stephens is quicker, slams the door and shoots back the bolt.

Colonel Lake yells through the door that there can be no escape. With his wife inside, Stephens cannot risk fighting it out and so pulls back the bolt, before racing up the stairs to his wife, Superintendent Ryan following. The revolutionary leader clearly wants to have a few moments with his wife before the arrest.

And now here he is, emerging from the upstairs bedroom, waiting calmly.

We have him!

In a heartbeat, an officer looks 'The Captain' of the Fenians square in the eyes and says, 'James Stephens, I arrest you, in the name of the Queen.'[33]

Stephens is sullen. 'You are my prisoner,' the officer reiterates, 'now get dressed.'[34]

So be it.

Stephens offers no resistance, as it would be pointless. In fact, it is only when his wife asks for his blessing to visit him in prison that he shows much emotion at all.

'You cannot visit me in prison without asking permission of British officials,' says he, 'and I do not think it becoming in one so near to me as you are to ask favours of British dogs. You must not do it. I forbid it.'[35]

One thing before going, however.

Whatever is about to happen, Stephens wishes to look his best, and, upon his instruction, one of the detectives retrieves for him, out of 'his splendidly-furnished wardrobe . . . a fine blue cloth coat, black trousers and vest, black silk scarf, and gloves of the same colour'.[36]

The other three Fenians in the cottage are soon under arrest, and all four are quickly conveyed under heavy guard to the Lower Castle Yard of Dublin Castle and lodged in the Police Commissioner's Office, until such times as a Justice can be roused.

•

The word quickly spreads around the city, and from there, to much of Britain – the authorities have Stephens – and there is no telling what might now happen.

It seems to most that The Rising is over, for while much of Ireland weeps, all England leaps with joy.

But is it *really* over?

Might this be the spark to set The Rising raging? Some of the answer might turn on Stephens' committal hearing, which is held just six hours after his arrest, in a room no more than 22 feet square packed full with government officials; led by the Magistrate, Baronet John Calvert Stronge, along with the Clerk of the Crown, the Attorney General, members of the press, and a dozen policemen and detectives, all of whom are armed.

And now, with his fellow prisoners, a heavily manacled Mr Stephens is dragged forth, to be placed on seats behind a table. The journalists crane their necks to get their first good look at him: the man, the myth.

'Who would not recognise,' the *Nation* asks, 'the reputed Fenian chief in that fresh-coloured man at the head of the table, with the quick, piercing eyes, and firmly-cut, decisive style of countenance?'[37]

To their amazement, he is not only calm, but 'sits tapping the table with his gloved hand',[38] and no signs of grief or depression are visible about him.

And look how well-dressed this dandy is, in his fine blue frock coat, black trousers and vest, black silk scarf, and gloves.

Arriving in a flurry of gowns, appearing for the British Government, is the famed Prosecuting Attorney, Charles Barry, QC – all wig, black robes, and grave demeanour.

And for you, Mr Stephens?

'I have employed no lawyer,' James Stephens says to Magistrate Stronge, from his seat, refusing to rise. 'Nor have I put in any plea in this case, neither do I intend to do so. By so doing, I should be recognising British law in Ireland. Now, I conscientiously and deliberately repudiate the rightful existence of British law in Ireland, and I scorn and defy any punishment it can inflict on me.'[39]

For you are talking here to the Provisional Dictator of the Republic of Ireland, and of course he will not kow-tow to underlings of a foreign power, who have no business in being in Ireland in the first place.

Sensation in the court!

Thunderous anger from the Crown's representatives. But for most of the rest it is simple wonderment. The hangman's noose is dangling about James Stephens' bald head, yet still he is brave enough to make such a speech.

It is inspirational, or terrifying, depending on where your loyalties lie.

Magistrate Stronge has heard enough, and after the briefest of statements by Mr Barry, the Head Centre of the Fenians is soon remanded in custody to appear at another hearing on the following Tuesday – where there is more of the same, with a few alterations.

And so to the first witness . . .

Why, it is none other than *The Irish People*'s envelope-licker . . . Pierce Nagle.

Stephens seethes at the sight of the snake.

The view of another of the Fenians is clear.

'It would be hard to picture a meaner or more untrustworthy insidious cast of countenance than Nagle's,' he will record. 'A black moustache and chin tuft of sickly growth, and lank black hair complete the picture of the oiliest and most repellent face that has ever adorned the person of a government informer.'[40]

Nagle looks all a'quiver as he takes his seat and dares not even look in the direction of Stephens until called upon by Magistrate Stronge to do so, to identify him. And even that hurried glance is enough to redden him to the brow.

The most interesting thing from the point of view of the press is Nagle's account of a letter he carried from Stephens to the Fenian leaders in the Irish town of Clonmel, where 'the Captain' – as he insisted he be called – declared that the 'flag of the Irish Republic must this year be raised'.[41] When something very close to a titter moves through the courtroom, an annoyed Stephens sharply exclaims, 'So it may.'[42]

Mercifully for Nagle, who clearly hates everything about this procedure, most particularly being under the gaze of Stephens, his testimony is quickly over and he is excused before more witnesses are brought forward over the following two days.

With the Crown's evidence concluded, Mr Stronge surveys the prisoners with a gimlet eye and inquires whether, perchance, they have anything to say for themselves before he commits them to trial?

James Stephens now indicates he would like to make some remarks and is not interested in the hoarse whispers of the concerned, distinguished lawyer sitting in the audience behind him that such remarks are not in order.

'You look on these matters as a lawyer,' Stephens says calmly. 'I look on them as a patriot.'[43]

Rising to his feet and folding his arms he says, 'I deny the right of the existence of British law in Ireland. I defy the punishment it might inflict on me.'[44]

So be it.

The magistrate has heard enough.

The accused are committed for trial at a Special Commission scheduled to begin hearing Fenian cases on 27 November.

All rise.

The prisoners are removed to the most secure premises for criminals and traitors in all of Ireland – Richmond Bridewell Prison.

No-one can escape from there, and certainly not Mr Stephens. Built in 1813, it has an 18-foot high perimeter of solid stone walls, with guard towers at regular intervals of 25 yards. Inside it has impassable corridors and cells, blocked as they are by heavy, locked iron doors.

But is it actually impenetrable, for a secret society that has its people *everywhere*?

The man who has taken over the leadership of the Fenians in what is hoped to be James Stephens' temporary absence – Colonel Thomas J. Kelly – does not think so.

•

Their boy, John Boyle is home, on a rare visit. Oh, how William and Eliza O'Reilly beam just to see him, just as he melts to see them once more. Ever and always he has been the best of sons, just as they have been the best of parents. Few families are closer than the O'Reillys of Dowth and just as it had pained both parents greatly to be parted from him once he had become a soldier based in Dublin, so too are they filled with joy to see him now, even for a brief visit, and even if it seems he is keeping something from them, something he has on his mind, but can't share . . . ?

They press, a little, but not too much. He will surely tell them in his own good time. For his part, it is a sanguine visit for young John. As much as he is delighted to be home, he regrets it is such a short time, and keenly aware that this visit might be . . . the last time. He has chosen his course to join the Fenians, and has no regrets. But there is no doubt that it is risky, and if his activities are discovered he will be lucky to escape with his life and the best he could hope for would be decades of imprisonment. Like a sponge, he soaks up every detail of his happy home in and about Dowth, the castle, the River Boyne, the schoolroom where his father teaches the clock . . . where is the old school clock? Oh. The old one has been changed. John Boyle O'Reilly regrets it. He loved that old school clock. Even when you go away for a short time things change. Except the love of his parents. And his love for them. When the time comes to go, he embraces them hard, noting with another pang of regret how frail his mother feels after recent illness from which she is not yet recovered.

Goodbye, our son.

Goodbye, my parents.

CHAPTER TWO

THE CIRCLE CLOSES

[John Devoy was] a man of weighty influence. Forbidding of aspect with a perpetual scowl upon his face, he immediately conveyed the idea of being a quarrelsome man, an idea sustained and strengthened by his manner of speech and gruffness of voice ... [His] friendships were few and far between, and had it not been for his undoubted ability ... he could never have reached the prominent place which he subsequently attained in the Fenian organisation.[1]

British spy Thomas Beach, on John Devoy

24 November 1865, Richmond Bridewell Prison, better a free bird than a caged hawk

It is a dark and stormy night – one of the stormiest in Dublin in recent times. The wind howls, the thunder booms, the lightning flashes, and the rain lashes – torrents of it, with the gusts of wind sending scudding waves down the nearly deserted streets of Dublin.

Ah, but in fact, they are not totally deserted. For now, nearing midnight, 10 Fenians approach the prison walls. A man here, a man there, a couple over there and several over the other side, all at a safe 150 yards back from the walls, ready to monitor and help proceedings, and get the word to Fenians around Dublin if they are needed.

And who is the man in the dark hat and heavy coat buttoned up against the sweeping rain, quietly going from watchman to watchman, to make sure all are in position? Why, of course, it is Colonel Kelly.

John Devoy himself gets into position near the section of wall whence the Captain is supposed to come. (The sparkle in the eye of the handsome lad's eye, this night? It is not just the excitement of the moment. It's the thrill that sweet Eliza Kenny has said yes! They are engaged to be married next year, and his spirit cannot be tamed. He feels as strong as the British lion. No, he feels *stronger*. Whatever the world can throw at him, he is ready for it. Like, right now ...)

All is in readiness on his side of the wall, hopefully everything that is meant to be happening on the other side is also going smoothly.

•

It is just before 1 am.

In the hospital ward of Richmond Bridewell Prison, a few ill prisoners are so fitfully sleeping that the hospital steward with the long flowing beard, John Breslin, keeps a weather eye upon them as he very quietly sits on his own bed, and changes shoes. For what he is about to do, he wants his regular shoes to remain pristine, as befitting a man who wishes to cover his tracks.

It's true that John Breslin is not a sworn Fenian, like his five eager brothers. No, he is too modest for the backroom posturing of the Brotherhood; it's simply not his style. But he *is* a *pure* Irishman, and so it is that, as he rises from his bed, he slips into his pocket three shiny new keys, which have come courtesy of the prison's night-watchman, Daniel Byrne, who had carefully made beeswax impressions of the keys to Stephens' cell and other relevant corridors.

Breslin leaves his room in the hospital ward, hugging the shadows as he goes through the darkened corridor with walls of solid stone, mounts the stone stairs to the second floor, where he walks to a heavy, inch-thick, double-locked door of hammered iron.

The prison clock strikes one. Flashes of lightning through the barred windows throw stuttering shadows against the old stone walls.

Against the crashing of thunder, his steps, though careful, are firm.

If at this point he is challenged he will have to invent a medical emergency to justify this late-night foray. A terrifying prospect for an average man, but not for the persuasive Breslin, who can charm himself into and out of just about anywhere with grace.

Either way, he has no right to do what he does now – slipping two duplicate keys into the dual locks of the door that leads to the solitary confinement cells. Silence is tantamount, for on the other side of the door at the end of the long corridor, there is an armed guard. Like a huge cat, Breslin pads along the long corridor with feline stealth and turns right into the shorter corridor, where the cell of Stephens is found.

Further complicating things is that right next to Stephens is an ordinary prisoner by the name of McLeod, who has instructions from the Governor still ringing in his ears to ring the gong provided if he hears anything untoward, like . . .

Like *that*! Now wide awake in his hammock McLeod is certain that he can hear the distinctive metallic grating of a large key being slipped into the padlock of his neighbour's cell. Sitting up, he strains to hear more.

Stephens hears the key, too. They have come. Standing up from his hammock, he is instantly ready, fully dressed in a black suit.

John Breslin opens the padlock that secures the wrought-iron barred door of Stephens' cell, carefully swings the door open and is soon shaking hands with the infamous revolutionary standing expectantly just over the threshold. Breslin indicates through sign language that Stephens must stay silent and tightly behind him. And, oh yes, here is a loaded revolver. We each have one. Any problems, and we will fight our way out.

Leaving the cell door wide open, the key in the padlock, off they pad, following the route that Breslin has put a great deal of effort into working out, steering clear of all guard checkpoints and delivering them unchallenged into the prison yard. Quickly now, they dash across the yard to the wall, where a ladder – used by the guards to light the yard lanterns – which night-watchman Byrne has placed there, assuring Breslin it will be high enough to easily get a man to the top of the wall. Grunting with the effort, making sure that Stephens stays clear, Breslin puts it up against the wall, only to find out it is six feet short! A lesser man would have wept with frustration, or howled with rage – perhaps both. But Breslin barely blinks, and simply swings into action.

Pointing Stephens towards an empty sentry box close by, he motions for Stephens to wait inside it, whispering, 'I will take care of everything between the sentry-box and the prison door. Shoot any man coming from the other direction.'[2]

Turning, he silently heads back across the yard, before disappearing inside the prison proper. He locates Daniel Byrne, and together they carry a couple of tables from the lunatics' dining room over to the wall near where Stephens waits. Stacking the tables flush on top of each other, they now put the ladder on top and hold it steady while the Captain scrambles up to the ladder. Stopping on the first rung, he turns and hands the revolver back to Breslin, to the latter's amazement. Does he not understand? If Stephens is spotted on the other side of this wall, his only chance is going to be to fight his way out. But Breslin bites his tongue. Even in a situation like this, you don't argue with the Captain.

Slowly now, Stephens ascends the wobbly ladder, swings his legs over the top of the wall, before dropping down onto the roof of a garden shed. With one last leap, he lands in the Governor's garden, and – as per Breslin's instructions – makes his way towards a pear tree growing close to the outer wall.

If all is going according to plan, on the other side of this wall, more Fenians are waiting to rush him away on horseback.

But are they there?

Using the arranged signal, Stephens picks up a handful of gravel and throws it over the wall.

John Devoy hears the smattering of pebbles through the tempest. The Captain!

Hearing the pebbles, another Fenian nearby, John Ryan, starts . . . well . . . he starts quacking like a duck in remarkably anatine fashion.

'Quack . . . *Quack* . . . QUACK.'

It is the arranged signal for all nearby Fenians – the Captain is close. (Still, just as the best-laid plans of mice and men can oft go awry, so too does it risk happening with ducks and men. For as John Devoy would later recall of their time waiting in the rain for the Captain to arrive: 'There was a genuine duck in a neighbouring garden that raised a false alarm once.'[3])

On the inside of the prison wall, Stephens can hear the strange quacking, but also something else – it is a muffled shout, followed by a whirr and a light thud against the wall. A thick rope knotted at two feet intervals now dangles on the wall in front of him.

Reaching out, he grabs it and gives a pull.

It is the Captain! On the outside of the wall, four Fenians, including Devoy, pull back on the rope.

A few more tentative tugs from Stephens' side, so hesitant that one of the Fenians on the other side feels compelled to call out: 'It's all right; we'll hold this end while you climb.'[4]

Stephens starts to climb, while Devoy and his men hold their end, taking the weight, gazing upwards waiting for their leader to emerge. There he is! First a dark blob appears at the top of the wall, followed by a larger blob, and it is soon apparent that the man himself is sitting atop the 18-foot high wall, peering down at the shadows below.

'Old man!' one of those shadows cries fondly in muffled tones.

But the Captain doesn't move. It is one thing to have scaled the wall from the inside with a rope. But how to get down this side?

Again, one of the shadows calls up: 'Drop down with your back to the wall, we will catch you.'[5]

After taking a deep breath, and saying a deeper prayer, Stephens does just that, inching his buttocks forward on the wall before free-falling feet first and landing so square on a flattened Fenian's chest that he leaves two perfect sandy boot marks on the man's buttoned coat. Just dropping in.

John Devoy catches the Captain's knees, others grab him under his arms. Their Captain is trembling. But he puts his feet on the ground, a free man.

Colonel Kelly and John Devoy welcome him warmly, while the men selected to be his personal bodyguards do so respectfully, awestruck to be in the Captain's presence. One of them, Denis Duggan, a carpenter who had been to school with Devoy and has been selected by him for the role because of his courage and calm when under pressure.

And they are under exactly that, right now. For they must get away, before the alarm is raised.

Colonel Kelly takes Stephens by the arm and leads him away at once. Crossing the road – their bodyguards tightly behind, gripping their revolvers in their coats and ready for anything – they turn into Love Lane and disappear into the wild night . . .

•

Inside the prison, Breslin and Byrne leave the tables as they are, and quickly, quietly return to their posts – Byrne to his watchman duty, and Breslin to his room in the hospital.

Breslin takes off his patent leather shoes, wipes them clean and puts them away. He dusts off his clothes, hops into bed and, as Stephens and Colonel Kelly are stealing away from the prison's outer wall, he is already fast asleep.

As for Stephens, he is whisked to one of the six houses that have been told to expect him that night – he will only decide at the last minute himself – and the sentinels disperse to tell the hordes of Fenians that instead of continuing to stand by, they must stand down and quietly scatter. The job has been done, and Ireland will be closer to liberation at sun-up than it was at sundown.

•

At five minutes to four in the morning, Mr Henry Philpots, the prison's Deputy Governor, is suddenly awoken by a furious pounding on his door. It is night-watchman Daniel Byrne and he is very upset. Doing his morning rounds, sir, he has discovered two tables piled up against the prison yard wall, and fears there has been an escape!

Come quickly, sir, come quickly!

The Governor himself is woken within minutes, and together they rush to the long corridor where . . . the cell door of the 'Chief Organiser of the Irish Republic', James Stephens, is ajar. On the floor is the padlock with a shiny new key still inside.

He is gone!

Quickly, Governor Marques orders McLeod's cell door to be opened. 'Did you hear any noise?' he demands of the convict.

'Yes,' the prisoner replies. 'About 1 o'clock in the morning I heard someone open the end door, come to Stephens' cell and unlock it.'

'Why did you not pull your gong, as I told you to do?' asks the Governor, looking as if he is about to burst.

'Because,' McLeod says, 'I knew whoever was doing this was likely to be armed, and could open my cell also, and take my life.'[6]

It is, frankly, a fair point.

•

Within the hour, the cry is going up all over Dublin, from one end of the ancient city to another.

'Stephens has escaped! Stephens has escaped!'

'From Richmond Bridewell Prison? When? How? Impossible!'[7]

There is, yet, a clear difference in the cries.

For the Irish, it is a cry of exultation; for the English, consternation.

Both ways, the legend of Stephens is expanded across all Ireland, Great Britain and America – and even in the faraway British penal colony of Australia – as headlines tell the story of the seemingly impossible escape pulled off by the shadowy military secret society known as the Fenians.

'The police and detectives went about the streets crestfallen and humiliated; while members of the Fenian fraternity could be pretty well identified by the flashing eye – the exultant countenance, the wild, strong grip with which they greeted one another.'[8]

Police go door to door in suspect neighbourhoods, ransack houses from top to bottom, front to back, even as the cavalry scours the country for any sign of the infamous fugitive, and every Irish port has ships boarded and searched by customs agents. Gunboats go out to fishing smacks and coasters, board them, and search them. Stephens' photograph and detailed description are circulated once more throughout the land, posters soon line every public wall, advertising 'One Thousand Pounds Reward' for anyone who can help capture the 'Chief Organiser of the Irish Republic', James Stephens, and 'lynx-eyed detectives'[9] are placed at every railway station to look out for him. It is to no avail.

In the meantime, at Richmond Bridewell Prison, suspicion falls on the warder who had been the watchman on the night, Daniel Byrne. When his house is raided, it is not just that a copy of the Fenian oath in his hand-writing is discovered, it is the part that is underlined: '. . . that I will yield implicit obedience . . . to the commands of my superior officers'.[10] He is arrested on the strength of it.

The charming and charmed John Breslin completely escapes suspicion.

27 November 1865, Green Street Courthouse, Dublin, 'the Fenian conspiracy'

Now, despite the humiliation of the British Crown over James Stephens' escape, it must go ahead with its Special Commission to try the swathes of Fenians still in prison. It gets under way with Judges William Nicholas Keogh and John David Fitzgerald presiding, each with glowering countenance.

Judge Keogh – Irish Catholic but determinedly loyal to the Crown and her laws – is clear about what they are accused of. It is nothing less than the 'overthrow of the Queen's authority, the separation of this country from Great Britain, the destruction of our present constitution, the establishment of some democratic or military despotism . . .'[11]

Arousing British loyalist sympathies thus, he goes on to give a judicial reminder: 'the object of British law is not retaliation – is not vengeance. It desires only to secure the safety of the lives, liberties, and the property of the people.'[12]

Thomas Clarke Luby is the first high-profile Fenian to sit in the dock, his trial starting on the second day, 28 November, and setting the precedent for the trials to follow.

In short, he can't win.

There's Pierce Nagle's testimony – the informing snake with the oily hair sits with his back to Luby, not daring to look at his former comrade. Then there's the stack of Luby's hand-written letters and documents openly discussing the Fenian movement and their aims, much of it found at *The Irish People* office.

In the grand tradition of Irish politics, Luby makes a valiant yet tempered speech from the dock:

> From the time I came to what have been called the years of discretion, my entire thought has been devoted to Ireland. I believed the course I pursued was right; others may take a different view. When the proceedings of this trial go forth to the world, the people will say that the cause of Ireland is not to be despaired of, that Ireland is not yet a lost country – that as long as there are men in any country prepared to expose themselves to every difficulty and danger in its service, prepared to brave captivity, even death itself if needs be, that country cannot be lost.[13]

He is summarily convicted and sentenced to 20 years of penal servitude. *Next!*

•

High and low, far and wide, Ireland's most famous fugitive is searched for. But there is no sign.

Stephens is, all this time, secreted in the basement of the home of an impoverished widow, Mrs Boland of Brown Street. She's the sister of *The Irish People*'s book-keeper, who had two months earlier warned Stephens of the paper's seizure by police. In all of her born days the woman would not have seen a thousand pounds, let alone possessed it, but not for ten times that amount, not on pain of death, would she reveal her guest.

Despite being in hiding, however, Stephens is nothing if not busy. For the question is put before the entire leadership of the Irish Republican Brotherhood: Is now the time for The Rising? While the people exult, and the British reel, should the call go out for all of their supporters to take to the streets, for all of their soldiers in all of their regiments to turn their guns towards the hated occupier and its supporters?

After all, right now, all of Ireland, it seems, is both aflame with resentment at the British occupiers, and inspired by the successful escape of their old Fenian Captain.

It is with this in mind that, two nights after his escape, Stephens convenes a meeting of his Dublin Centres and key American officers in one of their many 'safe houses'.

Together they must decide: 'Shall we strike, now or wait?'[14]

One by one, every man present is asked what he thinks is 'best to be done'.[15]

The vote goes around the table, with every Dublin Centre, and every American officer, casting a vote for 'immediate action', until they come to the Centre from County Wicklow, Denis Cromien, who argues for delay until they are better prepared. His comrades stare at him in disbelief. The circle is closing in on them and he wants to *wait*?

Still, it's only one vote against a dozen in support of launching The Rising.

All eyes now turn to Stephens.

Votes are fine, but it remains the province of the 'Provisional Dictator' to make the actual decision.

Stephens appears tired, more haggard and dishevelled than usual.

He looks around at his men, his lazy left eye narrowing, and announces his decision.

No. We wait.

Stephens' view remains as it was after *The Irish People* raid. They need more strength, more arms, more men and more money from the Irish–Americans.

With that in mind, Stephens must make his way to America, to rally for the cause, before returning in triumph to lead The Rising.

Quietly, the men around him fill with rage and . . . uncertainty about their leader.

One Centre, Joseph Denieffe, will later chronicle this moment, 'This resolution, to me, seemed simply a hocus pocus. Stephens plainly did not want to fight, and I made up my mind that he did not want to proceed any further; in fact, I concluded then and there that Stephens' work was done, and his usefulness ended on that night of November 26, 1865.'[16]

Colonel Thomas Kelly feels exactly the same. As do many others.

But the decision is taken and, at least for the moment, they must abide by it.

As for the Captain, he asks one of his Dublin Centres, John Flood – the son of a prominent Dublin shipowner – if he might have a quiet word? Stephens is drawn to the charismatic Flood, as are most Fenians. High-born, well-educated, he is a leader of men, and everyone likes him. He is, further, a fellow who 'always looked like a sailor or petty officer who had just stepped off one of Her Majesty's ironclads. He was invariably in great spirits and the picture of health, and was a man of resources, courage and aptitude for any emergency that might arise.'[17]

But now for that quiet word . . . John, over the past few months you've been instrumental in enabling us to smuggle American rifles into Ireland. Now, if you can do that, surely it is a relatively simple thing to get a man like me out of Ireland, yes?

Yes, Captain, that should be no problem.

Meanwhile, despite the Captain's reticence, the Fenians who remain free all over Ireland are ramping up for the fight. As John Devoy records, 'drilling went on more intensively and the whole organization felt that the long wished-for fight for Freedom was coming at last, with fine hopes of success'.[18]

With or without the Captain, who is apparently leaving them . . .

Early January 1866, Dublin, the net closes

Late on this wintry evening, manning a picket at Dublin's Royal Hospital, Private Thomas Hassett is doing his rounds, when a breathless comrade from the barracks – none other than William Foley, the soldier purloining the communications of General Sir Hugh Rose – arrives.

A quiet word, Tommy?

'Your time is up. [An armed] guard has arrived at the picket room to arrest you.'[19]

Very well then.

Hassett – as is always his wont, for he is a man of impulse – does not hesitate.

He puts his rifle to his shoulder, starts marching and . . . keeps going. His eyes forward, his back straight, his arms swinging, his step regular, onwards he marches through the streets of Dublin until, at ten o'clock, he reaches a house on Thomas Street in the city centre, where he knows a meeting of Fenians is being held.

Upstairs a council of rebels are indeed in full deliberation as to where to launch the first attack of The Rising when they . . . pause.

What is that?

Footsteps on the stairs!

The sound of a rifle butt, thumping on the floorboards!

Is this *it*?

The Fenians grasp their revolvers with purpose, and grit their teeth, ready to fight their way out, when they hear it.

Tap-tap, tappity-tap-tap-tap . . . TAP.

It is the coded signal, which indicates that whoever is on the other side of the door is a Fenian brother. Still the door is opened cautiously to reveal . . .

A redcoat!

Aghast, shocked, the revolvers are brought to bear and . . .

And wait. This is not a bust. He's smiling. Beneath that familiar peaked forage cap with the regimental number '24' embroidered on the lip, is a familiar face.

It is Tommy Hassett!

Coming into the room where the motley mob have clearly been smoking and drinking pots of porter, he lays before them on the table his entire stand of arms: his rifle and bayonet, knapsack, pouches and cross straps, his entire uniform and equipage, including 60 rounds of ammunition.

'Most of the fellows who desert for Ireland's sake,' says he, 'come to you empty-handed, but here am I, ready for work.'[20]

A Fenian is sent to a nearby store run by a Fenian and returns shortly afterwards with a fresh set of clothes and boots.

'The red coat was voted to the fire, and the belt and arms were stored away with a religious hope in the coming fight for an Irish republic.'[21]

By the following morning, the fresh-faced Hassett appears to be just another Irish civilian, even if he now looks more like 'a muscular Methodist minister'[22] than a regular Dublin lad.

17 January 1866, Dublin, enjoying the craic

On this chilly mid-winter evening, the two deserters from the 5th Dragoon Guards, the scar-faced swordsman Martin Hogan and the blue-eyed James Wilson, are out and about in Dublin, incognito, all rugged up against the biting cold, their hats pulled down hard over their ears.

Now that they have been 'gazetted' as deserters, and their descriptions have been circulated to Dublin police, they are in danger of being arrested at any moment. Still, they refuse to leave the city for safer climes, believing the long-awaited Rising is upon them. Their eyes scan the eyes of all those coming their way, looking for any sign of alarm, or recognition, and once satisfied, take a quick look behind. Again, nothing, and no-one looking their way. The coast is clear, so they duck quickly inside Peter Curran's Pub, at 1 Clare Lane, near the centre of Dublin, where the warm air immediately envelops them and the roaring fire by the bar tempts them. But on this night, the cockles of their soul are due to be warmed by something other than fire.

They make their way upstairs to a private parlour and tap the secret knock. The door swings open to reveal their fellow Fenians – most of them their former comrades, cavalrymen from the 5th Dragoons and 10th Hussars who are still serving, like the splendid regimental Centre, John Boyle O'Reilly, and the veteran Patrick Keating, who had way back in '48 been on the transport escorting the rebel leader John Mitchel as a convict in chains to Van Diemen's Land. (Now if Keating is looking deep in thought on this evening it is because he is himself seriously considering deserting. Just last month he'd also been a member of the military escort taking Thomas Luby over to prison in England and been so unnerved to see this once distinguished leader so shackled that he had burst into tears. His emotions had been noted by others in the escort and reported, and he has since felt like a marked man.) Also attending from the 5th Dragoons are William Foley and Patrick Foley, who share a surname but not a lineage, along with teetering Thomas Delaney, porter in hand – typically a little drunk, but at least he is there. Everyone in the room is under orders from John Devoy to attend and listen to their special guest.

Devoy himself rises as Wilson and Hogan enter, and he shakes their hands with great warmth. And who is this other fellow, with the war-weary but distinguished air, sitting with Devoy. Could it be the man they have come to hear?

•

It is. Captain John McCafferty, born 1838 in Ohio to Irish parents, had fought with distinction for the Confederates during the American Civil War.

John Devoy stands before the men, his thick black beard and his gravelly voice lending him the aspect of a man far beyond his 23 years. He makes a few introductory remarks about the Irish–American officer, his prowess in battle, how valuable he will be to their cause.

The men in this room, Devoy makes clear, have been handpicked to form the nucleus of a new unit, the Fenian Cavalry Unit.

The soldier Fenians grin approvingly. The Rising is truly coming.

With that, Devoy turns to McCafferty and assures him that all the men here are eager to learn.

'Are they all ready and willing to fight?' the Civil War officer asks in his soft drawl.

'They are,'[23] Devoy assures him.

Excellent. For the next 90 minutes the American holds the floor, telling of his experiences with 'Morgan's Guerillas', a force of cavalry raiders who eschewed set battle pieces, declining to confront the enemy where he was strong and instead hitting him where he was weak – again and again and again, behind enemy lines. Strike, and move! Strike and move again. Destroy his capacity of supply, blow up his weaponry, ammunition, and means of transport – and then melt away again, striking the next target before the enemy can even get a bead on where you are!

There is a stirring among his audience. What McCafferty is saying does not accord with their training at all. Does this man with the strange accent really know what he is talking about? He was, after all, on the losing side of the war. Martin Hogan, master swordsman, is particularly underwhelmed.

'Do you mean, sir,' begins Hogan, after McCafferty emphasises the need for guns, 'that you wouldn't use swords at all?'

'Nothing but revolvers,'[24] says McCafferty, quietly. It had been one of many lessons of the Civil War: horsemen with two six-shot revolvers were much more deadly in a close in-fight than a man with a sword.

Martin Hogan frowns, but says no more. Privately, he wonders whether this American import has ever seen a sword used properly.

Still, as the meeting goes on, and they ask questions, it is ever more clear that McCafferty really is an expert and his experience in actually fighting is very much to be envied. With him in the lead, they really could wreak havoc on the British forces.

Fresh-faced and optimistic, young John Devoy directs his precocious gaze upon this fine body of Irish patriots he has put together. They are strong, healthy, skilled in matters military and committed. Though he is their junior in years, he is their leader. And proud of it. He farewells them into the night with warmth.

The likes of Hogan and Wilson return to their safe house, while O'Reilly, Patrick Keating and William Foley head back to the barracks, with a renewed spring in their step. This is all starting to come together!

Not everyone, however, heads home. Patrick Foley of the 5th Dragoon Guards steals away from Peter Curran's Pub and into the night, careful he is not followed.

●

With all that is happening, John Devoy can see the writing on the wall.

After taking the night train, and trudging through the fields once more, he reaches a particular tree in a field near the Kenny household where Eliza is waiting for him and they fall into each other's arms. But he has come to say farewell, for the moment and foreseeable future. He is certain he is being watched, that the net is closing, and if it does he does not want her to be with him. So this is goodbye for a while. The two young lovers hold each other in the night, not sure of what it holds but only hoping it will be together.

•

10 February 1866, Dublin, the traits of the traitor

On this day in early February, the Crown's informer from the 5th Dragoon Guards is walking along a Dublin street when he stops still. That figure up ahead! The slope of his shoulders . . . the curious stutter in his stride . . . the angle of his head. He would know it anywhere!

Yes, it is Thomas Hassett, his former fellow soldier, who had deserted one month before – and is thought to have gone to the Fenians. Staying back a little, the informer follows Hassett to his lodgings house in one of Dublin's back alleys, then quickly goes to the police at Dublin Castle.

Within mere hours, the police surround the house and arrest Hassett along with other Fenians.

It does not take Hassett long to work out he has been done down by spies.

'[Down with] traitors,' he says on his way to the cells. 'If it were not for them we would have the Irish Republic long before now . . .'[25]

Before the sun goes down he is charged with treason and desertion.

For in that tangle of back lanes between Francis, Patrick and Nicholas streets in inner Dublin, the police know of dozens of small lodging houses where a poor man can find a bed and a filling meal for as little as four pence apiece. It is an obvious place for Fenian soldiers on the lam to shelter and lose themselves in the tangle.

But they can't always lose themselves, and certainly not on the evening of 10 February 1866 . . .

For on this night, another informer has recognised the upright swordsman Martin Hogan by his distinctive 'gait and appearance of a cavalry soldier',[26] and carefully followed him and his companion, James

Wilson, to their lodgings. Only a couple of hours later, Hogan and Wilson are asleep when six Dublin police burst through the door and arrest them. Within minutes, they are on their way to Chancery Lane Police Station and charged with mutinous conduct and desertion.

And they are not the only ones, as dozens upon dozens of other Fenian soldiers are fallen upon and arrested over coming days.

And so it goes on.

On 12 February 1866, the splendid John Boyle O'Reilly is looking out the window of Island Bridge Barracks in south-western Dublin when he freezes, a sliver of ice driving into his very soul. And there it is. One of his fellow Fenians in the 10th Hussars is being led away by an armed guard across the yard to the guardhouse, clearly under arrest. 'My turn will come next,'[27] he says quietly to himself.

Within two days, O'Reilly finds himself suddenly tackled to the ground in his quarters at the barracks. The authorities bind his wrists and, surrounded by an armed guard of six, he is forcibly led across the barracks square, where he is confronted by his Commanding Officer, Colonel Valentine Baker, who has always regarded O'Reilly as one of his finest men.

His face red, his lips spluttering a notably vile bile, Baker shakes his fist at his former protégé and roars 'Damn you, O'Reilly, you have ruined the finest regiment in Her Majesty's service.'[28]

O'Reilly smiles back. Either that, or he has struck a blow for Ireland, and will be one of those who has won a wreath that will be green forever.

For now, he is dragged away to Arbour Hill military prison, to await his trial.

A week later, nearing midnight, John Devoy is holding a meeting of military Fenians upstairs at Pilsworth's public house in Dublin's James Street when an urgent word is passed: there are two known detectives outside the pub, hovering with intent.

Devoy moves quickly.

'Leave quietly through a back door,'[29] he says calmly to his men. Most do just that, disappearing into the night, leaving just a handful with Devoy, as . . .

As the door bursts open and the two detectives rush into the room. Expecting exactly this, Devoy tightens his grip upon the handle of the revolver in his pocket, which he is about to bring to bear when one of his men cries out: 'Don't fire! There are a hundred policemen outside!'[30]

He looks out the window to see the swarming horde.

Devoy has been caught with 11 serving soldiers who have taken the Fenian oath, two deserters and four other civilians, of whom three are from the United States of America.

Everyone get your hands in the air . . . YOUR HANDS IN THE AIR!

Yes, one of the Fenians – James Byrne, a Centre – suddenly whips out a seven-chambered revolver and points it right at the head of a constable, but when a dozen guns are suddenly pointed at him in turn, he wisely decides against it, and lays down his weapon.[31]

Resistance would be futile, and Devoy, with all the rest – including Patrick Foley from the 5th Dragoon Guards and Devoy's old school friend, the carpenter Denis Duggan, who had arrived from London the previous year, to briefly be one of Stephens' bodyguards – are quickly marched out of the pub and through the crowd that has massed outside. All of the soldiers of the 8th Regiment have their bayonets drawn, ready to thwart any attempt by the crowd to release the prisoners, but no such threat emerges.

Within the hour the arrested Fenians find themselves in the cells of the Chancery Lane Police Station.

(An hour after that, Patrick Foley is quietly released.)

The next day the prisoners are transferred to the bowels of Dublin's Mountjoy Prison. John Devoy, for one, notices the absence of Patrick Foley,[32] and only now remembers a warning that he had been given about the risks of him being a spy.

Elsewhere, all over Ireland and England, other leading Fenian soldiers and civilians are arrested and dragged off to the cells. Among their number is Michael Harrington, a hard man's hard man, a veteran soldier of Her Majesty's forces for 22 long loyal years, mostly in India, before joining the Fenians only a few months ago – now arrested and placed in confinement at Arbour Hill military prison. At Richmond Barracks in Dublin, a remarkably tall soldier of the 61st Regiment, known to all as 'Big Bob' Cranston is arrested and dragged to a cell. As for William Foley, his activities, too – intercepting the correspondence of his master, General Sir Hugh Rose, and passing it on – have no sooner been discovered than he is dragged off to prison.

For the British authorities, such arrests are significant breakthroughs, but their major enduring frustration remains. Where is the leader of the conspirators?

If only they could claim James Stephens' public scalp, they really could claim to have crushed the movement.

13 March 1866, Dublin, Ireland, flight of the Wandering Hawk

The notably handsome Hansom cab proceeding through the streets of Dublin looks to be very nearly as grand as the two distinguished-looking older gentlemen inside, who are in turn matched by two liveried young bucks at the back, one driving, the other watching their surrounds.

For the moment, they are entirely unremarkable.

Ah, but look closer.

See the glittering left eye of the distinguished gentleman inside the carriage closest to us. Why it is none other than the most wanted criminal in all of Ireland, James Stephens! And, of course, right beside him, is the very man who had masterminded his escape from Richmond Bridewell Prison, Colonel Thomas J. Kelly, who is now masterminding his flight from Ireland itself. And the liveried young gentleman closest to us on the back is one John Flood Esq, the Fenian Centre with ample shipping connections, who always looks like a sparkling sailor or petty officer, no matter his dress, and who one comrade would describe 'as fine a specimen of Irish manhood as need be seen'.[33]

On the carriage goes, all the way to the small fishing village of Balbriggan, where the footmen leap to the ground, look around with care and . . . . . . open the doors . . . . . . and the two fine gentlemen alight. By the shore is a longboat manned by several worthies, and Stephens, Kelly and Flood climb on board, to be whisked away to a large lugger – a two-masted sailing vessel – anchored close by.

Still, they are not mere passengers, for the skipper of this lugger, Captain Nicholas Weldon – a friend of Flood's from boyhood onwards – soon has them hauling on the winch to get them under way, so as to fill out the manpower of his skeleton crew.

Once clear of the harbour, the lugger is soon making its way, bound for a port in the north of France.

Fittingly, for such an enterprise, a great storm arises from the south, causing the captain to alter course for Scotland. The lugger sails on north through the Irish Sea, amidst heavy squalls. A narrow shave is endured as they skirt a dangerous reef. At length, the anchor is cast after the vessel has run into the old harbour in the Firth of Clyde at Ardrossan. Flood, an experienced seaman, is cut severely on his hand but sails on. From there it is on to London by carriage before crossing the channel to France, Flood throwing authorities at Dover off guard with his perfect mimicry of an upper-class English accent. From France, Stephens and Kelly will soon be catching a ship to the United States.

For his part, John Flood quickly returns to Ireland, before crossing the Irish Sea once more, this time to take up his position as the Stephens-anointed leader of the Fenians in England and Scotland.

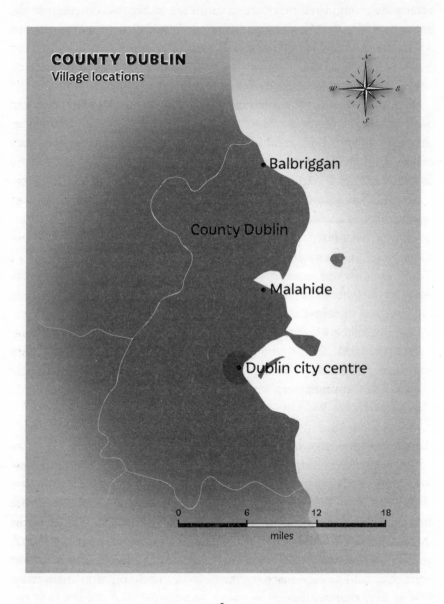

It is a quirk of the human spirit that those who have happy childhoods tend to remember sunny days, while those who have suffered long and hard more often recall thunderstorms and drizzling rain.

Often, sometimes all day and into the night in his gloomy cell, John Boyle O'Reilly thinks back on his happy childhood in Dowth Castle near Drogheda overlooking River Boyne. He remembers sunshine. He remembers long, lovely days learning in his father's schoolroom in the grounds of Dowth Castle, and then roaming the ruins that abounded all around and rambling with his friends in the green meadows that lay between the castle and the river just half a mile away, before swimming on hot days in its cool greenness.

He thinks of a particularly high spot upon *an móate*, where you can look out over the Boyne, over Rosnaree, to the Hill of Tara, to Newgrange and Knowth and Slane, and Mellifont and Oldbridge – the very same lands where the Irish lost to the forces of William of Orange in the Battle of the Boyne, 1690, and which led to the first famed flight of the Wild Geese.

It is a vision, he later recalls, 'that I carry forever in my brain and heart, vivid as the last day I looked on them'.[34]

Most particularly, he thinks of Dowth's graveyard, right by the old church. On a foundation stone of that old church, as a lad, he had laboriously etched his initials, 'J.B.O'R'[35] the only real mark he has made on the world to this point.

The mere memory of the place calms him.

'I should like to be buried just under that spot,'[36] he will later recount.

In many ways it is the contemplation of those glorious childhood days that inspires him now to write poetry in his cell, both to bring the old days alive, and perhaps to make his mark in another field.

•

That figure slowly going from cell to cell in the deepest, darkest sections of Arbour Hill military prison, in the centre of Dublin? The old fellow with the high bearing, and distinct military gait, I mean.

Why, it is Captain Fergus Whelan of the 8th Regiment, the man who has been charged with prosecuting the traitorous Fenian soldiers in the upcoming courts martial, and he is a man on a mission. That is, to break the Fenians before they are put in the dock, to get them to turn against each other and give evidence for the Crown, to help put the others away, and so save themselves.

His method is simple.

As all of the Fenians have been put on starvation rations – just enough to keep them alive – their morale is already low, and Captain Whelan is the first kind man they have come across in weeks.

And he wants to help them avoid the noose, really he does. And he shouldn't tell them this, but he decides to anyway.

William Foley of the 5th Dragoon Guards – the once-trusted messenger of the high brass – is offered his freedom if he gives evidence against his dear friend James Wilson and his companion Martin Hogan.

Turn on Wilson and Hogan?

The stout William Foley would sooner die, and tells the authorities so. Do your worst, but I will not be betraying my mates.

Moving on to the 10th Hussars, Captain Whelan goes to soldier after soldier, lying through his teeth: 'O'Reilly has informed on you. Your only chance of saving yourself is by telling everything you know.'[37]

O'Reilly himself has already told all?

Knowing O'Reilly well, none of them believe him. O'Reilly betray them? It is unthinkable.

Thwarted at every turn in getting John Boyle O'Reilly's comrades in the 10th Hussars to betray their Centre, Captain Whelan – on the evening of 26 June, just before O'Reilly's court martial is due to begin on the morrow – decides to have one more go with O'Reilly himself.

Many times Whelan has tried with the splendid soldier poet, and every time he has failed. But there surely can be nothing lost by making one last attempt.

In the most secure wing of Arbour Hill, Whelan makes his way to O'Reilly's gloomy cell, accompanied by an old warder who is a former soldier, one of the Pensioner guard, as they are commonly known.

'O'Reilly,' says Whelan, trotting out his usual spiel, 'you must save yourself by telling all you know.'[38]

Smiling, O'Reilly declines.

The old warder tries his luck: 'Yes, O'Reilly, you'd better do as the Captain says . . .'

O'Reilly shakes his head.

Well, that is it then.

Whelan storms out of the cell, saying he can do no more, and it will be for O'Reilly to face the 'dire consequences' of his refusal.

The instant that the coast is clear, the old warder, just before he closes the door, leans his head back in, and says to O'Reilly, in a low, stern voice: 'And, damn, I'd like to choke you with my own hands if you do.'[39]

There is never any risk of that.

CHAPTER THREE

COURT MARTIAL

GOD SAVE THE GREEN
Whereas in the year of the Irish Republic 1866, certain persons
(enemies of the said republic) styling themselves in Parliament of
Great Britain, and who pretend or imagine they have authority
over this Oppressed Nation, have ordered the arrest of all the
loyal subjects of said Republic by the suspension of an Act which
they call Habeas Corpus. Now, in order to let the usurpers see
that the Irish Nation will have their independence, and in case the
myrmidons of the so-called British law make any attempt on their
liberty, it is ordered that they do not allow it if possible. By order
of the Executive Committee, Irish Republic, 21st February, 1866.
God save the Green![1]

'Fenian' proclamation posted in Tuam, Ireland, February 1866

Things fall apart; the centre cannot hold . . .[2]

W.B. Yeats, 'The Second Coming'

Spring 1866, courts martial, Dublin and Cork, curse ye Fenian soldiers

And so the courts martial, designed to root out the 'Fenian conspiracy'
from the military once and for all – like plucking weevils from an infested
sack of flour, and crushing them underfoot – are to get under way
in Dublin's Royal Barracks, the oldest public building in the city, all
granite, mahogany, arcaded colonnades and the history of oppression
of the Irish people.

The charges are simple. Most of the Fenian soldiers who have been
arrested are charged with 'mutinous conduct . . . in that coming to the
knowledge of an intended mutiny in Her Majesty's forces . . . did not
give information thereof to his commanding Officer'.[3]

They are accused, furthermore, of engaging in 'conduct to the prejudice
of good order and military discipline in having . . . joined a treasonable

41

and seditious society, called the Fenian Brotherhood, having for its object the levying of war against the Queen and subverting of the government of the country'.[4]

Compared to their civilian Fenian counterparts, they are sure to receive heavier sentences.

Among the first to face court martial down Cork way is Thomas Darragh. Myriad witnesses – mostly soldiers of his regiment – come forward to attest to his efforts in getting them to join the Fenians.

Darragh denies it.

'With my 14 years' service,' he thunders indignantly from the dock, 'had I joined such a society, I would be more fitted for a lunatic asylum than a prison. My long service in Africa and China, and the high character I bear in the regiment, should be taken as proofs of my loyalty.'[5]

But it is to no avail, and on 2 March 1866, he is found guilty but no sentence is handed down. For the moment, he is dragged to the cells, to await his fate in isolation.

A little over a month later, the call goes out around the parade ground of his old barracks in Cork, and carries all the way through the bars of his cell, to his poor benighted self.

'*Parrraaade* . . . fall in.'

And so they do. Every battalion files onto the central square for this rare 'General Parade' of every soldier stationed in Cork, some 10,000 in all. Once they are all in, all standing to attention in serried ranks around three sides of the parade ground, the Commanding Officer of the whole district, Major-General John Bates, strides out to the centre.

'*Present . . . arms!*'

As one, 10,000 rifles are whipped up to the vertical, aligned with the centre of the body, before they clasp arms rigidly to the fore, a carefully choreographed blur of military movement, impressive for the fact that not a single soul is out of kilter either in motion or dress.

'Atennnnnnshun.'

Again, as one, 10,000 men lower their rifles, both arms falling instantly to their sides. And so they must stay, still as statues.

They are here for a very solemn, extremely formal occasion, hence their full-dress uniform, their shining brass, their highly polished boots, their grim demeanour.

And yet, even though they are highly disciplined soldiers who know that they must now stare directly ahead, there is many a'man who simply cannot help himself, as his eyes quickly glance toward Sergeant Thomas

Darragh, the Protestant 34-year-old father of two being dragged forth from the cells. Over his right shoulder, the men can see the firing squad post. It has a hook, up high, to hold him up by his handcuffs if he can no longer stand up himself. Many shudder at the thought.

With a soldier on each side, Darragh – wild-eyed, his dishevelled red mop atop his head, and clearly in shock – stands before the men whose uniform he has disgraced by his actions, a grim reminder of what happens to those soldiers who engage with Fenians.

'Thomas Darragh,' a decorated Colonel announces, 'you have been found guilty of Mutinous Conduct in Cork in not reporting an intended mutiny of Her Majesty's forces and secondly, with having about the same time joined a treasonable and seditious conspiracy called the Fenian Brotherhood. You are to be executed in the presence of the troops of garrison.'[6]

'Her Majesty,' the officer intones, 'approves the findings and sentence.'[7]

My wife! My children! My life on this earth! My country!

The Colonel goes on.

'However . . . considering your service and your previous good character, Her Majesty has been graciously pleased to commute the punishment to penal servitude for life in one of the penal prisons.'[8]

Darragh slumps with relief.

The guards practically have to carry him back to his cell.

•

Mercifully, Thomas Darragh has been saved by the growing view in the highest echelons of the British Government that, while they might be able to execute this generation of Fenians, such brutal treatment would only see the next generation larger, more alienated and more committed. A wiser policy, they have decided, is to simply banish them to the furthest reaches of the earth.

15 May 1866, New York, New York, an open conspiracy

And now the Wandering Hawk is not only safely landed in America, but also being given a grand reception from no fewer than 7000 American Fenians at Jones's Wood. Rising before them, his hands raised indeed like a mighty hawk about to take off on their thunderous roar, he starts to tell his story.

'Friends of Ireland's!' he begins, before recalling the history of the movement, the noble patriots who make up its ranks, the challenges they have faced.

The thousands in the audience hang on his every word, their cheers punctuate his every sentence.

'The organisation in Ireland,' he roars, 'towards the close of last year numbered 200,000 men.'[9]

The crowd erupts more violently than before – 'great cheering'[10] fills the air and fades.

Stephens goes on.

'Of that force, 50,000 men were thoroughly drilled, with a large proportion of men who had seen war, who had smelt powder on the battlefield, veterans, in short. Fifty thousand more are partially drilled men. The other 100,000 are undrilled; but if there is a man among you who thinks that 50,000 Irishmen, thoroughly drilled, and 50,000 more partially drilled; to begin with, would not constitute a force sufficient to meet anything that England could bring against us in Ireland, then indeed he is wilfully ignorant . . .'[11]

Of course, he is exaggerating wildly, wantonly even – revolutionary rhetoric of a proud leader far from home – but it achieves its aim. It rallies the American Fenians to *believe*, to send money and munitions, and to head over to Ireland themselves, ready for The Rising to come.

27 June 1866, mess-room of the 85th Regiment at Royal Barracks, Dublin, snakes in the ranks

All rise. Particularly *you*, John Boyle O'Reilly. For even if tomorrow is your 22nd birthday, today is the day your court martial begins. Colonel Sawyer of the 6th Dragoon Guards, acting as President of the proceedings, enters the room.

The ever-handsome O'Reilly calmly stares out at those who would do him down – including the scowling Prosecutor, Captain Fergus Whelan of the 8th Regiment – the very man who tried to get him to turn on his confederates.

The jury is a selection of 14 officers from other regiments who are watching proceedings carefully from behind a table at the side.

How do you plead, Private O'Reilly?

'Not guilty,'[12] the charismatic prisoner replies calmly. Despite having come straight from a prison cell, he still cuts a dashing figure as befitting one who had so loved looking at his own reflection.

'The enormity of the offence with which the prisoner is charged,' Captain Whelan begins gravely, 'is such that it is difficult to find language by which to describe it. It strikes at the root of all military discipline, and, if allowed to escape punishment which it entails, would render Her Majesty's forces, who ought to be the guardians of our lives and liberty, and the bulwark and protection of the laws under which we live, a source of danger to the state and all its loyal citizens and subjects, and Her Majesty's faithful subjects would become the prey and victims of military despotism, licentiousness, and violence.'[13]

Pausing theatrically, making sure that all in this courtroom appreciate just what is at stake here, he continues: 'Our standing army would then be a terror to the throne, and a curse, not a blessing, to the community.'[14]

Captain Whelan reminds the jury to fulfil their duty under the law and weigh the evidence carefully. But make no mistake, that evidence will be presented in abundance, starting with our first witness, Lance-Corporal Michael FitzGerald of the 10th Hussars.

'Do you swear to tell the truth, the whole truth, and nothing but the truth?'

He most certainly does.

Tell us, then, Corporal FitzGerald, of your key interactions with Private O'Reilly.

'I know the prisoner. I know Hoey's public house in Bridgeport Street. I was in it in the month of November, 1865, with the prisoner. He brought me there. I was introduced by the prisoner to a man named Devoy.'[15]

Corporal FitzGerald recounts how O'Reilly and Devoy had tried to persuade him to join them. He had agreed to do so, because to do anything less would be dangerous, while resolving to tell the authorities, which is partly how the whole plot had been exposed.

'The next time I saw him,' the Corporal goes on, 'was one evening I met him in town coming from the barracks. Some arrests took place that day, and I said, "This business is getting serious." He said it was, and that my name had been mentioned at a meeting a few nights before. I asked what meeting, and he said a military meeting . . . He added, "If you come home to-night I will take you to a similar meeting."'[16]

After Corporal FitzGerald's testimony, other soldier witnesses come forward with similar stories of O'Reilly and John Devoy recruiting from Her Majesty's ranks, though, for the moment, there remains a clear lack of soldiers testifying that O'Reilly personally spoke to them about Fenianism.

A Private MacDonald establishes one key point.

'When the prisoner told me to go to the public houses at night,' he tells the court, 'he used to say, "Go to such a house and you will meet John there, and tell him I am on duty."'

> President Sawyer: 'Who was John?'
> Witness: 'Devoy.'
> President: 'Then Devoy was a great friend of the prisoner?'
> Witness: 'He appeared to be.'

'Did I ever tell you,' O'Reilly intervenes, 'Devoy was an old friend of my family?'

'No,' the witness replies, addressing the judge only, 'he did not.'[17]

The President, Colonel Sawyer, has precious little time to be pleased at this answer, however, before the witness follows up.

'John O'Reilly never spoke to me about Fenianism, and I never heard Fenian songs in his company.'

The President is not pleased.

'Recollect what you say: Did you not swear that prisoner told you he was a Fenian?'

'He said he was one at Cahir . . .'

'Did you not state to the President,' O'Reilly intervenes once more, 'that I told you I *had* been a member of the Fenian Brotherhood while I was at Cahir?'

'Yes, that you had been a Fenian at Cahir.'[18]

Again, the President is not pleased. After more of O'Reilly's former comrades give evidence of varying worth – all falling short of confirming that he was himself actively planning revolution – the Commanding Officer with the 10th Hussars, Colonel Valentine Baker is sworn in. O'Reilly hasn't seen Colonel Baker since being arrested and frog-marched through the yard, where Baker had publicly blamed him for 'ruin[ing] the finest regiment in Her Majesty's service'.[19]

'I know the prisoner,' Colonel Baker says, while looking ruefully at the accused, in the manner of a disappointed father. 'He never gave me any information of an intended mutiny in Her Majesty's force in Ireland.'[20]

Very well, then. But O'Reilly has a question of his own.

'What character do I bear in the regiment?'

'A good character.'[21]

Which is something.

But whatever benign light shines on O'Reilly by this piece of good testimony, it is quickly dissipated by the next witness. O'Reilly looks up to see a familiar bullet-shaped head walking to the witness chair . . . surely not . . . is it him? The man known to the Fenians of Limerick as the charismatic water-bailiff, the towering, devout patriot John Kelly, takes his seat and is introduced by the prosecutor as . . .

'Constable Thomas Talbot.'

John Boyle O'Reilly's blood boils. Yes, the Fenians have been duped by a Dublin detective! Kelly's . . . no, Detective Talbot's uncanny knack for avoiding the police was a ruse! He has been filing reports to Dublin Castle all along. He now paints a picture of just how far the conspiracy goes, how it has infiltrated every regiment in the country, how the Fenians have in their possession weapons, maps, keys, money and *men* – traitors to be precise.

'Not a single regiment in the service is free from [this] rebellion,' he says, 'and part of the conspirators' scheme is the enlistment of revolutionary agents in the various branches of the British service. O'Reilly is just such an agent.'[22]

O'Reilly feigns calm.

Thankfully, Talbot does not give direct evidence on O'Reilly's activities, but the thrust of his evidence is clear: this conspiracy has gone a long way. If this court is going to do its bit to crush it, it must be ruthless.

But now the *pièce de résistance* of the prosecution.

Step forward, Private . . .

And here he is.

John Boyle O'Reilly stares as wee Patrick Foley of the 5th Dragoon Guards slithers across the room and coils his way round and up into the witness seat. The *snake*!

Of course. O'Reilly had been surprised a few weeks earlier to hear that Foley had been released only shortly after being arrested . . . and now he knows why. Foley was the informant among them all along.

Prosecutor Whelan, so puffed up with smug pride he looks ready to burst, invites Patrick Foley to tell the court of what he knows of the accused's involvement at gatherings of Fenians.

'I saw him in Hoey's public house about the 14th of January . . .' Foley begins, never looking remotely at O'Reilly himself. 'At the time I saw the prisoner at Hoey's, there were a number of people there, principally civilians. Devoy was one . . . Hogan and Wilson, both deserters from 5th Dragoon Guards, were also there in coloured clothes.'[23]

On another occasion, Foley says, in February, he was with the prisoner at Barclay's public house. They went to a private room in Barclay's, where

O'Reilly sat a table with some fellow Fenians – including Devoy – and Foley could hear what they were saying.

'It was on Fenianism and the probable fate of the state prisoners who were on trial at that time. There was also something said about electing a president as soon as they had a free republic.'[24]

A stirring in the court. Infamy! Talbot was right. Here are soldiers of the Queen talking about *electing* a *President*, when Ireland is a *republic*. Could anything be more traitorous?

'Was there at any of these meetings of which you spoke,' the prosecutor asks, 'and at which the prisoner was present, any conversation of an intended outbreak or mutiny?'[25]

'I object to that question,' O'Reilly interrupts, 'because the witness has already stated the substance of the conversations as far as he can remember. The prosecutor had no right to lead the witness, and put into his mouth the very words of the charge.'[26]

Very well then, the prosecutor reframes the question, and soon gets the answer he is looking for from Foley.

'There *was* a conversation of an intended mutiny that was to take place in January or the latter end of February.'[27]

And so it goes,

On 9 July 1866, the court delivers the only verdict possible – 'Guilty' – and it behooves the President to pass sentence upon John Boyle O'Reilly: Death. Mercifully, by this time it is established that the death sentence is likely only a formality, so there is hope. In the meantime, O'Reilly is marched back to his cell, a convicted man, still somehow managing to cut a splendid form as he goes.

•

Similar scenes are taking place, all over Ireland and Great Britain throughout the latter months of 1866.

In Dublin, Wilson, Hogan, Hassett, Kiely and Cranston also must face the devastating testimony of Talbot.

Talbot plays a key role in taking down the garrulous young soldier, James Kiely, who had casually blabbed about his uncles' pike nests down Dungarvan way. *Guilty!*

Patrick Foley, too, plays his part in bringing as many Fenians down as he can, testifying against James Wilson and Martin Hogan in particularly damaging fashion.

Foley testifies that he was in Hoey's that night of 17 January, and had seen Wilson and Hogan there, actively involved as the American, Captain McCafferty, had been teaching them new guerilla tactics.

In response, Wilson and Hogan make no defence. As with James Stephens, they refuse to recognise the authority of the court to ask them anything.

•

Down Limerick way, it has not taken long for the word to get out. Have you heard the news?

Water-bailiff Kelly, that lovely man who disappeared a few months ago?

Turns out, he was a spy for Dublin Castle all along! Kelly was not even his real name, and he is in fact Constable Thomas Talbot, giving Queen's evidence against no fewer than 200 of our brethren, most of them from here in Limerick! And that explains all those arrests of nearby Centres, and plots foiled, while he was among us!

He has made no apology for his treachery, saying only, 'It was necessary for my duty.'[28]

That traitorous *bastard*!

Well, his time will come.

3 September 1866, Royal Square, Royal Barracks, Dublin, English soldier to Irish felon

Awaiting his final sentence in his tiny cell in Arbour Hill military prison, John Boyle O'Reilly nevertheless remains defiant, leaving his mark on the military establishment which is hosting him by scratching into the wall of his cell with a nail.

> Once an English Soldier, now an Irish felon – and proud of the exchange.[29]

In the meantime, he continues to let his mind wander back to the many joyous scenes of his childhood. What happy times they were! And how far away from them he is now.

His parents, William and Eliza, had both had a strong literary bent, and always encouraged him, his two brothers and five sisters, down the path of exploring their own poetic prowess. Given that O'Reilly has never had so much time for the task as right now, he throws himself into it with a will.

He takes up the loose nail once more, and again begins to scratch at the wall of his cell.

> *We are born with scorn and insult.*
> *But the Saxon yet shall feel,*
> *The strength of Irish vengeance,*
> *And the points of Irish Steel.*[30]

Ah, but this proves to be just the first few drops of what will soon become a torrent, as John Boyle O'Reilly starts writing more and more poems on scraps of paper – the flights of fancy taking him ever more frequently out of his prison cell.

As it happens, on the very morning of his sentencing an angel of inspiration alights on his shoulder as he finds himself staring at the prison's clock ... *tick tock* ... *tick tock* ... *tick tock* ...

Reaching for the pencil, he is taken back to the last time he'd returned home on furlough to see his beloved parents back at Dowth Castle and had noted they'd changed the old clock in the old schoolhouse. Now, just contemplating that old schoolroom is enough to calm him, to give him spiritual sustenance, and the words begin to pour from his pencil. He begins ...

The Old School Clock
Old memories rush o'er my mind just now
   Of faces and friends of the past;
Of that happy time when life's dream was all bright,
   E'er the clear sky of youth was o'ercast.
Very dear are those mem'ries, – they've clung round my heart.
   And bravely withstood time's rude shock;
But not one is more hallowed or dear to me now
   Than the face of the Old School Clock ...

The words continue to flow, the poem taking shape beneath his ever-moving right hand.

•

Finishing it up, O'Reilly writes a quick note and gives his few precious scraps of paper to a friendly prison guard, entrusting him with the important task of giving them to a fellow Fenian convict he's befriended during his stay – a veteran of the American Civil War by the name of Murphy, who he knows is soon to be released – and ...

And quickly now, go, for here they come.

The rhythmic approach of many feet stepping in time indicates that the guard has been called out and, sure enough, O'Reilly and other convicted Fenian soldiers are now told to dress in full military garb, before they are escorted into Royal Square, Royal Barracks, where all of the troops are formed up, rigid in their ranks, ordered to watch this spectacle.

The Fenians stand stooped, blinking in the light.

John Boyle O'Reilly, however, gazes steadily back to those soldiers staring at him. He has done nothing wrong, knows it, and it is a point of honour to show it. In any case, he knows many of those soldiers are Fenians themselves, for he has personally sworn them in. And now an officer steps forward, and starts to read the charges proven against each soldier, and the sentence passed upon them, starting with O'Reilly himself who has, 'at Dublin, in January, 1866, come to the knowledge of an intended mutiny in Her Majesty's forces in Ireland, and not giving information of said intended mutiny to his commanding officer . . .'[31]

On the officer goes until he arrives at O'Reilly's sentence.

'Death.'

Even one as brave as O'Reilly must take pause at the word but, sure enough, just as had happened to others, he soon hears the merciful news: this original sentence of death . . . is commuted to life.

More merciful still, because he is still so young, his sentence is further reduced to 20 years' penal servitude.

And now, in front of everyone, to the slow rhythm of a drum, O'Reilly and the others must remove their once proud military uniforms – the very one that had filled O'Reilly with such pride that he would alter his route so he could better see his own reflection – and instead put on the garments hurled at their feet.

It is the ragged uniform of the convict – ill-fitting grey woollen tunics, trousers and rough leather boots. Next, the prisoners are chained to each other, to make their humiliation complete. Let this be a lesson to all.

This, this, is what happens to those who break their oath, turn their backs on their brothers-in-arms, and commit treason.

Cashiered from the Dragoons, now no more than a convict, shortly thereafter O'Reilly and his comrades are in the back of a sturdy black van rattling along behind six horses, with armed soldiers galloping along on each side, being taken to Dublin's Mountjoy Prison. It is the beginning of a peripatetic prison journey that will shortly see them transferred to Pentonville and Millbank prisons, both in London, before being transferred yet again to Chatham, Portsmouth and Dartmoor. Always the idea of the British Government is to keep the prisoners moving so that, even if an escape plan is conceived by Fenians on the inside or outside of thick walls, the men will be gone to a new prison before the plan can be put into effect.

•

By the dismal light of dusk coming through the bars of his Arbour Hill cell, Murphy opens the scraps of paper passed to him by one of the guards.

'My Dear Fellow', he begins to read, instantly recognising the elegant hand of his fellow inmate, that precocious prodigy, O'Reilly,

> I wrote 'The Old School Clock' today. If you can possibly give a copy to my father, do. He or my brother will tell you all about the 'Old Clock', etc. I was reminded of it by looking at the prison clock this morning.[32]

Murphy hides the note and the poems in the ventilator of his cell.

Autumn 1866, Dublin, discretion is the better part of valour

All is confusion, gloom, courts martial, convictions and also ongoing arrests. James Wilson, Martin Hogan, Patrick Keating, Thomas Hassett are all given life, while Thomas Delaney is given 10 years and William Foley faces five years' hard time.

In contemplation of what awaits there is a mix of resignation, misery and . . . *outrage* – much of the last extended to the spies and informers whose testimonies have put so many Fenians away . . .

But have they all come forward in the courts martial, or are there still a lot amongst us Fenians?

It is the question of the moment.

Who is a Fenian Republican, true to us faithful few and who are the loyalists to the Royalists? And of those who have been arrested and dragged away, how many have talked; who have they identified?

To this point, John Breslin, the key man with the keys in Richmond Bridewell Prison, had been able to get about his business, without the slightest suspicion falling upon him.

But how long can that go on?

Breslin must contemplate that when, in the autumn of 1866, he finds himself responding to suddenly pointed questions from the prison's

Governor as to what *he* was doing on the night that Stephens escaped. Has someone talked? One way or another it becomes obvious that if he does not flee, he risks occupying the very cell he had helped to vacate. And so he moves quickly – easy for a man unburdened by wife or children.

Gathering what money he has, and all the worldly possessions he can in a single bag, he slips on board the Holyhead boat at Kingstown, bound for Paris.

His escape proves to be just in time. Only days after he has disappeared, the Lord Lieutenant of Ireland issues a warrant for his arrest – with a reward of £2000 soon posted in the *Hue-and-Cry*.

From Paris, Breslin heads to the United States, where he is embraced by the American Fenians – *Gentlemen, a toast, to the man who broke Stephens out of Richmond Prison!* – and settles in Boston, taking a job as a humble railway freight agent.

What the future holds for Mr Breslin, he is not yet sure – and is only glad to have done his bit for the cause, and to have satisfactorily escaped the horror of incarceration at the hands of those British bastards.

Speaking of which . . .

The British authorities running the fierce penitentiaries of mainland England don't miss the opportunity to give their military deserter guests a souvenir to remember them by. Forever.

With little preamble, and no explanation – for the prisoner has no rights and may be treated as a beast of burden – prison guards bustle Martin Hogan into a small room, lay him out on a long plank of wood that comes up from the floor at a 45 degree angle, and has an inverted triangle at the top. While his legs are now manacled to the bottom of the plank, each arm is splayed along one side of the triangle and also manacled. The one-time champion swordsman of the British Army would have made short work of the lot of them in a free fight. But they are too many, and after months of incarceration, he is too weak.

He is at the mercy of merciless men.

To his horror now, one of the warders roughly opens his shirt to leave his chest entirely exposed. A call goes up, and Hogan will ever after remember the horror of what happens next.

In comes the prison blacksmith, with a bucket of hot coals. Out of the bucket he pulls a red-hot branding iron, on the end of which is the letter 'D'.

Oh my *Lord*! Is this it? Is he . . . ?

He is.

Before Hogan can even protest at the barbarity of it all, there is an instantaneous sensation of scorching heat as the brute brings the red-hot metal on to Hogan's bare flesh, a bright searing flash, and the smell of burning skin. His own . . . Forevermore he will bear the large letter 'D' over his heart. This is what we do to Deserters.

In their own prisons, Michael Harrington, Thomas Hassett and James Wilson are equally so branded.

•

As for the snake Patrick Foley, there is 'branding' of a different type. Yes, in his own mind he has helped lock up traitors, which is a good thing. But in the mind of the 5th Dragoons, awash with Fenians after all, *he* is the traitor, the one who has turned on brother soldiers, who has betrayed the bonds that unite them all. His life is, consequently, made hell. He is ostracised, bullied, all but spat upon. At mealtimes he sits alone. On the parade ground, there is active manoeuvring not to be the one standing next to him. In fact, it is not just the Fenian soldiers who detest him. Even loyalist English soldiers in the Dragoons despise the 'spy' in the regiment. Before long, in an effort to save him, Foley is transferred to England, but word of his activities will soon follow him there, too. He is a spy, who has turned on brother soldiers. He is *not* to be trusted.

For his part, Pierce Nagle faces such outrage at his duplicity that he flees to London, where he is badly beaten up by a group of men and hospitalised. Shortly after getting out of hospital, however, he is found hanging from the archway of a London bridge, with a knife in his heart. On the handle of the knife is the inscription: 'Death to traitors'.[33]

At least for Constable Thomas Talbot, there is no such opprobrium from his fellow detectives. He has done a brilliant job. But the same cannot be said for how most of the Irish population regard him.

For some, Talbot's cards are also marked, and many are eager to pin the Ace of Spades to his forehead.

•

Some agree with James Stephens that the Fenians should organise in America and make a mass landing in Ireland. Others continue to insist, with all seriousness, that a better option would be to invade Canada – no, *really* – subdue it, and make a trade with the British: We will free Canada, if you free Ireland.

Still others think that while both options might be possible, neither is possible now.

And it is the way of such things, with so many passions running in opposing directions, that the net result is a frustrated inertia, compounded by the fact that Stephens' leadership is under attack by both his comrade of the 1848 Rising, John O'Mahony, and also Colonel Kelly, who had been so instrumental in releasing him from Richmond Bridewell Prison. Colonel Kelly, particularly, is now all but openly moving against him, frustrated at Stephens' lack of will to bring on The Rising . . .

When Kelly writes to an American Fenian friend, he even reports of Stephens, the less than hirsute revolutionary:

> Little Baldy has at last given up the ghost, and acknowledged that if he came to Ireland the people would be certain to make short work of him. The rascal is in Paris, taking his ease with his wife, while the destiny of Ireland is in the balance. The money he squeezed from the men of New York, through you and others, under pretence that it was necessary to procure a boat, he coolly pockets . . . and denounces the Irish-Americans as 'dogs, dung and devil's scum.'[34]

In Ireland itself, the committed Fenians still at liberty are anxious for The Rising as never before. Their numbers now include many more Irish–American officers and soldiers, who for the final months of 1866 and early weeks of 1867 have been flooding back to the old country.

Most of them are distinctly underwhelmed by what they find – a dearth of trained men and a critical lack of arms, while from every pulpit the priests, forever conservative, are preaching peace, telling the population that they must turn away from the Fenians and bow to the authority of the British.

Still the rebels persist, and initially – despite there still being no sign of the return of Stephens, who is now rumoured to be somewhere in Paris – the date for The Rising is set by Colonel Kelly for February 1867.

19 February 1867, Dublin, Mrs Brown vs. John Devoy

After a year spent under lock and key in Mountjoy Prison awaiting trial, the mastermind Fenian recruiter, John Devoy, is finally brought before his accusers in Dublin's Green Street Courthouse.

How do you plead, John Devoy?

The young Fenian rises and in typical fashion retorts without hesitation in his gruff voice: 'Guilty, my lord.'[35]

And when the motions have been gone through, the judge reads the sentence.

'You, John Devoy, were appointed Centre for the military, and were engaged in the seduction of soldiers from their allegiance ... The sentence of the court is that you ... Devoy, be kept in penal servitude for 15 years.'[36]

As the newspapers report, he is but one of a list of Fenians being sentenced this day, with inevitable consequences:

> The prisoners exhibited great surprise and emotion
> on hearing their sentences. Baines burst into tears,
> and Power appeared to be almost paralysed. Not one
> of them said a word. The galleries were crowded with
> the wives, mothers, sisters, and other relatives of
> the prisoners, and it was painful to listen to the
> hysterical shrieks of some of them, or witness the
> silent sorrow of others.[37]

One of those so weeping is sweet Eliza Kenny of County Kildare, John Devoy's fair fiancée and apple of his eye. Of course, she had known the risks of falling in love with a Fenian. But it had been so many of the values he'd displayed as a revolutionary – his courage, passion and love of country – that had made her love him so in the first place. That, and his obvious love of her, and his care that she not be implicated in any way ... So of course she had accepted his proposal of marriage in an instant. And yes, typical of his selfless love, after his arrest he'd begged her over seventeen heart-rending pages to forget him, and their engagement – while adding a promise that he would marry her if she was still single upon his release – but she could not even contemplate it.

She would love him forever, whatever happened. But now this. Oh, how she weeps as he is taken away in chains.

And quietly, John Devoy weeps in turn.

What has he done to his dear Eliza, by being dragged off to prison like this? He weeps for her, for himself, for their lost life together.

•

After a delay of a few weeks, in the vain hope that more men, money and munitions will miraculously arrive, the new leader of the Fenians, Colonel Kelly sets the *final* final date for The Rising for 5 March 1867.

After all the waiting, all the false starts and frustrations, it is at last time to do this, to rise up and throw the British out.

Alas! On the eve of the action, the heavens themselves conspire against the rebels.

'Of all the nights that have ever passed over my head, that memorable night of the 4th of March,' one of those rising would recall, 'was the most furious that I remember. The wind blew a hurricane, accompanied by sleet and rain. The streets were deserted . . . and the only sounds heard were those of wind and rain falling in torrents.'[38]

After that comes the snow in such a furious flurry of flakes, going for so long – all through the night and next day – that everything is soon entirely covered in a thick blanket of white, uniquely well designed to prevent easy movement of everyone, and none more than revolutionaries needing to move quickly.

Nevertheless, at Kilbaha Coastguard Station, on Ireland's west coast, the attack goes ahead anyway. At five o'clock in the evening, six Fenians – including the Irish-speaking, Irish-breathing, dark-haired Thomas Fennell, charge into the home of the Station's Chief Boatman, John Wilmott, just as he is sitting down to tea with his wife.

They demand the station's arms in the 'name of the Irish Republic!'[39]

Rising to the occasion, Mr Wilmott first assures them calmly that he will do exactly as they ask and ushers them outside to the yard, away from his wife . . . before he suddenly-brandishes-his-loaded-revolver-and-fires just as his assistants arrive with guns of their own.

In the melee that ensues – which sees the Chief Boatman pistol-whipped and stabbed three times for his trouble – Thomas Fennell is shot through both the hip and testicle and is dragged away, while his crew have no arms to show for their own trouble.

Meanwhile, Fenians in Dublin make their move. No fewer than 600 of them, with guns, gather in the shattering cold of windswept Palmerston Park, before Captain Patrick Lennon.

'Fall in,' he shouts, 'form fours, shoulder weapons.'[40]

Yes, they are a little rag-tag about it, but enough of them know what to do that the others can follow, and very shortly they have indeed got their weapons on their shoulders and are on the march, four abreast, behind a green flag, and ahead of a horse-drawn ammunition cart bearing 17,000 rounds of ammunition.

Captain Lennon walks in the lead, with his second-in-command, Denis Duggan, beside him. (Though Duggan had been arrested with

Devoy, there had been a lack of evidence to convict him, and he had been released on condition he leave the country. He had complied by going to London to join the London Irish Volunteers, returning just in time for The Rising.)

Despite the howling wind, the snow, and the rain, the plan is to march towards the Wicklow Mountains, and have Dublin's military follow them out, allowing the Fenians who remain in the city to take it over. Other groups from other locations similarly head off, and the Crumlin police sergeant is shortly thereafter sending a message with a report that, 'the Dublin road is crowded with young men, all taking the direction of Tallaght'.[41]

As the rebels march towards their first target, the Stepaside Constabulary Station – just six miles out of Dublin – Captain Lennon looks down to see a 14-year-old lad, bearing a rifle, who has joined and is now proudly marching along with them.

Arriving at the barracks in the wee hours, the Fenian troops are frozen, but still willing.

Captain Lennon steps up to the door, and uses the hilt of his sword to rap upon it, calling on the police inside to 'Surrender in the name of the Irish Republic!'[42]

The police do not, and a bitter battle ensues, with many shots fired in both directions, and many windows broken. At one point the attackers throw straw through one of the broken windows and threaten to set it alight if the constables do not surrender. Still they don't, but the only fire that ensues is an escalation of the fire-fight already under way. The 14-year-old lad is a stand-out of the attackers, a testament to the courage of the rising generation, too.

In the end, so withering is the fire from the Fenians that the constables do indeed surrender, to be treated as prisoners of war.

Moving on, the freezing Fenian troops keep marching, and arrive at Glencullen, three miles to the south, where a similar siege takes place, with another fierce fire-fight, lasting more than an hour. This time the stand-out of the Fenians is Denis Duggan, with Lennon reporting to his superiors that he had displayed, 'great nerve and acted with the coolness of a veteran'.[43]

One problem is a local priest, who comes forward to harangue the Fenians, telling them to go home. That problem, at least, is quickly resolved when Lennon places the muzzle of his revolver to the temple of the priest and says, 'Fuck off home or I will give you the contents of this.'[44]

The priest goes home. But so too, soon, must Lennon's forces, as police reinforcements arrive, and those rebels who can, flee for their lives.

•

Something is stirring. In one of the darkest and dankest prison cells in all of central Dublin's Mountjoy Prison, John Devoy's senses tingle. As usual at this time of night he can hear the 'deep sonorous voices'[45] of the guards rumbling down the stone corridors, but on this occasion there is a note of alarm in their voices and an obvious urgency in their step.

Could it be The Rising?

Perhaps!

Minutes later, there are more hurried footsteps as tense guards rush by his cell, barking at each other. The very security of the prison might be in doubt because of unrest outside, and more reports are coming in. Mobs, on the streets of Dublin!

Yes, the time has come!

Devoy rises to climb up on his bunk and peer out through the small air vents cut into the thick stone wall of his cell. Alas, all he can see is the bleak, frozen winter-scape, and snow still falling – all of it so heavy you'd delay dinner plans, let alone a country-wide revolutionary plot. But, clearly, it is happening anyway.

A voice from within him gurgles up and whispers out loud: 'God help the poor fellows who are out tonight without overcoats or warm clothing. And what are they going to fight with?'[46]

•

At the village of Tallaght, about 10 miles out of Dublin, 200 marching Fenians armed with pikes and revolvers – their numbers including five brothers of John J. Breslin, the youngest of whom, Pat, is just 15 – find themselves blocked by a contingent of police, kneeling, with their rifles loaded. In the ensuing melee, two Fenians are shot dead.

Similar clashes, or at least skirmishes, with similar results, take place in all of Limerick, Tipperary, Cork, Monaghan and Louth. Much bravery is displayed across the board in what are mostly heroic defeats – with a few exceptions.

One such exception is in County Cork where a small band of Fenians, led by Captain John McClure, Peter O'Neill Crowley and Edward Kelly – the last an intrepid 26-year-old Irish–American who had arrived from Boston a year earlier – successfully capture the Coastguard Station at

Knockadoon, regarded as very likely, 'the neatest job done by the Fenians in the Rising'[47] for the fact that not a single drop of blood is shed for the taking of 10 prisoners and the capture of their rifles.

A small parenthesis here. Yes, the response of the British is savage and it will see Peter Crowley shot down in cold blood in Kilclooney Wood before the month is over, with McClure and Kelly captured – not surprising for the fact that no fewer than 300 British soldiers had been sent after them – but in the entire debacle of the 1867 Rising, Knockadoon will ever after stand as a rare success, while the episode in Kilclooney Wood would generate a famous verse from the pen of Irish poet, Dr Robert Joyce, with an even more famous final line:

> 'Twas down in wild Kilclooney, at the dawning of the day,
> The redcoats circled round the wood to catch their gallant prey,
> Young Kelly, and the brave M'Clure, and Crowley, stout and bold,
> Who slept as sleeps the lion-king in the rocky mountain hold;
> Perchance he dreamt that vision free within his wooden den –
> One true man, dead for liberty, is worth a thousand men![48]

Close parenthesis.

Overall, the problem for this Rising is that there is so little support from the people – with many trapped in their houses by the snow, even if they had wanted to join.

In Wales, a group of over one thousand Fenians under the command of Captain John McCafferty of the Confederate Army – and with the assistance of the resourceful John Flood, who remains in charge of Fenians in England, Scotland and Wales – have made their move. They attack Chester Castle – right by England's border with Wales – in a singularly brave effort to get their hands 'on the 25,000 stands of arms . . . known to be kept in storage guarded by a small body of English soldiers'.[49]

Once secured, the plan had been to race them across the Irish Sea to the Irish port of Wexford to arm the rising peasant army!

Alas! An informer has whispered to the British authorities and a 'welcoming committee' lies in wait, taking many prisoners.

Captain McCafferty and John Flood manage to flee and board a steamer bound for Dublin, only to find that, as they approach their berth in the Irish capital, both sides of the River Liffey are lined with police and troops. Grabbing a small boat, McCafferty and Flood and fellow Fenians try to escape – jumping into a waiting oyster boat – but are quickly arrested once they scramble ashore.

Everywhere that The Rising rises, the British loyalists are able to muster enough force to see a Falling.

Within two days, the *Irish Times* is able to give the news to its readers.

'The Fenian rising in the county Dublin,' it soberly reports, 'though attended with most mischievous results and some loss of life, has been a total failure. Throughout the country also it has been a disastrous and an ignominious failure. The overwhelming demonstration of military force paralysed all the efforts and frustrated the designs of the leaders.'[50]

There is only one positive note to the whole tragic affair.

'The one thing on which the country had to be congratulated,' Thomas Fennell would note, 'was that it failed so completely and so quickly as to cause little bloodshed. Every influence combined to minimize the waste of life.'[51]

Again the cells fill with failed Fenians, awaiting court martial or a Special Commission trial.

John Flood is convicted of treason felony, distinguishing himself by his eloquence from the dock upon being found guilty.

'The Attorney-General has alluded to me repeatedly as "that wretched man",' he tells the President of the court martial, the jury and the gallery. 'If loving my country through my whole life should make me wretched, I am wretched indeed; for I tell you now, and I tell the world that I not only abhor assassination, but I would rather go to my doom than be guilty of the moral assassination that has been practiced against me. I am ready, my lords, for my sentence.'[52]

That sentence is 15 years.

For his part, young Edward Kelly is sentenced to be hanged, drawn and quartered; that is, to be hanged, disembowelled, decapitated and cut into quarters. Not particularly fussed at this unkindest cut of all, Kelly makes a request from the dock that, 'all pleas for mercy on my part be disregarded as I am willing to die for the cause'.[53]

Surveying the wreckage of all their plans, the incarceration of so many good men, John Devoy, who had been forced to bid a melancholy farewell to his fair Ireland and his even more fair Eliza for good – oh, how he's wept – and been transported under the oppressive weight of British chains and irons to an English prison cell, feels bitterness towards the eternal and infernal delays and blunders which had brought them to this point.

Who is to blame?

Devoy has no doubts.

'It was [James Stephens,] the man who built up the movement and filled it with enthusiasm who was the chief cause of the failure. Perhaps it would be more correct to say that the situation got beyond him and that he had not the capacity to deal with it . . .'[54]

•

Despite all the arrests that follow the failed Rising, despite the destruction of their plans, Colonel Thomas J. Kelly is *still* fomenting revolution of his own, and while in Manchester to attend a Fenian meeting in early September 1867, is arrested while standing in a doorway in the company of another of the highest-ranking Fenians in England, Captain Timothy Deasy. They are quickly taken before a magistrate and remanded in custody.

A week later, on 18 September, in the prison van on the way from the police court to the borough jail, it so happens they must pass under that low railway bridge over Hyde Road at Bellevue, a singularly lonely stretch that sees little traffic.

Just as they are about to go under the bridge, all hell breaks loose.

For, now, a man leaps down from the embankment, pistol in hand and points it at the driver of the van and shouts out, 'STOP!'[55]

Rather making the point that this would be a good idea is the equally sudden appearance of no fewer than 30 armed men, who jump the stone wall that lines the road and swarm all around the now halted coach.

Far from resisting, the shocked driver falls off his seat, even as the accompanying police escort atop the van jump off and run for their lives. The prison van is now at the mercy of the bandits, bar one armed policeman inside with the prisoners, who holds the only key to the back door of the van. When he refuses the shouted instructions to open it, a shot is fired at the lock . . . at the very time he is peeking through the keyhole.

He slumps back, mortally wounded, and the back door bursts open.

Scatter, men, scatter!

Captain Kelly and his men gallop to freedom.

24 September 1867, Millbank Penitentiary, London

Picking coir – tough, unyielding, fibrous, dense, coarse, used to caulk Her Majesty's new steel ships – is a bastard of a thing, and like all prisoners, one of the Fenian prisoners, Denis Cashman, hates it. It is as monotonous as it is painful – causing blisters on his fingers, and an aching in his joints that goes right to the marrow of his bones and clear to the next morning when he starts again. Cashman is just so engaged in his cell, when he hears steps approaching . . . and now stopping . . . outside his cell door.

Suddenly, first the iron gate, and then the wooden door of his cell are flung open and a warder barks: 'Stand at ye gate.'[56]

Glad of *anything* that will break this wretched monotony, Prisoner Cashman – formerly the chief clerk of a legal firm – is instantly on his feet and standing at attention by the door, as Head Warder Handy and some of his acolytes cast a gimlet eye over him.

'Cashman,' Handy tells him without preamble, 'you are to be transported to Australia.'[57]

Cashman reels. To be sent to the other side of the world, away from his dear wife, Kate, and three loving children?

He opens his mouth to protest . . . but closes it again, to avoid the lash. He has no choice in the matter. He has been sentenced to seven years for treason, and must go where they tell him to go.

All he can do is return to picking the coir, in 'acute agony'.[58]

As he will later recall, a vision begins to haunt him: 'the tearful eyes & sorrowful face of my dear Kate, gazing at our dear children, who want her to tell them why their Pa does not come home'.[59]

What can he do?

He falls to the floor of his prison cell, and prostrates himself before God, praying that his family will be all right without him, that he will see them again, that somehow, his transportation to Australia will not destroy all that he holds dear in his life.

October 1867, Dartmoor Prison, the last of the convicts

Of course John Boyle O'Reilly has heard the whispered rumours that go from cell to cell, down the corridors and up and down the iron stairs, circulating with the freedom denied the inmates. They are absurd – something about a convict ship set to sail for Australia – and he refuses to believe them. After all, the east coast is by now closed to transportation.

And yet, there is one particular outpost of the empire's far-flung outpost, a speck on the map known as Fremantle – shark-infested waters on one side, deadly Australian bush on the other – where the authorities really are actively petitioning for convict labour. They could use the help; the settlement depends on it.

For the British authorities, it makes a great deal of sense. After all, following the attempted Irish Rebellion of 1798, where had Great Britain sent the Irish republican trouble-makers? Why, to Sydney Town, where most of them had never been heard from again, at least in terms of making trouble in Ireland. Oh yes, they had tried to stage a brief uprising of their own in Australia, the Battle of Vinegar Hill, in 1804, but that had been quickly crushed. The British had done the same with those rebels of the Young Ireland movement of 1848.

As for this last lot of traitors? The obvious course is to follow tradition. Let us send the worst of the Fenians to Fremantle, *the* most isolated settlement on earth, which means they will all but definitely never be heard from again.

And so a ship is commissioned and the usual array of criminal convicts selected to fill it, with 62 Fenians set to be transported with 218 other common prisoners.

Yes, for his part, John Boyle O'Reilly is still refusing to take the rumour seriously until . . . approaching footsteps echo down the corridor, there is the rattle of keys in his cell door and a prison official curtly informs him that you, John Boyle O'Reilly, are to be transported to Australia.

No longer than five minutes after that, he is in double irons clanking down that same corridor towards a Dartmoor conveyance that waits for him in the prison yard, and he is quickly embarked on what will be a long trip south to Portland Prison, in Dorset, which sits pretty in the sunlight atop the hill, overlooking the sparkling English Channel.

Always one to look on the bright side, whatever the circumstances, John Boyle O'Reilly is excited by what he immediately views as his most audacious challenge yet.

CHAPTER FOUR

THE *HOUGOUMONT* HUSTLE

A three months' voyage on board a British convict ship to an Irish political prisoner is an indescribable horror. It is utterly mono-tonous, and is only varied occasionally by hearing the cat on a convict's back, the funeral services now and again, followed with a splash and the fins of a shark or two darting after the prize; the constant rattling of chains on limbs and hands of the unfortunate convicts.[1]

Denis B. Cashman, Fenian convict and diarist

Considered as a man, the English gaoler is nearer to being a demon incarnate than a human being. Heart and soul he is dead to the veriest acts of kindness and for the wretches in travail under his charge he has but the mechanical coldness of never exchanging a pleasant word, never wears a gratifying cheerful smile, nor does an expression of sympathy ever shadow his sullen countenance.[2]

Thomas McCarthy Fennell, Fenian convict

7 October 1867, Portland Prison, Dorset, awake, ye fiendish Fenians

Can there be a worse way to wake in this world?

Either way, there is no doubt that a truncheon banging along the bars of the cells of Portland Prison at dawn on this cold morning does the trick. Instantly – for any tarrying will see the truncheon applied to them – 130 prisoners throw off the thin cotton covers they have been shivering under all night, rise from their planks and are soon standing outside their cells awaiting their next orders.

It does not take long.

The cry goes up: 'Chains! Chains! Chains!'

From bone-shudderingly bitter experience, the veteran Fenian prisoners like John Boyle O'Reilly know all too well how they of the clanking ranks must proceed and O'Reilly does his best to show the 20 most recently convicted Fenian countrymen fresh from Ireland what to do. They line up in groups of 20 – the political prisoners separated from the criminals – as prison blacksmiths put handcuffs on each prisoner and also chain the legs of the men together with 'double irons' – two iron bracelets on each ankle.

'The clamps that encircle [our] legs are made to wed the bone,' one prisoner would recall, 'so that the stockings barely fit between.'[3]

Those double bracelets are joined by a long chain that extends up to the wide leather belt around each prisoner's waist, from which a hook extends. The top of that chain is put over each hook. From the back of the belt, there is a link from which extends another chain, which joins to a link on the belt of the prisoner behind.

Still, just to be *doubly* double sure – *to be sure, to be sure* – once all the prisoners have their double irons on, the blacksmith attaches a chain to join whole columns of them together, 20 apiece.

'Forward there!'[4] rings the cry, rattling and rolling down the dark, dank corridor. The chained prisoners slowly shuffle forward – the 'convict shuffle' as it is called – vainly searching for a rusty rhythm to their heavy chains, as they grunt their way out into the prison esplanade.

John Boyle O'Reilly looks around with squinted eyes.

'It was a gala day,' he would later recall, 'a grand parade of the convicts. They were drawn up in a line – a horrible and insulting libel on an army – and the governor, and the doctors of the prison and ship reviewed them.'[5]

Once the review is over, not long before midday, the prisoners are formed into long columns of chains and start to clank their way out of the gates of Portland Prison and down the precipitous winding path towards the harbour, watched over by warders bearing truncheons and pistols – and grim-faced soldiers of the 13th Light Infantry.

Most closely watched of all are the military Fenians – the likes of John Boyle O'Reilly, Thomas Fennell, James Wilson, Martin Hogan, Tommy Hassett, Thomas Darragh, Michael Harrington, Bob Cranston and James Kiely – who form a group apart. They are the ones most likely to try to organise a last-minute escape – and none more than O'Reilly, who has already made three escape attempts since being locked away in England. The soldiers guarding the Fenians are thick on the ground, with their bayonets fixed. In the unlikely event that a prisoner could break free of his rusty irons, he wouldn't get five yards before being struck and stuck like a pig.

Tens of columns of convicts noisily clank and waddle across the cobblestones, drawing a crowd as they go – news of the transportation of the next lot of convicts to Australia has spread – down towards Government Pier Six, where a small steamer waits. A dozen burly sailors – coastguardsmen – stand by, ready to take the prisoners to their ship.

The Fenians are the caboose on this train of pain, bringing up the rear. Finally reaching the gangway to the steamer, their grim gaze goes across the waters to where a convict hulk awaits when . . .

When a shriek goes up.

From the crowd now, a young woman rushes out and throws her arms around one of the convicts on O'Reilly's chain. She's sobbing like a bereaved mother, weeping like a willow tree, her limbs wrapping around his whole body and refusing to let go. It is the sister of a Fenian, Thomas Dunne, who, after having been refused permission to see him through the legal process, has come all the way from Dublin to see him for a minute – and that minute is now.

Yes, the law says he is a traitor, but even the usually merciless guards can see he is a man who is deeply loved by his family, and allow his column to stop so he may have a few words with her. Given the chains on his arms, he cannot embrace her in turn, but at least can speak softly to her and lower his head to kiss her cheeks, to ask to be remembered to all at home, to tell them that he will be all right, that he is strong, and thinking of them all, and that Ireland will one day be free.

Too soon, however, the word is given and the guards must forcibly detach her from him. The woman stays, weeping, until the vision of her brother heading up the gangplank of the steamer waiting to ferry them out to the ship unleashes more shrieking,

'Oh God! Oh God!'[6] she cries in her thick brogue.

'From the steamer's deck,' John Boyle O'Reilly will record, 'we saw her still watching tirelessly, and we tried to mutter words of comfort to that brother – her brother and ours.'[7]

Among those watching are, in fact, two genuine brothers, Lawrence and Luke Fulham, a couple of ailing Fenian shoemakers from Drogheda, being transported for five years for treason. Unlike the unhappy Fenian gazing at his sister, they at least have each other, side by side in their hell, and draw some strength from that.

As the steamer slowly crests the swells and pulls out into the English Channel, away from the rocky shoreline of the Isle of Portland, the eyes of the Fenians are inevitably drawn back to the prison, perched atop the isle's summit, whence they staggered two deep in rusty chains. And the prison glowers menacingly back, its 'towers, angular walls and sloping abutments', the 'black moving sentinels' ever on guard in what Thomas Fennell knows too well is 'a mammoth grave of the living'.[8]

They know naught of where they are going, but they know what they are leaving behind. Surely, what awaits might be better?

After 20 minutes, the paddle of the steamer slowly draws to a halt before turning, *churning* back in the opposite direction, spraying white water all around as the boat nudges backwards alongside the huge hideous hulk of a ship proudly flying the Union Jack and the 'blue peter' – a signal the ship is ready to sail.

The black hull looms over them, displaying a broad arrow convict symbol painted in white, to remind them of what's ahead. Her name is the *Hougoumont*, named after the Chateau d'Hougoumont, which was occupied, fortified, and held by the British during the triumphant Battle of Waterloo. She is an 875-ton frigate, with a beam of 34 feet, a length of 165 feet and a hold that is 23 feet in depth. Once a troopship, she has been re-fitted to carry a cargo of convicts, with a fair measure of them already on board now. A week earlier, 150 odd convicts, 36 Fenians among them, had been brought down from Chatham, Millbank and other prisons to London, where they were taken on board. She has now arrived just off the Isle of Portland, her final stop in England, to firstly take on board this last lot of scurvy convicts, and, over the next few days, the other passengers who are taking the voyage to Fremantle.

Now, as soon as the common criminals have been mustered on deck and sent below, it's the turn of the Fenians. They are prodded like cattle up the gangway, dragging their chains as they go – only to be greeted on deck by lines of glaring Marines from Her Majesty's guardship *St George*. The government is taking no chances with these scheming, daring traitors.

Looking around him, John Boyle O'Reilly's attention is drawn immediately to the foremast, from which protrudes a black gaff – similar to the crossbar on Christ's cross. He looks closer. Yes, he knows what that is.

'This was the triangle,' he will chronicle, 'where unruly convicts were triced up and flogged . . .'[9]

On the gaff are 'iron rings which when the spar was lowered to the horizontal position corresponded to rings screwed into the deck'.[10] To these rings a man's irons are attached so he may be stripped and strung up as if to be quartered, ready to receive the cat's wrath.

And if that doesn't tame the unruly convicts, higher up, from a spar stretching out from that same foremast, hangs a brand-new noose, twisting idly in the wind.

A little forward of the noose and the whipping apparatus is yet another form of punishment, the solitary cells – small chambers on deck that measure just a little under three feet across, and just under five feet high. With no light, and little air, they are a claustrophobic construct, and the final bit of torture therein is an iron ring at knee height, through which the prisoner must pass his right hand, before it is handcuffed to his left wrist.

It means that for as long as the prisoner is in there – from one day to a hundred, depending on the severity of the sentence – he can neither lie down nor stand up.

Welcome to the *Hougoumont*, and it is great to have you.

•

The ship's blacksmith steps forward to knock off the Fenians' chains. Inevitably, it takes a great deal of time, meaning that many of those still encumbered with the ghastly links must answer the call of nature where they stand – which is problematic, when it requires more than mere urination. Men caught short make pleas to be allowed to at least loosen their pants to defecate there on the deck.

Some pleas are answered. Some aren't.

When they are answered, it is not simply a matter of the individual squatting.

For, so tightly are the men chained to each other that, as the Fenian who had been in the attack on Kilbaha Coastguard Station and lost a testicle for his trouble, Thomas Fennell, will record it, 'in a unison of handcuffs, he who is not in immediate needs is forced to accompany him who is, and in a stooping posture keep guard and witness the revolting spectacle till all manner of shame ceases to be a virtue. It is an occasion never to be forgotten, an occasion of loathing, barbarous brutality, from whose indecent gaze the savage might turn in sickening disgust.'[11]

Oh how their English gaolers laugh and sneer at them, while offering their jibes, which make their fellow gaolers roar with laughter.

'You'll have plenty of spare time and lots of leisure with which to clean shit and vomit out on the high seas!'[12]

Finally, however, Fennell, O'Reilly and their fellow Fenians have their chains removed.

But their relief is short-lived. Just moments after they are able to rub their aching, chafed, bleeding wrists and ankles to restore circulation, a barking warrant officer orders them below to the hold.

What hits O'Reilly first as he descends into these bowels of hell is, appropriately enough, the sheer stench, the bodily effluence of the prisoners who have been in the hold for days – an olfactory sensation matched by the sheer ugliness of what he sees now.

'The sides of the main hatchway were composed of massive iron bars,' he will recall. 'As we went down, the prisoners within clutched the massive bars and looked eagerly through, hoping, perhaps, to see a familiar face. As I stood in that hatchway, looking at the wretches glaring out, I realised more than ever before the terrible truth that a convict ship is a floating hell.'[13]

Instead of walls, there is an iron grate separating the prisoners into different compartments, which strengthens the impression of being animals trapped in a vast cage, bound for the furthest, emptiest and hottest continent on earth.

'Only those who have stood within the bars,' O'Reilly would note, 'and heard the din of devils and the appalling sounds of despair, blended in a diapason that made every hatch-mouth a vent of hell, can imagine the horrors of the hold of a convict ship.'[14]

Fennell will never forget his impressions as he looks around, his eyes struck by the ghastly, ghostly countenances of his fellow travellers, lit only by the sad sputtering of a couple of lanterns.

'Here then huddled together is an impenitent brood of human creatures representing every shade of crime and wickedness and whose equals the world never saw. An assemblage of vilest criminals composed of thieves . . . forgers, murderers and fiendish despoilers of character and virtue, with a handsome sprinkling doomed to oblivion – indulgent victims in the abomination of Onan and Sodom.'[15]

At least, however, this number includes some of their comrades from Fenian times in old Ireland, if only they could see them before entering blindly into the fetid, seething void.

O'Reilly stands stunned at the doorway to the cage, when through the semi-darkness of this demi-monde he notes a blob pushing his way through all the sweating bodies to open his arms and say in his distinctive way, 'Come, we are waiting for you.'[16]

With his eyes not yet adjusted to the darkness, O'Reilly can't quite see the man, but he would know that voice anywhere – it's his old friend from the 5th Dragoons, Patrick Keating. The new Fenian arrivals follow Paddy through the criminal quarters to a door leading to a compartment in the middle of the ship where, after a Fenian knock, the door opens and they are waved inside.

'Then the door was closed,' O'Reilly will later recall, 'and we were with our friends – our brothers. Great God! What a scene that was, and how vividly it arises to my mind now!'[17]

No, there will be no room for them all to sleep there, but they can deal with that later. All up, there are 17 Fenian soldier-convicts, among 62 Fenian political prisoners overall. Hail fellow Fenians well-met, as old comrades embrace, and share news of sentences, families and fates of friends, which goes on for some time until a tall dark figure arrives in their dim box. It is an Irish priest, a Father Bernard Delany, himself on his way to Western Australia for missionary work and who will be ministering to convicts, particularly the Fenians on this voyage. The men take to his quiet, open presence like geese to water, which is appropriate as things turn out, but already we are ahead of ourselves. Most importantly for John Boyle O'Reilly, courtesy of the good Father, he is soon in possession of paper and ink to write his precious poems.

(Such is the John Boyle O'Reilly charm, though nobody is sure if it's his disarming good looks or his fierce intelligence. Most likely, it's both. Or perhaps it is the mighty force of his incorrigible optimism, for he is not long in celebrating the new horizons opening before him on this long journey to the other side of the earth: 'Australia! The ship! Another chance for the old dreams; and the wild thought was wilder than ever, and not half so stealthy.'[18])

After just a few more days at anchor – *Oh! The freedom of moving about their assigned areas of the ship totally unchained! They spend hours on deck, bathing in the sun, drinking in the clean air* – the final contingent of passengers arrives and the *Hougoumont* sinks a little lower in the water with its full complement of 431 people ready to go: captain, chaplains, sailors, soldiers, wardens, 280 convicts – rebels, revolutionaries, rapists, murderers, thieves – and 108 passengers among whom are 44 Pensioner guards – essentially retired soldiers who have struck a deal to accompany the convicts as extra security, and then settle in Western Australia to work in the penal establishment there – along with 22 women, 34 children and one baby.

12 October 1867, the *Hougoumont* sails from England, Oh! Farewell

A nod for a nod.

Captain William Cozens gives a nod to the Bosun, who nods in return before bringing a cast-iron whistle up to his lips. And now, as Fennell will document, 'to the tune of "Arise ye dead", he blows a thrilling, piercing blast that startles all around, brings the sailors to their feet to a man, and promptly thereafter to their posts'.[19]

As the crew springs into action, Thomas Fennell observes in wonder from the portion of deck assigned to the Fenian convicts: 'Lively as bees from their hives, the rusty tars usurp the situation and clear the deck to assert their rights and privileges. All over they are astir: some nimbly creep aloft to man the yards, some to the bows, some to the lee and starboard tackle, while others ply the handspikes to the capstan . . .'[20]

With the handspikes in place, the sailors start to sing and push for all they are worth and then some, as 'the mournful cadences of the "sea song" chorused by all hands, rise above the din and clatter'.[21]

Around and around they go, the rhythm of the shanty building a physical momentum of its own, and as the capstan keeps turning the chains take the strain, the anchor lurches off the sandy bottom and starts to be hauled from the watery depths.

'Aweigh!' comes the cry at 2.55 pm. And still the men keep pushing, until finally, with a splash of defeated resignation, the anchor clears the water.

Fennell watches in wonder as they work.

'The [helmsman] puts the helm easy to port, sheets slacken, square sails adjust themselves, curling ripples appear in the blue waters at the prow.'[22]

For this first part of the journey they are closely escorted by Her Majesty's bristling gunboat *Earnest*. As English newspaper reports assure their good English readership: 'It is promised that an attempt at rescue will take place while the ship is *en route* down to the Channel. Should such an attempt be made no doubt the *Earnest* will give them a warm reception.'[23]

The *Hougoumont*'s destination, according to the same report, is 'New Auckland, Australia'.[24]

And yet, for the moment at least, escape is a long way from the Fenians' minds, as they, side by side with the British murderers and rapists who make up much of the rest of the convict contingent, stand swaying on their assigned decks, moving counter to the motion of the ship itself, and at least enjoying the salty fresh breeze on their faces, the liberating lack of leg irons.

Already the hierarchy of the ship can be told by the clothes of those on deck. Those up on the poop deck at the rear of the ship, dressed in the 'silks and broad cloth',[25] are the ship's captain and his officers, while up the other end, around the forecastle, are the bulk of the sailors, in their greasy pilot-cloth, who lounge lolling around while off duty. Amidships, meantime, are the soldiers 'in blue and red, warders in blue and gold' guarding the 'sad-looking dejected convicts in ill-contrasting costumes, brown smocks, knickerbocker breeches, long stockings and a four hand cap of the same material and cross-barred red, the entire suit beautified with quaint broad arrow stamps of different paints to contrast in colour with the garments'.[26]

As to the *Earnest*, satisfied there are no Fenian ships on the high seas about to attempt a rescue, it turns back to port. It is time for the regular rhythm of the voyage ahead to take hold.

'Down below to supper!'[27] comes the first of many such 4 pm commands, their first taste of discipline at sea.

'Presently,' Fennell records, 'the under-decks yawn like a weird sepulchre and the noise and clatter of pints, spoons and platters gives it the appearance of some extensive tin works whose most attractive feature is confusion and mismanagement, this starved out army of pent up convicts crowd around the rustic bunks without temporary seat or table to devour the miserable repast handed out to them.'[28]

For men who have been living in tiny cells on land, eating mostly solitary repasts, ship life – crammed cheek by jowl by towel with so many others – does not come easily. For one thing, a lot of the convicts are naturally violent men, who are not overly familiar with the ways of gentlemanly sparring should a fight break out. But there is one upside to the fact that the British authorities regard the politics of the Fenians as the most dangerous thing of all. That is, they separate the civilian Fenians from the common herd, not to protect them from the murderers, but to keep the Fenian politics away from *them*. It means that the 45 civilian Fenians are given their own compartment amidships, wholly separate from the criminals, and they may sail in relative comfort, right next to the hospital compartment. Alas, while the 17 military Fenians are allowed to spend time there during the day, when the time comes to sleep they must head to the criminal quarters, assigned to small airless compartments with eight rudimentary berths, 18 inches wide and six feet long, 'constructed of commonest deal boards in tiers of two, one above the other'.[29]

'The first few days of the voyage,' O'Reilly will note, 'are inexpressibly horrible. The hundreds of pent-up wretches are un-used to the darkness of the ship . . . depressed in spirits at their endless separation from home, sickened to death with the merciless pitch and roll of the vessel, alarmed at the dreadful thunder of the waves, and fearful of sudden engulfments, with the hatches barred. The scene is too hideous for a picture – too dreadful to be described in words.'[30]

Despite the hardships and their initial horror of the 'floating hell',[31] the truth is that both the civilian and military Fenians can take some heart from the fact that their treatment actually is a cut above and many lashes below that which is handed out to the common criminals. Simply the fact they are in a cordoned-off section with their backs to the hull means they can spend long hours chatting freely.

As Thomas Fennell records: 'The change in the situation from the bastille to the sea is too thoroughly appreciated on account of the many new and unexpected concessions it brings with it. To sit or saunter about with companions of your choice, to talk, dance, whistle, or sing without even a hint of restraint, and being up so late and long in the open air is a thing unusual – a resolution of fortune.'[32]

Helping matters even further is that some of the Pensioner guards on board once served with some of the Fenian soldiers, meaning they 'with comradely sympathy, alleviated their lot as far as possible'.[33]

The best thing of all is that, once at sea, there is no chance of them jumping off and trying to escape, so some of the Fenians are allowed up on deck to breathe deep the clean night air. As Thomas McCarthy Fennell will later recall, 'to be on deck is the uppermost, all engrossing thought . . . the ladders are ascended at break neck [pace] to indulge on the pure bountiful elements . . . Instantly, the gunwales are crowded with spectral figures, mute as the genii of the sea, but stark and deformed as the frightful ghouls of the spirit-land eagerly gazing on the copper-tinted phosphorus evolving from the sides of the great ploughshare and gurgling and boiling in elegant profusion in her wake.'[34]

Fresh air, the wind in their faces, like they have not known since being in the deepest depths of so many prisons. No, they are not free men, but it is all bracing enough that, just for a moment, they can imagine they are. After a time, though, bells ring once more and they are ordered to the hold for rest.

For John Boyle O'Reilly, there is only one upside of being in the stinking hold of a convict ship. At least you have time. In prison, your days run to the rhythm of regimented activity and austere solitary confinement, meaning that although you are serving time you actually have little to yourself. At least here he is able to while away hours doing one of the things he most loves to do, writing poetry, and in this case he addresses the subject dearest to all the convicts' hearts on this day . . .

On and on he goes, occasionally scratching out one word, and replacing it with another, and at other times scratching out whole lines and even whole stanzas, until the poem takes shape.

> *Farewell to thy green hills, thy valleys and plains.*
> *My poor blighted country! In exile and chains*
> *Are thy sons doomed to linger. Of God, Who didst bring*
> *Thy children to Zion from Egypt's proud king,*
> *We implore Thy great mercy! Oh stretch forth Thy hand,*
> *And guide back her sons to their poor blighted land.*[35]

John B. O'Reilly, *Hougoumont*, 12 October 1867

24 October 1867, Atlantic Ocean, may laughter light our days[36]

Nearly two weeks out, somewhere off the coast of Northern Africa, the weather is warmer. As the copper-plated hull of the *Hougoumont* pushes through the ocean, those on deck are able to enjoy that delightful interplay that comes from gurgling bow waves mingling with the flapping and occasional snap of the canvas sails.

It is no less than a symphony of smooth sailing . . .

Down below, it is different.

The hold is impossibly stuffy, even at night, and monotony is beginning to rear its needy head. And so the Fenians have a debate 'as to the best means of killing time and amusing ourselves during the voyage'.[37]

Theatricals are suggested, but there is no space for a stage.

Concerts?

Aye!

The men, led by John Boyle O'Reilly and the former Fenian leader of England, Scotland and Wales, who had smuggled James Stephens safely out of Ireland, John Flood – and to whom O'Reilly has become very close on this voyage – and Denis B. Cashman, agree. They will hold a concert each evening at six o'clock.

The first show is presented in two parts, featuring 17 acts, including Patrick Keating singing 'Freedom's War' and John Flood singing the aptly chosen 'She is Far from the Land'.

On this evening, as every evening thereafter, the concert concludes with all the Irishmen standing and joining in the singing of the anthemic 'Let Erin Remember', with everyone giving particular emphasis to the haunting words, 'Thus shall mern'ry oft, in dreams sublime, Catch a glimpse of the days that are o'er'.[38]

The Fenians in the audience, sitting on upturned pails and whatever else has come to hand, huddle in close to hear old Irish tales, sing beloved songs from their youth, and meet the performance of each of their friends with wild acclaim whether deserved or not, their eyes blazing in the dim yellow lantern light. (It is indeed a light-hearted antidote to the bloody floggings they witnessed this week, one of the criminal convicts receiving 48 lashes for impertinence. Denis Cashman records that the convict in question 'showed no mark of suffering. Prisoners cheered him at the last strike.'[39])

On the fifth evening, O'Reilly makes his concert debut, performing the poem he'd written while awaiting trial at Arbour Hill prison, 'The Old School Clock', telling the story of his happy childhood and the things in it which he can recall so clearly, and cherishes now more than ever, finishing with his final stanza . . .

> Yes, dear are those memories – they'll cling round my heart,
> And bravely withstand Time's rude shock;
> But not one is more dear or more hallowed to me
> Than the face of that Old School Clock.[40]

J.B. O'Reilly

The Fenians applaud heartily.

There's much more: 'Our Irish Flag' is sung by Michael Cody in his stunningly resonant voice, while John Kenneally recites the poem 'Fontenoy', about the great battle in France a century earlier, where the Irish had covered themselves in glory fighting *against* the British. The concert wraps up with a number from a Fenian named Sheehan, who stands and in his refined brogue introduces the title of his story. 'The Stolen Pig', he says with a flourish and a look in the eye that sends the men into fits of laughter, their roaring delectation staying constant through the splendid delivery.

In the moment, O'Reilly can't help but feel the sting of their exile. For such a fine group of lads, a talented lot of men with curiosity and character, to be condemned to the end of the earth with little to do and no association with civilisation . . . it's absurd. As he will later reflect, 'What a strange crop of felons Ireland has produced within the past two or three years – orators, poets, soldiers – men to plan skilfully and act daringly, and who meet disaster and humiliation with light hearts and even tempers. When the true character of those men comes to be known in England, there will be a strong reaction of public feeling there with respect to Fenian convicts, and we believe a unanimous desire for a general political amnesty.'[41]

And so it goes over the next week or so, as the Fenians continue to construct a world for themselves entirely removed from the one they actually inhabit. It helps. With the new marine life they are discovering – shoals of porpoises play in the ship's wake, whales and albatross abound – these nightly concerts are something good to leaven the bad, the storms, the gruel, the confinement, the boredom and horror at the regular spectacle of brutal lashings with the cat-o'-nine-tails, which leave the backs of their fellow convicts hanging in glistening bloody ribbons. It revolts their souls, rouses their already rebellious spirits to the point that, as one might expect given the reason they are here in the first place, the idea starts to take hold that perhaps they should stage their own Rising! As chronicled by Denis Cashman, John O'Reilly was 'father to a scheme to capture the ship, guards, convicts and all'.[42]

Yes, O'Reilly enthuses!

> We can simultaneously capture and disarm the officers and guards. Moving all at once, we can use every weapon, strangle all adversaries, stifle every opponent and give no quarter. To fail would be eternal disgrace, would entail death most shocking to the survivors, therefore, let no man shrink from duty till life is dearly sold, the gore complete and the last one dead at his post. Be victory or death the motto, for it is far better to perish in the unequal strife than await strangulation from the yardarm another day.[43]

Alas, alas, they are few, and the sailors and soldiers are many, and between the Fenians, aside from the formidable John Flood – who is a 'first-class navigator'[44] – there proves to be very little expertise to sail a ship of this size. And if they did succeed in taking the ship, and could sail her, they could clearly never return to Ireland because they would all be hunted down mercilessly! And what would they do with the families of the warders?

In sum, the plans come to nothing. This ship, thus, will deliver them to their fate, whatever that might be.

O'Reilly falls into a deep gloom as he is sometimes wont to do – a surprising deep streak of melancholy, in an otherwise joyous man. It is all his friends can do to lift him out of it, worrying what he might do to himself, but slowly they succeed.

The *Hougoumont* sails on.

•

What now?

It is a knock on the door of the O'Reilly family home in Dublin. Ever since their beloved son, John Boyle, had been transported to Australia, his parents, William and Eliza, have been in effective mourning. And it is not that visitors are not welcome, necessarily – as family and friends have been more than kind and supportive, often checking on them – but yes, sometimes they just want to be alone with their grief.

This particular visitor however, a neighbour, proves to be a joy. It is a long story, but Mr Vere Foster, an educator and philanthropist, has some contacts, including some who worked at Arbour Hill military prison. And it turns out that not long after their son had been transferred from there, on his way to Australia, a bundle of papers belonging to their son had been found in the ventilator shaft of one of the prison cells, and it included a poem, 'The Old School Clock', and a note asking that the poem be passed onto his family. And, well, here it is!

Both parents weep to read it, a paean to their once happy family, a testament to how well they have taught him a love of literature, an ability with words.

5 November 1867, the *Hougoumont*, Wild Geese take flight

By now, with the journey under way for nearly a month and the sheer crushing tedium of shipboard life starting to weigh heavily, the Fenians come together to debate new ways of dealing with their pressing boredom. The concerts have been grand, but not enough.

Perhaps . . . a shipboard newspaper?

It is Flood and Cashman who push the idea most assiduously, at least in part in an ongoing effort to lift O'Reilly's spirits. A shipboard newspaper really might do that.

Yes! Most of the Fenians are well-educated, able to write and edit, not to mention both recite and compose poetry. And while O'Reilly had worked through his teens at a newspaper, Edward Kelly, the spirited lad who helped in one of the only successful actions in the '67 Rising – capturing the Coastguard Station at Knockadoon, if only for a while, before he'd been one of the two heroes who'd fought to the bitter end at Kilclooney Wood, before being captured – had been a newspaper compositor. Cashman records in his diary: 'We held a meeting to see if we could start a newspaper – the meeting was composed of Con Mahony, J. Flood, Duggan, O'Reilly, Cody, Casey, Noonan & Self – we passed resolutions, appointed a Chairman & finally settled to start if we get paper.'[45]

Captain Cozens – a remarkably benign character for one in charge of such a ship – agrees, on the express proviso that the paper contain no political content, and so all is set. John Flood is appointed editor, O'Reilly sub-editor, while Kelly is manager, and Cashman is the penman and composer, writing it up, decorating the masthead and such.

Two days later, the industrious Fenians hold a second meeting, and debate the name for their new convict-ship rag.

Flood's suggestion wins the day: *The Wild Goose*, in honour of those Irish soldiers and patriots who were thrown out of Ireland and sent to France by William III, an exodus known in Irish lore as *The Flight of the Wild Geese*. They had become even more famous through the work of the great writer and patriot Thomas Davis, who ends the first stanza of his poem, 'When South Winds Blow' with the lines:

> *The Wild Geese fly where others walk;*
> *The Wild Geese do what others talk –*
> *The way is long from France, you know –*
> *He'll come at last when South winds blow.*[46]

Yes, of course, they are headed much, much further afield than France, now so far behind them – but still there is resonance with the name, an idea of common identity, most particularly the hunger to return to Ireland *when south winds blow*.

Now, to get their newspaper up and running, Father Delany, bless him, Oh Lord, is quick to provide them with much-needed paper and pencils, and they get to work, writing articles, poems and stories to fill their first edition.

After just four days of intense activity, on Saturday 9 November, passing within sight of the Cape Verde Islands, the first edition is 'published'. It is four sheets of white paper folded and bound at the middle to make an eight-page newspaper. Cashman's ornamental heading in bold capitals is entwined with shamrocks:

THE WILD GOOSE: A Collection of Ocean Waifs.

The first offering is an open letter by the publication's esteemed editor, John Flood, 'To Our Readers,' a promise from the *Wild Goose* to look over and protect the Fenians on their journey.

> From the frozen north, past the smiling shores of the Island of
> Destiny – where so oft I have lingered on luxurious lakes, brilliant
> in silvery moonlight, slept on the bosoms of its singing rivers, and
> shrieked in wild freedom o'er the Atlantic on adventurous wing –
> the leader of my flock – I have flown to cheer you on your weary
> way with my homely notes.[47]

There are stories, there are satirical news items – 'Nov. 2 Venus winked at the man in the moon. Diana threatened to scratch her eyes out. Celestial court greatly scandalized';[48] market updates – 'Tobacco not to be had at any price; holders unwilling to part with the commodity. Great demand for preserved potatoes and plumsduff';[49] answers to correspondents – 'Enquirer – Very little is known of the first settlers of Central Africa; but the supposition that it was colonized by an Irish chieftain named Tim Buctoo, appears to be as popular as ever' and 'Dick – It is spelled "Coxswain" not Cockshen. Where did you go to school?';[50] poems – the first published is John O'Reilly's 'Oh! Farewell!'; along with other articles, ideas, anecdotes, and one piece by Edward Kelly, letting the boys know what they might find at their destination.

Australia

> As our readers, we presume, would be grateful for a truthful
> account of the land to which they are going, and where they
> will probably sojourn for a lengthened period . . . it is, perhaps,
> superfluous to say that our statement may be implicitly relied on.
> *'Australia is surrounded by water, and the sun is visible there during*
> *the day, when not obscured by cloud . . . This great continent of*

the South, having been discovered by some Dutch skipper and his crew, somewhere between the 1st and 19th centuries of the Christian Era was, in consequence, taken possession of by the Government of Great Britain, in accordance with that just and equitable maxim, "What's yours is mine; what's mine's my own." . . . As an evidence of the advanced state of civilization among the natives, the consumption of oysters and ale (from which the name of the country is derived) is so enormous, that we smack our own lips at the bare idea, and fondly indulge in pleasing anticipations of the part we are destined to play in exterminating the molluscs of those vast seas, and draining the country of its genial potations.'[51]

At its end, Flood and O'Reilly are sure to fit in one last joke, as they do each week afterwards.

'Printed and published at the office, No. 6 Mess, Intermediate Cabin, Ship "Hougoumont."'[52]

Ah, how they laugh. The friendship between Flood and O'Reilly, established from the first days on the *Hougoumont*, becomes a deep and abiding bond as they create the newspaper and recognise in each other their same love of literature, of liberty, of having *fun* with your fellow travellers.

Now to mark the launch of their paper, John O'Reilly stands before his Irish brothers and reads the *Wild Goose* aloud.

Roaring laughter from the Fenian compartment can be heard rising up into the twilight sky, sailors aloft pause to wonder what's happening, Father Delany sits to the side watching on, beaming at the men and their good works. And so starts the weekly reading of the *Wild Goose*, which becomes better attended every week. Some of the fare even includes mildly political sentiment, with Edward Kelly – whose family had emigrated to the United States when he was young, before he'd returned to Ireland – reminiscing about having spent one 4th of July celebration in Boston, his account concluding:

Thus do the Americans commemorate their country's natal day. That night, sadly contrasting the position of my own country with that of the proud American republic, I fervently prayed that a happier day might dawn for my own native isle of the sea.[53]

And so it goes. As the days pass in these equatorial climes, the heat and humidity in the hold gets so oppressive that in an effort to alleviate the terrible stench, a stretch of canvas is configured above the hatches to catch the wind and drive it below, even as the convicts are set to scrubbing away the vomit, urine and faeces with buckets of hot water. Lime is sprinkled to soak up the damp. Sulphur candles are lit to fumigate the hold.

It helps, but some of the convicts ail badly anyway, none worse than Patrick Keating and William Foley, both of whom are struggling with the appalling conditions. James Wilson goes out of his way to nurse both men. Wilson goes back over a decade with the worthy Foley – who he describes as 'my poor but true and great comrade'[54] – and knows that Foley had refused to testify against himself and Hogan in return for mercy. Foley had risked life and limb to pass on General Sir Hugh Rose's dispatches; he deserves to be looked after. As to Patrick Keating, it is Wilson's view that he is a true patriot.[55] Brave, honest, resourceful, loyal – Wilson makes sure Keating always has water, food and rest.

The *Hougoumont* ploughs on. Very occasionally other ships are sighted on the high seas, going in both directions. But there is no contact.

The usual etiquette of the high seas does not apply when, like the *Hougoumont*, you bear the broad arrow on your hull.

A stinking, pestilent convict ship? We desire nothing to do with you.

The *Hougoumont* limps on, o'er the waves of woe, a leper of the seas.

Early December 1867, sailing under the Southern Cross

As Christmas on the high seas approaches, the Fenians note new constellations in the glittering night sky, including the famous Southern Cross, which they find strangely pleasing. For one thing, it heightens the sense of entering a new world, but more importantly for these Wild Geese hungering to one day return home when the south winds blow, it acts as a way-marker in the heavens, one by which they might guide themselves when the time comes.

On 13 December, the *Hougoumont* sails just to the south of the Cape of Good Hope, itself on the southern tip of Africa. The Fenians look out into the night void, trying to spot the glowing lights of the *Flying Dutchman*, that mythical ghost ship, doomed to sail the oceans forever, never allowed to make port – the phantom vessel that is no sooner sighted by others than it disappears into the haze.

As Cashman records, 'Passed the longitude of the Cape at 12 o'clock last night – we were looking out for the [Flying] Dutchman – no chance – so Jack had to make one.'[56]

'Jack', of course, is the man who in these few short weeks has become close to Cashman's dearest friend, John Boyle O'Reilly, to whom falls the task of writing a poem about the famed fable, and reciting it.

For that is just the way O'Reilly is.

'His personality was unique and charming,' a later contemporary will note of him. 'No-one could resist his smile, nor the exuberant flow of his generous, flattering words. At a dinner he was easily chief. Where he sat was the head of the table.'[57]

See now, as on the evening of 21 December as the *Hougoumont* continues to rise the massive swell of the Southern Ocean, the masts creaking with the strain of the billowing wind filling the sails, as the Fenians crowd around O'Reilly again, pushing into the circle of dim yellow light cast by the oil lamp that lights his fine features. All are ready to hear the final edition of the *Goose*, a full 16 pages for Christmas.

O'Reilly clears his throat, looks around, beaming at his brethren, and begins in his lilting brogue.

'Adieu,' he begins, reading John Flood's editorial. 'With feelings of regret I come, the last of the "Wild Geese," to bid you adieu. Week by week, one of our flock has tracked you across the ocean, and flown to you, if not welcome visitors, at least with an earnest wish to be both agreeable and welcome; and though few our number, and our visits having come to a premature end in consequence of the swift approach of the end of your voyage, I hope that, if not to all, at least to some, our appearance has been a source of some little pleasure . . .'[58]

O'Reilly pauses, clears his throat and starts again, diffidently:

'The Flying Dutchman,' he announces portentously, 'by John Boyle O'Reilly.'

> *Long, long ago, from Amsterdam, a vessel sailed away,*
> *As fair a ship as ever rode amidst the dashing spray;*
> *Fond loving hearts were on the shore, and scarfs were in the air,*
> *As to her o'er the Zuyder Zee they waft adieu and prayer.*
> *Her gaudy pennant streamed aloft, and as she skimmed the seas*
> *Each taper mast was bending like a rod before the breeze.*
> *Within her there were gallant hearts, tho' filled with sadness now,*
> *For still the lingering parting kiss was fresh on lip and brow.*

The Irishmen sit transfixed by the great man before them weaving tales of doomed sailors, tales they've known for years but never felt this chill, for their lot is not far off the doomed tars of the *Dutchman*.

O'Reilly reads his final lines:

> *But heaven help the hapless crew that impious sentence hears;*
> *The doom of those is sealed to whom that fatal ship appears:*
> *They'll never reach their destined port – they'll see their homes*
> *no more*
> *They who see the flying Dutchman, never, never, reach the shore.*[59]
>
> . . .
>
> . . .

Near silence.

All that can be heard is the creak of the hull that surrounds them, the splash of the bow pushing through the swell, and the flapping of canvas in the darkness way above. And now it starts. A clap, a cheer, a bravo, until the whole lot of them are wildly cheering!

Taking a mock bow, O'Reilly reads on, restoring the festive atmosphere with a series of Christmas numbers and some welcome news:

> We congratulate our readers on our rapid voyage since leaving England. It is probable that, with the continuance of such weather as we have had for some days we may arrive in Fremantle on or about the 8th January 1868.[60]

●

They are not far off the mark.

On the sparkling morning of 9 January 1868, the *Hougoumont* is pushing east at ten knots courtesy of a strong breeze under a cloudless summer sky when from up above in the crow's nest, the call goes out:

'Land ahead!'[61]

Those on deck immediately push to the bow, and sure enough there it is, less the land of their dreams than their nightmares, but at least it is land, 'a low range visible surmounted by a lighthouse'.[62] That range, they soon surmise from overhearing one of the sailors, is Rottnest Island, just off Fremantle!

Onwards the *Hougoumont* sails, until a pilot boat with seven crew comes to guide it towards port.

In the misty midnight hours, the *Hougoumont* slips silently into Fremantle Harbour, dropping anchor at 3 am.

CHAPTER FIVE

FREMANTLE PRISON

An hour later, the ship had approached within a mile of the pier at Fremantle. The surrounding sea and land were very strange and beautiful. The green shoal-water, the soft air, with a yellowish warmth, the pure white sand of the beach, and the dark green of the unbroken forest beyond, made a scene almost like fairyland. But there was a stern reminder of reality in the little town of Fremantle that lay between the forest and the sea. It was built of wooden houses, running down a gentle hill; and in the centre of the houses, spread out like a gigantic star-fish, was a vast stone prison.[1]

John Boyle O'Reilly, *Moondyne*

How many of the stout hearts now beating are destined to lay their bones in this land? How many will again tread the fair hills of Holy Ireland? Oh, for a dip into the gloomy dark future![2]

John Sarsfield Casey, Fenian convict, writing in his diary as the *Hougoumont* arrives just off the coast of Fremantle, 9 January 1868

Within the walls and world abroad farewell! The slam of the massive doors as they close behind, ominously reverberate through the empty halls and corridors and pierce the culprits with a peculiar thrill of horror that ever after keeps company with their troubled souls.[3]

Thomas McCarthy Fennell, Fenian convict

3 am, 10 January 1868, Fremantle Harbour, Western Australia, 'A land blessed by God and blighted by man'[4]

It is a strange thing for a ship to reach the end of a long voyage in the silent watch of the night, when most of those on board are asleep; when even those who are awake can see little of the shore bar a dim outline in the moonlight; when the only thing that remotely approaches the

85

exclamation mark that might be expected at the end of such a journey is the splash made by the anchor when it hits waters some 400 yards from the shore.

But such is the case as the *Hougoumont* nudges into position in the wee hours.

The ship secure, Captain Cozens returns to his cabin for some sleep, but he is up with the rest of the ship at dawn to gaze at Fremantle in the fresh morning light.

Lining the shore are picturesque beaches dotted with charming jetties and delightfully decorous fishing barks, before it gives away to shrivelled shrubs, then the usual collection of higgledy-piggledy houses and hotels on narrow streets that abound at most ports – though here, for some reason, the buildings are uniformly whitewashed.

But beyond them all?

Oh, the horror.

Like a turd on a rose, the enormous structure sitting atop the hill behind the town is a disturbing vision – a stone-cold penitentiary that towers menacingly over all that dares stand below. One feels bullied, just to look at it.

Built by convicts, it is made of limestone quarried on site, and comes complete with guard towers on all corners. It is totally out of proportion to all that surrounds it, and has no connection to the landscape on which it is situated. If good architecture connotes that a building looks to have grown organically out of its surrounds, this is the reverse. This is a huge transplant from somewhere else – some former inmates of London's Pentonville Prison recognise it immediately as a rough replica – and it could not be more jarring in appearance.

It is, of course, Fremantle Prison, originally known as 'The Convict Establishment', and now simply as The Establishment.

The mere sight of it is an affront.

'The native beauty of the place,' as one contemporary writer would describe it, 'is . . . blighted by the sight and defiled by the touch of the great criminal establishment.'[5]

The Fenians and their fellow convicts soon assemble on deck to be placed in chains, and shortly thereafter, an assault on all of their senses at once commences.

For, as the convicts are led down the gangplank onto waiting barges, the sun hits them almost as if their faces and bodies have been thrust close to a roaring fire. The sweat dampens their shirts and trickles down their legs. Up ahead on the wharves, the blinking convicts can see troopers in 'snow white uniforms mounted on capricious spirited steeds prancing along the creaking planks'.[6] Once they leave the barges to land on the wharves the convicts are pushed and prodded along by 'savage gangs of prison officers, supported by a detachment of "old fogies", Pensioner soldiers drawn hither more for ornament than real use . . .'[7] Beyond the mounted men in white, a bedraggled crowd from the settlement is gathering on the clear ground by the wharves to gaze at the newcomers. Yes, the locals are a miserable-looking lot – stunted, poorly dressed and withered brown by long years in this searing sun – but they are clearly interested to see arrivals more miserable and starved than themselves.

The Fenians are the last to arrive on the wharf, where they are mustered, ready to march up to The Establishment on the hill above them. For yes, we know all about you Fenians, and the danger you represent. You may have wanted to overthrow the order in Ireland and be a dangerous military force, but that is precisely why you have been sent here: to crush you, without killing you directly. But we are watching you, very, very closely.

Thomas Fennell stares up at the forbidding edifice, fearful of the future it holds: 'On dry land once again,' he records, 'the old ocean waves behind, but alas! the fretful foot, falls on a degraded penal soil – a vast prison land down by the antipodes'.[8]

And now comes the cry.

'Forward march!'[9]

Bloated with self-importance, more preened and puffed up than the horse he rides, the Commanding Officer of the Mounted Troopers – an enormous man, with a singularly bulbous red nose, going by the name of Major Charles Finnerty – leads off, as the convicts clank in ranks behind, doing the 'convict shuffle'. First, they must pass by the officials who stand to one side of the wharf – Chief Warders, Superintendents, Assistant Superintendents, the Prison Governor – reviewing the sorry lot England has sent them this time, and now they must pass through the pressing crowd who seem to be squarely divided into two camps – those who fear the Fenians and those who revere them.

Oh yes, the infamous Fenians are feared by the finer folk of Fremantle, who whisper tensely even as they part like the Red Sea to let the chained column through. The colony has been desperate for convict labour to sustain itself, but it never asked for revolutionaries to be sent, and many are unhappy about it.

But the former Irish convicts among the crowd? They have nothing but sympathy for the famous Fenians now traipsing and huffing and sweating and puffing in a suffocating cloud of dust, up and up dirt roads towards The Establishment.

They are, as Thomas Fennell will record, 'ankle deep in drifted sands. [We] pushed on in hot haste through clouds of dust and suffocating heat till at last the great prison gate swings apart'.[10]

Passing through the portals of the prison – a large gate, besides which, 'neath the glaring sun, equally glaring guards bristle like cacti – the clanking convicts snake their way forward. As they go, atop those prison portals, sentries keep their rifles trained upon them. Just let the Fenians try anything, and it will be the last thing they do. At last, the last of the Fenians arrive in the central parade ground, bordered on three sides by buildings – the three-storey cell-block, barracks, a Church of England chapel, guardhouses, some storehouses and the commissariat building, where 'Halt!'[11] is called.

Like the barren town they've just passed through everything in this prison is glaring white, almost designed to make you squint. Every building is white, as are the high walls, as is the ground on which they stand – crushed limestone trampled to chalky dust by convict boots over the years. Those rays of the sun that don't burn you on the way down, get you on the way back from the fierce reflection. Though a few trees offer dappled patches of shade from the glaring southern sunshine, none of that is offered to the new arrivals, and they stand, squinting, sweating, suffering, trying to take it all in, even as guards with guns surround them and stand staring back at them.

Before the newly arrived prisoners, standing upon a rostrum beside a flagpole from which hangs a languid and completely uninterested Union Jack, is a rather rotund, officious fellow with grey hair, dressed in what is clearly the uniform of all prison officials. He stands expectantly waiting for the last of the clanks in ranks to settle.

And hush now, for he is about to speak.

'I want your undivided attention. That is my first order,' he begins, in a flat, uninterested way. 'My name is Doonan. I am Superintendent of this prison . . . my word is law.'[12]

Menace in his words? Not a bit of it. Menace would imply he needed to impress upon them that he is serious – and he needs no such thing. He *is* serious, as serious as syphilis, as the convicts will discover soon enough if they doubt it. What they must understand is that there is no escape, this is the most remote, highest security penitentiary in all the colonies, there is no recourse but to obey every rule and every order – or face the consequences.

'No prisoner shall disobey the overseer or any other officer,' Doonan announces, starting his very long list of rules and repercussions. 'Or be guilty of swearing, or any indecent or immoral expression or conduct, or of any assault, quarrel, or abusive language, or smoking inside the cell, privy, cookhouse, washhouse, or workshops, or any talking or other noise during meal-hours and . . .'[13]

And on and on it goes.

John Boyle O'Reilly, standing in the middle of the briny throng of felons and Fenians, is nigh on bemused by the number of times he hears the words: 'the penalty of which is Death!'[14]

And now, onto the subject closest to O'Reilly's heart.

'Some of you will think of ways of escaping,' Doonan continues in his flat way. 'I will save you the trouble and tell you how. There are two ways of escaping from this prison, by land or by sea.'[15]

So you're thinking you can get away by land? Good luck. You will be heading off 'through the most cruel country God ever turned over to the devil . . .'[16]

You will be facing deadly deserts, shimmering salt-lakes, where the sun from above and below will peel your skin off before breakfast, and impenetrable bush that is home to so many venomous snakes they're only outnumbered by the maddening insects that will bite and sting you to a bloody pulp.

'You cannot live, you can go mad, you will die – unless I find you first. And I will, and you will be glad I did, and be grateful for flogging and the chaining.'[17]

Ah, but perhaps you think you can steal away on a visiting ship?

Well, to begin with there isn't an English ship's master on earth who would be so traitorous as to take you, and as they represent the vast majority of visitors to these shores, that will make it difficult for you. As to ships under foreign flags, they are all searched for stowaways before departure, and though you could try to swim out to them, the waters have more deadly sharks than the bush has poisonous snakes.

O'Reilly, for one, is interested to hear it. Of course there *has* to be a way. It is just going to be a question of finding out what it is.

But for now, like everyone, he must complete the paperwork of his confinement, as these walls, and the situation, start to close in. Twenty years to endure in this hell!

And now, consulting his register, a bored prison official starts to call out the numbers of the inmates.

'9644!'

A skeletal pock-marked pickpocket from Liverpool, Patrick Abraham, steps forward. Now, sign here . . .

Taking the pen, the all but illiterate small-time criminal concentrates on the dirty pages of the prison folio spread on a wooden table before him and carefully writes the only words he has ever managed to put on paper – his signature. And so his 'account' at The Establishment is effectively opened, just as it is for all new arrivals.

On the debit side is your name, your description as gathered in England, your prison number – which is your affixed arithmetical position in this whole soulless system – together with a notation of the crime or crimes which you have been convicted of. Now, off with your smock so we can confirm your marks, moles and other noteworthy features.

On the right side, we will record your behaviour, your punishments, the degree to which you have co-operated with The Establishment. We will note down all details of your life inside these walls, and on our chain gangs building roads and the like, and it will allow us, a decade or so from now, perhaps, to make decisions as to whether you might be worthy of becoming a ticket-of-leave man, able to live nearby, on the condition that you find work, regularly check in with us, and observe a strict curfew of ten o'clock at night. Alternatively, this ledger will provide evidence that you should never be released, should be left here to rot for the rest of your days.

'9645!'

Fenian Jeremiah Aher steps forward, and goes through the same procedure.

And on.

'9647!'

David Allison of Glasgow, serving 15 years for incest, steps forward.

'9732!'

Isaac Fernicough of Leeds, serving 15 years for raping an eight-year-old girl, steps forward.

'9779!'

Benjamin Jones also of Leeds, serving life for wilful murder, steps forward.

All the rest of the convicts can do is wait and wither in silence as the raging sun burns them, beats down on them and saps them, as the process of going through all 280 men must be finished before any of them can retire. Soon enough, O'Reilly hears his number.

'9843!'

He steps forward and signs, before undressing so his description can be confirmed.

'Black hair, brown eyes, oval visage, dark complexion; an Irishman.'[18]

The process drags on until the convicts hear the now familiar final numbers of their lot.

'9915!'

Military Fenian James Wilson steps forward. 'Height 5 ft. 8 ¼ in., brown hair . . . oval visage, fresh complexion. Marks. D left side; is a labourer. Fenian.'[19]

And so it goes. The huge scar on Hogan's left cheek, which had come courtesy of the scimitar of an Afghan warrior, is marked down, as is the fact that he has 'the gait and appearance of a cavalry soldier',[20] while Darragh's flaming red hair is noted, as is the tattoo on Cranston's arm of, yes, a Fenian cross.

With the roll call at last finished, the prisoners are finally herded towards the inner yard, where they are given leave to stretch 'their weary bones'[21] and even given a lunch of six ounces of brown bread and a pint of tea. The bread is wolfed down, the first fresh-ish food they've had since leaving England three months earlier.

But now, their milling about must end.

'Fall in double!' snaps the order, and the convicts slowly move back into line.

'Right face, march!'[22]

Thomas Fennell records the scene, 'three hundred despicable broken down forms toe the mark and like moving mummies are led to the bath house in an off corner of the yard'.[23]

Again, the first 30 men are herded inside, to find a long trough filled with water to a depth of 18 inches and partitioned into stalls, with the base of the partitions several inches above the stagnant water. 'Washing' themselves in such filth is a little beside the point, but they do the best they can, and once done they find themselves back in the parade ground, in two long lines, before the rostrum once more.

Superintendent Doonan stands before them and advises in portentous tones. 'You are to be addressed by the [Governor].'[24]

'Attention!' comes the aggressive cry, bringing a sudden silence as the men watch the Comptroller General of Convicts in Western Australia, Governor Henry Wakeford, step up. A short, florid man with a glaring countenance, still his most memorable feature is his gleaming shiny black patent leather boots, which are in such contrast to the whiteness all around. Not for nothing, as the convicts soon come to understand, is his universal nickname 'Boots'. Fennell finds his whole demeanour remarkable, recording that, 'his style, appearance and costume resembling the aesthetic paraphernalia of an actor in comic opera more than a high government functionary'.[25]

Wakeford begins in that upper-class voice of the born-to-rule Englishman:

> To you men it is needless to mention the fact that by your lawless conduct and behaviour in the Mother Country you incurred the anger and indignation of law abiding subjects. On this account you have merited your present fate, banishment from society, your native home and country to penal exile in a foreign land. You are beginning a new era of servitude, in many respects, perhaps, different to that which you were heretofore accustomed but let me impress upon you not to be deluded by false notions of expecting better treatment . . . Obey your superior officers is the golden rule, trespass on no injunction, avoid insolence and insubordination, do as you are bade, cheerfully and willingly and your good conduct will be one day rewarded by getting your sentences remitted as provided by prison rules and regulations.[26]

In unceremonious fashion – no bow, no more gems of penal wisdom, no last threat – he says to the officials around him, 'Officers file them off,'[27] and leaves.

The prison guards do not have to be told twice and are soon barking orders, snapping at the backs of the prisoners as they herd them up the iron steps to their cells on the top level inside 'the great bastille'.[28]

Jangling keys snap open heavy locks and each man is directed inside his own stone-walled room with a tiny grubby window letting in just enough light to reveal that it is only about nine feet high, seven feet long by four wide; a tiny stone cave. The black-painted, iron door is slammed shut behind them. Another jangle of keys, the bolts snap back to locked.

And so it begins, the new, unceasing rhythm of their lives.

Every morning, a bell tolls at 4.30 am, signalling that it is time to rise, dress in their prison garb, perform their ablutions with the stagnant water from their wooden pails, arrange their hammocks and bedding according to code, before a second bell at 4.45 am must see them standing to attention in their cells as warders unlock the iron doors and ensure that everyone is present and accounted for.

Now, *march*!

Down the iron staircases they traipse, and out into the prison yard, where they must stand in rigid lines – shoulder to shoulder, backs straight, and hands by their side ... *backs STRAIGHT, I said!* – while a second roll call of their numbers is conducted.

'9707!'

'Here!' cries Thomas Darragh in reply.

'9757!'

'Here!' Michael Harrington replies.

'9767!'

'Here!' calls Martin Hogan.

And so on, until the final report is made: All present and accounted for, sir!

'Sir' is most often Superintendent Doonan, effectively the Chief Warder, an Irishman himself who, according to his immediate superior, is a man of such 'sound judgment, industry and high principles' it probably makes him 'the most trustworthy and deserving subordinate officer of this service ... as to education, manners and conduct I think him well qualified to take charge of any convict prison or depot'.[29]

A few more barked orders and the convicts are on their way to the work stations – to the laundry, the kitchen and the vegetable gardens – to perform all the myriad chores such as painting, repairing and chimney-sweeping that go with keeping something as vast as The Establishment in good order.

Some of the men move relatively freely, others clank along, as their legs are chained to each other. More often than not, the 'chain gang' is assigned to break stones used for the macadamised road, while others shovel them into place.

Another barked order comes just before 7.30 am, and the men head back to their prison cells, where they must stand at attention, their backs to the outside of their black iron cell doors until their food – 12 ounces of bread, and tea that tastes like 'insipid slop'[30] – is brought to them.

They hold out their tin pint measures and bowls, their food is slopped in by a fellow prisoner, and they are given a few minutes to eat before it is time to head to the chapel and earnestly pray for forgiveness for their many sins.

At 8.30 it is time for the day's work proper to begin, including work further afield than the immediate environs of the prison, and they march off once more, some clanking all the way.

There is a break at midday for lunch, which, as one appalled warder notes, is served by 'placing the prescribed ration of meat & vegetables in tin plates which are handed to the men & on receipt by them hurriedly capsized onto towels (laid on the floor for their purpose) with which they dry their persons after washing; the plates being required for their soup or gruel. Thus the solid portion of their dinner is eaten off the towels, the liquid portion out of their plates.'[31]

At 2 pm the prisoners resume work, until they must return to the prison from 5.50 pm, with every man searched as he passes back through the gates by the careful if perpetually nervous and slightly sickly Gatekeeper, Francis Lindsey, or one of his charges, to make sure nothing is secreted on him. The men must then clang their way back up the iron staircases and be standing in their cells at 6 pm, when the supper of eight ounces of bread – two-thirds of what they receive at breakfast – and another pint of insipid slop is brought around, and they are locked in once more, left to eat alone in sarcophagal silence.

'This breakfast and that supper the year round without change,' Fennell notes, 'is enough to paralyse a mule . . .'[32]

After supper they may move around in the exercise yard smoking and talking until 7.30 pm, at which point they must gather to hear evening prayers and join the preacher in asking for God's everlasting mercy on their sinful souls, Amen. And now, just before 8 o'clock, they must return to their cells, account for their presence one last time – a quick 'all right'[33] to the warder's stern rap on the iron door – with all lights extinguished by 9 o'clock sharp.

Suddenly the silence of the tomb descends on the men trapped in their stone vaults, fighting the demons of the dark, their isolation, their distance from home, until at last some kind of fitful sleep takes them under until the morning bell, which always rings . . . too early.

All is routine, all is *system*, all is calculated to slowly press the life out of even the most defiant of prisoners, to make him understand that resistance is futile, that co-operation is everything, that his best, nay, his only option, is to keep his eyes down and submit to the will of The Establishment.

A single misstep – tardiness, slovenliness, noisiness, refusal to work hard, lack of respect for superiors, etc., and we know what to do with you, and what to mark in the ledger. And we are particularly watching you Fenians, you hard-line trouble-makers. The slightest sign of dissension from any of you, and you will be straight into solitary on bread and water.

But, fit in? Obey the rules? There are rewards.

Take the flaming red-headed Fenian convict Thomas Darragh, for example. Even though here for the worst of crimes – taking up arms to try to overthrow Her Majesty's Government – the fact is that he is one of the few devout Protestants in the prison, which practically makes him an Englishman. His reward will be that, after serving time on the chain gangs, he is made an assistant to the Church of England chaplain – nicknamed 'Amen-Timbertoe'[34] for his wooden leg. Darragh is even accorded the privilege of leading the prisoners in their evening prayers.

•

It is a strange feature of the human condition that sights which so recently seemed so alien, so out of kilter with everything ever seen before, can so quickly seem like the only world you know. All the rest must have been just a dream.

So it is for the newly arrived convicts as they become immersed in the rhythms of both The Establishment and – through work gangs – Fremantle itself.

The main street of this small burgh, just 3500 people strong, is the quarter-mile long High Street, off which come three or four cross-roads, the western end of which leads to the harbour. It's a hodgepodge of government buildings, a couple of churches, many small cottages and a few shops selling fruit, fish, meat and the like. But, mostly?

Despite having been settled 39 years before, the town looks very rough, and has, as one observer would note, an 'untidy, unfinished look inseparable from half-completed streets and unpaved footpaths'.[35]

The way it works, the newly arrived Fenians come to understand, is that Fremantle is more than just a penal settlement, it is a quasi-military settlement.

Built on the southern side of the entrance to the Swan River, part of Fremantle's role beyond port and prison is to stand sentinel for the bigger colonial settlement of Perth, a burgh of 5000 people, which is on the other side of the sandy banks of the Swan, some 10 miles upstream. For the few settlers and the many soldiers, there is a fair amount of traffic to and from Perth, in small steamers for the moneyed, and on 'Shanks's pony' – walking – for the rest. A newly constructed wooden bridge, some 300 feet long near the mouth of the river, gets you across to the other side.

Beyond those two settlements, known together as the Colony of Western Australia, lies geographical eternity, just as Superintendent Doonan had warned. To the north and south there is deep Australian bush. To the east is endless desert. And to the west, of course, beyond the vessels bobbing about in yonder anchorage, the small ships coming and going, lie Garden Island and Rottnest, and, beyond them, the gaping blue maw of the Indian Ocean.

As to the social hierarchy in the Colony of Western Australia, right at the top is the Governor of Western Australia, Dr John Stephen Hampton. A notorious flogger of prisoners and believer in the virtues of solitary confinement, in his time as Governor since 1862 he had imposed a strict cost-cutting regime and turned the prisoners into the workforce of choice for public works. He is a bastard.

Below him are the other high officials of Her Majesty's Government, including the Governor of The Establishment, Mr Henry Wakeford, followed by the officers of the military Pensioner regiments and the police force.

Then come the settlers. Most esteemed among them are an official group of civilian Volunteers who are even allowed to don the redcoat when assembled for state affairs of pomp and pageantry. And oh how they *love* that.

The settlers are followed by the ticket-of-leave men, those who have served time in The Establishment, and are now allowed to live in the community, on the strict conditions, after the bell from The Establishment rings out over Fremantle.

The lowest of the low – not counting the natives, because in these burghs they barely register – are the Fenians with the other 700 inmates of The Establishment. Over a short period of time, the Fenians come to know many of the old lags of the prison. Some have been here for a decade and a half and had actually helped to build it, quarrying the stone from the limestone hill previously found at the site.

'They were mostly men, healthy and strong, their faces and bare arms burnt to the colour of mahogany,' John Boyle O'Reilly will chronicle. 'Burglars, murderers, garotters, thieves, double-dyed law-breakers – but for all that kind-hearted and manly fellows enough were among them.'[36]

In fact, O'Reilly is struck by the distinct culture developing among these men, these so-called lowest of the low.

'No caste there,' he will note of the convicts' rapport. 'They have found bottom, where all stand equal. No envy there, no rivalry, no greed nor ambition, and no escape from companionship. They constitute the purest democracy on earth.'[37]

Of those that have been there the longest, O'Reilly notes a squinty, rheumy quality to their eyes. He learns they suffer from what the prisoners call 'Moondyne', a condition that comes from breaking big limestone rocks into little limestone rocks for years on end, which sees limestone dust settle in your eyes, causing long-term irritation so you never see quite properly again.

Inevitably, the newly arrived ask the older hands what chances there are of escaping.

The answer is not good.

Yes, there are attempts now and then, usually made by new arrivals who don't yet realise the complete futility of it. Most often, they try to make a break from one of the work gangs, when the nature of that work – getting down into a ditch, or getting onto a wall by Fremantle Harbour – means their chains must be removed. In these cases, one of the warders assigned to guard duty simply fires his rifle. It is not to shoot the fugitive, for there is no need. He will be caught soon enough. There is nowhere to run to, don't you see? The bush is no more than the extended prison yard. What's more, within 30 seconds or so, the rifle shot is answered by the boom of the gun in The Establishment, and a red signal flag is raised at the highest point on the hill to alert all in sight that a prisoner has escaped.

Mounted troopers in beautiful white uniforms, on duty for just such occasions, are quickly on their way, trotting on their steeds behind the black-trackers in garbs of kangaroo pelts. Once the black-trackers have the spoor, the gallop begins and it is usually over for the frothing fugitive, who is always brought back to the prison yard in chains, and while all the prisoners watch, 'tied to a triangle, by arms, legs, back, neck, so that he could not crouch or escape the dreaded whipping'.[38] The guards then lie the whipped, bloody shaking fugitive on his stomach, where he stays for days, his deep wounds festering into a painful, oozing repulsive mass of pus and gore.

'In a few cases extreme measures were taken – convicts were tumbled into Eternity through a trap-door. The populace could witness the hanging.'[39]

It is a severe, brutal environment, where everyone knows everyone and, most importantly, knows their place. Those who would try to buck against it will soon find out what awaits, *particularly* you Fenians who are here in the first place because you tried to rise. We are watching you very closely, and don't you forget it.

•

In Sydney, as it turns out on this 12th day of March 1868, they are not watching the Fenians closely enough, down Clontarf way, as the city turns out in force to greet Queen Victoria's visiting son, Prince Alfred, the Duke of Edinburgh himself.

His Royal Highness has just finished his lunch and is leaving the royal tent in the company of the Countess of Belmore, the Governor, the Chief Justice and their host and President of the Sydney Sailor's Home, Sir William Manning, when it happens. Out of nowhere, a ruffian, a low and cowardly cur carrying a pistol, rushes forward shouting, 'I'm a Fenian! God save Ireland!'[40] before firing his pistol right into Prince Alfred's back!

His Royal Highness falls to his knees, exclaiming 'Good God, my back is broken,'[41] while Sir William springs at the would-be assassin and manages to prevent a second shot being fired before the assailant is fallen upon from all sides.

'Lynch him!' the cry goes up, and a sailor even fetches a rope to do exactly that. But the Inspector General of Police, Superintendent John Orridge, and his men, ably assisted by the Chief Justice, are able to extract the bleeding wretch from their clutches and manage to push him onto a steamer so he can face the full weight of the law, not his own full weight jerking at the end of a rope – at least not yet. Even now though, the Fenian is not safe, so inflamed are the passions, for the sailors of the steamer also try to string the Fenian up and are only prevented from doing so by one of the Duke's own travelling companions Lord Newry and their own captain.

Prince Alfred, thank the Good Lord above, makes a complete recovery. But nothing can recover the Fenian name in Australia, never so besmirched as now. It is a warning to all. The Fenians are dangerous. They must be watched closely and, ideally, crushed.

•

The horror, oh the *horror* of this existence.

Some men of philosophical and poetic bent, who find themselves in prison, can embrace the 'life of the mind' to escape their oppressive stone walls, and exist on a plain above.

John Boyle O'Reilly is one such man; his preferred higher plain is poetic. He is in his cell right now, pouring out his pain in the gloom of a balmy evening, finding peace in pained verse.

> *Have I no future left to me?*
> *Is there no struggling ray*
> *From the sun of my life outshining*
> *Down on my darksome way?*
>
> *Will there no gleam of sunshine*
> *   Cast o'er my path its light?*
> *Will there no star of hope arise*
> *   Out of this gloom of night?*
>
> *Have I 'gainst Heaven's warnings*
> *   Sinfully, madly rushed?*
> *Else why were my heart-strings severed?*
> *   Why was my love-light crushed?*
>
> *Oh, I have hopes and yearnings –*
> *   Hopes that I know are vain;*
> *And the knowledge robs Life of beauty,*
> *   And Death of its only pain.*[42]

Mercifully for O'Reilly, there is something of a breakthrough. Little over a month after arriving in the colony, he is selected to go 100 miles south of Fremantle to the coastal outpost of Bunbury, where a gang of convicts is building a road through the Australian bush.

Sight unseen, O'Reilly is pleased.

Anything must be better than staying in infernal Fremantle Prison, frying in the whitewashed sun.

And so the sad day comes when O'Reilly must say goodbye to his brother Fenians, some of whom he has known for years, all of them for many months. Over that time they have fought together, served together, conspired together, voyaged together and suffered together. They have lifted each other's morale when all had seemed as bleak as blackness, and O'Reilly himself had been the one capable of lifting them all by his kindness and humour, his poetry, stories and, yes, his contributions to their newspaper – the *Wild Goose*.

And now he is suddenly leaving them?

It feels like they are losing an arm, a leg, their soul. The actual separation comes as the convicts are returning to The Establishment for their midday meal just as O'Reilly is heading out the gates.

'We waved him an adieu,' Cashman would later sadly recall, 'as we were bustled through the gates. Our hearts were heavy: we could not speak. A tear – well no matter.'[43]

In the traps that have been sent to take the new gang to the south, O'Reilly sits, with all his worldly possessions between his legs, waving them goodbye. He, too, is deeply emotional at the farewell to his brothers, but at least feels marginally better as with every clip and clop of the horses the vision of The Establishment diminishes.

Late summer 1868, on the road to Bunbury, 'This ghastly state of things is what you call Bunburying, I suppose?'[44]

John Boyle O'Reilly will long remember his experience in the Australian bush, most particularly his time with the road-gang around Bunbury, a settlement that had started as a whaling camp and grown into a small port.

'Had there been any moisture in the bush it would have steamed in the heavy heat,' he would record. 'During the midday hours not a bird stirred among the mahogany and gum trees. On the flat tops of the low banksia the round heads of the cockatoos could be seen in hundreds, motionless as the trees themselves. Not a parrot had the vim to scream.'[45]

Each day, from sun-up, to sundown, O'Reilly and the other 25 men in the gang – guarded by a couple of warders – must carve their way through the thick dry bush, taking axes to the trees, digging out the stubborn stumps, sometimes laying 'stone foundations to a depth of 18 inches covered with metaling and bordered with drains, constructed to a standard width of approximately 18 feet'.[46]

In the late afternoons, reeking of the sweat and dirt that covers every inch of their itchy skin, they return to the rough brushwood huts they have constructed for their central camp, to rest, eat, sit around the fire and talk, with O'Reilly lifting morale by telling stories and reciting his poems.

Yet never let it be said that the soul of a poet lends itself only to penning and reciting poems. For what is a true poet if not one who cherishes natural beauty, who finds inspiration in the world around, who seeks to preserve for the sake of posterity, not destroy for so-called 'progress'.

For one day, several months after arriving, O'Reilly and the rest, chopping their way through the bush, come face to face with a magnificent tree, a work of God, over centuries, towering above them to give them shade, spreading its branches wide in welcome.

Yes, a government surveyor has drawn a line on his map, which says this tree must be chopped down, but O'Reilly – though a humble convict, with no rights whatsoever – simply cannot stand it.

So persuasive is he with the warder in charge of the road-gang, so eloquent and inspiring, that the warder allows the tree might be able to stand, and the road go around it, if his superior, the local Bunbury government potentate, also agrees.

Dusting himself off to make himself a tad more presentable, O'Reilly goes to see the official in question and pleads that the magnificent tree be allowed to survive. The official is not persuaded, but at least amused enough by O'Reilly's presumption to mention it to his wife, who perhaps has something of the soul of the poet in her, as well. For she insists on seeing the tree, and with one glance is convinced it must stay.

Poets 2, Viceroys 0.

And so the road bends to the will of John Boyle O'Reilly. For this convict in chains it is a rare victory in an existence that continues to bounce between the brutal and the banal.

And the warders are not always so accommodating. Once, when O'Reilly is late returning to camp, an aggrieved overseer comes up with the perfect punishment.

'O'Reilly,' says the overseer, 'here is a letter for you.'[47]

O'Reilly gasps. For he can see the letter has both the familiar writing of his father on the front . . .

John Boyle O'Reilly
The Establishment
Fremantle, Western Australia

... and that the envelope has black borders, a sign that the contents will contain news of a death.

'Thank you,' says O'Reilly, holding out his tremulous hand.

With a wicked gleam, the overseer tucks the letter away and says, 'You will get it in six months.'[48]

•

At least in Bunbury some of John Boyle O'Reilly's many talents are recognised by the road-gang supervisor, Henry Woodman.

In truth, O'Reilly stands out from the other convicts, even the Fenians, for his education, his intellect, his sensitivity. And Mr Woodman is not the only one who thinks so, as his daughter also takes more than a shine to the good-looking young man.

Partly at her behest, and partly because O'Reilly is clearly the best qualified, Woodman takes O'Reilly 'off the tools' and gives him clerical duties, even making him a 'Constable', whereby he is trusted to oversee other convicts, deliver messages, take a horse into town for supplies, and all the rest. A red stripe is sewn onto his sleeve, the official badge of his office.

Such relative liberty doesn't deliver O'Reilly the black-edged letter that haunts his dreams, but it does allow him the chance to interact with others, including the local Aborigines, the Noongar people. At first they are flitting figures in the bush, who seem to disappear just moments after you spot them. Badly treated by many of the settlers and some of the convicts, they are fearful of white men, but ...

But over time the natives perceive that this one is different. He seems to wish them well, and they are right. O'Reilly does not regard them as savages. He sees himself as a man from a land that has been occupied by the British, against the will of the natives. The natives suffer the same fate. He has empathy for them from the first. Gently, with arms open wide to show he is not armed, with his bright expression and kind face, O'Reilly is able to gain their confidence, and even learn some of their words, and some of their ways, becoming particularly fascinated with their abilities to track animals through the bush. It is not just the outline of their feet in the sand. It is everything from freshly disturbed grass, to broken twigs, to overturned pebbles. He's not long in using what he has learned. By judging how big the broken twigs and sticks are he works out how big the animal is. By seeing how dried out the former underside of the pebble is, he works out how long ago a creature passed. To keep insects from biting, he takes the leaves of the lemon-scented myrtle plant and rubs them vigorously all over himself, just as he has seen the natives do. O'Reilly is hoping such skills might prove useful.

He is a long way from green, green Ireland.

Late 1868, England, lenience for Fenians

Perhaps, however, there might be another way to give the Fenians their liberty once more?

After all, England, despite her many sins, is not without decency, just as the halls of her parliament are not without decent men.

Some determined parliamentarians, led by Mr McCarthy Downing, the member for Cork, continue to agitate for amnesty to the Fenians, even gathering signatures on a petition that starts to grow in length. The first signatory of that petition is Edward Purton, the Lord Mayor of Dublin, who even comes to Westminster to present the petition to parliament. His point, and that of his fellow respected signatories, is that if the British wish to calm the population, they must show some leniency to the Fenians.

Late 1868, Koagalup near Bunbury, the cruellest cut of all

In Western Australia, the sun does not shine, it beats, even as the bush south of Perth – down Bunbury way – does not rustle, it roars.

Suffering 'neath the former, while in the thick of the latter, the roar comes from the bountiful insect life, the blowflies, crickets, dragonflies, bees and, most particularly, the bush's lead vocalists – the cicadas. Never are those insects more abundant than now at midday, for not only have the parrots and cockatoos taken shelter in yonder jarrah and gum trees, and the low banksias that abound all around, but the sweating convicts themselves are providing precious moisture worth buzzing around and celebrating. It is so hot, even the poisonous snakes that slither hither and thither in the less ferocious parts of the day have taken a siesta in whatever hollow logs they can find, while swarms of bull-ants have retreated to the shade.

Still the convicts work on, pushing the arteries of the expanding colony to the south.

'The primitive history of Western Australia is written for ever in its roads,' O'Reilly will recount. 'England sends her criminals to take the brunt of the new land's hardship and danger, to prepare the way for honest life and labour.'[49]

Yes, for O'Reilly, things are much easier than for the convicts on the tools, but the small bit of liberty he has secured does nothing more than make him desperate for more.

In the meantime, the black-bordered letter continues to crowd his every waking thought . . . until one day, the sneering scoundrel of a warder finally hands it over.

With wavering hand, John Boyle O'Reilly opens it to read the news. His beloved mother has died, nearly a year ago now.

O'Reilly weeps. All day and into the long lonely night, black as pitch.

John Boyle O'Reilly has known hard times before, has got through them, and even spiritually prospered. But never has he known bleak blackness like this, the sense that all of life is for nothing, that it is only a means to know more pain, that it is just not worth going on.

His dear mother, Eliza, is gone.

Devastated, despairing, pushed beyond his limits, numb, O'Reilly takes a knife and slashes his left wrist, the warm blood gushing down his legs onto the sandy earth.

Mercifully, as the *Inquirer and Commercial News* will later report, he is quickly 'discovered in a fainting state, and the necessary remedies were successfully applied'.[50]

Coming to his senses over the next few days, John Boyle O'Reilly becomes determined.

He does not want a small bit of liberty. He wants total liberty. He wants to live as a free man again. He is going to make a break for it – 'hook it' in convict parlance – and attempt to escape this hell on earth, or die trying.

But to where, exactly, when his starting point would be this deep Australian bush, 100 miles south of Fremantle Prison, surrounded by the ocean, the desert, 'the road that couldn't take him home'?[51]

That part he is not yet sure of.

It is simply his growing certainty that to stay here would be a slow death, intolerable to his spirit.

He decides his best hope is to first escape into the bush, survive the best he can, then look for opportunities to get out to a passing American whaler, with a captain who might risk taking him on board.

In his Fenian way, he takes a personal oath to keep it secret.

'No-one knew my mind,' he would recount. 'I had before seen so many fail that I concluded it was best to make the effort alone.'[52]

But is that indeed the best way?

On this particular day, the convicts receive a visit from a man beloved by them all, Father Patrick McCabe, a bush preacher like they don't make 'em no more, whose pulpit is effectively the back of his horse, and whose congregation is composed of whatever convicts and ticket-of-leave men he comes across as he roves his 'parish', which goes from the cottages of Perth all the way to the wild bush around Bunbury.

'His grand physical nature,' O'Reilly will recount, 'was joined to a spirit of the noblest heroism in his holy calling . . . His influence on the convicts was most beneficent and beautiful. A scholar and gentleman of the rarest accomplishments, he had at that time given 15 years of his life to the convicts.'[53]

For yes, while the convicts are treated as the scum of the earth, cast to its very end, Father McCabe treats each and every one of them as God's child and is always there for them, giving solace, counsel, and guidance to all, regardless of creed.

But his bond with John Boyle O'Reilly stands apart. The two get on so well that the good Father always seeks him out so they can talk long. On this day, Father McCabe rides to O'Reilly's hut, tethers his horse to a tree, and the two go for a private walk together in the bush.

O'Reilly tells him his whole plan, how he will steal away, lie low, then make contact with a whaler, to make good his escape.

For a moment, Father McCabe says nothing, the silence filled by the cicadas once more, roaring their applause or derision, it is unclear – but it is loud.

John Boyle O'Reilly grows nervous. Finally – it is only a few seconds, but feels like a minute – the priest speaks.

'It is an excellent way to commit suicide,'[54] Father McCabe says at last, before quickly changing the subject and declining to speak of it further.

Right after climbing into the saddle, however, ready to head off to the next camp, he leans down and says, *sotto voce*, 'Don't think of that again. Let me think out a plan for you. You'll hear from me before long.'[55]

Early January 1869, Chatham Prison, pass the needle

Can it really have only been three years ago that he was a free man, fomenting revolution all over Ireland, in charge of thousands of Fenian soldiers?

For John Devoy it seems like another lifetime.

In this first fortnight of the New Year, he is transferred to Chatham Prison in Kent, where he is reunited with many old Fenian comrades, including Jeremiah O'Donovan Rossa. Their special status as political prisoners is recognised at Chatham, and along with seven other Fenians they are kept a little apart from the other prisoners. Moved to a punishment ward, measuring 12 feet by eight feet, they spend their waking hours mending the dusty sandy stockings of the other 1500 prisoners. (Yes, it's a privileged position in prison.)

And yes, they say 'a stitch in time saves nine', but stitching eternally saves none of these nine Fenians. It is just endless dull work, and they can only dream of the day when they will once again be free. At least they have news that there is growing agitation from Ireland to grant amnesty to Fenians, and that is their best chance.

As it happens, so strong is that agitation that, before long, the man that wins a by-election in Tipperary is none other than . . . O'Donovan Rossa! It is true that the Prime Minister, William Gladstone, will rise in parliament shortly afterwards and successfully move for the annulment of O'Donovan Rossa's election on the grounds that he is currently serving time for treason felony but for the British authorities it is proof positive where public sympathies lie in Ireland concerning the Fenians. They have enormous support in Ireland and treating them too badly – as tempting as it is – risks causing another Rising. It might even be that the whole idea of keeping them in prison till they rot has to be reconsidered . . .

•

As to John Boyle O'Reilly's military Fenian brothers back up Fremantle way, they have now been for the most part separated from each other and scattered among work gangs of murderers, thugs and rapists – while the civilian Fenians at least are allowed to stay together in their own work gangs, separate from the common criminals.

In both cases, much of their days are spent with sledge-hammers in hand turning big rocks into little rocks, rubbing the dust from their eyes, building new roads and doing many of the myriad menial tasks necessary to build a dependent colony into a self-sustaining settlement.

'By Jove!' Denis Cashman writes home to his wife. 'Won't I know how to perform a bit of household work for you when I get out of jail. Washing, scrubbing, pumping, scouring, with 1000 other etc's.'[56]

Civilian Fenian from County Louth Patrick Wall is working on a road crew in the bush, as he explains to his parents: 'Well it may be called so, for really it is in a bush we live . . . We miss the beautiful green fields

The fiercely intelligent James Stephens was a founding member of the organisation that would come to be known as the Irish Republican Brotherhood. He was the first to appreciate that the path to victory was to convert the many thousands of Irish soldiers who were serving with the British Army to fight for Ireland instead. (Photograph by J.J. O'Reilly. Courtesy of the National Library of Ireland.)

Great patriot John Devoy was tasked with recruiting Irish soldiers to the cause. In 1865 he coordinated Stephens' escape from Richmond Prison and was instrumental in orchestrating the rescue of the Fenian Six from Fremantle Prison.

THE BRITISH LION AND THE IRISH MONKEY.

Monkey (Mr. Mitchell). "One of us MUST be 'Put Down.'"

Years of starvation and disease caused by the famine in Ireland increased animosity towards England and stirred many to the Republican cause.

('The British Lion and the Irish Monkey' by John Leech, April 1848 edition of *Punch* magazine.)

Informants in the ranks scuppered the chances of an Irish uprising and caused the arrest of Irish Republican Brotherhood leaders, who were taken to Mountjoy Prison, Dublin, to await trial. (Courtesy of Alamy.)

John Devoy was held under lock and key at Mountjoy Prison for a year before his trial in 1867. (Courtesy of Alamy.)

The *Hougoumont* set sail for Australia with 431 people including 280 convicts and 108 passengers. Among them were our Fenian prisoners, and 44 Pensioner guards who were set to take up employment in West Australia.

Denis Duggan joined the Irish Republican Brotherhood in 1861 and rose to lead one of the largest circles in Dublin. He was arrested on 14 February 1866 but a lack of evidence led to his release on the condition that he leave Ireland.
(Mountjoy Prison photographic collection by Thomas Larcom (1801–1879). Courtesy of The New York Public Library Digital Collections.)

Denis Duggan.

John Flood joined the Fenians in the 1860s, and soon rose to become a trusted deputy in the organisation. After leading the attack on Chester Castle, he was arrested upon his return to Dublin and sentenced to 15 years.
(Mountjoy Prison photographic collection by Thomas Larcom (1801–1879). Courtesy of The New York Public Library Digital Collections.)

John Flood.

THE WILD GOOSE.

A Collection of Ocean Waifs.

Vol. 1.] Convict Ship "Hougoumont," Saturday, November 9th 1867. [No. 1.

To Our Readers.

From the frozen north, past the smiling shores of the lakes, brilliant in silvery moonlight Island of Destiny,—where so oft I have lingered on luxurious lakes, brilliant in silvery moonlight, slept on the bosoms of its singing rivers, and shrieked in wild freedom o'er its verdant hills, — far o'er the broad Atlantic, on adventurous wing, — the leader of my flock, — I have flown, to cheer you on your weary way with my homely notes. All natured people may incline to call this cackling; but I scorn the insinuation. When the notes of a goose. — a mere tame slave of a creature — saved the Capital of mighty Rome, was that cackling? Ans(w)er!. Not that I mean to say that a wild goose has not a privilege to cackle sometimes, — for instance after having made a lay, and on many other legitimate occasions, of all which I intend to avail myself.

I've dipped my wings in the emerald spray of Erin's waters; scanned the pathless Ocean's waifs on my way hitherward, and with retrospective eye, have contemplated the land of pilgrimage and pride of the "Wild Geese" of other days,— to bring you memories of home and friends, of wives and sweethearts, and of scenes and songs of fatherland, ever dear to the wanderer.

I will aim to console you for the past, to cheer you for the present, and to strengthen you for the future. But it beseems not so shy a bird to promise too much, nor must I flatter myself that I shall be so welcome to you as one of more melodious throat or gaudier plumage; yet welcome I trust I shall be here where all else is strange, and that each new weekly visitant may be still more welcome,— welcome not alone for the news it brings to keep your memories green, but also that it may prove of interest to all to watch the changing flight of the flock, and read the mystic story they trace as they pass on their airy flight to the shores of that far, strange land of our destined exile.

The wanderer, far from those he loves, and all his heart holds dear,
Oft pauses, as he onward moves, to check the rising tear.
When thoughts of homeland bye gone days, come crowding o'er his brain,
Have soved the voice within, that says—hope on, we'll meet again.

While still onboard the *Hougoumont*, the Fenian prisoners, led by John Flood, created a hand-written newspaper to chronicle their journey.

Robert 'Big Bob' Cranston was a farmer before he joined the 61st Regiment of Foot. He joined the Fenians in 1864 and was arrested in 1866, receiving a life sentence. (Mountjoy Prison photographic collection by Thomas Larcom (1801–1879). Courtesy of The New York Public Library Digital Collections.)

Sergeant Thomas Darragh served in the 2nd Queen's Own Regiment of the British Army before joining the Fenians. He was arrested in 1865 and charged with failing to report mutinous conduct. (Mountjoy Prison photographic collection by Thomas Larcom (1801–1879). Courtesy of The New York Public Library Digital Collections.)

James Wilson was one of John Devoy's best recruiters. He was arrested in 1866 and sentenced to life imprisonment. (Mountjoy Prison photographic collection by Thomas Larcom (1801–1879). Courtesy of The New York Public Library Digital Collections.)

Michael Harrington served with distinction with the 61st Regiment of Foot. He joined the Fenians in 1866, was convicted in July of that year and sentenced to life. (Mountjoy Prison photographic collection by Thomas Larcom (1801–1879). Courtesy of The New York Public Library Digital Collections.)

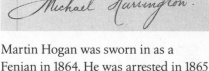

Martin Hogan was sworn in as a Fenian in 1864. He was arrested in 1865 and sentenced to life imprisonment. (Mountjoy Prison photographic collection by Thomas Larcom (1801–1879). Courtesy of The New York Public Library Digital Collections.)

Thomas Hassett joined the 24th Regiment of Foot in 1861. He took the Fenian oath in 1864, and was said to have personally sworn in a further 270 members of his regiment. He was arrested in 1866.

(Mountjoy Prison photographic collection by Thomas Larcom (1801–1879). Courtesy of The New York Public Library Digital Collections.)

John O'Reilly, 10ᵗʰ Hussars

John Boyle O'Reilly was a poet and journalist. After a brief stint in the British Army he joined the Irish Republican Brotherhood and recruited more than eighty soldiers to the cause. (Mountjoy Prison photographic collection by Thomas Larcom (1801–1879). Courtesy of The New York Public Library Digital Collections.)

After his escape from Fremantle Prison on the *Gazelle*, John Boyle O'Reilly settled in Boston, where he began writing for the Boston *Pilot*.

of the old land, as the appearance of the shrubs and trees are but an apology for the genial smile of our native green . . .'[57]

But unlike O'Reilly – and the other military Fenians like Wilson, Hogan, Darragh and the rest – the civilian Fenians at least have the comfort of each other. In a letter to his parents, Paddy Wall warms to the theme of how much he draws strength from his fine companions.

'In the evenings with my companions we arrange ourselves on benches round a camp-fire to hear some song or tale of the old land. So passes the time, just as if we were in as good circumstances as any wealthy freeman. So will it be with us whatever is our lot . . . When anything happens to one each person feels, so we cheer, comfort and console each other with a brotherly love.'[58]

Working on a road crew near West Guildford with Thomas Fennell, another convict, Eugene Lombard, takes a similar tone: 'We always try to cheer each other, crack a merry joke, and sing a song of love or war when seated together at our rude camp fire.'[59]

John Boyle O'Reilly hasn't seen Father McCabe in *months*. With any other man he would have started to despair, started to conclude that either the priest has forgotten his commitment to help, or recanted. But not with this priest. McCabe has told O'Reilly firmly that he will help, and the convict has taken him at his word. He will just have to wait, confident that this man of God will come back to him when it is time.

'Still, it was hard to think, hard to sleep for those months; and my trust in him kept me from working on my own plan, that had formerly made me happy.'[60]

All O'Reilly can do for the moment is keep about his business, and on this particularly hot mid-summer day, he is riding into Bunbury to submit the warder's weekly report to the government authorities at the depot, crossing a plain known as 'the Racecourse', when he hears a 'coo-ee' in the distance, and looks up to see a big, hard-hewn man walking towards him, bearing an axe and . . . mercifully . . . a friendly smile.

'My name is Maguire,' says he by way of greeting. 'I'm a friend of Father Mac's, and he's been speaking about you.'[61]

Very well, then.

O'Reilly says little in return – least of all acknowledging that the man in question had offered to help him escape. The burly man smiles some more to see such hesitation, and draws from his wallet a note penned by Father McCabe.

Very well then!

Father McCabe advises that, in eight weeks or so, the American whalers making their way back from the summer season in the Southern Ocean will briefly be stopping in at Bunbury for water and other supplies.

'I,' Maguire says, 'am going to make all arrangements with one of the captains for your escape.'[62]

Escape! To America!

Could it really be true?

O'Reilly offers profuse thanks and continues with his rounds, but such is his excitement, and nervousness, that for the next week, he can barely sleep or rest until he sees Maguire again. For, surely, something will go wrong. Perhaps the whalers won't come. Perhaps Maguire will change his mind and think better of running the terrible risk of helping a convict to escape and, when the time comes, will turn away from his commitment.

But, then again . . .

The next week, riding the same errand into Bunbury, here is Maguire hailing him once more, and this time, *beaming*.

'You'll be a free man in February,' he says, 'as sure as my name is Maguire.'[63]

John Boyle O'Reilly beams back. There is something about Maguire, known locally as 'Big Jim',[64] that simply inspires confidence.

But again weeks go by with no word until news is brought to the camp by a passing woodcutter. Three American barks, whalers all, have just come into Bunbury Harbour.

It is happening. It is *happening*!

Surely, surely, Maguire will soon appear, summoning him to Bunbury with the precious news that his ship has come in?

But no. The day passes with no word. And the next. And the next.

So devastated is O'Reilly that he resolves to immediately put into action his original plan. He will simply slip away, live off the land, trap wild animals, get water from the paperbark trees as he's learned to do, and see if he can survive long enough to get to the coast, perhaps build a raft, and, ideally, 'intercept the whalers as they sailed from Bunbury'.[65]

It is a desperate plan, but he is a desperate man. Yes, that is what he will do!

Just the next day, as he takes his weekly report into Bunbury, despite his worst fears, here is Maguire again, waiting for him in his usual position on the Racecourse.

'Are you ready?'[66] he asks.

Oh Jesus, Mother Mary, Joseph and all the saints included, I am ready.

Great. The whaler *Vigilant*, out of New Bedford, Massachusetts, is set to sail in four days' time, and her skipper, Captain Anthony Baker, has agreed to take you on board *if* he can find you afloat on something, just beyond Australian waters.

'He has even promised to cruise two or three days and watch for you coming out.'[67]

Big Jim Maguire has it all arranged.

He instructs O'Reilly to procure a pair of freeman's shoes, a crucial ruse as the native trackers could easily identify the indents of a convict's boot. Now listen to me, and remember everything I tell you.

You must leave your hut just after dark on the night of 18 February. Flee into the bush, keeping as much as possible to bare rock and running creek beds, to throw off the trackers. Get to the old convict station on the Vasse Road, where you must 'lie still until you hear someone on the road, whistling the first bars of that famed Irish tune, "Patrick's Day".'[68]

Again and again, Maguire has O'Reilly repeat every detail of the plan until he is sure that it is completely memorised, and there will be no misadventure due to misunderstanding.

CHAPTER SIX

THE ABSCONDER

The sun rose o'er Fremantle,
And the sentry stood on the wall
Above him, with white lines swinging,
The flag-staff, bare and tall:
The flag at its foot – the Mutiny Flag –
Was always fast to the line,
For its sanguine field was a cry of fear,
And the Colony counted an hour a year
In the need of the blood-red design[1]

John Boyle O'Reilly, 'The Mutiny of the Chains'

18 February 1869, down Bunbury way, a dash in the dark

When the sun finally falls, and the cool night rolls in, John Boyle O'Reilly is left only with the light from his one dim candle. Taking his pen in hand, the Irishman begins to write to his father in a hasty scrawl, informing him that tonight he will be escaping, and should he succeed, America shall become his new home, and . . .

And someone is coming!

It proves to be the warder, doing his nightly rounds. A single glance and a friendly nod confirms that O'Reilly is here, and so he moves on.

Alas, his fellow convicts, totally unaware of the importance of the night, will give him no peace. One is so oblivious as to join O'Reilly in his hut to borrow some tobacco and engage in some mindless chatter. The visitor overstays his welcome, but, thankfully, finally, he leaves just before full darkness sets in.

It is time.

Carefully removing his convict shoes, O'Reilly replaces them with the boots of a hapless free man. Dousing the candle, all is dark within the hut, and he quickly steps out into a night lightly lit by a soft half-moon and glittering stars – just enough light for a lone convict to make his way. With careful haste, he moves off into the moonlit bush, a flitting shadow among the shadows.

The murmurs and movements from the convicts' huts grow fainter and fainter as O'Reilly skulks through the night. He has only just begun, but he knows somewhere out in the dark is his next step towards freedom . . . not realising he has already been seen by someone just 200 yards away.

But there he is!

A man in the moonlight, coming towards him.

O'Reilly stiffens.

He is still so close to his own hut, that he is not obviously making an escape, and might be able to talk his way out of this, if challenged.

Oh. It is one of his fellow convicts, Kelly – a fellow transported for life – who he knows quite well.

'Are you off?' says he in a whisper. 'I knew you meant it. I saw you talking to Maguire and I knew it all.'[2]

O'Reilly is speechless. All his efforts at secrecy, and this fellow knows all! How many others know? With one shout from Kelly now, or waking the warden just a little later, he could destroy everything.

But, no. At least for the moment, it remains safe.

'God speed you,' Kelly says, putting out his hand, and shaking O'Reilly's in a vice-like grip. 'I'll put them on the wrong scent tomorrow, if I can.'[3]

Still without a word, though bursting with relief, O'Reilly moves off into the soft moonlight.

Three hours later, he comes to the old convict station on the Vasse Road, and lies down, out of sight, behind a great gum tree, resting, and waiting.

Around midnight, he hears it.

It is less *clip-clop* than *clod-clod* – that muffled sound that hoofs make on a bush-track.

Horsemen! Two of them.

Straining his ears, O'Reilly hopes to hear the opening bars of 'Patrick's Day', but . . . there is nothing.

Murmuring lightly to each other, the riders simply *clod-clod* on by – a couple of farmers, or mounted police, the escaped convict cannot be sure.

Not long afterwards, he again hears horses approaching, these ones at a much faster . . . clod.

Friends, foes, or indifferent?

The answer soon floats to him on the light breeze: the opening melodious bars of 'Patrick's Day', coming to him clear and low.

O'Reilly breaks from his cover behind the gum tree and is on the instant in the moon-shadow thrown by Big Jim Maguire, who introduces the man next to him as Father McCabe's close friend, the wealthy local land-owner William Moriarty.[4]

Wonderful! A resourceful man, *with* significant resources, Moriarty has brought with him one of his finest steeds, and hands it over to the escapee. After offering his profuse thanks, O'Reilly quickly mounts and they gallop off, towards the coast, intent on settlement before dawn, when his escape will surely be quickly discovered.

For hours they ride on in silence before, still in the silent watch of the night, Maguire, in the lead, calls a halt, dismounts, and emits a low whistle.

The whistle is returned, and within a couple of minutes they are joined by three men, two of whom prove to be Maguire's cousins. After they all shake hands with the escapee, the third takes the horses, leaving the remaining five men to form an Indian file – covering each other's tracks to hide their number – as they head off into the bush, proceeding for another hour until they come to a dry swamp near the ocean. Moriarty remains behind with O'Reilly, while Maguire and his two cousins quickly disappear.

'We are close to Bunbury,' Moriarty says to O'Reilly, 'the others have gone for the boat.'[5]

The men wait, silent, staring into the darkness that hides a wide expanse of shallow water known as Geographe Bay. Sure enough, just 30 minutes later, out in the western gloom, it is suddenly as if a match has been struck, as a light appears half-a-mile off-shore. It blinks off, comes on again, blinks off, comes on again and finally blinks off.

It is the signal. They push forward and find Maguire waiting for them on a little bridge across the road. The whaleboat is ready, bobbing by the shore. Maguire leads the way through thick mud that gurgles, slurps and sucks them in up to their knees. No matter, in just half a minute O'Reilly and the three Maguires are bobbing in the boat.

'Come on,' hisses Maguire quietly to William Moriarty still onshore, the one who was not of the Maguire family.

'No,' the man replies, his voice a'quaver. 'I promised my wife not to go in the boat.'

After all, if you are caught assisting or harbouring an escapee, the penalty is being tied to a post and given 100 lashes, before doing hard labour for 12 months.

'All right,' sneers one of the Maguires, 'go home to your wife.'[6]

Hauling softly on the oars, the small dinghy slowly pulls out to sea. The four men watch as Moriarty's forlorn figure on the shore fades into the darkness. O'Reilly bears him no ill will. He is no coward, just a brave and decent man observing the promise he made to his beloved.

After some long minutes, O'Reilly, who continues to watch out on the shore for the flitting shadows of warders – the ghosts of doom – is sure that they are far enough out to sea that the sound made by their oars is beside the point, and they are free to haul as strongly and noisily as they like. By the time the sun rises, they are so far from the shore that only the tops of the high sand-hills around Bunbury are still visible.

Their oars slap in the ink dark water of Geographe Bay, steering to a far-off point near the northern head of the bay where they can wait for the *Vigilant* to appear, 'and cut her off as she passes'.[7]

Rowing in shifts, they keep pulling till noon is nearly upon them, and they are nigh on exhausted. Without water or food – that part of the plan had somehow fallen by the wayside – they are parched and famished, none worse than O'Reilly, whose last meal had been at noon the previous day.

But at least they are nearing the shore, and they soon feel the crunch of the sand beneath their boots. Wringing out their clothes, the dripping sea-water is a grim reminder of their cracked lips and dry throats. The men secure the whaleboat and set off into the bush to find a paperbark tree, which, as O'Reilly knows, have been a valuable source of water to the natives since the Dreaming, as their fibrous husks store bizarre-looking 'humps' of rainwater.

There! What about that one?

The men quickly cut open the first suitable paperbark tree they see, only to find . . .

Nothing.

The long hot summer has taken a toll.

Surely the next one will have some water stored away, just a little?

Again, nothing.

Going from tree to tree, the men make their incisions hoping that it'll be the next one, or maybe the one over there, but the pain in O'Reilly's chest is becoming unbearable. He is burning from within, like his heart is the sun, radiating a great blistering heat inside his chest.

It is the thirst of a convict on the run in the Australian bush, precisely as Superintendent Doonan had warned them on that first blistering hot day on the parade ground at The Establishment.

Good luck making it 'through the most cruel country God ever turned over to the devil,'[8] he had threatened.

The men have no choice but to keep searching into the evening.

Finally, as the day's heat subsides, they find what they are looking for!

And not hidden in a paperbark hump but right here on the ground in front of them. It might only be a muddy pool at the end of a cattle-track, but it'll do . . . Like mad things they plunge their faces into it and gulp deeply . . . only to violently wrench their heads back and spit the rancid muck back into the toxic puddle whence it came.

There is only one thing for it.

One of the men knows a local in these parts, an Englishman called Jackson who is the hired keeper of a herd of cows, and lives in a log-cabin which is the only habitation within 40 cooees in any direction. The cabin is only a few miles away, and if they can make it that far, they will surely be all right.

Alas, alas, they cannot risk taking O'Reilly with them, for they cannot be seen with him. Once it is realised that he was the convict who got away it would put them all at risk.

So they leave him to wait their return by the rancid puddle, without food, without water at least until the next morning, maybe to the next evening, when the *Vigilant* would put to sea, and they could row him out to join it.

All the exhausted, agonised, starving, parched O'Reilly can do is lie down and watch his comrades wind their way away among the sand-hills until they disappear.

Try as he might to sleep, the blistering pain in his chest becomes so unendurable that he must rise and walk around, hoping against hope that he will see one of them returning.

'That time of suffering,' he would recount, 'I look upon as the worst of my life. At last, I remembered that the natives lived on freshly-killed meat, when they could get no water. I soon found a tree with possum marks, which I climbed, and pulled out a large possum. I found then, and afterwards, that this was indeed the very best substitute for water.'[9]

At last, as night falls the following day, Maguire returns just long enough to give him some chunks of cooked meat and a bottle of water, a blessed relief that allows O'Reilly to sleep on a bed made of branches spread upon the sand and . . .

And already it is morning, and the others are back. They head down to the beach. Arriving at 9 am, one of the men immediately climbs a high hill with a looking glass to see if he can spy the *Vigilant*. Just on lunch-time he is back, racing down the hill to report that it is on its way, 'under full sail, steering north'.[10]

Quickly now!

They push the sturdy whaleboat out and haul hard on their oars to get through the surf, a song in their souls. After all the trouble they have been through, their reward will soon be at hand.

John Boyle O'Reilly will soon be on his way, free!

All they have to do is keep rowing hard, so as to intercept the whaler before it reaches the headland.

And there she is!

It has taken two hours of hard hauling, but with a surprising sudden-ness, as if the space between far and near is a mere illusion, they find themselves right in the whaler's path!

They are so relieved, they stop pulling and wait for her to hopefully drop sails and pull alongside.

But, what now?

Vigilant suddenly alters course, seeming to want to avoid them.

O'Reilly is crushed, Maguire infuriated.

'Captain Baker gave his word as a man, and I cannot believe that he would break it. I cannot believe it! I cannot believe it.'[11]

One of the men bellows out, a hail that the boat *must* hear.

His voice echoes off the growing expanse of water between their whaleboat and the *Vigilant*.

Nothing. Stone-cold, motherless nothing.

O'Reilly and Maguire join in now, their voices adding to a chorus of desperate yells and cries for attention.

Still, the *Vigilant* moves through the water on her new course.

Can she not hear them? Are the crew deaf? Is Captain Baker blind? A charlatan?

Maguire rummages through the whaleboat, looking for something that might help, something that would make a signal.

There. A bright white shirt is no flag, but it is better than nothing.

He ties it to one of their oars and, hoisting it like a banner, begins to wave it around as the ensemble of male voices rises behind him on the whaleboat.

How can they miss us *now*?

The men yell and shout, wave their hands and stand aloft in their vessel, but the *Vigilant* neither slows nor strays from its course.

The whaler passes on through the water, their great hope turning to a dwindling speck on the horizon.

•

What now?

At the Bunbury Police Station, Sub-Inspector William Timperley has just received an urgent dispatch from the warden of the Vasse road party: Number 9843, John Boyle O'Reilly, has absconded.

Good Lord!

Timperley moves quickly, and while troopers and black-trackers are instantly dispatched to Vasse, others go to those whalers in the harbour to check for stowaways, and prod long bayonets into every nook and cranny.

•

Aboard the *Vigilant*, Captain Baker is frustrated. It had all seemed so simple, five days before. After the *Vigilant* sets off once more, you will see just off the northern head of Geographe Bay the man we want you to pick up, waiting with others in a whaleboat. And Baker has done absolutely as asked, even zig-zagging from side to side to maximise his chances of finding him, but he can see nothing. He knows from long experience it is remarkable how easily you can miss people in boats even when they are close to you – for they are frequently hidden by the swells – but still it is frustrating.

All he and his crew on the *Vigilant* can do is keep going. All crew on deck, all eyes in every direction. Keep looking!

Late February 1869, in the bush near Bunbury, a vigil for the *Vigilant*

For O'Reilly and his companions, reality is setting in. She is gone.

The weight of dashed hopes hanging heavy above every man, they turn the bow of the whaleboat towards the shore and begin rowing. There is no haste to their strokes, no enthusiasm as they row.

What now?

Maguire is the first to break the mood.

'We beach the boat and head to Jackson's,'[12] he suggests. It will mean that O'Reilly will be alone in the bush, once again left to the fate of this harsh, unforgiving land. Jackson will also have to be informed of their secret and O'Reilly's hiding place in the bush. It is not a plan without risks, but the men agree that, given the circumstances, it is the best way forward.

The crew row on with a grim determination. It is evening by the time they haul the whaleboat up onto the sandy beach, exhausted and exasperated.

The men comment that O'Reilly seems 'at home' in the sand-valley, and it is with warm words and firm handshakes that they wish him luck for the days to come. They assure him that, after returning to Jackson's, it won't be more than a week until they return with information about the next passing whaling ship.

They can trust Jackson as well, and it shan't be long before the old man comes with food and water. It will be okay, John.

As his companions head off into the distance, O'Reilly finds himself alone. It is a sombre experience to return to solitude after such a day, coming within inches of freedom only to have it slip away without an explanation.

But O'Reilly is not one to mope or dwell, he understands that there's simply nothing to be done. If false starts and a little loneliness are the price he has to pay for his freedom, then so be it. Fixing his bed for the night, the Irishman puts his head down to rest.

Night falls, and while O'Reilly sleeps soundly, it is a short peace.

He bolts up in bed to the sound of cries in the distant dark.

HALLOOOOOOOOO.

HALLOOOOOOOOO.

HALLOOOOOOOOO!?

Someone is coming. Those are not the calls of a lost traveller or a wayward bushranger. It is the character of these cries, in the middle of the night, and even more in the middle of nowhere, that the call is specifically for him.

To reply . . . or *not*?

At this point, any risks he takes have the potential to be dire, if not in fact fatal . . .

But now Superintendent Doonan's words ring through his memory. 'The penalty for which is death!'

True, it might be old man Jackson, but what if he's wrong? He would have nobody to blame but himself if he announced his presence and revealed himself to the authorities.

So John Boyle O'Reilly lies low, stays silent, waiting to see if the cries grow closer.

And closer they indeed come.

The sound is encroaching upon his hiding place, not far at all now. But suddenly, the cries change from halloo to his name.

'O'Reilly! O'Reillyyyyy! O'Reillyyyyyyyyy . . . !'

It is a kindly voice.

Taking a chance – surmising this can only be Jackson, as he answers the description, and clearly knows there is an escaped convict hereabouts – O'Reilly now calls back, and the two quickly find and greet one another in the dark.

Jackson recounts that Maguire and his cousins had visited him on his spread, given details of O'Reilly's predicament and where he could be found, and borrowed some horses before moving on. Jackson has brought food, and while O'Reilly takes it appreciatively, he thinks little of its taste. Jackson explains that he will return for O'Reilly when he deems it safe enough, at which point the Irish convict will be free to return to the ranch. However, the old man gives O'Reilly a stern warning that police troopers frequently visit the area, and may be counted on doing so now in the wake of an escaped convict. He must lie very quiet all day so as not to draw any unwanted attention.

O'Reilly finds Jackson to be a kind, warm fellow – a 'bloke', as the Native Australians call them – who has bounced from place to place in Australia, before washing up here by the Indian Ocean in this remote spot north of Bunbury.[13] He has lived many lives, once being in the service of Sir John Franklin when he had been the Lieutenant-Governor of Van Diemen's Land, before he had become the famous lost explorer who perished while attempting to navigate and chart a region of the Northwest Passage in the Canadian Arctic.

For his part, the old man is clearly thankful for the opportunity to talk to someone, and O'Reilly is more than happy to comply. The two talk until the wee hours of the morning, enjoying each other's company. At the first sign of the dawn, however, a barely perceptible lightening of the skies to the east, the old man stands and assures the fugitive that he will return when the time is right.

Yes, sir, and thank you again. Everything will be all right, I can find my own food and water.

Jackson nods, and leaves, the sound of his retreat fading in sympathy with the setting moon.

After snatching a few hours of profound sleep, O'Reilly wakes to the blinding sunlight and a need for food and water, to spare himself the need of consuming whatever Godforsaken thing Jackson had left him the previous night.

In the meantime, O'Reilly ruminates on his failed attempt at meeting up with the *Vigilant*. Was there some chance that Captain Baker really *hadn't* seen the whaleboat? If he hadn't, would he still be out there, looking in vain for a seaborne Irishman? Perhaps he can go looking for the *Vigilant* on the open sea?

Other than these idle thoughts, O'Reilly is safe, well-fed, and sanguine about his prospects. His only real trouble is a curious combination of suspense and boredom – with no pen and paper to relieve the latter through composing verse. When will Jackson return?

On the second day after the midnight rendezvous, the rising of alarmed cockatoos in the distance presages a visitor. As O'Reilly has learned from the Aborigines, the cockatoos do not even ruffle their feathers when they hear anything from their own natural world, which they have been familiar with over the millennia – not even for a mob of kangaroos. And that includes the Aborigines, who have a way of moving through the bush that is silent. But let just one rumbling, bumbling white man make his way through, breaking branches, turning over rocks as he goes, and the birds rise as one against the intruder.

O'Reilly hides, for the moment, suspecting it will be Jackson, but not willing to risk it.

It proves to be a shabby lad of 12 or 13 who, only moments after appearing, goes straight to the spot where O'Reilly had been with Jackson. O'Reilly does not recognise him, but the boy clearly neither means harm, nor is capable of doing much, and so the Irishman emerges.

The lad explains in his rough, mixed-up accent that he is Jackson's son. His father has sent him. Knowing he can trust him, O'Reilly asks him the question that has been gnawing at him over the last 48 hours.

A boat, lad? Do you know of anywhere I can find one? Not a heavy one, like the one that brought me here. I need a light one that I can manage alone.

For O'Reilly is now convinced the only explanation is that Captain Baker and his men must have been looking for him, but simply missed him. In that case, perhaps they are still out there, trawling back and forth? He *must* get back out there as quickly as possible.

'Well,' says the lad a little uncertainly, 'there is an old dory at the horse range further up the coast, buried in the sand.'[14]

Not long after the lad leaves, O'Reilly begins the long walk along the coast, almost seven miles, in the direction of the buried dory which he hopes will bring him into contact with the *Vigilant*. After what feels like an age, O'Reilly spots it. There! Though half-buried by the shifting sands, it is tied to a stake with a rope made of hewn paperbark, that fabulously versatile plant. But the tiny dory has seen better days, and will need some work before she is seaworthy. For one thing, long days under the sun in this blasted land have warped the wood. O'Reilly spends the night fixing the watercraft, using sheets of paperbark to plug holes, smooth out the bow and resurface any gaps – fashioning a type of coir, using precisely the same principles he had learned over many finger-blistering hours making coir while in prison in England. By morning, the boat is as watertight as O'Reilly can make it with the tools he has at hand – just his hands, powered by elbow-grease.

Stowing food and the bottle of water he has painstakingly collected from a big paperbark tree, O'Reilly pushes the boat into the water before climbing aboard himself. For all her faults and ramshackle repairs, the vessel is surprisingly light and easily pulled. O'Reilly glides through the water riding a northward current, towards the *Vigilant*, if it is still out here. By the fall of night, O'Reilly finds himself floating past the head-land, now well and truly on the Indian Ocean itself.

It is, at least, freedom of a sort.

He lashes most of his stash of kangaroo and possum meat to the back of the boat, so it doesn't rot, before taking a swig from his bottle of water and nodding off.

O'Reilly wakes the next morning to find . . . a great deal of his food missing and presumably in the bellies of sharks. The ravenous carnivores have left him with precious little, and what remains in the boat stinks to high heaven under the scorching sun. The heat is close to unbearable. O'Reilly decides to conserve his energy and falls back in the boat, choosing to watch and wait rather than row any further. The day passes slowly, another eternity of waiting for slim chances and vague hopes.

Waiting.
Waiting.
Waiting.
Sitting up, slowly.
Staring.
Can it be?
It is!

A white sail! And not just any white sail, it is the very white sail that O'Reilly had seen only a few days before. The *Vigilant* never left! And not only that, she is drawing closer to the little paperbark dory. They are so close that O'Reilly can see the men aloft on the lookout. At last!

But again ... the *Vigilant* does not draw quite near enough to see O'Reilly, or so Captain Baker would thereafter claim.

There is no sign of recognition, no altering of course, nothing, to give any indication that they have seen him, much less any intention to rescue him. Though the ship turns and comes by for another pass, the same thing happens, and by the time night falls it is disappearing into the distant gloom, never to be seen by O'Reilly again.

The muffled groan in the enveloping darkness is O'Reilly's. Twice in a week now, he has rowed to the open ocean in the vain hope it will lead to a rendezvous and a rescue. It is soon completely dark, and the absence of the baking sun has invited a cool air and mild dew to settle atop the tiny patch of the Indian Ocean in which he floats. O'Reilly is exhausted with the day's effort, but the change in climate has brought some life back into him. Back to the shore, then? It shouldn't be long before Maguire returns, and it would be a shame to be caught out on the ocean when he does. Pulling weakly at the oars until dawn, O'Reilly sees the sand-hills at the headland of Geographe Bay. There is still a-ways to go, and O'Reilly has now been rowing on and off for longer than any one man could be reasonably expected to row. By noon, the Bunbury convict finally has the paperbark dory ashore and tied up. His feet are back on solid ground, and so begins a most weary walk back to his spot in the sand-valley where he can at last sink down to the embrace of Mother Earth once more.

It feels like a lifetime ago that he changed his shoes and stole away from his hut – and a miserable life at that. Attempt after attempt, setback after setback, he is *still* no free man. And yet, his efforts have exhausted him to the point that he feels there is no more to be done than simply wait. O'Reilly no longer leaves the sand-valley, and begins falling into deep sleeps that take him through both night and day. There is nobody to disturb him, nowhere to go, certainly no adventures to the open ocean in search of unreliable sea captains.

All he can do is wait.

•

For the police searching for O'Reilly in the bush around Bunbury, the problem is not that no-one has seen him. It is that *everyone* has seen him. And they are giving tips to the troopers which are sending them to all points of the compass.

Typically, O'Reilly is as popular with the settlers, the ticket-of-leave men, and the district authorities as he had been with his fellow convicts. Most understand the truth – this man is not a criminal. He has committed no crime against morality, only against the laws that denied him and his land liberty. And if they can help in any way by insisting they had seen a man just yesterday moving through the bushes, out by the Thomson place, or perhaps it was further down, by the road to Albany, then it is all to the good. It is amusing to see the troops run ragged on their own instructions.

Early March 1869, Bunbury, Hathaway has a way

It is true that as a reporter for a provincial newspaper in the Colony of Western Australia, it is not often that one gets to wax lyrical, but on such precious occasions as a small handful of American whalers visiting all at once, this reporter down Bunbury way has already made an exception, chronicling chronicles for his readers accordingly:

> The beautiful bay looks quite gay with five large ships at anchor
> ... The American sailors, as a class, have proved themselves steady
> and well-conducted men – and this is the more to be appreciated
> by the inhabitants, inasmuch as Bunbury is now considered the
> rendezvous of American whalers on this coast. The good anchorage,
> the beauty of the townsite, the numerous beautiful gardens in the
> environs, growing every description of fruit and vegetable that the
> colony can produce; and last, though not least, the hearty welcome
> and hospitality of the people, have all tended to make this seaport
> a favourite resort for strangers ... [15]

A few days after anchoring in Bunbury Harbour, Henry Hathaway, Third Mate of the *Gazelle*, is strolling along the main street of Bunbury puffing on a fat cigar when he is hailed by a priest who introduces himself as Father Patrick McCabe.

'You're one of the officers of the whaling bark *Gazelle*?' asks he.

'Yes . . . ?'[16] the American inquires, taking another puff, and looking at the cleric evenly.

Taking Hathaway by the arm, the priest begins to tell him something of the story of John Boyle O'Reilly, how he had been sent here with common criminals, for nothing more than wanting Ireland to be liberated; how he had been plucked from the bosom of his family, placed in chains in the bowels of a ship, and forced into hard labour building roads, here at the very ends of the earth. Now, Mr Hathaway, does that strike you as fair?

No, Father, it does not.

Father McCabe looks the American sailor up and down through the cloud of cigar smoke that shrouds his head at all times. There is something about him to be trusted. The young man looks physically powerful – his rippling muscles straining his shirt – but also morally strong. There is a grace in his gaze which says this is an honourable man.

And so Father McCabe takes a chance.

'Would you be willing to take him aboard the *Gazelle*?'[17]

'You will have to see Captain Gifford,' Hathaway replies. 'He is in command of the vessel, and I am only the [third] mate.'[18]

'I've already seen him,' says Father McCabe, 'and he says he's willing if you are.'[19]

Oh. So that's the situation, is it? Hathaway understands immediately. Captain Gifford is a great man, who regards his Third Mate almost like a son, and rarely made any decision without considering him. Of course it stands to reason that Father McCabe would have approached the Skipper first, and that the Skipper would have deferred to him. It is the respectful way of doing it, rather than simply foisting a dangerous escapee – at least *potentially* dangerous, both physically and legally – upon the ship.

Now, the easy thing would be to say no. Why take such a risk? Well, the answer is, as Father McCabe has pointed out: O'Reilly's situation is unjust. And so Hathaway gives his answer.

'If Captain Gifford is willing I have no objections.'[20]

Excellent!

Would you like to meet him?

Hathaway would. Father McCabe promises to arrange it . . .

2 March 1869, Geographe Bay, O'Reilly says 'O' Henry'

Five days pass in a vague blur, none any more notable than the last until O'Reilly is roused from his deep slumber by a cheery voice.

Maguire!

The weariness in O'Reilly's bones is washed away in an instant, the warmth in Maguire's voice filling him with a fresh hope.

Maguire has brought Father McCabe's close friend, the local land-owner William Moriarty, who had helped them on the first night of the escape. O'Reilly beams to see them.

Moriarty takes one look at the emaciated fugitive and says: 'I am resolved to see you through this time.'[21]

It strengthens O'Reilly's determination to know he has such generous and loyal men by his side.

The men bring with them a brief letter from Father McCabe.

A whaling ship from New Bedford, Massachusetts, the *Gazelle*, is scheduled to set sail tomorrow. The Captain, David R. Gifford, has agreed to get O'Reilly away from the dreary existence of a convict in a foreign land. There will be no question about this Captain's loyalty either, as Father McCabe has paved the path of O'Reilly's exodus with legal tender. Captain Gifford is a whopping ten pounds richer, so surely there'll be no question as to his reliability.

But there is a catch, and it is one final reminder of O'Reilly's days in the convict camp.

It is about Martin Bowman[22] . . . one of the worst men to ever disgrace Bunbury – a cunning criminal transported to the colonies for one of a string of vicious assaults in England – who'd somehow managed to acquire a ticket-of-leave. The men know not how, but Bowman had become aware of O'Reilly's escape and had approached Maguire with a threatening offer. Either Maguire would help Bowman escape along with O'Reilly, or the police would be swiftly informed. Father McCabe has no choice.

The day before O'Reilly is to depart, Maguire returns, this time accompanied by . . . Henry Hathaway!

For the American whaling man, it is an exercise of great trust to accompany Maguire to this deep bushland, knowing he is breaking the law by meeting with an escaped convict, but Hathaway is a brave man, with an acute sense of right and wrong. And it is wrong that a man who has done no more than fight for the liberty of his nation be sent to these Godforsaken parts.

John Boyle O'Reilly sits on the sand before him, blinking up at the visitors and clearly 'in a bad way'.[23]

'He was all broken up,' Hathaway would recount. 'We cheered him up, and assured him that if he would put out to sea again that night we would pick him up the next day . . .'[24]

•

That evening, the menacing Martin Bowman stands before O'Reilly, Maguire and Moriarty, saying nothing, staring at them with calculating, cool eyes.

A violent bastard's violent bastard, the man cannot be trusted, but O'Reilly is determined to regain his freedom, and if this conniving convict insists on joining him, then so be it. Sleep does not come easy for any but Bowman, as the other men take turns keeping an eye on him throughout the night.

'He,' O'Reilly would note of this interloper, 'was all evil, envious and cruel; detested by the basest, yet self-contained, full of jibe and derision, satisfied with his own depravity, and convinced that everyone was just so vile as he'.[25]

Morning arrives without incident and the four ready themselves for what will be O'Reilly's third attempt at a rendezvous on the open ocean.

The men push out in the whaleboat once more, and watch as Jackson and his son wave them off. The men only hope that Gifford's instructions will prove more worthwhile than Captain Baker's did.

And look there!

At noon, the men spy the white sails of not one, but two ships on the horizon. As they come into sight, O'Reilly and the men realise the boats are heading directly towards their whaleboat. There is no waiting about, no sudden change of course, the ships are well and truly there for *them*!

From the crow's nest of the *Gazelle*, the second of what proves to be two American whalers, the cry comes:

'Boat on the lee bow!'[26]

A great hail bellows out from aboard the *Gazelle*.

'John Boyle O'Reilly, come aboard!'[27]

Yes, and you too, Martin Bowman, we suppose.

The beaming Third Mate, Henry Hathaway, takes the cigar hanging from his bottom lip and introduces the crew to the hero of the piece, the fighter for the freedom of Ireland – that's him, O'Reilly. The men aboard the *Gazelle* cheer and clap, ecstatic to have him with them! O'Reilly will be treated like a returning hero, and will bunk in the cabin of Hathaway himself. Meanwhile, the scoundrel Martin Bowman is sent forward to live among the crew, expected to work in exchange for the *Gazelle* tolerating his presence aboard the ship.

It is time for Maguire and Moriarty to leave. Clambering down the side of the ship and back into the whaleboat, Maguire pauses once he has found his footing and cranes his neck to look up at O'Reilly.

'God bless you; don't forget us – and don't mention our names till you know it's all over!' he cries out.

O'Reilly is only able to answer through tears of gratitude, elated with his successful bid for freedom but sore at the prospect of being apart from such gallant friends who have risked so much on his behalf.

•

Have you heard the news! Jack O'Reilly has gone! He's escaped!

It is enough to gladden the heart of any convict, and none more so than those with the privilege of knowing O'Reilly – who know how truly aggravating his escape will be to British prestige. Certainly, there is no guarantee yet that he has got away, but as the days pass with no sign of him being hauled back to prison, their hopes rise. And when Father McCabe is able to, *very quietly*, get word to them about the whaler, they – equally quietly – rejoice.

And yet there is nothing quiet in the reaction of the British authorities, as they move with savage fervour to crush whatever ideas O'Reilly's fellow Fenians might have to try the same thing. Greater surveillance of the gangs is put in place with stricter conditions and ever more severe punishment for even minor transgressions. It is hard to bear, and as a contemporary would report of the sapphire-eyed James Wilson at the time, 'He looked like a man that had to put up with a great deal of annoyance, as I believe he has, from his warder, who is continually reporting him for the slightest cause.'[28]

In truth, it is all the strong-willed Wilson can do to keep his temper, but for the moment he has no choice but to bear it, as escape is out of the question.

As for the efforts of the British authorities to hunt down John Boyle O'Reilly and that scoundrel Bowman, it does not take long for their early suspicions to crystallise into a grim conviction. They must have escaped on one of those American whalers that occasionally visit this otherwise sleepy port. It's the only way. So – by sending a message on the next ship going to Adelaide, which is the hub of Australia's cabling network to the world – the authorities circulate a notice throughout the outposts of the British Empire in the Indian Ocean. They are given notice that two convicts have escaped from Fremantle, and are likely aboard the *Vigilant*, *Clarice* or *Gazelle*, all of which were at the Colony of Western Australia around the time of O'Reilly's escape. Yes, they *must* be on one of those ships, so you must look out for them and search them thoroughly should they come into your port.

As for making sure nobody ever escapes again, the authorities bolster the police force specifically devoted to patrolling and enforcing the law on the waters. As the *West Australian Times* reports, 'It cannot be expected of our land police to do double duty, but persons here reasonably expect the Government to supply proper surveillance, and no harbour is in greater need of a Water Police crew.'[29]

Within 18 months, after local petitioning, the ranks of the Water Police of the Colony of Western Australia – responsible for keeping track of all persons arriving and departing, ensuring that customs laws are observed and seeing that *no more prisoners escape* – are increased so as to cover Bunbury, too. The newly installed Superintendent of the Water Police, John F. Stone, a former Clerk to the Police Magistrate of Perth and the Crown Solicitor, does his best to ensure that the Bunbury Water Police have enough experienced hands to ensure smooth sailing, with enough young blow-hards to keep those sails filled.

•

John Devoy's spirit remains unbowed by Chatham Prison's sombre, impenetrable walls.

In early spring 1869, he avails himself of the opportunity to write a letter to his beloved *pater*.

> *Dear Father –*
> *. . . I am not the man to sit down and cry over my misfortunes, or let my spirits be damped . . . A cheerful heart and a strong will can carry a man through any amount of suffering, and if experience be any use in helping to bear it, I can fairly claim to be a veteran . . . I consider it little short of a miracle that I am alive at all. Well, I find I am nearly at the end*

of my bit of paper, and had better finish. With best love to all, and to
friends I need not name, I remain, dear father, your affectionate son,
John Devoy.[30]

21 April 1869, Swan River Quarry, broken men breaking stones

Sometimes, a man just snaps. Sometimes, years of deprivation, of injustice, of cruelty, pile up on a man and when the dam wall breaks, pity help the other man who happens to be standing nearby.

On this day the man who breaks is the Fenian master swordsman-cum-convict, Martin Hogan.

Beneath the beating sun in the dust-filled quarry by the Swan River, Assistant Warder William Munday sneers at Ireland and the Irish, when Hogan decides he can bear the sneering no more. Hogan doesn't like Munday; nobody does.

And in truth, as James Wilson will recount, Hogan had it in his heart, 'to kill a warder that spoke slightingly of Ireland',[31] but for the moment contents himself by throwing down his tools and refusing to strike another blow.

For his trouble, Hogan is sentenced to spend the next six months in solitary, chained in a darkened cell, with an insistence that strict silence be maintained. After just three months of such treatment, however, Hogan is a whimpering wisp of his former virile self, the purple scar on his emaciated cheek appears twice the size it once did, now that his fat and flesh have melted away under the Australian sun. Even the British authorities must relent. He is released and sent out on a different work party. His fervour for Ireland, for liberation, is in no way diminished, it's just that he now keeps his head down, and swallows his tongue, whenever the rage rises. Of course, he is not the only one suffering . . .

Other Fenians are ailing, too, both physically and spiritually. Physically, the poor diet, the constant work, the lack of proper rest, all combine to sap their strength, and age them before their time.

Spiritually, the loss of liberty tells on a man. When your day-to-day existence is unleavened by even the tiniest ray of hope, when you are exhausted beyond redemption, when you are continually haunted by your failure to have protected your family, who are now alone and defenceless, on the other side of the world, without you – and it is all because of your own actions – it can break a man as surely as the sledge-hammer they are eternally wielding breaks even the strongest of rocks.

Spring 1869, Indian Ocean, the south wind blows for one lucky goose

Often in the evening, and soon enough every evening, aboard the *Gazelle*, Henry Hathaway sits with his new friend 'Boylo', as he now calls him, talking and smoking on the deck by the old donkey boiler – the stove used to boil the whale fat.

As waves slap the hull, the wind moves through the rigging, and the moonlight shows the billowing sails and the sparkling ocean, they puff on Hathaway's cigars as they spend hours, days, weeks, and *months* talking of their lives, their loves, their faiths, their hopes for the future.

They grow as close as brothers, the American endlessly impressed at the sheer character of the man, his learning, his spirit of generosity, his kindness.

'O'Reilly was a true and a brave man,' he would later recount. 'No-one can point his finger to a mean act that he ever did.'[32]

Hathaway, now in his late thirties, tells of growing up in the beautiful whaling capital of America, the port of New Bedford in Massachusetts, the sixth child of ten born to his blacksmith father, Braddock Hathaway, and his fine wife, Harriet. From an early age they had encouraged him to pursue his passion for going to sea, and at just 14 years old, he had done exactly that, heading out on what would be the first of many whaling expeditions that had taken him the world over. But also, there was the sadness he'd known. Along with two of his older brothers, he'd enlisted in the Union Army in 1863, only for his eldest brother, John F. Hathaway, to have been killed in the Battle of Gettysburg, and have his corpse looted of everything, including his clothing. And that is how they had found him, naked and dead, 'the only thing he had on was a white sheet'.[33] It is the saddest thing Henry had known in his life. He has a sweetheart, Catherine Perry, and intends on marrying her and settling down, once they get home from this voyage.

John Boyle O'Reilly in turn talks of his own background, growing up in a fine family in Dowth Castle, a place so beautiful and green it would break a boy's heart just to gaze upon it. He talks of soldiering and poetry, of joining the Fenians, of meeting John Devoy, and of the grand plans they had had for The Rising, of his banishment to Western Australia.

'Ireland is not content to be a slave, therefore she will never consent to be a part of the British Empire,' he explains to his friend. 'Smitten she has been with fire, sword, and famine for six hundred years by a powerful, unscrupulous enemy; but subjugated she is not yet.'[34]

Yes, I and my brother Fenians have paid a high price for joining the fight, but *you*, Henry, have saved me, for which you will have my eternal gratitude.

15 May 1869, The Establishment, no more of the hard cell

Today is the day. Earlier in the year, the British Prime Minister, William Gladstone, had tried to lessen some of the ongoing heat coming out of Ireland by granting a partial amnesty to a handful of *civilian* Fenian prisoners incarcerated in English jails. It does not extend to soldier Fenians who are still regarded as mutinous traitors, nothing less. But it does include some of the men in Fremantle. And on this day, 34 of the 62 Fenian convicts who had arrived on the *Hougoumont* in January 1868 – those whose crimes have been judged as less traitorous than those who served in Her Majesty's forces – are granted a 'Free Pardon'. They are free to go.

Though they can barely believe the news, it means that the likes of Denis Cashman and the Fulham brothers are ushered towards the prison gates and, once on the other side, are free to do whatever they like ... this side of the law. Unlike ticket-of-leave recipients – who often end up working for settlers for just above starvation wages, with little rights and no capacity to travel freely – there is little restriction for those given the Free Pardon: no curfews, no need to report to authorities, no restriction on movement.

Now, while nine of those released – including the Fulham brothers – decide to stay on in Western Australia, in part because they barely have two shillings to rub together, let alone the money required to return home, the 25 others decide to return to the green hills of Ireland, or try their luck in America.

Oh, what a scene when the time comes to depart – with two carriages organised to take them to Albany, from where they will catch a ship to Adelaide, Sydney and then north to their new lives!

The burgeoning Irish community in the Colony of Western Australia – many of whom had donated funds to help the Fenians pay their way across the seas – has turned out in enormous force and colour to farewell their finest.

'Anything equal to the excitement attendant on their departure,' one of those leaving will recount, 'has not been seen in West Australia since its foundation as a colony . . . First came a splendid cavalcade of ladies and gentlemen on horseback, mustering probably some 25 or 30, the gay costumes of the former forming a striking contrast to the more homely attire of the latter. Next came the [carriages] containing the departing exiles, drawn by four horses . . . the rear being brought up by several carriages crowded with friends and sympathisers.'[35]

Of course, after the excitement of it all, comes the long haul over very rough roads, many of them under construction by convict gangs that include those Fenians they are leaving behind – the likes of Thomas Darragh, Martin Hogan, James Wilson, Thomas Hassett, Michael Harrington and Bob Cranston – working their picks and shovels 'neath the hot sun, as the victorious cavalcade comes through.

'Yes,' one of the men in that cavalcade will recount, '[here] are the brave men condemned by courts martial in '66 and '67 . . . without the hope of [seeing again] the old familiar faces of a fond father, a loving mother, or perhaps a fair-haired, bine-eyed maiden, sighing for the presence of that loved one amidst the green hills of holy Ireland.'[36]

Are they allowed to converse?

Technically, no.

'The mean, petty tyranny of the narrow-minded and ignorant autocrats of Swan River pursues these gallant men to the last,' the local paper documents, 'and to prevent the chance of speaking a word in private, or even enjoying the melancholy pleasure of grasping the hands of each other for perhaps the last time in this world of woe, the mounted trooper [forbid it]; but thank Heaven and our own good fortune, this cruel design was frustrated, and in spite of the watchfulness of the escort, the released State prisoners had the extreme pleasure of conversing for a few minutes and bidding a sorrowful adieu to their much-persecuted, victims of English courts-martial.'[37]

For those left behind, it is a bitter-sweet moment, similar to when John Boyle O'Reilly had escaped. Will there ever come a time when we, too, can set our sails for home, or at least for America? Or are we condemned to be in this Godforsaken place until we drop?

At least one Fenian soldier who does not have to ask that question for the moment is William Foley, who, just days after the others have left, is granted his ticket-of-leave on grounds of ill health. In many ways this soldier who had once run messages for lords and high brass now becomes a messenger for his locked-up Fenian comrades, as he remains in close touch with them, knows all the guards and is a trusted presence around them when they are out and about.

•

Cometh the dawn, cometh the vision splendid. For there it is, dead ahead over the translucent blue of the Indian Ocean . . . the white-tipped waves lapping onto the white sands of the beach.

The *Gazelle* drops anchor in the port at Rodrigues,[38] an English island in the Indian Ocean. It is an island no different from any of the others that the *Gazelle* has stopped at along her six-month journey from the headland near Bunbury convict camp.

Except . . . for the whaleboat rowing towards them bearing several soldiers surrounding a very distinguished-looking visitor in a long blue coat, with a bicorne hat that would have done Napoleon Bonaparte proud, and laden down with enough brass to make a cannon – clearly the British Governor, Sir Henry Barkly, accompanied by his guard.

Hathaway is standing aft, right by John Boyle O'Reilly, as the boat bearing the Governor pulls alongside, and it is His Excellency himself who calls up.

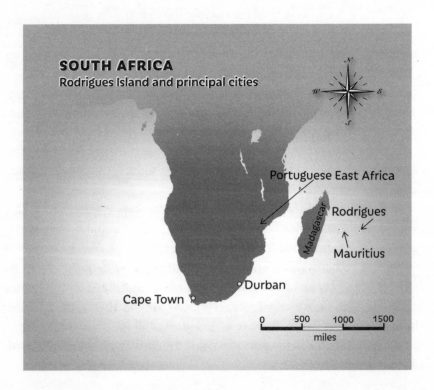

SOUTH AFRICA
Rodrigues Island and principal cities

Portuguese East Africa

Madagascar

Rodrigues

Mauritius

Durban

Cape Town

| 0 | 500 | 1000 | 1500 |

miles

'You have on board two convicts from Bunbury – John Boyle O'Reilly and Martin Bowman.'[39]

O'Reilly barely breathes, but Hathaway is quick to rise to the occasion.

'We have Bowman all right,' he calls to Governor Barkly, 'he's forward. But the other man you're after. I guessed he jumped overboard. He gave his name as Soule.'[40] (It is impromptu genius. A reprobate by the name of John Soule had jumped ship from the *Gazelle* several months earlier, and the Captain still has his papers on board – which he hands over to these inquisitors.)

Forthwith, the soldiers board and arrest Bowman, who feels singularly grim about things. Just as he is about to descend into the Governor's whaleboat, a prisoner of Her Majesty once more, he turns to O'Reilly and says, after a strange pause, 'Good-bye, shipmate.'[41]

Both Hathaway and O'Reilly divine his less than divine meaning.

Bowman's going to snitch – going to trade his knowledge for his life. Once the whaleboat is gone, O'Reilly's usual calm crumbles into a hot-headed panic. He is bereft, convinced that he will shortly be in chains once more.

But Hathaway rises to the occasion once more.

'Keep cool,' he tells the Irishman, 'and I'll fix it somehow.'[42]

And after much contemplation, he really does have an idea. What about the crockery locker under the stairs on the deck below? It is a hidden locker, known by very few, and it might possibly be big enough to secrete Boylo!

Returning to his cabin to get a screwdriver, he very quietly, when no-one is around, removes the two screws that hold the locker cover in place. Could it hold the Irishman?

Perhaps.

Equally quietly now he tells Boylo: 'Go down and see if it is large enough to hold you.'[43]

A short time later Boylo is back. 'It was a tight fit, but I can do it all right.'[44]

Right then.

When it grows dark, you must 'go and get the old grindstone on the deck, and have it handy to throw overboard, and throw your big, soft hat at the same time – before you go and hide in the closet. I will do the rest.'[45]

That evening, O'Reilly goes aft while Hathaway goes for'ard to talk to the watch.

First he points to the figure of O'Reilly by the stern, and tells them to keep their eye on him, for he is worried. After the Governor's visit, the man is desperate and there is every chance he will try and do away with himself.

After all, he notes, 'he tried to kill himself in Australia, before we took him off'.[46]

Hathaway now moves to not only block his men's view of O'Reilly, but to divert their attention to something by the bow when they all hear it . . .

SsssssSPLASH!

'What is that?' Hathaway roars with alarm.

Whatever it is, it's sinking quickly. All anyone on deck can see are bubbles rushing up to the surface, and a solitary hat bobbing idly.

'Man overboard!'[47] comes the cry.

'It's O'Reilly,' yells the watch. 'He has thrown himself overboard.'[48]

Hathaway races down the stairs and screws the crockery locker in place – Boylo already secreted inside – then shouts: 'All hands on deck!'[49]

Immediately, all over the *Gazelle*, cries ring out, as the order is repeated – a chilling choir of alarmed voices rising in the night as the crew jump from their bunks and scramble up the stairs. Someone is drowning!

Who?

O'Reilly.

Not O'Reilly?

O'Reilly!

No more than a minute later, a boat filled with sailors is lowered down the side of the ship. Paddling towards the floating hat, they are quick to realise the terrible news – it is too late. There is no sign of O'Reilly. There are no more bubbles, no movement under the surface.

There is just one sailor who swears, nay, *swears*, that while peering into the depths he had seen the face of O'Reilly peering back at him.

•

The following morning, an irate Governor Barkly arrives back alongside the ship, demanding O'Reilly – for after Martin Bowman had told everything, he now *knows* the Fenian is on board – *and* an explanation for why the *Gazelle* is flying her flag at half-mast.

The men are sombre, sorrowful, they hang their heads in his presence. Speaking to the officers, Governor Barkly is informed that the man he is looking for is the very same man who jumped overboard last night.

Knowing that his real identity would be uncovered, the grief was too much and he chose to take his own life rather than be recaptured. The Governor's policemen question the genuinely grieving crew, trying to ascertain the veracity of this convenient disappearance.

But they discover no sign of farce or false play. It is real. Why, right there, by the for'ard hatchway, you can see his wet hat! And these sailors are clearly deeply upset.

The Governor has no choice but to accept the account and take his leave, whereupon the *Gazelle* is quick to weigh anchor and set sail. But Hathaway is sure to wait until they are well out to sea and Rodrigues has sunk below the horizon before making his move.

'I guess I'll go below,' he says casually to the Skipper, 'and get a cigar.'[50]

Below decks, he makes straight for the crockery cupboard, screwdriver in hand.

And there is his friend! Boylo!

His face is as 'white as chalk . . . eyes as black as night', peering up at Hathaway, looking 'like a wild man'.[51]

With a groan, O'Reilly moves his tortured limbs for the first time in 12 hours.

'What now?' he asks, voice tremulous.

'Come out of that,' says Hathaway.

'What do you mean?'

'Don't stop to ask questions, man,' says the Third Mate. 'Get out of that and come up. You're safe for this time. Land is almost out of sight.'

O'Reilly crawls out and stretches his aching limbs.

'Now,' says Hathaway, 'go and shake hands with the Captain.'[52]

Off to the side, smoking his cigar, Hathaway watches closely as O'Reilly tentatively approaches the sad-looking Skipper, his hand out-stretched.

With just one look, the Captain pales, as if he is seeing a ghost, and now – when he realises that, miracle of all miracles, the Irishman is alive – bursts into tears.

Not long afterwards, though, the Captain – as astonished as he is delighted – is laughing heartily at the ruse of his clever offsider, once it is all explained. The rest of the crew feel the same, and the news quickly spreads.

O'Reilly is ALIVE!

He is risen again, and walks among us, still!

The *Gazelle* sails on, away from Governor Barkly, away from Martin Bowman, away from their troubles.

And there will be no tombstone for John Boyle O'Reilly at Rodrigues. Just a grindstone at the bottom of the harbour . . .

June 1869, off the Cape of Good Hope, leviathan vs. Irishman

Oh, but John Boyle O'Reilly has seen nothing yet in this regard. For while most men in his position, making their way back from the edge of the abyss, might be expected to steer clear of all dangerous activities just on principle, Boylo is not like that.

It has been a month or so since the near miss with the Governor at Rodrigues, and the *Gazelle* is after whales in the Atlantic when the keen eye of the lookout high in the crow's nest spots a pod of them not far off the ship. O'Reilly tells Hathaway that he wishes to go with him, out on the whaleboat, to see for himself what it is all about, and to help pay his passage.

True friend that he is, Hathaway demurs, telling him, 'You better stay by the ship.'[53]

But no, O'Reilly insists in hushed tones and Hathaway silently nods. (When closing for the kill on whales, silence on the ship is all, and not only must everyone whisper, but boots are removed to prevent any chance of the pod taking fright from strange noises.)

Quietly then, the two firm friends sit side by side in one of the two whaling boats lowered, which pushes away from the mothership in search of the aquatic leviathans. Over the next three hours they are pulled some 12 miles away from the ship and . . .

. . . and thar she blows!

About 200 yards off, they suddenly see a smoky drift of sea spray drifting lazily skywards, and, sure enough, there he is: a gleaming raft of barnacled black skin moving along the water's surface; a very big whale, clearly a bull, perhaps 60 tons worth! His black skin is rent with deep scars from battles unknown.

Well, the whale's about to have a battle to the death right now, and the tension on the whaleboat rises, six men in an open boat about to take on a massive whale.

The men pull hard, the steersman expertly brings them towards the whale's lee side, but it is the other whaleboat, led by First Mate Frederick Hussey, which gets there first. The tension is excruciating as the life and death battle – six men in an open boat, going up against a beast twenty times their collective weight – is about to begin. Hathaway and O'Reilly watch carefully as Hussey rises up, gripping the iron harpoon with intent. He draws it back and hurls it high at the flank of the whale, the Manila rope curling through the air after it.

Got him!

'Fast fish!' shouts the harpooner. Brace! Brace! Brace! Sure enough, after thrashing wildly the beast disappears under the dark surface as the rope snakes from its coil, and they prepare to be pulled along for miles, on what is known as a 'Nantucket sleigh ride', until the beast is weak enough to be killed by a lance. Strangely however, for the moment, there is nothing. The men in both boats lean portside looking at the flat, oily circle of water where the whale has submerged, meaning . . .

Meaning O'Reilly, for one, is not looking when the black hump suddenly surfaces *behind* his boat and for its death throes chooses to bring its massive tail down on the vessel, not once, not twice, but *four* times in as many seconds. The men dive into the chilling roiling sea and swim for their lives as their boat is reduced to flotsam around them. Hathaway has the good luck to grip onto the boat's thwart, the only part still solid enough to support a man. The rest of the men thrash wildly in the cold water in their heavy clothes, desperate to get away before the whale resurfaces with a vengeance.

Instinctively, Hathaway looks around for O'Reilly and . . .

'Oh my God! Where is Mr O'Reilly?'[54] he shouts.

'There he is, on the other side, underwater,'[55] says one of the crew, treading water by Hathaway's side. Hathaway can barely believe it, but it's true. There, floating lifelessly *beneath* the surface, amid scraps of smashed-up boat, is a single Irish convict. There is no sign of the whale. Hathaway throws himself under, clinging to the thwart with one hand and grabbing the waterlogged O'Reilly with the other, hauling him up, up, upwards to the air, before using the last of his strength to get him onto a large piece of driftwood.

It is grim. O'Reilly is as lifeless as a rag doll. Against that, Hathaway reasons, why didn't he sink? He must have air in his lungs! Hathaway has a desperate idea, and starts to punch his friend in the stomach – and is immediately rewarded by O'Reilly expelling some sea-water and letting out the tiniest of coughs. He's alive! And O'Reilly's reward is a bigger punch in the stomach. Every cough and groan thereafter sees O'Reilly get another joyous thumping. He *is* going to live!

Henry Hathaway keeps going until the *Gazelle* arrives and rough hands reach down for two of them. Now, and only now, does Mr Hathaway give in – collapsing on the deck, once it is established that John Boyle O'Reilly will live.

•

Henry Hathaway can feel the familiar rocking of the ship. He slowly opens his eyes to the dim morning light, to discover he is on his bunk, in his cabin.

But the rest of this feeling? The overwhelming grogginess in his head, the crushing fatigue? Never has he felt anything like it.

Dimly, and painfully, as thought pushes through his clouded mind, he remembers.

Yesterday afternoon. The whale.

Boylo, being hit . . .

Boylo!

Is he alive?

With enormous effort, the Massachusetts mariner looks over to the adjoining bunk, where he is instantly relieved to see Boylo. And he is awake, looking back at his friend.

'Narrow escape . . .'[56] says the Irishman.

Hathaway acknowledges with a painful nod that it had been just that, and now drifts back into that state which is somewhere between deep sleep and unconsciousness.

•

Sail ho! Just a few weeks later, the *Gazelle* runs into an American ship, the *Sapphire*, off the Cape of Good Hope. Sailing under a Captain Seiders, it is heading towards Liverpool then straight on to the USA. O'Reilly and Hathaway agree it's the fastest way to America – the *Gazelle* must keep on whaling, and is, in any case, very likely on the authorities' watch list after their recent encounter. Yes, his best chance for survival. Captain Gifford hands O'Reilly the papers of John Soule, the long-gone deserter – and also slips him 20 guineas to help him establish himself when he gets to America. O'Reilly can repay it when he can.

•

For Henry Hathaway, it is like he is missing an arm. Without Boylo constantly by his side, just as he has been over the last five months, everything is . . . rather empty. Taking pen in hand, thus, he starts to write his friend a letter, which he can post at their next port.

Ship Gazelle, *July 29, 1869.*

DEAR OLD FELLOW:
I am now seated at the old donkey, where we've sat side by side for the last five months, more or less, and have been reading over some of your pieces of poetry, and it makes me lonesome, although we have not been parted as yet hardly three hours, and thank God we have lived and parted as friends; and thinking, perhaps, in after years you would like to know the transactions of the remainder of this voyage, I shall endeavor to write a little, once in a while, hoping it may prove interesting to you. Most everybody on board is talking about you, and they all wish you good luck in your undertaking, and all that I have got to say is, 'Good speed, and God bless you!'[57]

•

Aboard the *Sapphire*, John Boyle O'Reilly must contemplate his next move. As the next port is Liverpool, taking him into the very maw of the English Lion, it is obvious that discretion will be the better part of valour.

Mercifully, he is helped in this endeavour by the ship's crew and some of the passengers, and, courtesy of one of the passengers, is able to find a safe retreat in Liverpool until a quick passage is secured for him aboard the American ship *Bombay*, which is sailing directly to Philadelphia.

O'Reilly is warmly welcomed by all of the Americans, and none more than the Captain who, on the late afternoon of the second day after sailing from Liverpool, calls him on deck and points to the western horizon, where he can see a heavy bank of black cloud, below which the sun's golden rays are falling.

'We are near the coast of Ireland,' Captain Jordan tells him softly.

O'Reilly's heart swells with love and pride before drowning in melancholy.

'They were sad words,' he would later write of the Captain's kindness, 'Ireland was there, under the sun; but under the dark cloud also ... Home, friends, all that I loved in the world were there, almost beside me – there, "under the sun," and I, for loving them, a hunted, outlawed fugitive, an escaped convict, was sailing away from all I treasured – perhaps, forever.'[58]

CHAPTER SEVEN

A RED LETTER DAY

I shall never forget the first time he spoke to me about his prison life. He was all alive with the most vivid indignation – he was a great storm out somewhere, a great sea pushing up against the shore.[1]
Walt Whitman, reminiscing about his friend, John Boyle O'Reilly

16 December 1869, New York, all the New World's a stage

Eyes to the stage, and hail the conquering hero.

It is none other than the escaped Fenian everyone has been talking about, you know the one, John Boyle O'Reilly, the one who made his escape from Fremantle Prison, that hell on the other side of the world.

Up on the stage, O'Reilly acknowledges the roar of the crowd, 2000 strong in the lecture theatre of the Cooper Institute in Manhattan's East Village. He also acknowledges the calls of encouragement coming from those with him on the stage, the leadership of the Fenian movement in America.

'*Céad míle fáilte!*' they call in Gaelic. 'One hundred thousand welcomes to the United States of America!'

O'Reilly is the embodiment of a precious, if rare, victory – a lone Fenian convict on an American whaler striking a blow against the British Empire, and gaining wide newspaper coverage for his exploits – and it is now for him to tell his tale.

His audience listens, rapt, tittering at his occasional wry asides, and shuddering with him as he recounts some of the more callous of his experiences – '"You will get it in six months," the warder said to me.'[2] O'Reilly gives them just the right amount of detail to make them feel as if they had been there. The man is a natural story-teller, and what a story he has to tell!

At story's end, the crowd stand as one to clap and cheer the hero of the hour.

'They cheered me and crowded round,' O'Reilly would recount to a friend, 'and blew me up till my head was in the clouds, and I couldn't see the sensible ways of the common world.'[3]

Many ask if he plans to stay in New York, but he tells them no.

He has already decided it is not for such as him. At this moment he wants two things: to be of service to the movement to liberate Ireland, and to make a living to keep body and soul together, hopefully as a poet, or journalist, or both.

Upon advice, he soon heads to Boston, which has a large Irish community, and a thriving culture of arts, literature and journalism. He has 'not one farthing'[4] in his pocket, and nothing with him bar some letters of introduction and high hopes for a fresh start in this opening month of the new decade.

Not that it's easy for all that.

'I found that there were two distinct classes of Irishmen in America,' he would recount.

> One the class that makes all the noise, gets up the 'hurroo boys' when a chance offers; and the other the class of respectable men who mind their own business and prosper. The first class do all the talking and ranting about Ireland – they are the 'Fenians' – but they do no more for her. The latter class, the men who make respectable positions, are a credit to her, though they don't tell you so. With this respectable class I found that the reputation the others were giving me – of being a rabid, fire-eating desperate Fenian – was a bad recommendation. I could get no decent employment, and for six months I walked about doing nothing, getting deeper and deeper into debt, and kept from starvation only by an occasional lecture.[5]

Ah, but now here is something different. In the spring of 1870, O'Reilly lands a freelance job for the Boston *Pilot* newspaper which by its own estimation is 'the leading Irish-American Catholic Journal of America'.[6] The paper really couldn't have found a more experienced correspondent for the subject at hand – O'Reilly is being sent to cover an invasion, by American Fenians, of Canada, launched from the tiny Vermont town of Franklin, right on the border.

Another Rising!

Yes, it has come to this.

The American Fenians' reckoning is that if they can just gain control of a good chunk of Canada, they could trade it for British occupation of Ireland – and have the brutes pull out.

Alas, the thousands of men previously reported to be gathering turn out to be no more than 500 men under their commander, General John O'Neill. Though well-disciplined and drilled for battle, the Irishmen are no match for the United States Marshal for Vermont, General George P. Foster. Arriving at 11 on the morning of the planned advance over the border, he informs the Fenian leader, General O'Neill, that they are breaking the laws of the United States, and must stand down from this 'unlawful proceeding'.[7]

But General O'Neill merely smiles and continues trotting around on his fine bay steed, before giving the order: 'Fall in!'

'Soldiers,' he says with pride, 'this is the advance guard of the Irish-American army for the liberation of Ireland from the yoke of the oppressor. For your own country you now enter that of the enemy. The eyes of your countrymen are upon you. Forward, march!'[8]

But, exactly as US Marshal General Foster had warned them, the Canadians open a heavy fire on them.

'Almost at the first discharge,' the correspondent O'Reilly will report, 'Private John Rowe, of Burlington, Vermont, was shot through the head, and fell dead in the center of the road. The Fenian troops, without deploying, returned the fire for a short time, and then fell back,'[9] over the border some 300 yards and behind the farm-house of one Alvah Richards. (Whether or not Mr Richards has a cabbage patch is unknown, but the battle is looking to be going the same way as it had back in 1848 at Mrs McCormack's.)

This is not going well.

Some of the Fenians continue to move forward regardless.

'The men were filing over the exposed ground between the road and the hill, when the heaviest firing of the day was opened on them,' O'Reilly will dutifully report. 'Francis Carraher fell by the roadside, shot through the groin, and, in an instant after, Lieutenant Edward Hope went down in the field, and Mr O'Brien fell dead, with a Canadian bullet through his heart. When the troops gained the hill, they got the order to advance to the front and open fire. They advanced, but before they had reached the position which General O'Neill wished them to occupy, they fell back again under the close, steady fire of the

Canadians. It was evident then that the troops were too few to achieve anything . . .'[10]

General O'Neill, who has been in the thick of the action from the first, tries to rise to the occasion.

'Men of Ireland,' he thunders from a safe spot on the US side of the border. 'I am ashamed of you. You have acted disgracefully; but you have another chance of showing whether you are cravens or not. Comrades, I will lead you again, and if you will not follow me I will go with my officers and die in your front.'[11]

And yet, even as he is preparing to do that, the US Marshal, General George Foster – who has just arrived at the Irish lines with an orderly – has other ideas.

Placing his hand on O'Neill's shoulder, Foster says, 'I arrest you by virtue of my authority as a District Marshal of the United States.'

'Sir,' exclaims General O'Neill, 'I shall resist your arrest.'

'It will be useless, sir,' replies General Foster.

'But, sir, I am armed.'

'So am I,' says the General. 'John, open that carriage door. Now, Mr O'Neill, get in or I will throw you in. I am going to take you to St Albans, right through the midst of your men, and if you make the slightest outcry I will shoot you dead.'[12]

Well, when the General puts it like that, he has a point, and O'Neill goes quietly after all, pausing only to tell his men quietly, 'I leave you now under command of John Boyle O'Reilly.'[13]

O'Reilly is stunned as all eyes now turn to the man who had come here as a journalist only, but whose obvious military experience and strong personality has made General O'Neill turn to him as the solution to their problems.

O'Reilly himself is not sure and it appears that neither is O'Neill's Chief-of-Staff, General John J. Donnelly, who walks several yards away, places his head in his hands, and weeps for Ireland, for General O'Neill, for what has happened to them. It helps.

But there really is nothing that can help this debacle, as after more skirmishing, O'Reilly meets the same fate as General O'Neill, as he is arrested and placed in the local jail cell.

Yes, it is a disaster for the Fenian movement in America – and very nearly a catastrophe for the stunned O'Reilly, who is now face to face with the horrifying realisation that he is already back inside a jail cell . . . after everything he has done, the risks he had taken to get *out* of prison.

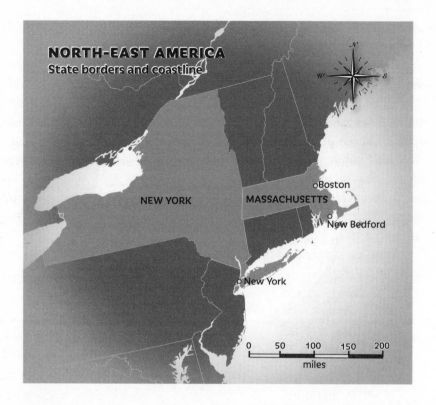

In the end, however, the whole episode proves to be an embarrassing disaster for the Fenians in America, but a triumph for John Boyle O'Reilly, who, once he proves he had been there as a journalist, not a combatant, is released within two days.

He returns to Boston, where he proves himself a good enough writer to capture the whole event in his extended reports for the Boston *Pilot*. And it's not all roses, for he is a strong enough man to bitterly criticise the thinking which had led to the whole calumnious quagmire in the first place.

Still, after O'Reilly has spent a month doing odd jobs for the paper, the editor approaches him with an offer.

'Mr O'Reilly, let us make an engagement for a year.'[14]

Aye, sir, let's.

6 June 1870, Western Australia, today's the day in Toodyay

Thomas Hassett has had a gutful.

Ever since John O'Reilly escaped this hell on earth on the edge of nowhere, Hassett has been on fire to do the same. Day and night working and recovering from working, it is all he can think of, and it is all he can do *not* to act on it.

Boylo had had a real plan before he ran away, an American whaler waiting for him, while Hassett has no such means, he cannot ignore the fire in his belly a day longer. He must try. And so, seeing his chance while working in a road party up Toodyay way – 60 miles north-east of Perth, by the Avon River – he slips into the bush and keeps going.

Now, on that momentous night five years ago back in Dublin, when he had been warned the British were coming for him, he had simply taken his stand of arms and marched in full kit out of the barracks, along the streets, until he reached the relative safety of a Fenian haunt. But that won't do on this occasion. There is no place of relative safety. Or just plain old safety for that matter.

And so he runs as fast and as far as he can. He trips over roots, leaps over fallen trees, startles flocks of birds, and doesn't look back.

The alarm is raised and the mounted troopers and Aboriginal trackers are soon on his trail. Still, despite his lack of a real plan, a combination of fury and fear make Hassett very fast indeed and, by wading through creeks to disguise his tracks, and moving at night over roads where the few traces he might leave are soon erased by the wheels of wagons and ruts, he is able to make his way to Perth, to knock on the door of the surviving Fulham brother, Lawrence – Luke had died of tuberculosis a few months earlier.

No matter that harbouring an escaped prisoner means that Lawrence, as a former prisoner himself, risks being put back in The Establishment for ten years. When a fellow Fenian needs help, there is no choice. He takes Hassett in, hides him, and shares what meagre resources he has.

•

And here is the irony.

Though Tommy Hassett is a pursued prisoner on the run, he is doing better than a nominal free man.

William Foley, who was ailing so badly that he was released on a ticket-of-leave back in May 1869, *still* has no money to return home, and is too weak to get proper work. Even from prison, his dear friend James Wilson follows his fortunes and will later report that he 'was left not only to remain in this land of tears and toil, but was reduced to a state of starvation and forced to sleep at night in a horse's manger with scarcely a rag to hide his nakedness or a bit to satisfy his cravings of hunger'.[15]

Yes, such is the fate of those soldiers who are judged to have committed treason against Her Majesty. William Foley, who had once been so trusted as to be the personal messenger for the Commander-in-Chief of Ireland, General Sir Hugh Rose, is now living in a manger with nothing but a loincloth and straw to keep him warm. He shivers through the night, his wasted body no longer providing the flesh to keep him warm, scratching his sun-burned skin and praying to the good Lord above . . . the very saviour borne of precisely these conditions.

•

It is one thing for many in the British Government to be content to leave the rest of the captured Fenians to simply rot in their prisons in perpetuity, but the British public – Irishmen necessarily among them – and much of the rest of the world, take a different view. There is a growing view that the better option is simply to grant them *all* amnesty, and expel them from British shores.

Yes, that's it, let them go to America, where republicans go.

In the House of Commons, the surge to purge the prisons of Fenians and get them to America is so forceful that, in the end, the British Prime Minister, Sir William Gladstone, cedes to it.

Keeping the Fenians in prison has simply become more trouble than it is worth – particularly at a time when the whole Irish question has settled down, and Great Britain's interests are for the moment not in danger of being torn asunder.

Taking his steel-nibbed pen in hand, thus, Gladstone signals to the Lord Mayor of Dublin and his confreres – who had visited London in recent times to agitate for an amnesty for the Fenians – of the forth-coming decision of his government.

Downing Street,
16 December, 1870

Gentlemen,
I have to inform you that Her Majesty's Government have carefully
considered the case of the convicts now undergoing their sentences for
treason and treason-felony, and that they have recommended to the
Crown the exercise towards them of Royal clemency, so far as it is

compatible with the assured maintenance of tranquillity and order in
this country.

They will, therefore, be discharged upon the condition of not
remaining in, nor returning to, the United Kingdom.
W. E. Gladstone[16]

There is to be one exception, however.

To make this amnesty compatible with the 'maintenance of tranquillity and order', those released will not include the military Fenians, those Irish soldiers who'd been serving with the British Army. It is the strong view of the Duke of Cambridge, Commander-in-Chief of the British Army – and he expresses it forcefully to no less than his beloved cousin, known to others as . . . 'Queen Victoria' – that releasing those disgraced soldiers would weaken the discipline of his forces. And it would be no good for the Irish people, who are a very child-like people, who need an always firm hand, sometimes applied vigorously, to grow properly.

'The fact is,' he writes in his elegant hand to the venerable monarch, 'that the Irish people are very impressionable people. They are very easily guided to mischief by bad and designing persons, but they are as easily guided to good . . .'[17]

No, the point must be made that for such as them, treasonous soldiers, there will be no forgiveness. And so they must remain in prison, rotting.

Christmas 1870, Chatham Prison, Kent, deck the halls

It has been an arduous five years for John Devoy, a peripatetic prison sojourn, being transferred from prison to prison, filled with dull routine and long hours in his cell, pining for his lost love, Eliza Kenny, contemplating his life.

But now, a lightly rumbling rumour about a general amnesty for the Fenians makes its way through the gates of Chatham Prison, along its stone corridors, through its iron doors and between the bars of his cell. Following it by a few days is a warder who comes to Devoy's cell to advise that the Governor of Chatham Prison wishes to see him.

Standing at attention in the Governor's office, shortly afterwards, the prisoner receives the news.

You, John Devoy, have received a conditional pardon, by the grace of Her Majesty. You will be released from this prison within days. You will be supplied with a suit, five sovereigns and a saloon passage to take you over the seas to America. A condition of your release is that you must leave Britain and Ireland for that matter, until such time as your sentence would have been completed.

Do you accept?

YES! One hundred thousand times YES!

Will you take this pen and sign it right he–?

Oh, I see.

The Governor has no sooner shown Devoy the 'patent pardon' – the document to formalise his release, and his commitment to leave the country – than the Irishman's signature is upon it. He is in turn given a document of his own, signed by the Governor – a parchment with a heavy wax Royal Seal – confirming his authorised release.

From here, everything happens with bewildering speed.

After being escorted back to his cell, he packs up his few belongings, and as soon as the following day – in the company of four other Fenians, including Jeremiah O'Donovan Rossa – he is placed in a carriage and taken to Chatham Railway Station, where, in the company of the Deputy Governor of Chatham Prison, the Irishmen board a train bound to London, then another to Liverpool, where . . . where, out on the Mersey, the steamship *Cuba* waits. By 10 pm they are on board, still under guard but able to eat and drink like free men.

The following morning, the suddenly friendly Deputy Governor gives each of them five sovereigns, almost as a farewell gift – nearly a sovereign for every year of their incarceration, if you like. After shaking their hands, he is gone, leaving them under the care of two of his deputies, who themselves leave the ship just before it heads out over the Atlantic proper.

And that's it.

They are free men.

Mid-January 1871, New York, *céad míle fáilte*, one hundred thousand welcomes

Sailing up the Hudson River on their way to berthing at New York, John Devoy and his fellow Fenians scan the day's newspapers and realise for the first time just how much news their release and impending arrival has created.

The members of New York's large Irish community are beside themselves with joy, as witness the . . .

What was that?

Cannon boom from the shoreline.

'Ship ahoy!' the cry goes up.

A sailor lowers a ladder down to the government cutter that has come alongside the ship, and up climbs a uniformed gentleman as fleshy as he is friendly. He steps aboard and, taking Devoy's hand, presents himself as the Collector of the Port of New York.

'On behalf of the Government of the United States,' he says, 'I welcome you, and your companions, and extend to you the hospitality of free America.'[18]

It is the beginning of an armada of vessels heading their way filled with well-wishers and representatives of the now splintered Irish political movement in America, all eager, once on board, to lay claim to the 'Cuban Five', as the exiles become known. All wish to host them at a grand reception, and actual jostling and shouting breaks out amidst the warring parties as to who should have the honour. Vicious insults fly.

'For God's sake,' John Devoy bursts forth, taking habitual command, 'recollect that there are French, German and American people on board, and stop this wrangling. If you don't know how to behave as gentlemen, or don't care to do so, leave this vessel.'[19]

When they won't, the Cuban Five leave them, retreating to a cabin to consider whose invitation to accept while, as twilight starts to fall, in the large dining room of the steamer, the warring tribes continue to insult each other. At length, Devoy and his fellow exiles decide not to join the discordant fray of Irishmen at all, but will disembark on the morrow and stay in a hotel, just until they find their feet.

The next day they land in Jersey City, where grand carriages await to take them, behind a 100-strong cavalcade of horsemen, the Legion of St Patrick, to the grand Sweeney's hotel, where they will stay for the next six weeks.

Now for Devoy and his fellow Fenians, it is one thing as newly released prisoners to be disoriented by their sudden liberty, but in this case, it is quite confounding.

Only a fortnight earlier their lives had been all rigorous routine in Chatham Prison: tiny cells, little light, yes sir, no sir, slops, chores, slops, work, slops, lights out.

And now?

They are the heroes of New York. A throng of no fewer than 3000 besiege the hotel foyer, and access to the exiles has to be restricted to those who are known personally to them, city officials or noted friends of the Fenian cause. But as the *Irish Canadian* newspaper reports: 'Of course this excepts the ladies, all of whom were shown upstairs.'[20]

Of course. For men who have been in prison now for four and five years, the ladies are *more* than welcome. (Even John Devoy, ever-pining for his dear Eliza, who is surely married by now, enjoys the company of the fairer sex, a delight he has been denied for far too long.)

As to the reception, it takes place under the auspices of the *Clan-na-Gael* – the family of Gaels – the phoenix that is rising from the ashes of the irreparably fractured Fenian Brotherhood, with most of its adherents hailing from Dublin, Cork and Limerick. A more secretive movement than the Fenian Brotherhood, they have grand plans for the liberation of Ireland, but keep those ambitions hidden under the guise of being a mere social organisation of Irishmen. John Devoy beams from behind his manly black beard to find among their leadership his old friend Peter Curran, who had been such a boon to them, back in Dublin days, providing one of the back rooms of 'Curran's of Clare Lane' for Fenian meetings.

In extremis, Curran had fled Ireland during the second Fenian crackdown of 1867, and had re-established himself here in New York. Devoy and Curran talk deeply, and the hotelier comes again a week later when the Cuban Five are given a 'Grand Procession' – they sit in open carriages driving down Fifth Avenue, as the people roar for 'the martyrs to Irish republicanism'[21] now freed.

'The inclemency of the weather,' the New York *Herald* reports to its heavily Irish readership, 'did not prevent a grand and memorable ovation of the people of this great city. It can scarcely be much of an exaggeration to say that 500,000 citizens expressed by vociferous cheer on the streets of our city yesterday the joy of America that these last exiles of Ireland were safe from the farther prosecutions of the hated, hypocritical English.'[22]

8 February 1871, Fremantle Prison, earning his stripes

Gatekeeper Francis Lindsey has never liked being the prison flogger. It gives him no pleasure at all. In truth, it positively revolts him. He simply does not like hurting people, even criminals.

But on this occasion?

It is different.

While on duty, he spots two prisoners trying to get over the wall of The Establishment and quickly brings his rifle to his shoulder, aims, and fires. One prisoner falls to the ground, shot through the lung. The other surrenders.

Lindsey has proved himself. He *can* do this. Shortly afterwards, he is promoted to Warder.

•

Inevitably, it takes several months for the official documentation confirming the Conditional Pardon of the civilian Fenians to reach The Establishment, but on this momentous day of March 1871, the remaining nine civilian Fenians are set free. Among their number is the man who helped sail Stephens to safety, John Flood – whose original sentence of 15 years has ended at just five years – along with Thomas McCarthy Fennell and Edward Kelly.

On this otherwise great morning, those released must say a sad farewell to their military comrades. Hogan, Darragh, Harrington, Cranston, Wilson, Kiely, and the ailing Keating watch them walk out the gate with heavy hearts. Yes, those departing promise not to forget them, to agitate for their release – or even rescue? – but there is no telling when that will be. To help the civilian Fenians on their way, the authorities dig as deep as they can, as deep as these men deserve, and give them . . . £1 each. With this, and whatever money the Irish community can raise for them, they may go forth wherever they choose bar Ireland and Britain, and make what they can of the rest of their lives.

The heavy gates close behind the released Fenians, and the military Fenians are ordered back to their cells, where each of them contemplates the long years ahead.

Many other Fenians, since the first round of Free Pardons, have already been granted a ticket-of-leave – which means that they are no longer incarcerated, but are bound by certain conditions restricting their freedom. However, they are free to seek hired positions, and this suits the settlers well, giving them a sure supply of cheap, desperate labour.

It leaves just seven Fenian soldiers still in prison, those who are regarded as having committed active treason against Her Majesty, and for that reason there can be no forgiveness.

As far as the British Government is concerned, they simply must stay there, and rot.

They at least take some solace in the fact that now, nearly a year on, their mate Thomas Hassett is still at large and for all they know might have made his way onto a whaler, just like John Boyle O'Reilly, and now be a free man living large in America.

•

John Boyle O'Reilly, in under a year at the Boston *Pilot*, is on his way to establishing himself as a major force in American journalism and letters, initially focusing on purely Irish matters.

And the Irish in America sure can generate appalling headlines. Like when the Protestant 'Orangemen' of New York parade through the Catholic quarters of the city, shouting 'To hell with the Pope'[23] and the like, which provokes a riot in which four people die.

O'Reilly thunders in the *Pilot*: 'Events have at intervals occurred in the history of this country which have justly called up a blush of shame on the faces of patriotic Irishmen; but we doubt if they ever have received so great a reason for deep humiliation as during the past week.'[24]

After recounting the riot, started by the taunts of the Orangemen, and finishing with the Catholic Irish banding together to set upon them with sticks and stones, O'Reilly goes on.

'Is not this cause for deep humiliation? Earnest men have laboured for years to remove that bitter old taunt of our enemies – "You cannot unite." Why must we carry, wherever we go, those accursed and contemptible island feuds?'[25]

The fact that O'Reilly is disgusted and says so, sees the Irish community regard him more highly still. This is a man to be reckoned with, a man worth reading.

•

He's been hiding for 11 months – moving from house to house of petrified ticket-of-leave Fenians – but now, Thomas Hassett is finally ready to make his escape, the best he can. His best hope, he decides, is to get to Bunbury where Boylo had got away from, to see if he too can get aboard a whaler.

Alas, to convince the wary to transport him, hidden in their wagons, will take a small bribe, and the combined resources of his hidden network of Irish friends sees him with just – *dot three, carry five, subtract four* – 20 shillings. It proves to be just enough and, though half-starved, once in Bunbury he is again secreted, this time by an impoverished family of Irish settlers.

As his friend James Wilson would later recount the story, 'alas, time had changed since O'Reilly was there; money was then in abundance but now gaunt poverty stalked across the land, but still the warm Irish heart was there, and they did what they could'. [26]

At last, it is all for Tommy to make his escape on an American whaler – in this case, the *Southern Belle*, in return for £30 to be paid to her skipper. Alas, alas, though that figure proves to be beyond his capacity to pay, in the middle of the night the desperate Hassett swims out to the whaler at anchor in Bunbury Harbour, hauls himself on board and hides . . . only to be found shortly afterwards and handed over to the Water Police.

Dragged back to The Establishment, Hassett is sentenced to six months' solitary confinement, followed by three years of hard labour in the chain gang right by the prison – the last part of the sentence a little beside the point for one already serving a life sentence with hard labour.

How long can this agony endure?

•

John Devoy has landed on his feet.

Courtesy of his stature among the strong network of Irish people in New York and his own literary skills, he has quickly secured a job as a journalist for the very pro-Irish New York *Herald*, covering both the city's affairs, and whatever comes up concerning the Irish community.

As to how he can help the cause back in Ireland, his dear friend John Boyle O'Reilly proves free with his advice. In a series of letters to Devoy in New York, the rising journalist makes clear his disaffection, starting with correspondence in late January 1871.

> John I hate that infernal name – Fenianism. It has done us more harm than thoughtless men can see. Had we been called Republicans or United Irishmen or ought else we would have retained respectability – but that meanly sounding word with its associations of defeat, dissension, and trickery has been a millstone on the neck of our nationality for years past.[27]

A fortnight later, after Devoy has delivered a heavily publicised lecture in New York, calling for the Irish in America to rise once more, O'Reilly offers counsel: calm down. Do not presume the Irish across America can match the fervour you have encountered so far in New York. Do *not*, John, throw yourself into the American Fenians.

I left their confounded organisation when I ceased to believe in it, and every individual Fenian seems to consider the man an enemy who does not believe with him – but I would wish to see you and all the gentlemen who have been released have as many friends and as much respect as I have in Boston. Fenianism in New York is a power, and interested knaves will defend it and sneer at the quiet neutral element I speak of but, believe me, that Fenianism is a devilish poor representative organisation for Irish nationalists – or rather no organisation at all.[28]

Devoy has an enormous affection and respect for O'Reilly, and values his counsel. He had been appalled at the fracturing of the Irish independence movement he'd found in America, and all the attempts to persuade the newly released prisoner to join a particular splinter.

'Do they think,' Devoy had asked a reporter, 'that by dangling the dollars before us they can influence us? We are not children, nor have we been in prison for the Cause to fall into the hands of a buyer.'[29] And yet far from shunning the *Clan-na-Gael*, the newly released prisoner not only joins it, but throws himself into it – and is soon welcomed into its leadership circles. What he desires most of all is peace with the other factions of the Irish independence movements. Yes, what they need most urgently is unity – followed by a tangible achievement, something to galvanise the Irish diaspora.

Mid-May 1871, Fremantle Prison, nostalgic news and clues

In his cell, Martin Hogan sits on his bunk, transfixed, reading a newspaper cutting smuggled into him by Father McCabe. In the late afternoon there is just enough light coming through his small barred window to make out the words. It is from a New York journal, and tells of a reception given to the released Fenian prisoners now welcomed to the United States by the *Clan-na-Gael*.

Yes, they're out! Released . . . *free* men . . . while Hogan and the rest have been left here to rot. While they are overjoyed for the likes of John Devoy, it remains a bitter pill to swallow, that they have been left here and seemingly forgotten.

Also of interest about the article is the fact that it mentions Peter Curran, in whose public house Hogan had met with fellow Fenians. How inspired he had been that night! How moving had been their words! And it even allows Hogan to surmise where Curran is living, which gives the prisoner an idea . . .

•

Now it is Peter Curran, in his hotel in New York, who sits there transfixed.

For he has received a letter, from a man he knew quite well, five years earlier back in Dublin, but whose circumstances have now changed. It feels like a letter from long ago, and far away . . .

Perth, Western Australia,
May 20th, 1871.
My dear Friend:
In order that you may recollect who it is that addresses you, you will remember on the night of January 17th, 1866, some of the Fifth Dragoon Guards being in the old house in Clare Lane with John Devoy and Captain McCafferty. I am one of that unfortunate band and am now under sentence of life penal servitude in one of the darkest corners of the earth, and as far as we can learn from any small news that chances to reach us, we appear to be forgotten, with no prospect before us but to be left in hopeless slavery to the tender mercies of the Norman wolf.

But, my dear friend, it is not my hard fate I deplore, for I willingly bear it for the cause of dear old Ireland, but I must feel sad at the thought of being forgotten, and neglected by those more fortunate companions in enterprise who have succeeded in eluding the grasp of the oppressor. If I had the means I could get away from here any time. I therefore address you in the hope that you will endeavour to procure and send me pecuniary help for that purpose and I will soon be with you. Give my love and regards to all old friends – Roantree, Devoy, Burke (General), McCafferty, Captain Holden, O'Donovan Rossa, St. Clair and others, not forgetting yourself and Mrs., and believe me that, even should it be my fate to perish in this villainous dungeon of the world, the last pulse of my heart shall beat 'God Save Ireland.'

Direct your letter to Rev. Father McCabe, Fremantle. Do not put my name on the outside of the letter.
Yours truly,
Martin J. Hogan.
Erin go Bragh![30]

Only minutes after Curran reads it he is on his way to see his dear friend John Devoy, now prospering at the New York *Herald*. Surrounded by clattering typewriters, Devoy takes it with interest and immediately notices the Bunbury postmark, and that it comes from a 'Father Patrick McCabe'.

Devoy opens the letter and reels. Hogan! The mighty swordsman. Of course he knows him well, and is overwhelmed with guilt to hear of his grim fate.

'Most of the evidence upon which the soldiers were convicted,' Devoy would later recount, 'related to meetings with me, and I therefore felt that I, more than any man then living, ought to do my utmost for these Fenian soldiers.'[31]

But how? What could be accomplished in New York, to help men cast out by the British Empire to the outer reaches of hell?

It is something he will have to reflect on.

July 1871, Dublin, the Ace of Spades

The confident bullet-headed bull of a man striding down Dublin's Hardwicke Street, nearing midnight of this summery night of mid-July 1871?

Why, it is none other than Thomas Talbot, who has prospered remarkably since his days spying on the Fenians. Now Head Constable, he is highly regarded within the police force for his accomplishments, and – the fellow coming the other way? Talbot barely notices him, right to the point that the fellow pulls out a gun, aims it at Talbot's head and pulls the trigger. A flash, a bang, and a searing pain in his neck. Such a bull of a man is he, however, he doesn't even go down. Instead, with blood gushing between his fingers as he tries to stem the flow, he gives chase.

As it happens, the would-be assassin is soon stopped by suspicious passers-by – something about that fellow running down the street with the revolver in his hand, chased by a bleeding man, tells me something is amiss – and Talbot is rushed to the hospital, where, despite fighting it all the way, he dies four days later.

That account, at least, has been settled . . .

CHAPTER EIGHT

BOLD FENIAN PLOT

Out of Ireland have we come.
Great hatred, little room,
Maimed us at the start.
I carry from my mother's womb
A fanatic heart.[1]

W.B. Yeats

For is not this a living tomb? In the tomb it is only a man's body
is good for the worms but in this living tomb the canker worm
of care enters the very soul.[2]

James Wilson in a letter to John Devoy

1872, New England, the question is, how?

To orchestrate a breakout, John Devoy needs to know how Fremantle Prison operates, where its weak points are and what record there is of successful escapes. Of course, Devoy consults his dear friend, John Boyle O'Reilly, who is enthusiastic to help however he can, but O'Reilly had spent so little time in that dreadful place before escaping that he is of little initial help. O'Reilly advises Devoy to speak to men with more experience of The Establishment to determine the plan's feasibility.

So it is that Devoy seeks out two of the Fenians released from Fremantle who have now settled in America, John Kenneally and Thomas McCarthy Fennell, the latter of whom is living nearby in the town of Elmira, where he owns a bar.

Fennell is eager to help, delighted that the American Fenians are at last moving to do something to help his brethren still so cruelly incarcerated on the other side of the world.

Devoy lays out the specifics of his plan, at least as far as he has worked it up.

'We should send from twelve to fifteen carefully selected men, fully armed, on a ship calling at an Australian port, get them ashore in some way unobserved . . . and take the prisoners off, by main force if necessary.'³

Well, that much is easy for Fennell to react to.

No.

To do so would be somewhere between madness and carnage and would probably result in there being no Fenians left alive to save.

No, Fennell has a much better idea. They need finesse, not force. To start, they must have their own ship, under their own control, ready to be positioned so that the escaped Fenians can make a dash for it when the time is right. And clearly that ship must have a legitimate reason to be in or around Fremantle, so it will need to have a cargo, or a purpose – one that will not arouse suspicion. Perhaps, Fennell suggests, it could be an American vessel 'loaded with grain or some other cargo and later pick up the prisoners'.⁴ From there, a way must be found to get the Fenians on board – stealth is paramount, Fennell cautions, his dark features narrowing like the peak of his thick black hair to emphasise the importance of his point – and then you must quickly get away.

You need to have been in Fremantle to understand the power of The Establishment, he tells Devoy in earnest. The height of the walls, the number of men and guns there to keep them secure. The men will have to be stolen from under the guards' noses.

Devoy listens carefully. Fennell makes a great deal of sense. But he is not sure that a simple cargo ship will work. Perhaps they could take a leaf out of O'Reilly's tale of the whaler, with the whole operation overseen by a strong whaling man? Beyond everything else, the very qualities that make a good whaling man – courage, derring-do, physical hardiness, endurance – would be the very qualities required for this exercise.

Happily, when Devoy journeys to see John Boyle O'Reilly in Boston – to dine with him and his new wife, Mary, who is pregnant – the now fast-rising journalist and poet agrees heartily from the first.

He not only knows it can be done that way, he would be surprised if it can be done in any *other* way. It is such a remote part of the world, there is little cause for vessels other than whalers to visit, and any other stated purpose would immediately arouse suspicion and, quite likely, surveillance.

For Devoy, it is food for thought. But irrespective of whether they buy or lease such a vessel and hire a crew, it will be an expensive exercise.

Where are we going to get the tens of thousands of dollars needed?

27 May 1872, House of Commons, London, let them eat slop

Sir George Samuel Jenkinson, the conservative High Sheriff of Gloucestershire, has the floor.

'Is the report in the *Times* today,' he asks Prime Minister William Gladstone, 'that it is the intention of the Government to grant an amnesty to the remaining Fenian convicts on the occasion of the approaching visit of the Duke of Edinburgh [to Australia], correct?'[5]

'No,'[6] the Prime Minister replies with conviction.

He is now firmly of the view that the more vociferous conservatives are right, and leniency to those Fenians who remain in prison will not solve 'the Irish Question'.

For the foreseeable future, those Fenian soldiers rotting in Fremantle will remain there. As far as William Gladstone is concerned, the British Government will be handing out no further amnesties.

If the Fenian soldiers in Fremantle are going to be freed, it will not be through the benevolence of the British Government.

•

It is the beginning of a long series of meetings for John Devoy and the leading patriots in the *Clan-na-Gael*. Their passion for doing something to free the Fremantle Fenians is growing. It is now a matter of stoking broad enthusiasm for the idea, and finding some general agreement as to how best to proceed.

But it proves very frustrating.

As the months pass and the frozen winter of 1872 meets the hopeful spring of '73 and there is neither enthusiasm nor general agreement – it's as O'Reilly had warned from the outset, the *Clan-na-Gael* is a troubled organisation, with little capacity to agree it is Sunday, let alone unite to do something on a particular date on the other side of the world.

For the moment all Devoy can do is write back to Hogan and affirm he has received the letter, while also noting the bitter truth: we are just not capable of mounting a rescue at this time.

Courtesy of the good Father and his billowing black smock, the other Fenians also smuggle out letters asking to be rescued, some of which are sent to the Fenians in Ireland.

The sapphire-eyed James Wilson takes the rare liberty available to him to send a letter directly to Devoy.

Fremantle
Western Australia

4 September 1873

To Mr. John Devoy.
Dear Friend,
I sit down to write to you with the liveliest feelings of satisfaction. I was delited [sic] to find that Martin Hogan had opened up a communication with you. It was the thing of all others that we most wanted, for we are under the impression that you would have devised some scheme to get us out of this if you had have known the real position of affairs with regard to us; now there is not the least thing in the world to stop us getting away from this place if it is managed properly, the whole amount of the population of this country is only twenty-four thousand.

There are some ports where whalers are in the habit of calling and several other towns in the interior of the country. You perceive at a glance that the number of inhabitants in any of these places are not very great. The great portion of the people are in and about the capital, Perth, and the chief seaport, Fremantle, where there is situated the convict establishment. There is a guard of Pensioners at Fremantle and also Perth. There are about three hundred strong all told. This forms the whole disposable force of the colony; with a few police. So you see that it would not be much risk for any vessel, whaler or otherwise, to run in on some pretence or other. And if we had the means of purchasing horses [we] could make through the bush to the coast where the vessel might be and so clear out . . . I can't forbear to mention Patrick Keating who had been sick in hospital for eighteen months and was on the point of death when the clergy interfered and the governor gave him a ticket-of-leave to try as a last resort to save his life . . . I must tell you that we are much altered in appearance, that from young men we have become old ones . . . Will you be so kind as to let Jack O'Reilly know that we are still alive please to convey to him our best wishes for his happiness and also that we would like to hear from him . . . We have just heard a piece of news that fills us with the most unbounded delight. We hear that 'Nagle' of accursed memory is shot, let us know if the news is true . . .

Yours, etc.,
J. Wilson[7]

Anxiously waiting for a reply as the days, weeks and months drag on by, Wilson is at least given permission by the warders to visit and look after his old friend Patrick Keating, who is now ailing so badly he has been put in lodgings in Fremantle so that his illness does not disrupt prison routine.

Wilson tries hard, trying to get his friend to eat, to get his strength back, but there's little he can do.

Only a short time into the new year of 1874, Patrick Keating slips into eternal sleep.

'The finest man amongst us named Patrick Keating is dead,' Wilson will report in another letter that is smuggled out. 'A truer son of our dear Motherland was never reared on her green bosom.'[8]

Wilson cries bitter tears for his friend. How much longer can all of them go on in this hell? Why has no-one come to their rescue?

There are now just eight Fenian convicts left in Fremantle Prison, if you count Thomas Delaney, who has been granted a ticket-of-leave but keeps being sent back for various atrocities committed while drunk. How much longer must they all *rot* here?

'Month after month we were waiting with eager eyes and beating hearts the arrival of the mail,' James Wilson would painfully recount, 'expecting to hear . . . what we were sure would be glad tidings; but we were doomed to disappointment.'[9]

It is deeply frustrating. For as time goes on, they are becoming ever more convinced that it *would* be possible to get away if only they could get help from their former brothers-in-arms . . .

July 1874, Baltimore, *Clan-na-Gael* convention, *Erin go Bragh!*
Order.

Order!

You have the floor, John Devoy . . .

For 30 minutes, in his low, passionate voice, Devoy gives the 61 delegates gathered in the room a summation of the situation in Fremantle, where brave servants of the Irish Republican Brotherhood lie in chains, only for the fact that free Irish patriots like themselves have done nothing to save them.

And that, friends, is not right. We must save them. We must mount a rescue mission to pluck them from those furthest reaches of the British penal system, and restore them to freedom. I have in mind a plan to rescue them.

Something between a low rumbling and a muttered grumbling rises from the room. A rescue mission? To the other side of the world? How? With whom?

Though he cannot go into specifics – for reasons of security, and for the fact that for the moment he only has the broadest of plans – Devoy at least talks of the conditions in Western Australia and how, one way or another, those who they send to facilitate the escape will obviously be needing access to a ship to get themselves and the released prisoners away. How they will get them out of the prison in the first place has not been worked out yet.

Whatever we do, it will take money. Will you go back to your own people, in your own branches, and ask them to provide that money? If we, as a movement, cannot help organise something like this, what are we here for?

There is silence in the room as he finishes. No-one moves. No-one speaks.

Knowing that he has them, Devoy decides to finish them, and takes from his pocket the letter written by Martin Hogan, and reads it from the top, inevitably giving special emphasis to these words:

'But, my dear friend,' he intones with enormous gravity, 'it is not my hard fate I deplore, for I willingly bear it for the cause of dear old Ireland, but I must feel sad at the thought of being forgotten, and neglected by those more fortunate companions in enterprise who have succeeded in eluding the grasp of the oppressor . . .'[10]

Devoy sits down.

Still no-one breathes. No-one moves. No-one speaks.

And now one delegate stands up, and starts to clap.

And now another.

And another!

Within seconds it is only Devoy who stays seated as the delegates stand, stomp their feet, and cheer, crying out, *'Erin go Bragh!'*[11]

Devoy has his answer.

Yes, the *Clan-na-Gael* will do its best to raise the money that Devoy needs.

And he, together with fellow Fenians John W. Goff, James Reynolds, Patrick Mahon and John C. Talbot, is formally voted to chair the committee to oversee the entire operation.

It has gone better than Devoy could possibly have hoped for. Light of heart, quick of foot, determined of spirit, the Irish revolutionary leaves Baltimore, knowing there is much work to be done.

•

In such an exercise, trying to enter a strange and distant world and achieve the extraordinary, the counsel of John Boyle O'Reilly remains invaluable, and a sure star by which to steer. And that counsel doesn't vary, as he writes to Devoy:

> *The only way to do your work clean, run, and well is by a New Bedford Whaler. The more I think of it the easier does it appear to me. Above all things you should keep your means of proceeding a secret. The crowd may know [what] you are doing; but they ought not to know what half a dozen men should know – how it is to be done.*
> *Yours sincerely*
> *JB O'Reilly*[12]

•

In short order, all across America, wherever the Irish congregate, the fund-raising for the 'Rescue Fund', as it is known, starts.

'Not knowing how much money would be needed,' Devoy would recount, 'all that could be done was to issue the appeal and start the work of the collection. The only part of the plan agreed on was that a ship should be sent to Australia, but whether one should be chartered or bought outright we had no idea nor was there any knowledge of the probable cost. But we went to work, hammer and tongs, to get all the money . . .'[13]

Each branch of the *Clan-na-Gael* has a fund-raising committee and each member is not only obliged to make his own donation, but also to approach others.

In this time of near economic depression, with languishing industry across the board and major unemployment it is not always easy, as noted by one member in a letter to Devoy, 'We have a great deal of apathy . . . My instructions were not to ask from anyone save Brothers in good standing. Now I can get more money from outsiders if I solicit them, men too that if my own liberty was at stake I would place more confidence in than in many of my "Brothers".'[14]

When the ailing revolutionary leader of 1848, John Mitchel – he who according to *Punch* was a mere pesky monkey to the great British lion – receives $100 for a lecture in Boston, he donates it to the cause, noting to Devoy, 'the good Irishmen who are interesting themselves in a good and sacred work – which I need not more particularly specify, but which calls forth all my sympathies – will certainly allow me to make my humble contribution towards the fund which is to go to that noble cause'.[15]

The money trickles forth, in dribs and drabs, but it is not enough. Devoy needs something to further galvanise support, and miraculously, it arrives in an unlikely looking package.

For it is another letter, in a notably scungy envelope.

Fremantle,
Western Australia.
15 June 1874

Dear Friend,
... What a death is staring us in the face, the death of a felon in a
British dungeon, and a grave amongst British ruffians. I am not ashamed
to speak the truth, and it is a simple truth, viz., that it is a disgrace to
have us in prison to day.
A little money judiciously expended would have sufficed to release every
man that is now in Western Australia ...
... Now, dear, Friend, remember this is a voice from the tomb. For is
not this a living tomb? In the tomb it is only a man's body is good for the
worms but in this living tomb the canker worm of care enters the very
soul. Think that we have been nearly nine years in this living tomb since
our first arrest and that it is impossible for mind or body to withstand
the continual strain that is upon them. One or the other must give way.
It is to aid us in this sad strait that I now, in the name of my comrades
and myself, ask you to aid us in the manner pointed out. We think that
you can do it if you will ... If there were any other way of getting
out of this difficulty; I would not apply to you, but our faith in you is
unbounded. We think that if you forsake us then we are friendless indeed.
There are now in prison in the colony, 7 life sentenced men ... The
names of the 7 men who are actually in prison out here are as follows:
Martin Hogan, Thomas Hassett, Robert Cranston, James Kiely,
Thomas Darragh, Michael Harrington, and James Wilson.
So, dear Friend, I will trust this matter to your kindness and will now
conclude by assuring you that whether this appeal succeeds or not that
the greenest spot in our memory is connected with you. And that we never
forget that we are still Soldiers of Liberty.
With respect to all friends, believe me to be,
Ever fraternally yours,
James Wilson[16]

A few evenings later, Devoy rises before his branch members gathered in a large room at a New York hotel and reads Wilson's letter to everyone present, pausing before and after the words, 'We think if you forsake us, then we are friendless indeed.'[17]

The effect is electric, as this voice from the tomb speaks directly to these Irishmen in New York, making each one realise how lucky he is to be there, and what his duty is.

Finally finishing, Devoy puts the letter down, and shouts, 'These men are our brothers!'[18]

On the spot, many hundreds of dollars are raised, or at least committed, which confirms Devoy in his view. If this is what comes from the letter being read to one section of the *Clan-na-Gael*, why not circulate copies to the chiefs of all 86 branches now operating throughout the United States? And copies of Hogan's letter can be sent too, and copies of the resolution taken by the Baltimore convention, so that the fund-raising committee can let all 7000 members be aware of precisely what is at stake, and the resources needed for their 'Rescue Fund'.[19]

It is true that if just one of those members is a British spy, then the whole thing will fall apart, Wilson and Hogan will likely be severely punished, and security on all the military Fenians vastly increased. But it is a risk that must be taken. At least they keep actual details of the plans tight to themselves, with Devoy later noting that only the ten on the committee could have given a rough summation of the plan, and of them 'only five knew the intimate detail'.[20]

Within weeks of the mail going out, in meetings across America, local chiefs of the Clan are standing before their members and reading in their own hushed tones these words coming from a brother in another world.

Wallets are opened, money is collected. Emissaries are sent to New York with wads of cash, and for the first time in three years of trying, the thrilled John Devoy can actually start to move from the problems of mustering the political will and necessary money, to the nitty-gritty of how such a rescue operation might work, who might lead it, when they might depart.

Monday, 1 February 1875, offices of the Boston *Pilot*, hail fellow well met

Mr O'Reilly? You have a visitor.

Fine. Please show him in.

The man being ushered into the office of the Editor of the Boston *Pilot* – for John Boyle O'Reilly has done well for himself since arriving in Boston five years before – is not only familiar with how newspapers work, as he works himself for the New York *Herald*, but, of course, he is more than familiar with the man himself.

Looking at O'Reilly now, how well he remembers that night, a decade earlier, when they had met at the Royal Barracks in Dublin. Back then, O'Reilly 'wore the full-dress dark blue hussar uniform, with its mass of braiding across the breast, and the busby, with its tossing plume, was set jauntily on the head and held by a linked brass strap, catching under the lower lip'.[21]

Not now.

Now, O'Reilly is a civilian, and he looks to be a whole lot more than ten years older, with greying temples, and suffering in the lines in his face that bespeak his story.

The two shake hands heartily, as ever – they have seen each other several times in the last four years, and kept up a regular correspondence – and exchange news, before John Devoy gets down to the subject of his visit: rescuing their fellow Fenians from Fremantle Prison.

O'Reilly is as enthusiastic as ever for the action to free his comrades, and very pleased that the plans he and Devoy had discussed by letter are crystallising. It is excellent that Devoy has indeed decided on a whaler.

And he knows just the man for Devoy to talk to about what kind of a whaler to get – his dear friend Captain Henry C. Hathaway, one-time Third Mate of the *Gazelle* and now with the police at the port of New Bedford, the centre of whaling in America, some 60 miles away. Hathaway knows whaling intimately, O'Reilly says. More importantly, he can be trusted.

'If you can wait until tomorrow, I can come with you, and personally introduce you to Hathaway.'[22]

Agreed!

Devoy excuses himself, but rejoins O'Reilly later at his house. This time the two are joined by Denis Cashman, one of the Fremantle Fenians who had been freed in the first amnesty in 1869 and now lives in Boston. They talk late into the night, as Devoy soaks up every detail that he can about Fremantle Prison, whaling in the area, how O'Reilly managed his escape, what level of security the authorities have to guard against prisoners fleeing, and so forth.

As it happens, O'Reilly is side-tracked at the *Pilot* office the next morning and cannot accompany Devoy to New Bedford, but he at least provides his comrade with a strong letter of introduction, asking his dear friend Henry to treat Devoy with all possible kindness, as he is a good man, on a great mission, and can be trusted.

Devoy departs in the company of the two members of the committee who have come on this mission with him, James Reynolds of New Haven, Connecticut, and John W. Goff of New York.

●

In the damp dark bowels of The Establishment, Wilson, Harrington, Hogan et al continue to despair that they have been forgotten. They have smuggled letters out over the last *four years* and received some fine words in reply. But they have not got the word they have been seeking – that help is on the way. Those gnarled D-shaped scars on their chests which had originally stood for Deserters – and proudly so – now stand for Deserted, making them despondent and frustrated.

3 February 1875, New Bedford, dear Henry has a way

New Bedford?

The one-time capital of world whaling, now well past its peak – as the market for whale oil has been cut by ever more use of oil from the ground – proves to be a picturesque port regardless. The harbour is a riot of vessels and sails, the waterfront populated by sailors of all stripes, the skies filled with caterwauling gulls drawn by the fishing trawlers unloading their nets.

In such a place, filled with strangers from all over the world, the tall bearded figure making his way through the throng attracts no attention at all, which is just how this new arrival likes it, most particularly when he makes his way towards the police station.

As introductions go, it is a curious one.

Most strangers who are visitors to Henry Hathaway in his role as the foreboding, forbidding Captain of the Night Police at New Bedford come accompanied by his police underlings and have handcuffs on. But not this fellow. A good-looking sort of man, with a strong Irish accent, he introduces himself as John Devoy, a journalist from the New York *Herald,* and . . .

'And I am a friend of John Boyle O'Reilly's. I have a letter from him, for you.'[23]

At the very mention of the name, Henry Hathaway looks up to give this stranger a fresh appraisal. 'Boylo?' You have come at the behest of *Boylo*? That changes everything. Taking the letter, he reads it while puffing on his ever-present cigar, and once finished, tells Devoy quietly: 'Follow me.'[24]

Hathaway leads Devoy to the courthouse and quickly locks the door. Devoy begins his hushed pitch.

We Fenians need your help. We need a whaler to buy or to lease, and a Captain, and a crew, and John Boyle O'Reilly says you are the man who can help us. (And on first impressions, Devoy can see why. Hathaway is striking from the first. 'Splendid physique,' he would recall of the hardy old whaler, 'handsome, honest face; quite English-looking. Wears only side whiskers; very reserved in manner; speaks low and slowly, but every word fits. Never without a cigar in his mouth. Eighteen years to sea, whaling all the time.'[25])

Captain Hathaway is sympathetic. Of course he knows all about the situation of the Fenians in Fremantle Prison, as his dear friend Boylo had given him every detail over many months at sea, and many times thereafter. He knows their existence is horrifying, and that it is a cruel and unfair punishment for desiring no more than the liberty of their own country.

Now he believes he can help them get a whaler for a reasonable price – no more of this nonsense about leasing one, because you couldn't fit it out the way it needs to be – and he knows just the man they need to lead the whole escapade. His name is George S. Anthony. He's a local whaler just recently retired from the sailing and whaling game after 15 bountiful years. He's just married, you see, so now he's working as a mechanic at the Morse Twist Drill Works, a machine shop of some magnitude, at the cutting edge of working with metal.

True, he has never actually captained a ship, rising only to First Mate before coming home to settle down, but don't let that concern you. This man is as fine a whaler and a sailor as any man in New Bedford, and will make a fine Captain. Plus, he has grit, true freedom-loving Yankee grit, which is exactly what you need for something like this.

But will he do it?

Hathaway's view is that Anthony is restless working as a mechanic, that deep inside him the siren call of the open sea is beckoning. The man is a swashbuckling seafarer by nature and, though now devoted to his new wife and child, might be amenable to the cause if it is presented to him in the right manner. It is true that he has not a drop of Irish blood in him, and as a matter of fact, is not even a Catholic – being a devotee of the Quaker religion – but still Hathaway insists that he is the man they are looking for.

To delicately approach him, Hathaway suggests talking to Anthony's father-in-law, a local whaling agent by the name of John T. Richardson, who is a friend of Hathaway's and can also be trusted – and as it happens, Richardson can help you purchase a whaler, too.

Thank you, indeed, Captain Hathaway. Devoy warmly shakes his hand, arranges to meet him on the morrow, bids him good night and returns to his lodgings, where Reynolds and Goff await.

Moving swiftly, Devoy and his comrades make some careful investigations of their own, using their contacts in the area, and seek independent assessments of George S. Anthony. Without stalking him, particularly, they are even able to observe him close up and assess the cut of his jib. He seems, at least, able and competent. No-one has a bad word to say about him, and it is obvious that, whatever else, he is highly regarded as a sailor and a whaler.

After more meetings with Henry Hathaway, and then one with the whaling agent John T. Richardson – who, though also a Quaker, proves to be untroubled in this instance by the possibility of facilitating something so potentially violent as a prison breakout – things fall into place.

After four days, Devoy, via the father-in-law, asks for a meeting with Mr Anthony, face to face, in a port store owned by Mr Richardson.

'Come to the store this evening,' Richardson tells his son-in-law a short time later. 'There will be two or three men there whom I wish you to meet.'[26]

•

Quiet!

That was a knock on the door at 18 South Water Street, New Bedford.

Out the back of the store – full of whaling lanterns, coils of rope, sails, harpoons, oil-skin pants, hoods, shirts, beanies, boots and warm waterproof jackets – several men are sitting around a large stove, warming their hands and feet.

The door is carefully opened and only once the visitor's identity is confirmed is he let inside.

George Anthony nods in greeting at his father-in-law and Captain Hathaway. A couple of the others he notes as fellows he has observed around the store over the last few days. One of them comes complete with both a great air of quiet authority and a magnificent set of full black whiskers that cover at least half of his face. Captain Anthony introduces the man as John Devoy.

George Anthony shakes hands with America's leading Fenian, as he does with the other men to whom he is introduced, allowing them to get a good look at him.

A tall man of singularly solid build in his early thirties, he looks like one of those whalers who, should a fight break out with his crew, would likely be the last man standing. A Quaker he might be, but at first glance it looks more to be in the way of an earthquake than anything else. He is not a man to mess with, and that strong air of quiet but overwhelming strength about him is exacerbated by his black hair and oddly black eyes, that seem to look right through you. The only colour in him is from his rosy red cheeks, which shows good health.

But to brass-tacks, Mr Anthony. Please take a chair.

They all need to talk and, using a method that the Fenians had often used at meetings where newcomers were among them, the fellow with the black whiskers says in an Irish brogue, 'It's just as well to sit in the dark',[27] before extinguishing the lamp.

Should Anthony snitch, or have loose lips with someone he never should have trusted, it will be difficult for him to tell them just who it was who said what.

In the darkness, Devoy takes the lead, first swearing Anthony to secrecy and extracting a formal promise that what is discussed here will never be discussed outside these walls, not even with his wife.

Somewhere between bemused and bewildered, Anthony agrees, and Devoy proceeds to give a quick potted history of the situation in Ireland, how the English had been there for centuries and how, in its own way, Ireland is trying to do now what America itself had accomplished a century earlier, in the War of Independence – break free of England. You will appreciate, Mr Anthony, that those who sign up to do that in Ireland are not criminals, but patriots! Enamoured of liberty, just like the Yankees! And yet here is the situation, many of these patriots have been shipped off on a convict ship to the furthest reaches of the British Empire, to Fremantle Prison in Western Australia, where they rot with common criminals, including murderers, rapists and highwaymen.

But our men are *not* criminals, he emphasises, and we want to break them out. We will break them out. All we need is a whaling man of your ilk to take a ship that we will provide, manned by a crew that you will pick, all the way to Western Australia, doing just enough actual whaling along the way to allay suspicion. You will depart as soon as the whaler is fitted out and your crew is sorted. Your job will be to get your whaler just off the coast near Fremantle, keeping it in international waters – at which point you will be beyond the reach of British law – and then receive a longboat coming from the shore where our own people, who will arrive in Fremantle ahead of you, will have the escapees waiting. You must then simply bring them back to America! And you will be well paid for your trouble, and the risk you are taking.

The men can't see the burly whaler in the dark, but George Anthony is impressed. He's almost grinning.

Yes, these Irishmen are talking about doing something that might be, technically, a criminal operation. But they certainly don't talk like criminals. These are educated, high-minded men, speaking with patriotic fervour. And their leader also talks of paying him a very handsome fee for his trouble. When Devoy is done, others have their say on a few matters and now, even in the darkness, all eyes turn to where they know George Anthony is sitting, as they await his response.

'I need some time in which to consider the proposition,'[28] says Anthony evenly.

'You can have a day,'[29] replies John Devoy.

The American rises, pulls on his woollen jacket and his beanie down low over his ears. Bracing himself for the blast of wintry air, he heads off into the night, walking briskly up the hill towards his home. Behind him, the moonlight glints off the waters where as many as 100 whalers are bobbing in the harbour. Is that the life, so recently abandoned, he really wants to return to?

He still has much thinking to do as he quietly opens the door to his home off Dartmouth Street, and nestles into bed beside his cherished young wife, the fair Emma – more than a decade his junior at just 20 years old – with their baby daughter, Sophie, sleeping beside her. It is a contemplation that goes well into the wee hours and bleeds into the next day.

On the one hand, he would love to go to sea again, and this is not only an extraordinary opportunity to do so, in highly adventurous fashion – but it would be his first command. On the other hand, he is newly married, and a family man now. And there is the added factor that when George had been just eight years old, the news had come through that his whaling father, Humphrey, had drowned at sea after his schooner *Henry Curtis* had been swept onto the rocks, and his mother had never quite recovered . . . while he had been haunted by the tragedy of it ever since, raised with the help of his aunts and uncles. Giving up whaling for the birth of his daughter had been a salute to his commitment not to put his own family through such an enduring agony. To add to that – his mother has been very ill of late.

Does he have any right to embark on such a risky venture, which may well see him shot dead or placed one cell along from the Fenians for many years to come? But are these Irishmen, these 'Fenians' down in Western Australia, truly lawfully held? Certainly not under any moral law that Anthony recognises. Mr Devoy's arguments had been compelling. The Fenians are no guiltier of a 'crime' than the Founding Fathers of the United States, who had hungered for their country's independence from Great Britain and fomented revolution 100 years earlier – it is just that the Fenian revolution had not yet succeeded.

But should he be getting involved in a fight that is not his?

And what of the terrible dangers he would inevitably face?

All day long, George Anthony continues his internal debate, still not sure what his final decision will be, until the hour approaches.

•

Quiet!

A knock on the door.

Again Anthony is admitted to the back of the store. Again he is ushered into the circle of chairs around the stove. But this time there is no extinguishment of the lamp. To hear his answer, they need to see the whites of his black eyes.

You have the floor, Mr Anthony.

'I will go,'[30] he says simply.

The collective sigh of relief is palpable – no suitable alternatives to the Massachusetts whaler had surfaced. But the profuse thanks and jubilant congratulations do not last long. They have much to decide, to plan, to facilitate; where to get the whaler they need, how much they can spend, and how Anthony and his father-in-law may access the money needed . . .

Ah, yes, the money.

The rough figures that have been worked out – some $5000 for a whaler, and twice that to fit it for an 18-month voyage – is well beyond the funds currently available, and even beyond that which has been promised. As it stands, in fact, as Devoy will acknowledge, 'but a small percentage of the money needed had been turned in'.[31] In short, the

Irishmen who have promised to donate are having a hard time actually emptying their pockets.

Between them, Hathaway, Richardson and Anthony might have the answer. Why not do some actual whaling? If everything goes really well, whaling won't just pay for the expedition and authenticate their ruse, it could even turn a profit, which would allow them to pay the crew their normal share of 'the lay', with a big bonus for the Captain, on top of his regular pay.

Of course, it would not be possible to borrow that much money to buy the ship against the mere possibility of future earnings, but in the short term things can be arranged.

For, all these years on, Devoy's *Clan-Na-Gael* comrade and co-Chair of the rescue committee, James Reynolds, is still haunted, and angered, by the horror of Ireland in the late 1840s, the starvation, the death, the pitiless English reaction. Yes, he had escaped at the age of 16 to come to America, and had since done well in the brass founding trade, but nothing could quell his enduring outrage at what had happened to his homeland. Now, there is a chance to strike a blow, and he is in a position to do something to help. He does not hesitate.

By mortgaging his home and placing a 'chattel upon his household goods',[32] he says he will be able to advance $4000 of the initial outlay needed to buy a whaler.

It's a boon, which will give Devoy time to collect some of the money promised, and raise some more.

The planners continue to talk late into the night, with Anthony, Hathaway and Richardson taking the lead on what kind of whaler they will need, where they should start looking, and when they might be able to get away.

And so it goes.

Starting with the recommendation of John Boyle O'Reilly, John Devoy and his fellow Fenians are placing all their trust, all the hopes of the *Clan-na-Gael*, and the fates of the poor Fremantle Fenians, on three Americans – Anthony, Hathaway and Richardson.

'[None] of these three men had, so far as we knew,' Devoy would recount, 'a drop of Irish blood in his veins, but they undertook the work they were asked to perform as readily as if they had been sworn Fenians.'[33]

The talk goes late into the night, and by the next morning, Devoy and his men have left for New York, a trio of Irish men o'war heading south under full sail.

•

In their wake, George Anthony, Mr Richardson and Captain Hathaway are busy finding an affordable whaler. They inspect various vessels. The *Jeannette*, a New Bedford whaler, is too expensive. The *Sea Gull* is a clipper from Boston, which, though commendably fast, is also in need of urgent and expensive repairs – which, even if they could afford, would delay them. The *Addison*, then? It used to be a whaler, and though now running as a packet ship, ferrying people and goods between Boston and Fayal in the Azores, it could be easily re-fitted. Yes, but they will have to wait until it returns from its latest voyage to even see it.

Very well, perhaps the *Catalpa*?

Do tell.

They are all vaguely familiar with her, as she had started life as a whaler based in New Bedford, but is apparently now being used as a cargo vessel. As a matter of fact, she has just returned to Boston from the West Indies with a cargo hold full of mahogany logs, and most importantly, she's for sale. Her name is inspired by the name of a type of tree native to North America.

Together, George Anthony and his father-in-law board the first train going to hurry up to the Massachusetts capital, and quickly arrange to look her over where she lies, moored by Orient Heights. Once they have made their way there, first by buggy – through streets filled with carts loaded with building materials and workers as the city rebuilds from the Great Boston Fire of 1872 – and then by ferry, they are impressed at first sight.

For there she is!

At just over 200 tons, and 90 feet long, by 25 feet wide, with a depth of just over 12 feet, and three masts, she is a substantial vessel. She's not a classic whaler, as she has been fitted out as a merchant bark – complete with poop deck and double topsails – but modifications can be quickly made for whaling purposes, if they can but buy her and get her into dry-dock.

How much?

Five and a half thousand dollars.

Having put in his notice at the tool works, the newly christened 'Captain Anthony' – it really does have a ring to it – estimates that it will take another $15,000 to get her ship-shape. Telegrams are sent, and pleas sent out. It is manageable. Just.

The bottom line is the bottom line, and after a quick exchange of coded telegrams with John Devoy in New York – and a quick trip to Boston by Henry Hathaway to get his confirmation that he, too, thinks it a good buy of a good vessel – things start to fall in place. Most importantly, they receive the authorisation they need from the committee.

On 13 March 1875 Irishmen and friends purchase the whaler, *Catalpa*.

Or, more accurately, James Reynolds purchases the *Catalpa*, and the ship's papers are summarily registered to his home address in Connecticut – something that attracts some interest from the New Bedford whaling community, who wonder who this new entrant into the market can be.

The delighted Henry Hathaway writes to John Devoy in New York using an agreed code word for the *Catalpa*:

New Bedford, March 15, 1875

To John Devoy, Esq.
Dear Sir . . .
I hope you had a good look at the Horse in Charleston and was satisfied with it.
I think it's a tip top bargain. I liked the looks of him first-rate and think will bring more than we paid for him any day. We have already been offered $1,000 more than we paid for him, but I think he will more than pay for himself this coming season on the track. We are going for him this week . . . I think he will cost us nearly $17,000 [overall], but we will try to do our best and make everything count. We have commenced this morning in earnest and will pay for the Horse today. I hope you will be punctual in sending the fodder, as grain is on the rise here . . .
How did you like the looks of the man that we chose to take charge of the Horse? He is the right man for it.
Yours in haste
H.C.H. Capt.[34]

Hiring a makeshift crew, Captain Anthony is able to bring the bark down from Boston Harbor to his own New Bedford, and within days he has it up on blocks at City Wharf.

It must be ready, he tells the workmen, to go whaling for a period of at least 18 months, and perhaps as long as two years in both the North and South Atlantic. They will need a blubber deck to be able to cut up the whales they catch – and let the blood drain away – together with all the equipment to boil the carcass down to extract the oil. A layer of copper is laid down aft of the masts, to protect the deck from the heat when a 'tryworks' is built above it – essentially an enormous brick oven into which huge copper kettles are laid. When fired up, these 'trypots' will be able to boil down the whale flesh we feed into it, producing the oil, which is a whaleman's liquid gold. Most mariners simply call it a 'donkey boiler', just as Hathaway had taught Boylo when they would sit by the *Gazelle*'s boiler, smoking and chatting late into the starry, starry night.

Above the whole thing, the carpenters get busy building a roof through which pokes the chimney, so there will be some protection from the weather. To protect the *Catalpa* itself from the ocean and wood-eating shipworm, the entire hull is also covered in a sheath of copper. This won't entirely stop seaweed and barnacles attaching themselves, but at least will diminish them, allowing the whaler to move smoothly through the water for, hopefully, the entire voyage.

And when will that be, Captain Anthony's tearful but understanding wife, Emma, asks him, holding wee Sophie in her arms.

If all goes well, my love, we will be back well before the end of next year. You must never breathe a word of this to anyone, but . . . we are due to be in Fremantle by late January or February of next year. There we will be collecting some Irish prisoners and it will take us as long again to return. We will be back before you know it, in the later months of 1876. I will miss but one Christmas with you!

With Emma's reluctant blessing, Captain Anthony throws himself into preparations. The *Catalpa* must be ready for the long haul, so she needs accoutrements, and plenty of them. We are going whaling, so we not only must have three whaleboats, and whaling gear including harpoons, we need solid davits built on deck, so we can easily lower those whaling boats and then retrieve them when it is done. As to getting the carcasses aboard to be cut up and then boiled down, we must have rope and chains, together with plenty of firewood to get the flames beneath the trypots roaring.

We'll also require quarters for the sailors, and special holds built on deck for all the extra sails and rigging we will be needing for the long trip ahead.

All day, and into the night by lanterns, there is the sound of sawing and hammering, scrubbing and rubbing, and hauling and bawling at those falling behind, as Captain Anthony also oversees the 'stowing' of the ship, making sure that all supplies are stowed where they should go.

New sails are brought aboard, along with a spare anchor, and a modern marine chronometer to determine longitude. Now, specifically for the whaling, planks of special wood and iron hoops are purchased and hauled into the hold so the coopers can make barrels to hold the whale oil. Captain Anthony also oversees the purchase of harpoons to first strike the whale, and lances to kill them up close. And we need blubber spades – razor-sharp pieces of steel attached to long handles which are specifically designed to separate the blubber from the bone, so we can cut it into pieces and feed it into the boiler.

Enormously strong oak davits are bolted on deck and, using the pulley system suspended from them, four new and freshly painted whaleboats are pulled into place and secured. Meanwhile, all the existing rigging is tarred to make it more weatherproof, and new rigging stowed against the likelihood that the weather will eventually get to the original stuff anyway.

And, of course, there are the food supplies – including chooks and pigs to go in makeshift pens now being built on the quarter-deck – as well as hammers, nails, bolts, screws, saws, chisels, cutting spades for the carpenters and smithies, and huge grindstones so the tools may always be kept sharp.

Oh. And we will need a couple of new American flags so that, come the time, we can show who we are, and where we are from. Make sure they are enormous ones, so they can be seen from afar and stow them in my cabin.

Each night, Captain Anthony returns home late and exhausted to Emma and Sophie, reflecting how odd it is that a man should be working so hard to facilitate the readiness and refinement of something which, when it is ready, will take him away from those he loves most in the world.

And then back to work, on the morrow at dawn.

At least for the comfort of the Captain, two small cabins on the starboard side have had a dividing wall removed, to make the Captain's cabin, while another room for the First Mate is fashioned directly opposite, while the Second and Third Mates can share a cabin next to him.

The key question Captain Anthony has been considering, of course, is who those Mates should be, most particularly the First Mate.

Anthony has in mind a long-time sailing companion and 'bosom friend'[35] from Nantucket, Samuel P. Smith.

But there is a problem. Like Anthony, Sam had recently left whaling behind, hoping for a more secure family life onshore – he has his eye on a young local lass, Amy – and it is far from sure that he can be persuaded.

At least for Second and Third Mates, Anthony is able to secure the services of Mr Antoine Farnham and Mr George H. Bolles, two swabbies from New Bedford.

As for the rest of the crew, he has two key requirements – no Irish, and no English. Which leaves a selection of itinerant sailors who happen to be in New Bedford at the time – and from whom Captain Anthony draws together a 23-strong crew made up of assorted Malays, Kanakas and 'Black Jacks' as African sailors are known. They are signed to a base salary of around ten dollars a week, plus a percentage of the proceeds once the whale oil is sold.

With none of them, not even the First Mate Samuel Smith – for he does finally agree to come – does Captain Anthony share the truth of what they are about. This is for basic reasons of security, as the fewer who know, the less chance there is that the plot will be discovered. It is also for the crew's own protection. If their plan is found out, those who don't know can legitimately claim innocence due to ignorance.

There will come a time, of course, when they will all have to be informed, but he will deal with that when the moment arrives.

As to the inevitable queries from New Bedford's tight-knit whaling community about this new whaler in their midst, John T. Richardson is happy to tell anyone who asks, and there are many: 'Captain Anthony is going where he has a mind and will stay as long as he pleases.'[36]

Oh.

That answer makes a certain amount of sense. On reflection, it is quite possible that Captain Anthony has got wind of some rich whaling grounds, so perhaps he is merely being protective of the secret.

•

By the end of April, all is in near readiness for departure. For the princely sum of $19,010 – contributed in mostly small sums by Fenians across America – the *Clan-na-Gael* now has a ship-shape whaler, re-fitted and victualled. And they have a Captain and most of a crew ready to go.

There remain just a few final decisions to be taken before they can depart. Of these, the key one is who should be the *Clan-na-Gael*'s eyes, ears and voice on board? They must choose between two men, the coach-maker turned carpenter, Denis Duggan, and a shoemaker Thomas

Brennan. Both are desperate to go. But John Devoy is insistent that it be his old schoolmate, Duggan, and his authority holds sway. Duggan will go on the journey listed as a carpenter. Brennan does not take it well, and is absolutely insistent that he wishes to go anyway . . .

Too bad.

In the final week before departure, there is one final obstacle as Captain Anthony's beloved mother's health takes a dive. It is out of the question to leave when she just might be on her death-bed, and there is a two-day delay until she has sufficiently recovered and Captain Anthony announces he is, in fact, ready to go – with the day selected being the first anniversary of his blessed marriage to Emma, 27 April 1875.

John Devoy takes advantage of having a day off from his work as night editor of the New York *Herald* to journey to New Bedford to give Captain Anthony his final instructions before his farewell.

'You will cruise until fall, about six months, in the North Atlantic,' he tells him formally. 'Then you are to put in at Fayal [in the Azores], ship home any oil which you may have taken, and sail at once for Australia, where we expect you to arrive early in the southern autumn of 1876. You are to go to Bunbury, on the west coast, and there communications will be opened up with you from our Australian agent . . .'[37]

All is set for departure on the morrow.

CHAPTER NINE

ON THEIR WAY A'WHALING

Their sufferings touched my heart, and I pledged my word as an American sailor to aid in the good work to the best of my ability.[1]

The Western Australian, 9 October 1895

29 April 1875, New Bedford, bound for glory

John Devoy stands alone on the shore, stroking his thick black beard thoughtfully, gazing with no little pride at the *Catalpa* bobbing among an armada of whalers about a half mile off-shore. This is really happening. Other men wait for their ship to come in. The bearded one has been waiting for his to go out, been working towards it, and now it is really about to set off on the journey of his dreams! Hopping into the whaleboat that has just pulled into shore, Devoy is rowed out to bid the *Catalpa* and Captain Anthony a fond farewell. He boards her to find the crew scrambling hither and thither, making the usual last-minute preparations. Captain Anthony is a man in his element, barking orders with glee. And if perhaps Samuel Smith raises a quiet eyebrow at Devoy's unexplained presence – just as he has noticed his mysterious hovering over the affair in recent weeks – he keeps it to himself. It is none of his business, and he places his trust in his friend and commander, Captain Anthony, now talking quietly to the bearded stranger.

For his part, Devoy feels no little sadness that he is not joining them, and silently fears for what might happen if it all goes wrong. Is he sending good men to their deaths? Is he consigning more good men to be left to rot in prison?

There is no way of knowing.

Devoy will stay with them for the first hour or so of the journey. All he can do is stay out of the way, and watch the burst of activity around the deck.

'Anchors aweigh!' comes the cry. The two anchors of the *Catalpa* are hauled from the water and the bark is bobbing freely.

The crew of the *Catalpa* bounce around like a bunch of enormous squirrels responding to the repeated commands of the First Mate, Samuel Smith. They run up the rigging and out onto the spars to unfurl the sails.

When each of his commands has been completed, the cry comes back: 'All gone, sir!'[2]

To passing fishing vessels just entering the harbour, this freshly prepared whaler bearing two signal flags – 'JTR' as the initials of the ship's agent John T. Richardson, and a 'C' for *Catalpa* – presents a magnificent sight, heading out on the beginning of what is surely a long voyage. Her clean white sails bulge to the task, her rigging is freshly tarred, her woodwork all painted and the stray bursts of sunshine through the cloud are reflected from the water onto the copper hull, which reflects it in kind . . .

The bow – made strong enough to crush Arctic ice – surges forward in a manner that throws white water endlessly tumbling outwards in graceful arcs, as if bowing to the boat's majesty.

And look there on the deck!

It is that well-respected figure in the local whaling community, George S. Anthony. Everyone had been surprised at his sudden retirement from whaling after his marriage and before he had achieved the rank of Captain, and so it is good to see him not only back, but also achieving his destiny, Captain of such a fine vessel.

Already the mighty whaler is moving at a good clip, and only an hour after weighing anchor, the pilot boat that has guided her out of the harbour prepares to turn back.

'Stand on the port tack two hours longer,' says the pilot's Captain, 'then tack out and you will be clear of land. Good luck.'[3]

The instructions seem all so very routine – plebeian platitudes of the maritime world – for what Captain Anthony knows is one of the most daring, and certainly longest distance, prison breaks ever attempted. But yes, thank you.

Devoy accompanies the pilot back most of the way, before parting company on a rowboat which takes him back to shore.

Watching the *Catalpa* recede into the distance, his heart is haunted by that achingly familiar sense of loneliness. Sweet Eliza. He tries to get her out of his mind, and has always found that the busier he is, the better he is able to cope. But as ever, at reflective moments like this when one grand project is under way and he is yet to shift onto the next one, when he feels at his most powerless and vulnerable, the memory of her always grips him: her smile, her scent, her *feel*. And rarely has he felt so vulnerable and powerless as now, nor so worried, as he watches the *Catalpa* sailing off on a dangerous mission of his design. What would Eliza say to comfort him?

Ah, but what a fool he knows himself to be. For he has heard she is married back in Ireland. He must not yearn for a married woman.

And yet he does.

A small parenthesis here: John Devoy has been misinformed, leading to a tragic misunderstanding. Not only is Eliza not married, but she is still waiting for him, believing he will send for her when the time is right. Against all the insistence of her parents, sister and friends, she continues to believe that she will fulfil her destiny, and marry John. Close parenthesis.

Having farewelled Devoy, Captain Anthony's focus turns to what lies ahead, even Martha's Vineyard slips by on their port quarter, a blur of near-Irish green in the distance. How many wonderful times has he had there with Emma, and how long before he can do it again? How big would little Sophie be by the time he returns?

As darkness falls so does his mood.

It had been one thing to be onshore in recent days, around the likes of John Devoy and other Fenian conspirators. Their enthusiasm and excitement at the prospect of executing one of the great heists of history had been infectious.

But now, they are gone.

Now there is no-one to talk with about the challenges ahead, not even Duggan, who is playing the part of an American carpenter. He is alone with the responsibility of taking this 'hulk of a whaleship to defy the mightiest naval power on earth'.[4]

The more that Captain Anthony thinks on it, the more he descends into what he will describe as 'the depths of despondency'.[5]

The turbulent weather on this night matches his mood perfectly: powerful dark gusts make everything shake. Within the hour it has built up to half a gale, which sees the *Catalpa* plunging up and down in heavy seas.

All Captain Anthony can do for the bark is shorten the sails and steer to the wind.

All Captain Anthony can do for himself is to try to push the darker thoughts away, to concentrate, focus all of his energies on completing the mission successfully so he can return to Emma and Sophie as quickly as possible.

The *Catalpa* plunges on.

•

With the *Catalpa* now under way, one crucial decision remains for John Devoy and his co-conspirators to maximise the chances of success.

The question is, who should be their man on the ground? They need someone to go to Australia to make contact with the Fenian prisoners, and examine ways to safely break them out. They have time, but not much. The plan is to send their chosen agent on one of the steamships leaving from California to Sydney, which is a much faster route than Captain Anthony's, who is sailing a longer route via the Cape of Good Hope, while doing some whaling, then across the Indian Ocean from there.

Yes, they have time to get their man in position in the Antipodes, but not much.

And who exactly?

On that subject, John Boyle O'Reilly maintains strong views, having already written from his Boston home to Devoy in New York, that the man who should go is Devoy himself. But there is a real problem with Devoy going.

If he suddenly disappears from view, it will invite speculation among the British agents in America – many of them operating out of the British consulate in New York and known to be closely watching him – that he has possibly gone on a rescue mission, and it might also generate dangerous speculation among the Irish community as to where he is.

'In fact,' Devoy will recount, 'my disappearance would have at once indicated that I had gone to Australia, and the consequent loose talk would almost certainly have ruined the chances of success. I gave up the idea.'[6]

Ever and always, the Clan must comport themselves in a manner where secrecy is paramount.

What's more, there is the ongoing issue of raising funds. It is a complicated matter, with many of the commitments having been made to Devoy personally. Without him in New York, there is no guarantee that the money will actually arrive.

But if not Devoy, then *who*?

It is Devoy himself who comes up with the suggestion. Why not John Joseph Breslin, the very man who had managed to spirit James Stephens out of Richmond Bridewell Prison then avoid any suspicion for almost a year before fleeing to America? Initially the quietly spoken Irish patriot had settled in Boston, but in a simple twist of fate, he has just arrived here in New York. Some of the *Clan-na-Gael* members have only heard gushing mention of Breslin, but one proper look at his background, and they just know that no-one could do better.

'He was,' Devoy would recount, 'familiar with the British prison service, was a man of fine presence, good manners, high intelligence and very unusual decision of character. He was ideal for the job, and, on my proposal, was unanimously chosen for the chief command of the rescue expedition.'[7]

Ah, but will he accept?

The only way is to ask, and on this particular evening after work, Devoy, with Goff in tow, heads to the address he has been given on New York's South Street on the Lower East Side, to knock on the door of an exceedingly modest flat.

Perhaps 20 seconds later they are rewarded with the sound of footsteps approaching . . . the door opens the barest crack and they see a face appear.

Oh. It's you.

The door opens wide, and a smiling John Breslin welcomes them into his humble abode.

The conversation takes only a short time, and from the first Devoy is impressed.

For there is a calm charm about this man Breslin, an intelligence, a presence that nigh casts a spell. While physically he is impressive – tall with chiselled Romanesque features and a flowing salt and pepper beard – it is his highly cultured manner that is most arresting. As courtly as the Queen of England, more noble than the nobility, more educated than an encyclopaedia, he could pass for a baron, were it not for the fact that he remains as humble as a potato with no hint of pretension. The glances and nods between Devoy and Goff confirm that they have come to the same conclusion: he's *perfect*.

Which is one thing.

Whether he'll do it – after they explain the whole plan, including the fact that the *Catalpa* is already on its way – is another.

As a man who is still being actively searched for by British authorities, with a large reward offered for his capture, will he leave the safety of the United States and return to the British Empire, where even being identified, let alone engaging in something as risky as another prison break, would see him immediately thrown in a cell . . . ?

Well, next time, could they give him a hard question?

For when Devoy puts the proposal to him, the response is immediate. Of course.

For far from being dismayed at the very idea of such a thing, far from expressing any concern for his own well-being if he embarks on it, the likely loss of his liberty and even life if it goes awry, John J. Breslin is eager from the first. There is only one complication arising, and that is not from him.

For in short order the delicate matter will arise . . . ahem . . . that he belongs to the United Irish Brotherhood, a rival Irish liberation movement to the *Clan-na-Gael*.

Devoy and Goff themselves are under instruction to insist that Breslin can only lead the rescue operation if he joins the Clan. It is no small thing to ask such a man to leave the organisation he is with, to join another so he can risk his life for the latter. And it is even more problematic when, as Devoy and Goff know, Breslin hadn't even joined the IRB when it was at the height of its influence in Ireland. Yes, he'd been willing to put his life on the line by quietly rescuing its leader, but he'd never sworn the oath. So will he join the Clan now . . . ?

'It took,' Devoy would recount, 'some delicate negotiation to overcome his scruples. He finally was taken in . . . and all obstacles were removed.'[8]

John Breslin, along with Captain Anthony, will have joint control of the whole operation. He'll be the Clan's man on the ground in Australia, with the task of working out how best to free the Fenians and get them on board the *Catalpa*.

(Not so quietly, the shoemaker Thomas Brennan – who'd already been passed over to go on the *Catalpa* in favour of Denis Duggan – is appalled once more, and has a fair measure of support among some power-brokers. As a long-time member of *Clan-na-Gael*, he believes *he* has the right to the role, and can scarcely believe it has gone to Breslin, who had only joined the Clan to fill the position! *Outrageous*.)

In the meantime, money continues to come in from all over the United States, with no region more generous than California, which raises no less than $7000 – representing half of the money raised to date from the entire country – a lot of it from Irish gold-miners in the Sierra Nevada.

That money, however, comes with one 'very earnest request'.[9] In return for their largesse, they would like to select one of their own to accompany whoever it is that the East Coast picks to lead the whole venture. Despite John Boyle O'Reilly's reservations, Devoy agrees.

With one proviso . . .

'Unless I approve of the man they select,' Breslin tells Devoy, 'I will decline to accept his services.'

'You shall be at liberty to do so,'[10] Devoy replies.

•

Ever and always, the first days of a long sea voyage establish the rhythm of the ship, with the Captain assigning roles, setting standards and overseeing performance, insisting that things are done his way.

In the case of Captain Anthony, working with an entirely new crew, on a new boat, the process is even more intense than usual, as time and again the crew is called aft as he sets out his expectations of their shipboard life in general – no drunkenness, basic orderliness, strict discipline in following orders of the Captain and his Mates – and that they will catch a lot of whales. It is with the latter in mind that, when the wind happens to fall away, he orders the *Catalpa*'s three whaleboats be lowered into the water, and their newly assigned crews are set to practising manoeuvres as if closing in for a kill on a whale.

Captain Anthony's first entry in the *Catalpa* log-book owes no little to the tale of the whale:

> Thursday, Apr. 29th, 1875 . . . Crew all on board. For several days thereafter all hands were busily employed in getting the vessel ready for whaling.[11]

True, when it comes to the finer points of whaling, Captain Anthony actually has other things on his mind – as catching whales will be little more than a sideshow to the main event – not least of which is that when he uses his newly purchased chronometer to perform navigational calculations, it turns out that instead of being on the high seas, the *Catalpa* is in fact on a peak of the Catskill Mountains in upstate New York.

Yes, they are heading to the other side of the world with a singularly dodgy navigational instrument. They will just have to do their best to fix it, and not get lost in the meantime.

A week after leaving, they come across their first pod of whales. Captain Anthony launches the whaleboats.

By the steering-oar, it is Anthony himself who goes out after the kill, urging his men to haul ever harder on the oars to get them close enough.

'Come down, Mopsy, come down. You, big Louis, pull! Toby, pull! What do you say, men? Come down all together. Pull away, my men, pull away!'[12]

After 40 minutes of hard hauling and bursting blisters for this first hunt of the season, they are beside an admittedly small whale – but it will have to do. One of the sailors raises what the crew call a 'whale iron', but land-lubbers call . . . a harpoon. It's a shank of iron some three feet long that has a cruel razor-sharp barb at one end with two smaller barbs folding back on the shaft like the flukes of an anchor, and a coil of rope at the other.

The harpooner, a massive man with biceps like cantaloupes, draws his right arm back and waits his moment.

NOW!

Aiming at the point just under the animal's blowhole, the harpooner hurls the whale iron fast and true, the rope uncoiling in its wake. It sinks so deep into the flesh of the whale that it sticks fast.

For a frozen moment all is still, and now, as expected, the whale reacts, thrashing its massive tail and rolling.

The cry goes up.

'Stern all! Stern all, for your lives!'[13]

Hearts pumping, lungs burning, the crew haul on their oars with everything they have, backing the boat away from the whale, which is thrashing its massive tail more than ever.

The men brace for their fate. Now! After a shallow dive, the agonised whale surfaces and streaks away. An immense shower of spray engulfs the men as they are wildly bounced across the ocean in the wake of the beast, on what whalers know as a 'Nantucket sleigh ride'.

Aboard the *Catalpa*, Samuel Smith barks orders for the whaler to follow close – tragically, the history of whaling includes a litany of tales where the whaleboat is dragged so far and so fast that contact is lost, and the men are never seen again.

Now, as the harpooned whale weakens, the whaleboat crew haul on the line to drag themselves closer to their quarry, to deliver what they hope will be the *coup de grâce*. The 'lancer' steps forward with his cruel-looking instrument – a six-foot long lance with an eight-inch sharp steel blade at one end – and plunges it several times into this denizen of the deep. The aim is to pierce the 'life' of the whale, the tight coil of arteries around the lungs, which is found about two yards beneath the whale's blowhole. Once you get the lance into that and the whale starts blowing blood through its blowhole – with the whaler's cry going up 'Chimney's afire!'[14] – you know it hasn't got long.

For now, with every last beat of its agonised heart now pushing the last of its lifeblood out into the boiling maelstrom of the ocean, it weakens ... before at last rolling 'fin out' – always the final act – bobbing in the water.

But the seriously hard work is only just beginning.

First, they tow the carcass to the side of the *Catalpa*. Using heavy ropes, the sailors lash the beast to the starboard side of the ship, its head towards the stern and its tail secured by a chain to make sure there is no chance that their prize will drift away. The crew then move quickly to erect a cutting platform made of planks from which to begin the task of stripping the blubber.

Now one of the most experienced of the whalers is lowered over the side by rope, and expertly straddles the dead whale. The most important thing now is to stay clear of the shark-infested water and he is careful not to slip as he rams a hook through a hole cut near the whale's head. After connecting the hook to the pulley by another length of strong rope, his work is substantially done, and, pale with exhaustion, he is hauled up on deck. Now the others get busy and with their heavy exertion and the help of the flensing knives, the hook and the pulley, the slowly rolling whale is peeled open like a fruit.

The flensers now get cracking, using 15-foot long-handled flensing knives – strong wooden rods, with curved blades at the end, like a whaling man's scythe, reaping their bloody harvest – to cut enormous chunks of blubber called 'blanket pieces' from the carcass. Each blanket is about as wide as a man, 15 feet long, and between a foot and two feet thick. They are hauled on board, where they are cut into very fine slices called 'bible leaves' and then laboriously fed into the copper trypots, above the roaring fire of the tryworks. Men slip in their bare feet through oil and blood.

With the work going around the clock in six-hour shifts, the whale blubber is boiled for oil, which is poured into barrels before 'being lashed to the rail on the ship's side to cool before being stored below'.[15]

All up, the sailors are soon drenched in whale oil themselves, their hair and skin completely covered in the grisly after effect of dismantling the biggest animal in the world.

'You are compelled,' one contemporary account runs, 'to breathe in the fetid smoke of the scrap fires, until you feel as though filth had struck into your blood, and suffused every vein in your body. From this smell and taste of blubber, raw, boiling and burning, there is no relief or place of refuge.'[16]

At least, however, they are able to get 20 barrels of oil from the whale, before throwing the remains of its carcass over the side. Back at New Bedford, that oil will sell for nearly $47 a barrel, and be used to grease machinery and fuel lamps across the United States. (True, that price had fallen in recent years, as the discovery of how to extract petroleum from the land in 1859 had started to cut right into the market for whaling oil, but $47 dollars a barrel is still handsome enough.)

•

John Breslin?

It is not *despite* his extraordinary achievement and renown in breaking James Stephens free that he is quiet, understated and reserved, it is likely *because* of those very qualities that he was able to pull it off at all. He just does not look or sound like a man who would contemplate such an act, let alone achieve it.

'A man of few words, of small acquaintance,' John Boyle O'Reilly will say of him, 'earning his bread in unassuming ways. Few knew, and to few were shown, the culture and refinement behind the modest exterior. In thought and appearance eminently a gentleman; in demeanour digni-fied and reserved.'[17]

The more John Devoy has got to know him in recent weeks, since Breslin has committed to going to Australia, the more he is convinced they have picked the right man.

As to his potential right-hand man, the Californian Clan have decided upon the enthusiastic Thomas Desmond, an Irish patriot living in San Francisco who had made it known to the Clan that he is available to assist any venture they have, in any manner they see fit. If Breslin approves of Desmond, that is.

On opposite sides of the American continent, the two men begin to make their preparations.

Late afternoon, 13 June 1875, *Catalpa*, thar she blows

The bad news is that some of the *Catalpa* crew are getting restless at the lack of success – and sometimes a seeming lack of interest in success – in catching and boiling down whales. One crew-member in particular, Cyrus Hill, broods menacingly on the subject, and is clearly an influence on the others. As men on a tiny base-pay only, they are counting on whales for their 'lay', their share of the proceeds.

The good news is that, suddenly, in this late afternoon, deep in the North Atlantic Ocean, the cry goes up: 'Thar she blows!'

Look, things don't work out exactly as planned. When First Mate Samuel Smith is put in charge of one of the boats and indeed gets close enough for the boat-steerer to throw the harpoon right into the whale, it turns out he is too close, for one of the death-throes of the whale knocks Smith into the water with a severely cut head. Dragged out of the water by his crew, only just conscious – he manages to revive enough to crawl to the other end of the whaleboat, grab a fresh lance and finish the job on the whale before collapsing. The next morning, despite a headache that is equal of ten hangovers at once, and feeling very weak, he insists on overseeing the cutting in and boiling down of the whale.

The crew are at least pleased to have caught their first whale in a month, while Captain Anthony is impressed by Smith's strong character. He is not sure what awaits them, but is at least confident, 'that when the supreme test came I would have at least one man behind me upon whom I could rely to the uttermost'.[18]

19 July 1875, Jersey City Terminal, Breslin departs

To the unsuspecting eye, the tall, elegant and imposing figure, refined and poised, who has just given a dollar to the porter to load his luggage onto the carriage at New Jersey's principal railway station – just across the waters from Manhattan – is likely just another businessman, which is precisely what John Breslin wants to appear to be.

Just hours before, Breslin had been given his final instructions by John Devoy. At least this time there is no need to get key replicas and smuggle them into the prison, no need to change shoes, no possibility of a gong in the neighbouring cell, no prospect of short ladders and tall walls . . . not just yet, anyway. No, with this one you have to begin by taking the train to San Francisco where you will meet up with Captain Thomas Desmond – a carriage-maker who is commander of the city's military companies of the *Clan-na-Gael*. True, you will likely have to wait a while in California until the last of the monies are gathered to see you on your way to Australia, and the last few loose ends are tied off, but it should be no longer than a month at most.

Travelling together, but apart, you two will catch a steamship to Sydney, and make your way from there to Fremantle, where you are to make contacts on the ground – John Boyle O'Reilly has recommended Breslin track down his former confidant, Father Patrick McCabe – and figure out a way to break out our boys from the most remote prison on earth, and get them to a rendezvous point with the *Catalpa*, which should be arriving in early March. Once the *Catalpa* arrives, you will make contact with Captain Anthony and go from there.

Okay, not so simple. But certainly different from the last one. We have all faith in you. Good luck.

•

Hulloa!

Sixteen-year-old Harry Passmore would recognise Thomas Darragh anywhere. And it's not just the flaming red mop that frames Darragh's freckled face. Why, he's known Thomas since the days his father, George, had been in charge of one of the chain gangs building the Albany Road. Thomas had always been one of the friendliest convicts. And now, as Harry delivers lemonade from his father's new shop to customers in Fremantle, here is Thomas again!

It is something of a surprise to see a man who he had last seen in chains now out and about in Fremantle. Harry knows for a fact that Thomas had not been liberated in the amnesty of 1871, as Harry had looked out for his name, and there had been no sign. But the explanation is simple.

Thomas – who is in turn stunned to see how much young Harry has grown from those old days on the Albany Road, making him think wistfully how big his own lad in Ireland must be now – tells the lad he is now head gardener at the private home of The Establishment's new Governor, William Fauntleroy, meaning he gets a fair measure of liberty beyond its walls.

It is the beginning of a growing friendship between the pair, as Harry starts to bring Darragh soft drinks and the older man tells him ever more of his life in Ireland – most particularly his wife and two children who he hasn't seen for over a decade – and his hopes of one day returning to the old green isle to be with his family at last.

13 September 1875, farewell to San Francisco

Sadly, squaring away finances has proven to be a matter of *months*, not weeks.

But at last it is all done and John J. Breslin, travelling under the pseudonym of 'Mr James Collins', engages passage to Sydney, Australia, for himself and the enthusiastic patriot, Thomas Desmond, who is just five years his junior at 37 years old, and whose fervour for the freedom of his native-born country reminds Breslin of his die-hard brothers. Desmond is a strapping man, his fair Irish skin turned bronze under the Californian sun. Breslin is impressed from the first, and he immediately sends a telegram to Devoy saying that he approves of the choice. Desmond is not much of a talker – which is exactly the way things should be, for such an exercise as this – and perpetually has the air about him of one who wants to get on with the business at hand.

Now the two are travelling together on the good ship *Cyphrene* – Mr Breslin in First Class, if you please; Mr Desmond in Second Class – across the Pacific Ocean, bound first for Sydney, where another Fenian awaits.

Though Breslin and Desmond are able to talk over their plans, they are careful to do it behind closed doors – and even then they keep to their chosen accents and personas. Breslin ... *ahem, Mr Collins* ... is a wealthy land-holder and mining magnate living in America, the type of man who sports a gold pocket watch on a fob chain, while Desmond chooses to be from Vermont, and is accustomed to measuring time by the sun rising and falling on his long work day.

Mid-October 1875, Sydney Town, you can take the Fenian out of Ireland, but you can't take Ireland out of the Fenian

It is the way of such things.

While it had been one thing for the English to scatter their fiendish Fenian convicts to their most isolated outposts around the globe in the hope of splintering them to oblivion, it has inevitably meant that the seeds of Fenianism have taken root all through the British Empire, so that a travelling Fenian can count on friends in every port.

Not long after arriving in Sydney, thus, John Breslin and Thomas Desmond – following a lead given to them by John Devoy – knock on the inner-western Sydney door of Edward Kelly.

Yes, Kelly. The very Fenian who, as a young man, had so distinguished himself in the taking of Knockadoon Coast Guard Station and the battle of Kilclooney Wood, before being a long-time resident of Fremantle Prison until being granted amnesty in 1871.

He beams to see them. One hundred thousand welcomes!

They are, after all, all sons of Ireland, meeting in a place far from home, and now embarking upon important work for the old country.

Kelly has been expecting John Breslin for some time, as letters from California had forewarned him, in coded language, of just who was coming, and broadly what the mission is. Since receiving those letters, Kelly has been busy galvanising Fenians on the east coast of Australia, raising money for an unspecified mission that will strike a blow for Ireland against the British Empire. Gazing upon Kelly's wasted form, after so many years of imprisonment, Breslin is once more moved by this wonderful spirit of the Fenians, that sees them continue to fight for their cause, right to the last gasp.

Yet another inspiration is one of Kelly's best friends and fellow Fenian, John King, who had saved the English the trouble and fled Ireland in the middle of the wave of arrests following the seizure of *The Irish People* newspaper in 1865, and come straight to Australia. Since that time, King has made his living selling groceries, foraging for gold up Bathurst way for seven years, and working in a quarry in Petersham – as a cover for his real role, raising money for the Fenians. That afternoon, after meeting Breslin and Desmond, Kelly takes them to meet his energetic and always smiling lieutenant.

King is returning from working at the Petersham quarry – sitting atop a carriage bound for the city – when he sees Kelly with some strangers, all of them sitting atop a carriage coming the other way. Kelly signals for him to alight.

Certainly.

John King is introduced to John Breslin, the man who had organised James Stephens to escape from Richmond Bridewell Prison! (In the world of the Fenians, the story has become legend.) They greet each other with the warmth appropriate to revolutionaries meeting on the other side of the planet to the land of their birth, now engaged in a grand venture to help move the revolution forward.

Breslin makes clear to his beaming interlocutor that their plan is well advanced, that a whaler is already well on its way, and that he and Mr Desmond here are heading to Fremantle to work out the best way to get the Fenians from the prison, and onto the whaler. The most important thing now is secrecy ... and money. Though that part of the plan has not been fully crystallised, it is clear that they will need more resources.

That is all right. The Australian Fenians are here to help. As it happens, they had been raising funds to launch an escape plan of their own – to 'charter a steamer, man her with our own men, go to Fremantle, rescue the prisoners and take them to the French settlement at New Caledonia'[19] – but given how advanced the American plan is, they are happy to throw in their lot with them, and do everything they can to help.

Within a 'coupla days' as the Australian residents so curiously say it, here is another Dublin Fenian, Michael Cody – the one-time notable on the *Hougoumont*, beloved for his renditions of 'Our Irish Flag', who'd been released in the second amnesty. He has come down from his Queensland mining town upon receipt of Kelly's carefully worded telegram. Together with Kelly and King, Cody goes about raising funds carefully, quietly, contacting fellow Fenians and, without ever going into specifics, making it clear that a blow is about to be struck for Ireland, and money is needed.

In the meantime, the Australian Fenians have £200 already gathered, which is handed over to a deeply appreciative Breslin, with the promise that whatever more they can gather quickly will be soon on the way, including money coming from their Irish brothers in New Zealand. Yet another Sydney Fenian is immediately dispatched to Wellington to collect that money and bring it back. It is decided King will follow Breslin to Fremantle in a couple of months, by which time the *Catalpa* will surely be about to arrive. He will not only give him more money, but also possibly stay on, to see if he can do anything to help with the plan decided upon . . .

Breslin and Desmond take their leave of Sydney, thus – catching a ship to King George Sound, Albany, some 250 miles south-east of Fremantle – with some satisfaction. It is all starting to come together.

Late October 1875, Azores, a barren roll call to roll off the barrels

The good news for Captain Anthony is they have successfully made it to the Portuguese colony of the Azores and anchored off the port of Fayal, where – 'neath the towering fortress atop the cliffs that glowers over all maritime visitors – the crew rolls off 210 barrels of sperm oil to be shipped home. The profits from that will already help to offset the cost of the whole venture.

The bad news is that it is not only the barrels that are heading home. For as soon as Anthony has paid the crew their wages to date and given them shore leave, the majority of them desert.

It is not that Captain Anthony has been harsh on them – far from it – so much as they do not wish to spend another year on a ship catching so few whales. They want to make money or go home.

And another problem is that Denis Duggan, the official representative of the *Clan-na-Gael* on the *Catalpa*, far from helping the Captain, takes some of the crew with him on a drunken rampage through Fayal. Duggan himself becomes so drunk that he falls out of the boat no fewer than three times on the way back to the ship. For all that, Duggan is one of the few in the crew who actively wants to continue.

Still, as no port worthy of the name doesn't come complete with a variety of sailors happy to go anywhere for the right amount of money, Captain Anthony is able to scrounge together another crew, composed of Kanakas, Portuguese blacks and Malays. After a little subterfuge in smuggling them on board – as the better part of them are without passports – the *Catalpa* is almost ready.

Captain Anthony?

It's Denis Duggan, now sobered up and even regretful, who wants a quick word. For he has received word from none other than Thomas Brennan – the man who he had beaten to be the Clan's representative on the ship – advising that he, too, had made it to the Azores, was now on the island of St Michael's, and would arrive on a steamer at Fayal the following day. He has, he says, a late clearance from the Clan to come and expects to be included in the crew.

Well, then.

'I think we have all the crew we need at present,' Captain Anthony says. 'Mr Brennan may get left.'[20]

It is not something they discuss, but both men understand. There is something about Brennan that is trouble, and they do not need trouble on this whaler. They need to get away before he arrives, and now move to do so.

Heading to the Fayal Custom House, the skipper quickly receives clearance and they are on their way before the evening sets in. By the next morning they have worked their way through the main passage to the open ocean when they see it.

It is the steamer, heading to Fayal.

And there on the deck is a man looking their way that is surely Thomas Brennan!

Catching Duggan's eye, Captain Anthony offers something between a smile and a grimace – at the very least an acknowledgement that they have had a narrow escape from having an unwanted guest.

In their wake they leave Thomas Brennan who is now steaming marginally more than the vessel that bears him. But that is his problem, as Captain Anthony is simply relieved to be leaving him behind.

The plan now, Anthony tells the crew, is to stop over briefly at Tenerife before trying their luck on the famously rich whaling grounds around the River Plate, the estuary formed by the merging of two rivers near Buenos Aires. Though relieved to be again under full sail, still Captain Anthony is heavy of spirit. To this point, the only thing the crew have been told is that they are going 'whaling'. None of them apart from Denis Duggan knows the true purpose of the voyage, and it's weighing on the Captain. He must, at least, explain the lie of the land to the First Mate. If Smith understands the mission, and agrees to do all in his power to help complete it, that will be wonderful.

If not, it will be crushing.

It might very well be touch and go, and there is a real chance he could lose him.

So it is that a few days out from Fayal, as a pleasant evening settles on the high seas, and the *Catalpa* sails gracefully towards Tenerife, that Captain Anthony asks if he might have a quiet word with his First Mate in the Master Cabin.

Of course, Cap'n.

Please take a seat.

'Mr Smith,' Captain Anthony commences, carefully, albeit with no prelude, 'you shipped to go whaling. I want to say to you now, before we get to Tenerife, that the *Catalpa* has done about all the whaling she will do this fall.'[21]

Mr Smith gives him a look – *what?*

What can the Captain mean by this?

Already embarked, Captain Anthony has no choice but to haul up the mainsail, and surge forward to the truth. Taking a breath and steeling himself – for the skipper is about to tell a brave man of great calibre that he has been entirely deceived – he goes on.

'We're bound to the western coast of Australia to try and liberate [some] Fenian prisoners who are serving a life sentence in Great Britain's penal colony. This ship was bought for that purpose and fitted for that purpose, and you have been utterly deceived in the object of this voyage. You have a right to be indignant and leave the vessel at Tenerife. You will have the opportunity when we arrive there, and if you go I can't blame you. But this ship is going to Australia, if I live, and I hope you will stay by me and go with me. God knows I need you, and I give you my word I will stand by you as never one man stood by another, if you will say you will remain in the ship and assist me in carrying out the plans.'[22]

It is not in Mr Smith's nature to stare open-mouthed at anything. He has travelled the Seven Seas and seen most of what this world has to offer – the good, the bad, the ugly. But on this occasion, his jaw is on the floor. For of course he'd had no idea that this venture was about anything other than whaling. And while hunting those dangerous aquatic beasts in the far reaches of the world had been one thing, this is quite another. Finally closing his mouth again, he takes in Captain Anthony's look of anguish – which way is he going to jump? – and gets serious. For he has questions, lots of questions, perhaps more questions than the skipper has answers for, though he does his best.

What kind of prisoners are we to rescue? What obstacles will we be facing to see them released? What are the consequences if we are caught? What kind of men do we have already on the ground? Will they have already fashioned an escape plan by the time we arrive? And so on . . .

Captain Anthony tells all he knows and adds an important assurance.

'If there is any trouble with the authorities, I will exonerate you completely from the conspiracy and proclaim that you shipped to go whaling . . .'[23]

There is not a lot more to be said.

Samuel Smith must reflect on his decision, and so he does, sitting silently for several minutes. Finally, he rises and offers the skipper his hand. 'Captain Anthony,' says he, 'I'll stick by you in this ship if she goes to hell and burns off her jib-boom.'[24]

The skipper cannot ask for better than that, and it is with infinite relief that he pumps Samuel's hand heartily in gratitude. The two now talk late into the night, as the Captain answers all of Smith's queries and fleshes out all the plans as they stand.

Set together for the long journey, there is only the matter of their troublesome chronometer to dampen the mood.

16 November 1875, chug-chug-chugging into Fremantle

John Breslin has been on better small screw steamers in his time.

Still, in this far-flung realm of the British Empire, making do with what you have is what you do, and Breslin, with Desmond somewhere in the Second Class section, must do it with the best of them.

Having been deposited at Albany by the good ship *Pera* three days earlier, Breslin and Desmond are now aboard the *Georgette*, once a 200-ton collier, but now serving as a steamer 'mail-ship' to serve the needs of the West Australian colony from Champion Bay on the far north-west coast, to Albany in the south – carrying passengers and mail to the many intermediate ports between.

With two masts and a single screw, the steamer *Georgette* is to a fast schooner what a donkey is to a racehorse – unglamorous but reliable and able to proceed in all weather, which is all that is needed in these parts.

The *Georgette* is chugging along with too little speed for Breslin's liking. He is eager to get to Fremantle, yet they cannot be going more than four knots at maximum.

But, finally, on this shining morning of pristine perfection, here is Fremantle before them.

As they expected, it is far from an imposing vision. A small settlement only, it is built around its harbour and composed mostly of a motley mélange of shops, shacks and cottages, all of differing wooden constructions, with the major coherent theme emerging, a very Australian one – this'll do.

There are, however, several far better buildings of government construction – led by Customs House – made substantially of sandstone, together with a few double-storey residences that are clearly for richer folk. Nearly everything is covered in a curious dull whitewash to reflect both the glaring Australian sunshine and the fact that this is mostly a government settlement.

John Breslin's gaze is drawn up to Fremantle Prison on the hill overlooking the town, a menacing monolith of limestone that towers over everything, throwing an enormous shadow in these morning hours. At Fremantle, the sun will only come up when the prison says it can, and the people of the 3000-strong settlement move through their day essentially to the prison's rhythms. As a matter of fact, Breslin and Desmond can see sad-looking groups of bearded men of bronzed hue who are clearly the convicts – recognisable for their dull grey uniforms, marked with the ubiquitous arrows – plodding around in work gangs, fixing roads, loading lumber onto the docks, and building stone walls. Obviously, there is every chance that some of these men are the same Fenians they have come to liberate – Hogan, Harrington, Hassett, Wilson, Darragh, Cranston and Kiely – which is why Messrs Breslin and Desmond, each in his own way, roundly ignores them. And those grim-faced, uniformed men with guns who surround the convicts are obviously the warders whose job in life it is to prevent precisely what Breslin is planning. But, we'll see.

Alighting at the jetty, Mr 'James Collins' loudly orders the best carriage that Fremantle can offer. Though only a short distance, he wishes to have himself and his fine leather luggage up to the Emerald Isle Hotel, a serendipitously named Fremantle establishment which will accommodate him in its best room, at least until he can get his bearings.

Thomas Desmond, meantime, fashioned as 'Thomas Johnson'[25] – not even a 'Mr' for him – is soon seen toting his tired trunk and trudging the 14 miles along the low road to the 6000-strong settlement of Perth, where he will secure work in his normal trade as a carriage-maker and effectively disappear into the muddy mass of the colony's lower classes.

Not Mr Collins, this wealthy Irish–American, though.

In no time, he establishes himself as a man about 'town', such as our town is. So well-dressed! Such a gentleman! Such charm! And so wealthy!

As a matter of fact, one of the maids at the Emerald, Mary Tondut, has seen a legal document he'd 'inadvertently' left out, from an American bank extending him a line of credit for a hundred thousand dollars.

('I believe,' Breslin will later note, 'my West Australian reputation as a millionaire is chiefly due to the fact that this document was "with intent to deceive" left loosely in my room so that it might be read.'[26])

Yes, apparently, he is here looking for 'investment opportunities' in mines, timber and agriculture. He is, in short, a man like we don't see often in these parts, a man worth getting to know.

As a matter of fact, Fremantle's own 'Governor', William Robert Fauntleroy, the Governor of Fremantle Prison, is quick to make his acquaintance and the two get on well together from the first.

We don't get many gentlemen in our settlement, Mr Collins, and it is a pleasure to meet you.

Yes, there is excitement in these parts this very week, for the fact that the explorer Ernest Giles has just completed – for the first time in history – an overland expedition from Adelaide to Perth, proving it can be done. But you, sir, have come from even further, and you, too, will be feted, as a man of means who must be encouraged to make investments in our settlement, which is nothing less than the most isolated colony on the entire planet.

Well, to Breslin's eyes it looks as one might expect of an isolated colony: a little scrub, but mostly white sand. Ever after, he will treasure the story of a 'new chum' arriving in Fremantle to exclaim, 'This is a very fine country', to which a nearby Irishman replies, 'Begorra, you may well call it a fine country – you could put it all through a sieve!'[27]

However, it is not as if Mr Collins has no feeling for the servant class. A case in point is the buxom dark-haired hotel maid Mary Tondut, with whom he is often seen in warm conversation. Ah, but the wealthy investor is a pious man for all that, and is immediately a noted worshipper at Fremantle's Catholic Church on Adelaide Street.

Mr Collins, one altar boy would recall, 'naturally came to my notice . . . by his engaging personality and good humour'.[28] In fact, the entire congregation soon comes to know him well, and regard him highly as 'a man of independent means touring the world in a leisurely fashion, idling a month or two here and there'.[29]

Despite his obvious wealth, as the same altar boy would recall many years later, '[He] mixed with all worth the knowing, irrespective of class or creeds . . .'[30]

No, not the convicts, as that is forbidden in any case. But to the poor free settlers, yes, and even to the ticket-of-leave men.

The Yankees are just like that, don't you know? They have grace, not airs and graces like their British counterparts. Though far from common, they do not mind talking to the mere commoners.

And look, there is Mr Collins talking to one now . . .

In low tones, John Breslin – having established from John Boyle O'Reilly that his obvious liaison point, Father Patrick McCabe, has unfortunately been transferred to a parish in South Australia – takes a chance with this Fremantle resident, a native of Ireland. After careful conversation has established that the sympathies of this resident are with a free Ireland, Breslin turns the conversation to the Fenian prisoners he has heard about, and is *fascinated* to hear of a ticket-of-leave soldier Fenian living nearby, one William Foley. The poor fellow is struggling badly, apparently, both financially and with some kind of heart disease that has kept him in hospital recently, but yes, he would be easy to find . . . ?

Not long afterwards, Breslin is speaking in even *lower* tones behind closed doors to William Foley, formerly of the trusted personal messenger of General Rose. Breslin establishes the two things he needs to know. Firstly, that Foley knows all the Fenian soldiers still inside and is in regular contact with them – and as he also knows all the guards, he is a frequent and unremarked visitor around and about the various work parties to see his old friends. And secondly, Breslin establishes that Foley's sympathies for the cause have not wavered.

Very well then . . .

> *You will remember your Fenian oath, Mr Foley – that you did solemnly 'swear, in the presence of Almighty God, that you will do your utmost, at every risk, while life lasts, to make Ireland an*

Independent Democratic Republic; that you will yield implicit
obedience, in all things not contrary to the Law of God, to the
commands of your superior officers, and that you shall preserve
inviolable secrecy regarding all transactions of this Secret Society
that may be confided in you. So help you God!' You acknowledge
that it still applies, yes? Well, I am not what I appear. I am of the
Fenian Brotherhood. I need you to get a message to our fellow
Fenians, inside the prison, particularly James Wilson. Tell them
that we have received your letters. Tell them that I am here, and
that I am not alone. Tell them more help is on the way, and that
I will be in contact. And, finally, I need you to organise for me
to meet James Wilson . . .

'I asked no questions,' Foley will later recount, 'and [Breslin] told me
nothing which I had not a right to know.'[31]

He is a Fenian soldier still. A Fenian Captain is on site, giving orders,
and they will be obeyed.

What Foley tells Breslin in turn is encouraging. For Breslin must
understand that the warders are not *all* against the Fenians. Three of the
warders, Foley says – the Principal Warder Thomas Davis, Warder James
McMahon and Assistant Warder Fred William Craggs – are themselves
Irish Catholics. Now this is not to say that they are sworn Fenians, but
nor are they without a certain natural sympathy for the Irish cause.
Through careful conversations, William Foley has worked out just who
he can trust. Breslin need not worry. He can get to the Fenians, even
when they are inside the prison.

Breslin is delighted to hear it. The two shake hands quickly, and
move on.

19 November 1875, off Tenerife, off calculations

Now that is more than passing strange.

Given that the peak of that Spanish colony off the coast of Africa,
Tenerife, is well over 12,000 feet high, Captain Anthony knows from
previous experience that it can be sighted, looming above the clouds,
from as far away as 90 miles when the weather is clear. According to the
calculations he has been making with his newly repaired chronometer,
he should be spying it dead ahead, any hour now.

So what on earth, *where* on earth, and why on earth . . . can he see
it some 60 or 70 miles off to starboard?

Clearly the chronometer will need correcting if they are to navigate across the Indian Ocean to Fremantle in the lower southern latitudes and their roaring winds.

Altering course, the *Catalpa* is able to drop anchor off the port by the evening of 20 November 1875, her Captain still shaking his head at how close he had come to missing Tenerife entirely.

Denying the crew the liberty to land, on the grounds they might not return, Captain Anthony is quick to head ashore to organise fresh supplies – sugar, flour, potatoes, fresh water and firewood – for the long and mostly unbroken journey to come.

Captain Anthony also purchases a huge supply of planks – spruce boards and joists – so that when they have the escaped prisoners on board, together with the agents sent to Fremantle ahead of them, their carpenter and *Clan-na-Gael* representative, Denis Duggan, can oversee the building of more accommodation for them on deck. To those of the crew who raise their eyebrows at such a quantity of timber, Captain Anthony is clear: it is for mending the boats.

But still, Skipper, so much?

Yes. Keep loading.

As the victuals are loaded, Anthony notes that the American schooner, *New Haven*, is in port, and takes the opportunity to board her. He spends the next three days using her accurate equipment to correct his chronometer's faults, taking sights and fixing the rate, in the hope that it will keep exactly the *right* time, *all* the time.

On 25 November the *Catalpa* is on its way once more . . .

•

Are you sure, William, are you *sure*?

William Foley is sure. And he tells his dear friend James Wilson one more time. The Fenians from America. They have arrived, James, they have arrived!

Again and again, Wilson squints his quizzical blue eyes and questions him for every little detail. What did the man look like? What was his accent? Did he say anything beyond the fact that his letter had been read, and he had been sent by John Devoy?

William Foley answers to the best of his ability, but must be fast. While the warders don't mind him having a quick chat with the convicts on work details, they will not countenance actual work time being cut into. And so the conversation is brief, before Foley must move on. But the job has been done.

James Wilson has got the message. His communications from the 'living tomb' have been received. He and his fellow Fenians have not been forgotten. Their Fenian brothers in America have organised themselves, and before long they will be able to break them out of this hell.

James Wilson goes back to shovelling. This time it does not hurt, as his heart sings. He cannot wait to tell the others.

•

It is simply one of many invitations that Mr Collins is receiving these days, but it has to be said this one interests the American investor more than somewhat. Superintendent Doonan of The Establishment wonders if Mr Collins would like to inspect his prison?

Why, yes. It would be a pleasure.

And what an interest he shows! And how quickly he absorbs everything! And how clever are his questions.

It is rare indeed for Superintendent Joseph Doonan to be in the presence of someone who has a genuine interest in what he does, but this fellow Collins is charm itself. Over two full hours, they go from floor to floor of the prison, past nearly every cell, 'all the corridors, both chapels, punishment cells, hospital, cookhouse, workshops and storeroom'.[32] Collins is even interested in the history of The Establishment and fascinated to be told that there has only ever been one successful escape.

Do tell?

Yes, just once. One of the Fenians got away on an American whaler, but we have since tightened supervision. Although we continue to send Fenian work parties on remote jobs, they are now accompanied by a heavy guard contingent. And every American whaler in these parts is also watched. Either way, this whole place is a natural prison, you see. Even if a convict could get out of these walls it is bordered by trackless deserts on one side, impenetrable bush on two other sides, and the Indian Ocean on the other. There is nowhere to go!

Mr Collins nods thoughtfully, clearly impressed by the English wisdom in placing their prison in such a place, and choosing such a fine fellow as Doonan to be at the coal-face of keeping the prisoners secure.

Encouraged by the visitor's obvious admiration, the eager Superintendent goes on, pointing out how important it is to maintain eternal vigilance when we have such *dangerous* prisoners as the Fenians. After all, it was a wretched Fenian who tried to assassinate Prince Alfred over in Sydney.

'Look here, Mr Collins,' the Superintendent says, pointing at two convicts the way a stockman might show off his prize bulls. 'This here is Bob Cranston and Michael Harrington, former British soldiers who committed treason by trying to bring down the Queen.'

Mr Collins looks them up and down carefully, his lip curling in clear disdain, as the two Fenians stare sullenly back at him.

Thank goodness there can be no chance of them ever getting out. Which brings Mr Collins to an interesting question for the Superintendent.

What *do* you do if someone tries to make a run for it?

The Superintendent is happy to tell him.

We always have troopers with saddled horses ready to pursue the escapees, and we have black-trackers on permanent standby. Mr Collins is even introduced to one of the troopers, a notably barrel-chested young fellow by the name of 'Big John' McKenna, and the 'investor' is able to gain a strong impression of just how competent these fellows are. And when it comes to the native trackers, they could follow a chicken over solid rock, let alone a criminal in chains. We always get our man.

I'll bet you are good shots with those pistols and rifles of yours, Mr Collins ventures, and that your aim is deadly?

Not at all, the Superintendent demurs. We don't even practise much, there is simply no need. We *always* get our man.

Mr Collins is not at all surprised. He finds the place, 'very secure and well-guarded',[33] and feels it a privilege to have been given such a comprehensive tour.

Thank you, Superintendent Doonan, and good day to you, sir.

Good day to you, Mr Collins, and it has been a pleasure.

•

The *Catalpa*'s long voyage continues. The last month has been uneventful, bar the small bonanza day of 19 December, when they had succeeded in taking three small whales. Crossing the equator on Christmas night, they continue to push to the south until 11 February, when they reach Latitude 41° South and start to sail east – when suddenly things turn far more eventful than they'd like . . .

The *Catalpa* gets stuck in a 'cross-sea', a phenomenon caused when strong weather systems send waves in opposing directions, frequently crashing into each other with shattering force. Woe betide any vessel that finds itself in the middle of such a maelstrom.

In all of Captain Anthony's born days he has never seen anything like it, later noting the waves as 'the most treacherous and menacing',[34] he had ever experienced.

The wind howls like a banshee, the ocean roars and their tiny whaler is tossed around like a tiny cork, at the mercy of forces beyond their control.

'The combers, coming in opposite directions, came together with reports like a clap of thunder, and the danger of a sea striking the deck was looked upon with no little apprehension.'[35]

That apprehension turns to outright fear when, shortly after dawn the next day, under the weight of the wind, one of the topsails splits and shreds, reducing manoeuvrability.

They only just manage to survive the roaring night.

It is a battered but not shattered *Catalpa*, thus – with the crew doing running repairs – that finds out that afternoon that it is not alone on this great Southern Atlantic.

For, just a couple of miles off, sailing in their same broad direction, albeit on a different tack, the crew spy, not just a whaler, but a New Bedford whaler, the *Platina*, sailed by a dear friend of Anthony's, Captain Walter Howland. What is more, the *Platina*'s shiny copper hull reveals she can only have left Massachusetts bare months before.

By the next morning, Captain Anthony is able to board the *Platina* – as hungry for news from home as he is reluctant to give his own news.

But Captain Howland insists . . .

'What under heavens are you doing here, Anthony?' he asks, genuinely stunned. 'You're the last man I expected to see out here. I thought you intended to make a short voyage in the North Atlantic.'[36]

Yes, well . . . Anthony can only lamely say he had decided to venture further.

For his part, Howland advises he's heading around the Cape of Good Hope to try their luck in the waters around the Seychelles.

Captain Anthony evinces great interest, maintaining he might go there too, and takes notes while Howland gets out his charts and shows him possible routes, but, clearly, Anthony's peer is not convinced. For after Captain Anthony also pumps him for news from home, Captain Howland keeps coming back to what is truly on his mind: 'Say now, honest, what are you doing here?'[37]

There still being no answer he can give, Anthony keeps changing the subject.

Now, when it comes to the crews of the two ships mingling, and trying to exchange information, the fortunate thing for Anthony is that his crew doesn't have any. They do have questions, however, and are stunned to hear that they are not, in fact, off the coast of Patagonia as they had thought.

'I tot we long time getting that River Platte,' Captain Anthony hears one of his Portuguese mates saying, in his thick accent. 'I tink maybe old man go to New Zealand catch whales. I there once. I tink nice place.'[38]

As it happens, that Portuguese mate is one of the few members of the crew to take the news that they are nowhere near the River Plate calmly. Led by that troublesome sailor by the name of Cyrus Hill, the others are up in arms, and it takes some effort for the skipper to calm them – at least for the moment.

At last, as the sun starts to fall well down on its western arc, it is time to wave farewell once more, and off they go, with Captain Howland still suspicious.

•

There goes Mr Collins.

In these hot summer days he has been out and about with his hired trap and fine horses, which he secures as required from Henry Albert's stables in Fremantle. Sometimes he goes to Perth, and on a couple of occasions has dropped by Sloan's Carriage Factory in Mary Street, Perth, where 'Thomas Johnson', now known to all as 'the Yankee', is seen to tighten the nuts on the axle, to ensure all is in order for some big trips Collins has planned.

Clearly, Mr Collins is a man on a mission, looking to invest in any or many local projects, from wool to timber and gold. Much of the timber industry is based around Rockingham to the south, while the gold is more to the east of Perth, and the wool interests lie in the district of Guildford and further that way to the north-west in the land on the Avon. As it happens, the Yankee also likes to travel the colony's long empty roads. It gives the two men the opportunity to reconnoitre the whole area around Fremantle, and nowhere are they more interested than windswept Rockingham Beach, just 20 miles south of Fremantle . . .

But, moving on. Most such excursions are day-trips for Mr Collins, and he is back that evening.

(Quietly, he frequently meets up with William Foley, who has proven to be a Godsend in keeping in touch with the Fenians, passing messages back and forth. It is important to Breslin that all of them remain aware of his broad plans and progress, so they will focus on the need to remain disciplined – and gain as complete a trust as possible from their gaolers.)

•

It has taken a great deal of organisation, but at last John Breslin has organised his first face-to-face encounter with James Wilson.

It came courtesy of Foley carefully making contact with the Irish Catholic warder Fred Craggs and his wife, Elizabeth, a nurse at Fremantle's hospital. The Craggs – like so much of the Irish community in Western Australia – do not regard the Fenians as real criminals and are sympathetic to the cause, and so things fall in to place. A part of Fred Craggs' responsibilities at The Establishment are the prison stables.

As Breslin sees the weary-looking Wilson approaching, he catches his eye, looks at him meaningfully, and then slips behind the stables.

Only a few seconds later, Wilson comes around the corner, and the two warmly shake hands.

But there is little time.

Breslin must be quick in his remarks. A whaler is on the way. It should be here by next month at some point. We are going to break you out, and will need your co-operation. It is very important that you all behave well, and continue to be allowed out on your work details, for that will be the key. When the time is right, we will have two traps, with fast horses, ready to spirit you away to a beach, where a longboat manned by sailors will take you out to the whaler, which will be lying in international waters. If we are all quick enough, we will have you on the whaler and gone before the authorities can properly react.

Wilson absorbs the message and furiously shakes Breslin's hand in gratitude. He is about to head on his way, when something occurs to him.

'Some money would be of service to us . . . ?' he asks, hopefully.

'How much do you want?'

'A pound a man would be quite sufficient?'

'Won't you be searched?'

'I am in no danger of being searched.'[39]

Breslin hands over the money then and there, with some final admonitions.

'You must destroy all letters received from me, and on no account let any man know anything of the intended escape but the men [concerned].'[40]

Wilson agrees, and they part, the convict with a spring in his step.

•

It is a bitter decision to be made, but all of Wilson, Cranston, Harrington, Hogan, Darragh and Hassett agree.

Though they are tremendously excited at the news of the arrival of the American Fenians to save them – and more than pleased with the pound each they have to spend on some contraband grog courtesy of friendly warders – they must proceed very carefully from here. Obviously, the danger is that the prison authorities will find out before they can get away, and so . . .

And so they must discuss the one of their number whose notoriously loose lips could indeed sink ships . . . their ship. It's James Kiely, the Chatty Cathy who had blabbed at length to Constable Talbot about his uncle's pike nests before The Rising. Apart from everything else, Kiely has become so close to Governor Fauntleroy – working for him and his family as a personal servant, and gained extended personal privileges because of it – he feels more like one of *them*, than one of *us*.[41]

And so the six Fenians decide to keep the whole plan secret from him. Kiely is to be left out.

'They were afraid to let him into the secret,' one person close to the Fenians at the time would recall. 'Much as they wanted to take him with them they were frightened that if they let him know, he might happen to mention it.'[42]

Easier to eliminate from their plans is the last civilian Fenian among them, Thomas Delaney, who, though he had been granted a ticket-of-leave, continues to be sent back to The Establishment for public drunkenness. He is a terrible man on the grog and they cannot risk telling him of the plan. His own freedom will come with simple sobriety, without need to engage in an elaborate escape.

As it happens, however, Wilson also has some explaining to do at his next meeting with Breslin, on that very subject: sobriety.

For Breslin has learned, as he will recount, 'that Hassett had been found lying drunk in the cell with a bottle of liquor and some twelve or fourteen shillings in his possession, for this he had been punished . . . and I looked upon his case as hopeless . . .'[43]

It can't happen again. Wilson agrees.

When they can, Breslin and Wilson continue to meet.

Their one point of major disagreement is over the manner of getting from Fremantle to Rockingham Beach.

Wilson insists they should all be on horseback. 'If we are pursued we will have a better chance of escape,'[44] he argues, as if his life depends on it. Because it does.

Breslin, however, is equally insistent in return: 'It would be difficult to obtain horses enough for you all without exciting suspicion, and it would also be difficult to use them for the same reason since we must make our escape in the daytime.'[45]

Breslin wins. This is his show.

Early in the new year, 1876, Highclere Castle, England, troubling news

Henry Howard Molyneux Herbert, the 4th Earl of Carnarvon, 'Lord Carnarvon', is quietly referred to as 'Twitters' for some rather mesmerising nervous tics he possesses that roam his bushy face like will-o'-the-wisps through English forests, stirring the natural growth as they go. Just when you think they've settled on his bushy chin, they start racing up his side-burns before . . . nay . . . taking a quick detour across his moustache.

It is a phenomenon entirely disconnected to whether he actually is nervous, but on this day it would be fair to say he is not at his calmest.

As the Secretary of State for the Colonies, Lord Carnarvon is respon-sible for the security and administration of all of Her Majesty's realms across the British Empire, and he has just received some troubling infor-mation from one of the Empire's network of spies that some kind of breakout is planned for the Fenians in far-off Fremantle. Look, it may be nothing. It probably is nothing. The idea that the Fenians would be able to mount a prison breakout in the most remote part of the British Empire, and actually spirit convicts away, is preposterous.

Nevertheless, Lord Carnarvon has administrative ardour in his bones. He has received a warning. There can be no harm in at least passing it on to Governor Fauntleroy in Western Australia. And so he composes a telegram to be sent, via the circuitous route over Asia, then cabled undersea to Darwin, then Adelaide, then on a fast boat to Albany in the Colony of Western Australia where it can be cabled to Fremantle or Perth, advising that 'money has been collected in this country and Ireland and a scheme set on foot for the purpose of assisting the escape from Western Australia of certain Fenians (I believe Military) now in the colony.' Those 'charged with carrying out this attempt have either lately sailed for Western Australia or may do so by the mail steamer which brings this dispatch'.[46]

Lord Carnarvon adds strict instructions to his warning. Governor Fauntleroy is to take whatever precautions he sees fit, but he is not to make an open warning to gaol and police authorities, as it would be very bad for morale to even think that the British might be genuinely concerned by such a thing. Tell one or two key officials only, advising them to keep it secret.

•

In his role as the wealthy investor Mr Collins, John Breslin has talked much about the prospect of speculating in gold fields.

But, after no move on his part to buy any mines, the curiosity of the Fremantle locals is aroused once more as to what he is up to. And so he starts to talk more seriously of sheep stations. Again, the good burghers of the port town are held off for a short time, but eschewing this field he lets it be known he is now interested in exporting timber . . . before moving back to the possibilities of gold, or perhaps sheep, which does indeed manage to 'pull the wool over their eyes' for a short time.

But in the end, he becomes aware that questions are being asked.

To really be an investor in these affairs he needs to be going on more than day-trips to possible stations, mines and forest, and so now he takes himself off on a fortnight-long journey inland, visiting Guildford, York, Northam and Newcastle.

(Besides the need to quell the questions, such a long excursion – as much as he is now not-so-piously enjoying the fair favours of the flesh allowed him by the sweet Mary Tondut – helps break the tedium of day-by-day waiting.)

Mr Collins arrives back in town just in time to farewell William Foley. He is seriously ill, so his many friends in Fremantle have rallied to raise the money to send him to America, where he will find refuge and support. He has been a faithful servant to the Fenians, and Breslin is sorry to see him go. At least, by now, he has established a way to talk to Wilson without Foley as intermediary.

For his part, Foley is glad to be going, but sad to be leaving his fellow Fenians still in prison. When he visits Wilson to say goodbye, he asks his old friend how he should correspond with him in future.

'Don't write to us anymore,' Wilson says quietly. 'I am confident we shall all follow you soon.'[47]

It is the first clue that Foley has that a breakout must be imminent.

As it happens, two days later Foley sees Wilson heading down to the wharves with a gang of convict workers, his kit bag on his back. Both men are so overcome they cannot speak, and do not even attempt to. All they can do is 'exchange a silent but hearty shake of the hand'.[48]

Before departure Foley has rendered Breslin one last great service, putting him in touch with someone who can fill his role and communicate with the Fenians practically at will should he get desperate.

Her name is Elizabeth McCann, a beautiful young woman in her early twenties, born to a well-known family of free Irish settlers. William Foley has known her for the last five years since his release and come to trust her – she is brave, and an Irish patriot.

With Foley gone, Breslin begins to use her services, giving her small tasks and errands to do until he, too, believes she can be counted on, and can replace Foley when it comes to contacting the convicts and those warders who are with them. She is, after all, a local teacher, whose many young students are the offspring of the warders, which brings her into regular contact with them. And she is so young and so beautiful, who could believe she is actually working on a prison breakout?

'Often I was trusted with the task of passing letters, and an occasional half-sovereign, through to the Fenians in gaol,' Miss McCann will recall. 'They were handed to me, and I passed them on to friendly officers, who saw that they reached their destination safely.'[49]

And Breslin's trust is not misplaced.

'I did not even tell my own mother that I knew of the plot. I was fearful if I breathed a word, it would be upset, and the plan miscarry.'[50]

In fact, so trusted is young Elizabeth that she is even let in on the issue of Kiely. They like him. They want him to come, too. But far from being able to keep secrets, he is simply the type who likes spreading them around, so they cannot risk it.

As it turns out, as the last weeks of summer play out, Elizabeth is called on more and more by Breslin to contact the Fenian prisoners. As the Irishman will recall, 'the communication with them had become difficult, and they were not so easily to be found when wanted'.[51]

•

His Excellency the Governor Sir William Cleaver Robinson – who had taken over from Dr Hampton as the ruling force of the Colony of Western Australia – is a classic example of what the Irish call a 'Shoneen', an Irish blue-blood aristocrat, likely more steeped in the virtues of the British than the British themselves.

Most recently the Governor of the Leeward Islands, he had left because it was 'a remote settlement at the fag end of the world',[52] and he has been in . . . . . . Perth . . . for around two years. Though he is last word on what does or doesn't happen in the Colony of Western Australia, administering a colony is not his passion in life. Art is. And poetry. And philosophy. And, most particularly, music and composition . . .

As a matter of fact, one of his compositions, 'Remember Me No More', has become something of a favourite across much of the British Empire.

> If to remember me would give thee pain,
> Remember me no more . . .[53]

He has delighted in its success and, as ever, is eager to compose more. In fact, as a broad rule, he is usually doing one of two things: engaging in one of his artistic pursuits, or feeling resentful that his duties are calling him away from one of his artistic pursuits.

That's not to say he lacks patriotism to Great Britain. In fact, he has it in spades. Born in Ireland, the son of a British Admiral, he is arguably more 'British than the British'. He is a man of the old school with 'strong Protestant proclivities',[54] governing in the manner of the old viceroy class – 'when he says "yea" or "nay", he means it . . . a thorough red tape ruler',[55] one contemporary would later write of him.

But his art is his passion, and every moment away from it hurts his soul . . .

Right now is a case in point, as he must meet with one of the most important figures in the Colony, himself a Governor of his own domain, The Establishment. But this is not a social occasion.

Governor Robinson has asked to see Governor Fauntleroy to pass on a veiled warning. Word has come from the Home Office. Now, because of the High Security classification that had been placed on Lord Carnarvon's dispatch, he is not at liberty to divulge details. But he can tell him that Lord Carnarvon has had wind of some plan hatched in Ireland to break the Fenian prisoners out of The Establishment.

Both men are, frankly, stunned and disbelieving of the news. A plan from the other side of the world to break prisoners out, here?

It surely cannot be, and Robinson is heartened by Fauntleroy's own reaction: extreme scepticism, followed by a commitment to tighten everything up anyway. He will report back.

Very well, Governor Fauntleroy, and thank you.

Governor Robinson returns to his artistic pursuits.

•

The *Catalpa* is in Latitude 39° 46' South, Longitude 31° 54' East, 5000 miles off the coast of Western Australia, where the morning sun shines brightly enough to warm you and the breeze is just fresh enough to cool you.

The man in the crow's nest calls below – a vessel ahead![56]

Within three hours they are alongside the mighty three-masted bark and Captain Anthony is close enough to hail the *Ocean Beauty*, seeking permission to board.

Of course, of course!

Shaking Captain Anthony's hand with some vigour, the Captain of the *Ocean Beauty*, James Seagrove, welcomes him aboard and they retire to his cabin, as the two crews keep the vessels moving forward together, within hailing distance.

The *Ocean Beauty*, it turns out, left Liverpool just over two months earlier and is on its way to New Zealand. As to the Captain, he is, in the image of his ship, a big, billowing entity, who, though he might have seen better days, bears such stories of those days that he is a happy presence, and Captain Anthony feels nothing if not welcomed.

But, to the true reason he has sought to board her. For the fact is, his aim is not just friendly, and in recent days he has become ever more focused on the fact that he lacks what he now most needs, a detailed chart of the Australian coast. Perhaps, he asks his host, you yourself have already made many voyages in these parts?

'Been making them out here all my life,' Captain Seagrove replies. 'Why, I was [with] a convict ship, the *Hougoumont*, and carried a shipful of prisoners to Australia in 1868.'[57]

The *Hougoumont*?

The name seems strangely familiar to Captain Anthony and he pauses for a moment to reflect on where he has heard it before. Suddenly it comes to him.

The *Hougoumont*!

Of course, the very ship that took the Fenian prisoners to Western Australia!

The coincidence is extraordinary. Blithely unaware, however, of the significance of the occasion, Captain Seagrove starts to tell stories of those days.

Why, let him tell you about the most significant of those prisoners – John Boyle O'Reilly.

'You may have heard of him,' says the master of the *Ocean Beauty*, 'for he escaped in one of your whale-ships.'[58]

Why, yes, as a matter of fact, Captain Anthony *has* heard of him. But say, speaking of Australia, how do you think we will go when we get there, re-fitting the ship, and taking on board fresh provisions?

No problems with either thing, replies Captain Seagrove, and nor would there be any problem with getting fresh crew-members, should he need them.

'Have you a sheet chart of the coast you could spare me?' Captain Anthony asks, reaching the point of this whole exercise as casually as he can.

'Lots of them,' replies the Captain, delighted to help out. 'Here's the roll I used when I was master of the *Hougoumont*. Help yourself. You're welcome to any you want.'[59]

Eureka!

Captain Anthony is soon in possession of a precious chart showing all the key features of that part of the West Australian coast that is of most interest to him, from the Swan River and Perth, to Rottnest and Garden Islands, to Fremantle, Bunbury and all the way down to the Margaret River.

Confident that he has the winds of good fortune blowing his way, and not just because the sails above are starting to flap and it is time to go, Captain Anthony bids his benefactor farewell, receives a cheery 'God speed' in return, and is rowed back to the *Catalpa* positively *beaming*.

'What's happened?' Samuel Smith asks upon his return.

'Would you believe it? I've just been given the very chart which was used by the Captain of the *Hougoumont* to land the prisoners we're after at Fremantle. The Captain little thought it was to be used in taking a ship there to rescue the same men.'[60]

Ah, how they roar with laughter as the Indian Ocean slips backward in the night, the stars sparkle brightly o'er the moonlit swell, and the *Catalpa* surges towards the shores of Australia.

CHAPTER TEN

ARRIVAL IN FREMANTLE

It is pretty hard work to crawl into the lion's mouth and turn around and crawl out again without exciting the suspicion of the lion.[1]

Captain George S. Anthony, in the *Freeman's Journal*, 24 July 1897

Mid-March 1876, Indian Ocean, may the wind be always at your back

Sail, on the for'ard quarter!

It has been a long haul, made all the longer in the last ten days by a gale blowing from the south-south-east that would blow a dog off a chain, the tits off a mermaid.

At last however, the gale has eased, and they've been sailing on calm seas with fair winds pushing them in the direction they want to go, and they veritably leap towards their goal.

They reach the island of St Paul – the rough halfway point between the southern tip of Africa and the west coast of Australia – on 15 March to re-victual in a couple of days, and push on from there. Captain Anthony tells the crew they are indeed on their way to the rich whaling grounds around New Zealand, and as he is the only one taking the navigational measurements, there is no-one to dispute it . . .

•

Never in his life could John Breslin understand atheists.

The idea that all the beauty in this world is simply an accident?

The notion that genuinely bad people won't be punished in the afterlife?

That good people, who repent of their sins, won't be rewarded in heaven?

Preposterous.

And then, of course, there are the *miracles*.

And this day is a case in point.

Desperately low on funds, aware more than ever that his whole façade will fall apart if he cannot continue to live lavishly, he has been praying for a breakthrough, and . . .

A gentle knock on his door.

He opens it to find John King, the smiling Fenian he had met in Sydney, the one who had given him the precious £200 to bolster his coffers. King, straight off a P & O steamer, has no sooner come into the room than, *still* beaming, he heaves his heavy portmanteau onto the table with a clunk and unbuttons his shirt to remove from around his waist a money-belt, which he places beside it. He opens both to reveal a hefty £384 in gold sovereigns, gathered from Fenian sympathisers on the east coast and Fenian goldminers in New Zealand.

Oh, the relief! The pure *joy*, of knowing he can continue.

Breslin plucks out £20 worth and gives it to King for his return voyage home, but King begs to stay, eager to help in any manner that he might be required. He is travelling under the name of 'George Jones', a goldminer who is about to head to the great north-west, following reports of gold being discovered in those parts.

Breslin concedes.

As it happens, King proves to be very useful to Breslin, for just a couple of days later, two strangers appear in Fremantle – an 'Alfred Dixon' and a 'Henry Hopkins'.

Making contact with Breslin, they make clear that they are from Ireland and they are here to help.

John Breslin is not so sure.

Are they, in fact, English spies sent to entrap him? Breslin makes no admissions to them, but explains the situation to King, who smoothly takes the matter in hand.

'I will find out about these men,' he tells Breslin with a smile, 'I will make myself known to these men as the head of the enterprise, and if they turn out false the most they could do with me would be to throw me in prison.'[2]

It actually makes sense, as this would leave Breslin free, and with the *Catalpa* due to arrive shortly, there might still be some chance of pulling it off. The authorities might even feel that, with King in custody, the plan has been thwarted, and relax their guard.

Breslin agrees, and King departs to find the strangers.

In fact, King is certain that he has already met them. Breslin's description matches perfectly a couple of fellow passengers he'd briefly met in Albany's Quarantine Station on the way over.

It does not take long. In a settlement as small as Fremantle, where so many of the settlers are ticket-of-leave men required to be in their homes by 10 pm each day, King can easily spot the travellers on the deserted streets.

And there is one of them now, 'Dixon', walking up High Street! King introduces himself, reminding him they had already met.

'He did not remember me at first, or at least he pretended not to. We strolled along talking on various subjects until we reached the outskirts of the city.'[3]

And now it is time.

Turning to 'Dixon', King asks him frankly: 'What are you doing here?'[4]

What? Shocked, Dixon pauses for a moment before replying.

'I have an uncle in Champion Bay and I am going down there in a few days to engage with him in the business of sheep raising.'[5]

But King will not have it.

'I know all about your plans,' he says, 'and just what you are in Australia for.'[6]

Oh yes, he does. You are here to break the Fenian convicts out of The Establishment!

'You must be dreaming!' Dixon replies, thunderstruck. 'You have been misinformed.'[7]

But still King insists, while going on to say that he is all in favour of it, as he is not only a Fenian himself, but wishes to help with the breakout.

'I,' King says, 'am in a position to do you a lot of good in an undertaking of this kind.'[8]

Again, Dixon pauses, before finally replying.

'I will meet you on the beach in half an hour and give you my decision.'[9]

Clearly, he wishes to consult with his travelling companion, but King is satisfied. If they are British spies, he will know soon enough. Returning to the Emerald Isle Hotel, he tells Breslin the situation.

'Use your own judgement,' Breslin tells him, 'as to whether these men are to be admitted to our confidence.'[10]

A short time later, King is standing in the moonlight on the white sands when Dixon and Hopkins arrive. King looks over their shoulders. There is no sign, yet, of any police come to arrest him.

'We have decided to accept your offer,' Dixon tells him simply. To further prove their bona fides, Dixon shows him some papers which, as King will recount, 'proved conclusively to my mind that he was all right and was really acting as an agent for Irishmen in England and the old country in a plan of escape for the Irish prisoners in Fremantle'.[11]

In essence, it proves to be Breslin's second miracle in nearly as many days. For King now brings Dennis McCarthy and John Walsh – their real names – back to Breslin's room, and the five are able to talk late into the night, trading notes on both of their schemes.

The new arrivals, it turns out, have also come in response to letters sent from the Fenian convicts, but their plan is still at the embryonic stage. They are not only delighted to find that the American branch of the Fenians are so far ahead of them, but happy to throw their lot in with the Breslin plan and offer to help in any way they can. This includes handing over the £1000 they have brought with them – together with a collection of pistols and rifles, with ammunition. All up, in the space of a few days, Breslin has gone from facing penury and penitentiary to having an embarrassment of riches and excess of manpower.

It's perfect.

Over many hushed discussions, the men plan the particulars.

Come the time, Walsh and McCarthy, heavily armed, will cut the telegraph wires that connect Fremantle to both Rockingham and Perth, then stay in Fremantle to act as a rear-guard if trouble starts. For his part, King can also remain in Fremantle as a mounted rear-guard, ideally catching Breslin and the convicts up to advise whether or not the alarm has been raised.

In the meantime, they decide to take many excursions in their traps, to practise what they will do on the day, to understand how long it takes to get from one spot to another, to be familiar with what obstacles might come their way – while also making enough trips to other spots that their particular interest in Rockingham will not stand out, should anyone be watching them closely.

•

In the meantime?

In the meantime, as much as John Breslin doesn't understand atheists, nor can he quite grasp the insistence of the Catholic church that congress outside of wedlock is a mortal sin.

Simply put, it's just not the way he's built. And it is *certainly* not the way that the voluptuous Mary Tondut – 'stately with beautiful features'[12] – is built, thank the Lord.

For late one night in his room at the Emerald Isle, when they are resting after another session of intertwined turbulence, she confides that some time in these last months, there has been a . . . not so immaculate conception. And you are the father, James Collins.

Mary Tondut beams. Abandoned once by the father of her five-year-old daughter, Louisa, this charming man has swept her off her feet, and now she is carrying his child she is more hopeful than ever that she can build a future with him. John Breslin remains hopeful of exactly that, while more than ever aware that the complications of his personal life are assuming a nature that could threaten his entire reason for being here in the first place. More than ever he is anxious for the *Catalpa* to arrive, so they can get the whole mission under way and the following morning, as ever, heads off early to stare wanly at the bulletin board outside the Telegraph Office, gazing at the shipping arrivals. This morning, as ever, it is the same thing – no *Catalpa*.

But, this morning, at least, there is news of another whaler arriving at Bunbury.

The *Canton* comes from New Bedford, so he cannot resist.

Going inside, Breslin sends a telegram asking the Captain of the *Canton* if, perchance, he has 'news of the *Catalpa*',[13] also out of New Bedford.

The answer comes back the next day – 'No.'

Look, going to Bunbury will accomplish little in turning up information that the bulletin board and telegrams can't provide, but to John Breslin it just feels right. As charming as the many charms of Mary Tondut are, he simply has to do something beyond waiting. And so he catches the mail-coach down to Bunbury to find that out beyond the pleasant settlement's long jetty there is . . . no *Catalpa*. At least he is able to make the return journey to Fremantle aboard a small commercial coasting vessel, *The May*, which allows him to further familiarise himself with the coastline the *Catalpa* will be operating along – if it ever gets here.

17 March 1876, St Patrick's Day, The Establishment, a missive to the father

Spending St Pat's Day so far from his native Limerick is always going to be a miserable affair for the swordsman Martin Hogan. But when you spend it on the road-gang during the day, and in your tiny cell at night, that misery is deep.

And yes, he lives in hope that this man Breslin who has arrived will be able to do something for him. But long years in this hell-hole have taught him the virtues of dampening expectations to save his weakened soul, to keep from unravelling entirely. He cannot allow himself to count on it, and so writes a careful letter to his surviving parent.

> *My Dearest Father, I received your letter of November which gave me some comfort to hear from you and I am so happy that you enjoy your health. You say, dear father, write every mail, if possible. I am not able to do that. I will do my best to write every two months. Months and days pass away from me in my long suffering that often I wish to Heaven that the day I received sentence of life that it was death. It would keep me out of long years of misery. Dear Father, you ask me did I get the ticket of leave. I will not for some years to come. Dear Father, send me nothing, no matter what kind it may be. Anything my dear mother has left me keep it till I get it in my own hands. Keep good heart, dear father, I will write a long letter next time.*
> *Your fond son,*
> *Martin J. Hogan*[14]

27 March 1876, off the coast of Western Australia, the *Catalpa* closes

Land ahoy!

Aboard the *Catalpa*, most of the crew believe the land they can spy up ahead is New Zealand and not Cape Naturaliste, on the south-western tip of the Australian continent. As a matter of fact, the Second Mate, Antoine Farnham, tells them all he recognises the promontory as being New Zealand from his previous visit to these parts.

Quietly, privately, the skipper is caught between the exaltation at finally approaching Australia, and the realisation that he is about to embark on the most testing escapade of his life.

Just who he will meet onshore is anyone's guess, but he presumes they will be watching for his arrival, and make contact. That is, if their plot has not been discovered? Perhaps they have been arrested, and he is now at risk?

For the moment, as darkness starts to fall, there is no way of knowing and he simply must wait.

He gives the order to drop anchor for the night in the shoal waters of Geographe Bay.

Dawn breaks, bright and beautiful.

Captain Anthony and his crew sail into Bunbury Harbour, squinting at the silhouetted form of the township taking shape as the sun rises from behind, first peeking over the rooflines then beaming down on Bunbury proper.

At first glance it looks to be exactly what it is – a relatively neat, small provincial settlement, boasting several government buildings, a few commercial enterprises, from shops to ship-wrights to public bars and hotels, and dotted with small brick cottages in scattered allotments, all nestled on marshy lowland leading down to the inlet of a broad estuary. A humble outpost, clinging to the coastline on the edge of the Empire. Its 300 or so residents live off whaling a little and surrounding farms a lot, and are generally prosperous.

The *Catalpa* drops anchor near the long jetty that pokes out into the calm harbour.

And say, where are we?

A boatload of Water Police row out to the ship. Pulling alongside, and climbing aboard, their head officer provides the answer . . . Welcome to Bunbury . . . some 100 miles south of Perth . . . in Western Australia!

In *Western Australia*, you say?

Some of the crew know that there has been a problem with the dodgy chronometer, messing up navigational calculations . . . but this is *ridiculous*.

Yes, Captain Anthony has some explaining to do.

Yes, I suppose I should have told you. But I've simply changed my mind, and decided to stop here, instead. No more, no less.

Fortunately, after such a long voyage, the sailors are more desperate to get ashore than they are insistent in learning why that shore is in Western Australia, but still the Massachusetts Captain is careful. This close to their goal, he simply cannot risk the desertions that so often go with making port, and so he allows only his most trusted men to accompany him in the whaleboat as they pull towards the jetty. The men disembark, with strict orders to be back here to meet the whaleboat by 5 pm this afternoon . . . or face the consequences.

Yes, Cap'n. And so they scatter.

Back aboard the ship, several of the men left behind glower. *Months* on this tiny tub, taking very few whales, making very little money, and now they have come to a port where there is grog, and no doubt women, and they can't land? It is *outrageous*!

For his part, Captain Anthony – less inclined to rush to bars, and no interest in whorehouses and the like – takes his time, first visiting

Customs House, a neat government building by the wharves, to officially report his arrival, his cargo, the names of his crew-members, and receive permission to remain for a week or so.

That permission is granted by an official with a gimlet eye – American whalers have been the cause of troubles in these parts – and Captain Anthony thereafter wanders the streets, looking for he knows not what. Hopefully, it will be less a matter of him finding someone, than letting word spread that the *Catalpa* has arrived, so someone will find him. All day long he looks meaningfully at every approaching face, and though many people smile back at him, and even welcome such a fine-looking sea-faring man to their fair burgh, no looks linger long and no-one seeks to take him aside for a quiet chat.

By the time he gets back to the ship that evening, his morale is low.

Has there been a miscommunication, a misadventure, a mistake? Something is amiss.

6.30 am, 29 March 1876, Fremantle, glad tidings on the tide

There!

Every morning for the last month, John Breslin has scanned the bulletin board of Fremantle's Telegraph Office.

Every morning for the last month, his despair has grown as the days have passed – but today, he sees gold.

For there it is, in small print, all but leaping out at him.

BUNBURY.—March 28.—Catalpa, from Whaling grounds.[15]

He moves quickly.

•

Another beautiful morning. Another excursion into Bunbury, this time with different members of the crew.

On this morning, however, no sooner has Captain Anthony set foot on the jetty than there is, yes, a lad looking at him meaningfully, and even approaching him! A single, fine-looking, man, rowed to shore by four sailors, must surely be the skipper of the whaler it has come from . . . ?

'Are you Captain Anthony?'[16] he asks, a little uncertainly.

With the Cap'n's nod of affirmation, the lad gives him an envelope containing a telegram.

Captain Anthony tries not to rip it open with unseemly haste. But the instant the lad's back is turned he devours every word.

Electric Telegraph, Western Australia.
Bunbury, 29th March, 1876.

Time, 10.40 A. M.
By B. W. The following telegram received here from Freemantle Station.
To Captain Anthony : – Have you any news from New Bedford? When
can you come to Freemantle? J. Collins.[17]

Oh, the relief!

Clearly, everything is on course.

Hurrying to the Telegraph Office, he wires to Collins:

No news from New Bedford. Shall not come to Freemantle.
G. S. Anthony.[18]

For going to Fremantle would mean abandoning his crew to their own devices and he is not prepared to risk their desertion, and thereafter being obliged to recruit a new crew – no doubt most of them from the British Empire – for the delicate task that remains. No, he must stay here for the moment.

At least, however, he is prepared to get a room at the local hotel, certain that this 'J. Collins', albeit under some other name, will surely be making a visit. In the meantime, one of the local shopkeepers, interested to meet an American, mentions in passing that they have recently been visited by another American, a fellow of enormous wealth, who seems to go prospecting in these parts.

'He is,' says the fellow flatly, 'the finest man I ever met.'[19]

'What is his name?' asks the mariner.

'Mr Collins,' replies the shopkeeper.

By happenstance, Captain Anthony is in this same shop the following afternoon when the clatter of hoofs and the creak of a carriage announces the arrival of the mail-coach from Fremantle.

'Why, there's the very man I was telling you about!' says the shop-keeper pointing through the dusty pane of his shop window. 'Come up to Spencer's Hotel and I'll introduce you.'[20]

Captain Anthony doesn't mind if he does.

Arriving at the hotel a few minutes later, they ask for Mr Collins, who is soon coming down the squeaky stairway, to arrive very shortly after his grand flowing beard.

Captain Anthony and Mr Collins shake hands politely, but no more than that. Even though each man is delighted to have found the other, and very much likes the look of what he sees, it simply would not do to embrace, clap each other on the back and express their sheer relief.

But now that the introductions are made, and the explosions of joy suppressed, let us get a good look at each other.

Mr Collins, it must be said, is a splendid man, elegantly turned out in a tailored suit, with tightly coiffed hair and – it's mesmerising – a stupendously full beard. He is the very picture of a wealthy man who not only enjoys that wealth but looks like wealth enjoys him. He wears it so lightly it's charming.

For his part, John Breslin sees a surprisingly young sea-faring man, still in his early thirties . . . a tanned, windblown mariner with piercing black eyes, who looks the very picture of what a man should be for this task. The shopkeeper returns to his store, while the two Americans sit down for supper, followed by cigars, still without uttering a single word to acknowledge their common purpose. It is important that they look the part of men from the same part of the world, catching up with news from home, and not be seen to be having an intense conversation.

But both men can only stand so much.

'Perhaps you'd like to take a walk, Captain Anthony?' Breslin asks him.

Why, yes he would.

In the dark night the two walk out onto the long jetty, where they can be neither seen, nor heard.

But only when he is sure that they are totally alone does Breslin allow himself to burst out of character. He grabs the Captain's hand once more – as if they are meeting for the first time – pumps it vigorously and says, 'How are you?'[21]

The short answer is, every bit as delighted and relieved as you!

Quietly, the Irishman confides his many fears of the past weeks, how he was certain that the *Catalpa* had been lost or waylaid, whereupon Captain Anthony tells him of everything that has happened in the 11 months since they left Massachusetts – including his crew deserting and the prolonged storm which had so delayed them.

But now it is time to get down to tin-tacks.

Breslin tells Captain Anthony of the lie of the land and just how he plans to get the prisoners to the *Catalpa*. The good news is that the Fenian prisoners they are after spend most of their daylight hours working outside the prison. The bad news is that since our friend John Boyle O'Reilly escaped, the authorities have doubled their guard on our boys. Prisoners as important as the Fenians are never put on remote road sites anymore, but kept close to the gaol, so they can be safely marched back to the cells every night.

Nevertheless, by launching a liberation raid at the most vulnerable moment, Breslin is convinced that they can be sprung, and put in a couple of fast traps to get them quickly to the south.

After consultation with James Wilson – the two have managed several meetings behind the stables since their initial one – Breslin confirms Rockingham Beach, some 20 miles south of Fremantle, as the rendezvous spot. Wilson worked on a road-gang down that way so is familiar with the area and everything he has said proves correct. It is true that there is a tricky set of interlocking reefs just off the shore, but the beach itself is perfect: it's isolated and always empty, and the sand is firm – ideal for them to run their traps onto and make a quick getaway.

One final bonus is that with Garden Island standing sentinel just half a mile off the beach, it means that the *Catalpa*, hovering on the other side, will be invisible to whatever inquisitive eyes there might be onshore.

If Breslin can get them to that beach in the morning could Captain Anthony undertake to be there with a whaleboat and crew, to row them out to the *Catalpa* in international waters?

Instead of being just three miles off the coast as originally planned, Mr Breslin has decided it would be better to make it 'fourteen or sixteen miles'.[22] At that distance, not even those on top of the lighthouse at Fremantle, and certainly none of those in vessels engaging in normal traffic up and down the coast would spot a ship hovering and become suspicious. Most importantly there would be no risk of drifting too close to the coast, where they could be legally apprehended, and risk coming a cropper against the many reefs that abound all around.

No, better for the bark to stay well off the coast, and have the whaleboat cover the stretch in just four or five hours.

'I am perfectly willing to do what is required of me,' Captain Anthony replies carefully, 'but have some difficulties. My crew are in a discontented state and attempting to desert.'[23]

It can be done, yes, but he will have to proceed carefully, to ensure his men settle.

Capital! In the meantime, Breslin has another idea.

It is important that Captain Anthony becomes familiar with the coastline south of Fremantle, without snooping around in the *Catalpa*. So why not come with him on the colonial mail steamer, the *Georgette*, which would be returning to Fremantle the next day, 1 April? The New Bedford whaler readily agrees, happy to leave his crew under the watchful eye of First Mate Smith.

If all goes according to plan, Breslin continues, we can pull this off about a week from today, say Thursday, 6 April . . .

All up, it has been a highly productive evening and as the two walk back to their hotel, both have a great deal to contemplate.

•

Major Finnerty again.

Governor Robinson is displeased. Once more a formal complaint has crossed his desk at Government House, concerning one of the more rambunctious of his functionaries, Major Charles Finnerty, who also fills a role as one of Fremantle's Resident Magistrates. A report in the press has it that, from the bench of the Petty Sessions on 13 March, Major Finnerty had addressed a Roman Catholic priest attached to Fremantle Prison, whose testimony in a particular case he doubted: 'I suppose you have received absolution in this world and the next, and may come here and state what you like.'[24]

His Excellency is appalled, and writes a stiff note to the Major accordingly, 'I can hardly think that a Resident Magistrate of your standing and experience would make use of language so injudicious and unnecessarily offensive to a large section of the community.'[25]

As it happens, Major Finnerty and his supporters will maintain that there had indeed been a mistake, and, radiant in the ruby red glow of his ardent indignation – for many of his underlings use his snout as a barometer of his mood: pink for mere irritation, red for rage, and a previously unknown shade of deep purple in moments of carpet-biting fury – the Major himself wastes not a minute in dashing off an explanatory epistle to the Governor with his side of the story.

Several letters of correspondence later, the Governor is somewhat accepting of the explanation, though he does not withdraw his initial remarks, instead deigning also to censure the behaviour of the priest involved. Ultimately, it does not alter His Excellency's view.

Major Finnerty is something of a hot-head, whose temperament does not always lend itself to the cool administration of justice.

1 April 1876, All Fools' Day, Bunbury Harbour, better a witty fool than a foolish wit[26]

All hands on deck to greet the Captain!

And the distinguished-looking visitor he has with him.

In short order Captain Anthony and First Mate Samuel Smith are showing Mr Breslin all over the *Catalpa* to give him a feel for what awaits once he and his accomplices, together with the Fenian Six, come on board.

Satisfied that the *Catalpa* will be able to accommodate them come what may – at least once they build a few new cabins on the deck, once at sea with the freed convicts – Captain Anthony and John Breslin are rowing back to shore, in plenty of time to catch the *Georgette* to Fremantle, as planned.

But wait!

Who is this?

For no sooner are they walking along the jetty towards the *Georgette* than they spy a familiar figure walking towards them. That lope! The way he bobs his head when he walks.

It can only be Thomas Brennan – the well-connected shoemaker who'd been passed over for command of the expedition in favour of John Breslin. And what a story he has to tell. And with what intensity he does tell it.

For yes, that had indeed been him at St Michael's, whose ship had been coming in just as the *Catalpa* was going out. But, entirely unperturbed, he had resolved to get to Australia by other means, and join them there. So, deciding to return to London, to catch a steamer from there, he had first stowed away on a ship bound for Liverpool, only to be discovered by an outraged Captain, who wanted to deliver him to Liverpool police, and would have, if not for the fact that Brennan had jumped overboard in Liverpool's River Mersey Harbour, whereupon he very nearly drowned, only to be picked up by a rowboat and taken to shore.

From there, he had indeed secured passage on a steamer to bring him to Western Australia, first landing in Albany thence to Bunbury, and now, here I am!

Yes, here you are.

Truthfully, John Breslin is underwhelmed. Is this Brennan a fool? It takes but one fool to unravel any plot, and Brennan is certainly going to lengths to do just that . . .

'I had already more men than I could conveniently undertake to provide for,' he would recount, 'and, again, he could not go on board the *Catalpa* at Bunbury without exciting suspicion, so I determined to let him come on to Fremantle, and then to do the best I could for him.'[27]

How to tell a man who had gone through such adventures just to join them that he is surplus to requirements, that they already have all the men they need? (And frankly, that Breslin does not like the cut of his jib in the first place.)

They cannot. The risk in enraging a man who knows nearly everything – and how he would react to being told 'No' in Australia, after having already been told 'No' in America and St Michael's – would be too great. And, after all, Brennan is a sworn member of the *Clan-na-Gael*, a body that is their ultimate master. All they can do for now is curtail any potential damage Brennan might do by taking him with them to Fremantle. But, careful. While Captain Anthony will be coming aboard as a guest of 'Mr Collins', they both must keep their distance from Brennan while on board.

In the meantime, Captain Anthony, who under the circumstances is happy to present himself for what he is – the Captain of yonder whaler – introduces himself to the *Georgette*'s Captain Michael O'Grady.

A Captain from Boston, you say? Well, welcome aboard, Captain Anthony! Even before they set off Captain Anthony is in the pilot-house with his new friend.

Fortuitously, O'Grady is himself an Irishman – hailing from Limerick – which, beyond meaning he might have sympathies for the Fenian cause, at least means he doesn't mind a chat, and so it proves!

O'Grady is 27 years old, and not only had he taken over as Captain of the *Georgette* two years earlier as his first commission, but three of his brothers are also Captains. He loves the maritime life, and is fascinated to hear more of Captain Anthony's experiences on his whaler, and happy to answer the American's many questions as they get under way.

While Anthony absorbs every morsel of information he can, the loquacious *Georgette* skipper talks of shoals and currents, tides and reefs, and he points out landmarks and shows Anthony the bearings he will need should ever his whaler need, say, to take him into yonder inlet. Ah yes, there is Garden Island, lying as a rocky sentinel off Rockingham Beach. Be careful there, for the tides that swirl around the island and the many reefs that lie to its north and south are treacherous. Using Captain O'Grady's own spyglass to better study the contours of how the land meets the sea, Captain Anthony is careful to show equal interest in Rottnest Island and other principal landmarks.

At noon the following day, the *Georgette* chug-chug-chugs into Fremantle Harbour and Captain Anthony's gaze is drawn towards the extraordinary prison that stands glowering over it. It is an arresting vision, a reminder that, though they have come far, and accomplished much, the real work, the real risk remains.

Are they really going to try to spring six Fenians from the steel jaws of a British penal system powerful enough to build a prison of proportions like that?

Apparently so . . .

And it really is going to be even more tricky than first thought, for, on this bright Sunday morning, the squinted eyes of both Captain Anthony and John Breslin come upon an unexpected sight – a British gunboat, HMS *Conflict*, which has apparently just arrived. Just look at her. She's a schooner-rigged vessel with two large guns on deck, capable of blowing the *Catalpa* out of the water with one salvo, and must have at least 30 armed men for crew. Her speed, though, is the main concern. For her sleek lines and fore-and-aft masts bespeak a vessel shaped precisely for speed. Captain Anthony supposes she's capable of at least ten knots. While it is possible, just possible, the *Catalpa* might out-sail her in a strong wind, there would be no chance in the current light winds. If it came to the *Catalpa* being discovered trying to make a quick departure with escaped convicts, they would be run down like a sick rabbit by a rabid dog.

Mr Breslin and Captain Anthony exchange grim glances. There is much they have to discuss because if they keep to their current schedule, and the *Conflict* is still here, it could ruin everything. Hurrying to the Emerald Isle Hotel, Breslin is quick to present Captain Anthony to their co-conspirators, John King and Thomas Desmond, the latter having just arrived on the cabled summons of Collins to greet – O *Captain! My Captain* – the presumed master of their salvation.

Immediately, Breslin sends Desmond down to the wharves to chat with some of the sailors, and he soon comes back with news. The *Conflict* is here on its annual visit and will remain for at least a week, and perhaps as long as ten days, before heading around the coast to Sydney. Meantime, another gunboat is expected in Fremantle shortly, intended to take Governor Robinson to visit the north-west coast.

Things are starting to get a little complicated. They will need a window of opportunity in the next fortnight, when neither gunboat is present.

Whatever else, their previous plan of launching the escape next Thursday morning, 6 April, will have to be delayed.

To settle his thoughts, and his spirits, by imbibing some, Captain Anthony retires downstairs to the bar of the Emerald Isle Hotel, where he soon falls into conversation with a young mounted constable known as 'Big John' McKenna for his barrel chest and massive biceps but certainly not for his height, as the 22-year-old who joined the service only two years before is an unremarkable five feet, six inches tall. The American buys him a drink and they pass a pleasant hour together, talking of Captain Anthony's life as a whaling man and, more particularly, McKenna's life enforcing British law in Western Australia. For the young constable, the American is good company and proves to be fascinated by everything that McKenna does.

•

The well-known Perth solicitor, Mr Nathaniel Howell, will ever afterwards recall it as one of the more curious matters in his career. The client being ushered into his office presents himself as Thomas Johnson, a carriage-maker from Sloan's Carriage Factory, which makes this one of the few times the 45-year-old urbane Mr Howell has been asked for legal advice by a common worker. More curious still, Mr Johnson seeks to pay for the advice he seeks with the gold sovereigns he casually places on the table, and . . .

And yes, Mr Johnson, what advice is it that you seek? And herein the third curiosity. Mr Johnson, who does not claim to be a maritime man, who has no connection with any vessel, and who offers no explanation for his interest, wishes to know about 'the limit of neutral waters'[28] in Western Australia. As in, how far does the jurisdiction of the colony extend into the Indian Ocean?

Bemused, for it is not a question that comes up often, Mr Howell advises him. The writ of British law extends to three miles from the coast and all who commit crimes or misdemeanours this side of that line will be answerable to British authority. Beyond that line you are in international waters, and answerable to the laws of the nation under whose flag the vessel sails.

There are nuances, and Mr Howell goes into some of them, but that is the essence of it.

Thomas Johnson thanks Mr Howell, and takes his leave.

•

John Breslin looks left, looks right, and now ducks behind the stables to find James Wilson waiting.

Mercifully.

In recent weeks, face-to-face meetings have been difficult, but there has never been a more important engagement than this one. Breslin bursts forth with the news. The whaler has arrived. All is in order. We will break you out in a few days. Every man must be on his best behaviour to ensure there is no chance of punishment, no change from your regular routines. Don't even pack your few precious, hidden possessions. You and your fellow Fenians will have to escape with the clothes on your back and nothing more. Everything must stay exactly the same. There cannot be the slightest hint of preparation on your part, not a single word of farewell to a soul, are we clear?

We are clear.

The conversation does not take long, and John Breslin is soon on his way once more. A few minutes later, James Wilson also reappears from behind the stables.

•

Out and about on the streets of Fremantle, young Harry Passmore suddenly sees his friend Thomas Darragh in the distance.

He'd know that shock of red hair flaming around above a convict uniform anywhere. As it turns out, the warm-hearted convict has been looking for Harry and has something to tell him. Do not bring me soft drinks anymore, thank you.

'I am leaving,'[29] Thomas tells him a little emotionally, without elaborating. And, young Harry, I have a gift for you. It is a small compass to hang on your watch chain as a memento of our friendship.

Supposing that Thomas must be being transferred to another district, Harry pumps the convict's proffered hand and thanks him profusely for giving him such a kind gift.

It's all a little odd.

•

It is time for John Breslin to familiarise Captain Anthony with the escape route, and show him the selected point of departure.

On this sunny Monday afternoon, the day after arriving back in Fremantle, all of Breslin, Anthony, John King and Thomas Desmond head south in 'Mr Collins's' trap and make good time over the first ten miles as two fine horses pulling them along – *a'canter, a'canter, a'canter . . . awaaaaay* – on the macadamised 'Fenian road', substantially built by the men they are wanting to free. It takes just 40 minutes to cover that distance, but then the road becomes sandy and heavy over the next seven miles, and, after passing the Rockingham Hotel, eventually becomes a mere sandy track of four miles leading to Rockingham Beach. The whole trip takes a little under two-and-a-half hours.

'Now, this is the place,' says John Breslin, alighting, 'where we propose to bring the men, and where we expect you to meet us with a boat.'[30]

Now while an 'X' might mark the spot on the map, here on the ground Captain Anthony feels he can do better, and, finding a long chunk of plank – fresh flotsam – he jams it vertically into the sand well above high-water mark.

'Let it be understood,' he says quietly, 'that this is the place where I will meet you with my boat if God spares my life.'[31]

It is set then, with the only matter remaining being the timing of the breakout. Returning to Fremantle, Breslin and Anthony take earnest rest from their hot endeavours, and in the evening discuss just how they will communicate with each other and synchronise their movements when the plan is in action. They need a code, as they obviously cannot talk openly through the telegraph.

The key arbiter of when they make their move will be when the gunboat leaves Fremantle. They agree therefore that when *Conflict* leaves, Breslin is to send a telegram referring to a friend – 'N' or 'S' – having gone home, which would be the clue that the gunboat has left to the north to Champion Bay, or the south, on its way to Sydney, via Albany.

Next, when Captain Anthony replies, confirming the hour of his departure, he is committing to having the *Catalpa* off the coast, and a manned whaleboat on the beach, 48 hours after the telegram is sent. Yes, there is a risk in making such a commitment as the distance between Bunbury and Rockingham – 100 miles – means that a combination of headwinds, tides and misadventure could prevent the *Catalpa* being there.

But what choice do they have?

At a certain point, and they are there right now, they must take their chances – throw the dice and trust that the Gods of Justice are with them.

In the meantime, it is important that both men, just like the Fenian convicts, behave normally. As this includes separate invitations for the next day to both men to the table of the Governor – the very man upon whom they now plan to visit the greatest humiliation of his career – they must accept, as it would be an unthinkable affront not to.

Still, as the dinner is at Government House in the company of some of Perth's leading merchants, Captain Anthony is more than a little nervous as he and Breslin arrive, within a few minutes of each other, still pretending to an only slight acquaintance. Here he is about to wrest six prisoners from the jaws of the British lion, about to dine in the lion's den beforehand?

Is this really a good idea?

Surely the authorities must suspect something?

Has he really covered his tracks?

It would take only one informant, just one, and it would be all over.

No. Stay calm. You are all right. Here is the dinner table, and you must simply sit down with all the rest, and prepare to toast Her Majesty Queen Victoria and . . .

And one of the officials has just placed a hand on Captain Anthony's arm.

'Excuse me, sir,' says he, 'but what is your name and business, and what are you doing here?'

The American is in shock. It seems that he is about to be arrested . . . ?

Suddenly John Breslin hovers close, and with extraordinary calm explains to Captain Anthony, with a broad smile, that this is a mere 'custom of the country'.[32]

Honoured guests, like Captain Anthony, taking their place at the Governor's table for the first time, are simply invited to tell the gathering a little of who they are, and what brings them to this part of the world.

Oh.

The Massachusetts man is able to babble a few anxious words about whaling, and the honour he has to sit at this table . . . before doing exactly that.

Much of the meal goes by in a blur, as he contemplates the sheer horror of what might have been. Instead of freeing the Fenians, he would likely have been placed in a cell by their side, there to rot for years before seeing Emma and little Sophie again. Oh, how it would break their hearts!

It is a stark reminder that beyond the exhilaration of planning a heist, there is a real risk involved.

This point is further emphasised the next day when Captain Anthony goes into Fremantle to buy a coastal chart from the hydrographic office and is made to answer a long series of questions as to just *who* he is and *why* he is here.

Captain Anthony comes to understand – the British are not stupid. They are aware of the risk he and his kind pose. He is being assessed and watched.

It is a point that underlines the importance of Breslin's instructions as to what he must do now. Return to Bunbury.

'Overhaul your vessel,' Breslin had told him. 'Paint her, and be in no hurry to get your wood and water on board, as we must wait until the gunboat has sailed.'[33]

•

It is time for Governor Robinson in Perth to report to Lord Carnarvon in England just how secure everything is at The Establishment. And it really is. Since his first conversation with Governor Fauntleroy in January, he has had weekly contact and been completely assured that there are no foreign agents in the area, and certainly no sign of anyone attempting to contact the prisoners, or any sign the Fenians themselves are restless. In fact, when the subject had been delicately raised at Fremantle Prison, the response had been clear, when it came to the military Fenians.

'But they are the most trustworthy men we have.'

Exactly.

In sum, Lord Carnarvon need have no fear.

The Fenians are being watched. And the plot to escape will end in failure.

Friday, 7 April 1876, Bunbury, trouble ahead

The exhausted figure climbing down from the Bunbury mail-coach after 32 hours solid of bumping along from Fremantle is, of course, Captain George Anthony, returning to his whaler and his men. In his bag he has £60 in gold, given to him by Mr Breslin to buy supplies and ready the *Catalpa*.

The next few days are hard for both Captain Anthony and his men, as the ship is loaded to the gills with enough food and water to get them all the way back to America without stopping to replenish at any port – though the skipper can't tell them that. The reason they must work so hard, hauling such quantities, is because the skipper says so, that is all. Grumbling, the men comply. A mysterious man, this Captain. They like him all right, as he is fair, but he can be very, very curious. Like the way he keeps looking around him all the time, and gazing to the shore.

Is it him, or is he being watched?

Are locals suspicious that the ship has now been here for well over a week, and shown no eagerness to get back out to sea to continue whaling? Are some of them suspecting that the *Catalpa* might be here for another purpose?

One way or another, it seems extraordinary how often in conversation with some of the older settlers of Bunbury the subject of the only successful escape – John Boyle O'Reilly, his name was – comes up.

'Is there any chance for others to escape?' Anthony asks, idly.

'Impossible,' they say flatly, 'for since then a stricter watch is kept over the men and there is no chance for any others to get away.'[34]

Do tell. Very interesting.

Captain Anthony takes it all in, hoping to betray no particular interest, but their certainty is unsettling. Samuel Smith feels the same.

'We had to be always on our guard,' Captain Anthony would recall of his tight conversations with his First Mate, 'and preserve the utmost secrecy, for a stranger is watched all the time, and one word or little whisper would spoil the whole thing. It is pretty hard work to crawl into the lion's mouth and turn around and crawl out again without exciting the suspicion of the lion.'[35]

Danger in this exercise comes not only from without.

For, making matters worse, is that even as his crew continue to give the *Catalpa* a fresh coat of paint and re-fit, even as they load her up with fresh supplies – including fresh water, potatoes, onions, and salted meat – it is obvious that they are more than restless over Captain Anthony's continued denial of shore leave – unless they are under the specific care of the First, Second, or Third Mate.

It is a real worry, all right. For if they are annoyed now, still believing that they are about to head to New Zealand, how the hell will they feel when, inevitably, he must tell them that the whole thing is a sham? Just what will they say when he says there are no whale profits to come, and the reason they have come all this way is to aid and abet a prison breakout, something the British will see as a criminal exercise?

As it happens, some of the crew beat them to it as, only a few days after he has returned, Captain Anthony and Samuel Smith are onshore when they notice that the colours of the *Catalpa* have been lowered to half-mast – a sign of distress – and when they look closer, they can see two boats coming their way from the ship.

The first is filled with four crew-members making a break for it – including the eternal trouble-maker Cyrus Hill – the second boat, with the Second Mate and loyal crew-members, is in hot pursuit. Captain Anthony goes straight to the police and the men are quickly detained, and – bar the ringleader, Joseph McCarty, who had struck an arresting officer and was taken into custody for his trouble – returned to the ship, where they are chained in steerage. If ever there was a sign that Captain Anthony had been right in not entrusting his secret with the crew, this was it. For how damaging would that information be now, in the hands of a man like McCarty, bartering for his freedom?

(In fact, after the trouble-maker has served his seven days for assault, he will be set free, and try to come back on board, but Captain Anthony will not have it. He has been trouble ever since he joined them at Tenerife, and the ship is better off without him.)

Early Tuesday morning, 11 April 1876, Fremantle, his ship has sailed

John Breslin stops.

And stares.

It is gone.

HMS *Conflict* is no longer tied up to Long Jetty. Wandering down to the jetty, Breslin is soon engaged in casual conversation with some of the dock-workers. Oh yes, the *Conflict* had departed at dawn, bound for Albany as her first port of call, before heading all the way to Sydney.

Breslin moves quickly, heading to the Telegraph Office.

•

Coming down the Bunbury jetty at noon on Tuesday, 11 April, is a lad bearing a telegram. Trying not to betray his eagerness, Captain Anthony rips it open and reads: '– Your friend S. has gone home. When do you sail? J. Collins.'[36]

Breslin is ready and awaiting word from Captain Anthony.

The Massachusetts skipper heads to Customs House to secure clearance to depart – a formal process where he must declare that customs duties are in order. (Yes, they come aboard, and are assiduous in searching for stowaways – which includes thrusting sharp objects into every dark corner, between bags, under every overhang, but with the lack of screams in reply, the Customs men seem convinced that the affable American is a fit and proper person to depart these shores, with precisely the crew register he has submitted, on board, with no extras.)

Anthony then pops in at the hotel, about to head to the Telegraph Office to send a telegram to Breslin, when word arrives.

Officials from Customs have seized the *Catalpa*!

Once again convinced that the whole thing has come unstuck, a nervous Captain Anthony bustles back to Customs House, only to find that the issue is a barrel of pork that had not been properly cleared.

It takes some doing, but finally the officers agree that he is free to go. Alas, on this day, at least, it is too late, and they must wait for the morrow.

Still nervous, Captain Anthony writes his note at the Telegraph Office with a slightly shaking hand and sends it off to J. Collins of the Emerald Isle, Fremantle.

> *I'll sail to-day. Good-by. Answer, if received.*
> G. S. ANTHONY.[37]

Breslin answers immediately:

> *Your telegram received. Friday being Good Friday, I shall remain in Freemantle, and leave for York on Saturday morning. I wish you may strike oil. Answer, if received.*
> J. COLLINS.[38]

Oh.

Fair point.

Breslin is carefully drawing the skipper's attention to the fact that, as the prisoners will be in their cells on Good Friday, that day won't work. So they must plan for an escape on Holy Saturday. Quickly, Captain Anthony replies:

> *Yours received. Did not start to-day. Wind ahead and raining. Sail in the morning. Good-bye.*
> G. S. ANTHONY.[39]

And there certainly is wind ahead, for all that. A devastating wind, as it turns out – and the worst kind for Bunbury Harbour – lashing the coast from the harbour's exposed north-west, sending enormous rollers that have been building all the way across the Indian Ocean buffeting into the *Catalpa*. Even as Anthony clambers awkwardly aboard, the wind howls through the rigging.

What had been mere 'white horses' scudding across the harbour when he had left to send the telegrams are now watery battering rams, turning his whaler into a bucking bronco. Worse still, one glance at his barometer tells him the air pressure is falling fast. This is only going to get worse. Throughout the tempestuous afternoon, all they can do is hold on and pray for it to ease, but St Brendan the Voyager, patron saint of sailors – who also happens to be an Irishman, from today's County Kerry, to be sure – does not appear to be in a listening mood. For, as night darkens, so do the clouds, which unleash their fury in devastating sheets to slap the sailors' faces, a painful rebuke for venturing onto the overflowing deck.

In the open ocean, of course, there are a dozen ways to ride out a storm, all turning on the way you set your sails, and the course you set to or against the wind, with or against the waves. But not here, not fixed to one spot in the harbour as the waves continue to smash into and over the side of the *Catalpa*, a series of hammer blows so strong they threaten to break the anchor cable . . . which would see the bark hurled on the shore and smashed within seconds.

The cables hold, but the anchors don't. A series of sickening lurches and the men on board can feel themselves hurled ever closer to the sucking sands of the shore as the anchors shift on the sea-bottom.

Though the ship survives, *in extremis* – breaking one of the anchors in the process – sailing in such an enduring storm is out of the question, and Anthony must send a follow-up telegram . . . if he can.

He arrives at the Telegraph Office on Good Friday morning – the storm ever so slightly abated – to find it shut.

Religious folk are at church. The rest are at home.

Sick at heart – there could be nothing worse than Breslin springing the prisoners free and arriving at Rockingham Beach to find no whaleboat waiting for him – the American starts pounding on doors in the small settlement until he finds the woman he needs.

Will she open the Telegraph Office, so he can send a telegram?

No, says the woman.

'It would be useless, since the Fremantle office is closed.'[40]

It would need a stronger person than this woman, however, or at least one of meaner spirit, not to give in to Captain Anthony's earnest, nearly tearful pleas, and she finally agrees to open up, and try to send the telegram, even though she knows it to be a waste of time. 'Tis Good Friday after all.

Taking the key in hand, she starts tapping . . . - - - . . . - - - . . . even as she continues looking meaningfully at the Captain with every passing minute that they receive no response.

•

In faraway London, Lord Carnarvon is relieved.

It is a telegram from His Excellency Governor Sir William Robinson of the Colony of Western Australia, giving all assurances in response to his previous warning that there may be an attempt afoot to spring the Fenian soldiers from Fremantle:

> *The eight [Fenians] who are in prison will be carefully watched by the Comptroller General [Fauntleroy] and I think I may assure Your Lordship that any scheme of the nature referred to which may possibly be set on foot will end in total failure.*[41]

Lord Carnarvon takes him at his word.

•

The sound of snorting horses and that uniquely clutter-clattering of iron wheels rolling over the gravel road brings John Breslin immediately to the curtains in his room at the Emerald Isle Hotel.

It is him!

As promised, the ever-reliable Thomas Desmond has arrived from Perth in a four-wheeled trap pulled along by two fine horses.

That trap will be ideally suited to carry three convicts on the morrow, just as the trap that Breslin has secured, together with the finest pair of horses on offer in Fremantle, will do the same.

Breslin has already taken them out for a trial trot, and all is in top condition.

Everything is falling into place.

Breslin's only concern is that Captain Anthony will suffer misadventure. If he is not on Rockingham Beach at the time promised, in the spot promised, then all is lost, and Fremantle Prison would shortly be receiving

some new long-term inmates. Oh, how the British Empire would love to have back within its grasp the man who had freed James Stephens.

He is confident he can fulfil his side of the equation. And he is fairly sure that the Fenian prisoners will do their bit – remain calm, and seize their moment.

To bolster them, he has Elizabeth McCann convey them a letter with final instructions. They are to all behave well. *Nothing* should be different. They must not say goodbye to anyone. Most crucially, they must find a way to get away from their work details on the morning of the breakout and get to the gum tree by the piggery as close to eight o'clock as they can make it. The traps will be waiting until nine o'clock, ready to whisk them away.

Having sensed the rising anxiety among the men, Breslin concludes with a line which will hopefully give them some steel: 'We have money, arms, and clothes; let no man's heart fail him, for this chance can never occur again.'[42] He is right. Now or never. Now, or stay rotting in this living tomb.

Wilson takes one last look at the message, then tears it into small pieces before eating the lot. Before lock-down, he moves to whisper word of the message to the others.

McCann returns and conveys the message to Breslin that they have received his instructions.

All is in readiness.

•

'I told you it would be of no use,'[43] the lady in the Telegraph Office says finally, and prepares to shut down the instrument when . . .

When she is interrupted!

. . . - - - . . . - - - . . .

There is someone in the Fremantle office, after all!

Sitting down once more, she listens for a moment, and gives Captain Anthony the news.

'They are taking the message. An operator happened in.'

Caught right in the middle between shouting for joy and fainting with relief, Captain Anthony actually shows reasonable calm – like the peaceful eye of a storm – expressing his gratitude to the woman once more, before dictating his message:

> *J. COLLINS, ESQ.:—*
> *It has blown heavy. Ship dragged both anchors. Can you advance money,*
> *if needed? Will telegraph again in the morning.*
> *G. S. Anthony.*[44]

Hopefully, Mr Breslin will interpret this as Captain Anthony intends. For the problem is not getting more money, but more time. If necessary, can we have a few more days?

•

Mr Collins, a telegram for you.

Good Lord!

Dragged both anchors? A forewarning that Anthony might need money? This sounds terrible. It sounds as if the *Catalpa* has gone onto the sand bar and might be stuck for weeks. Have all their efforts now come to naught?

Inwardly, at least, Breslin slumps.

He must get another message to the prisoners that the planned breakout for the morrow is delayed. Such messages cannot always be quickly organised. The worst thing would be if one of them behaved in a dangerous manner – leaving a message in their cell, doing *something* – on the reckoning that it wouldn't matter anyway, as they would soon be on their way. And yet, just as the Lord taketh away, so does he giveth . . .

For there, now, is Big Bob Cranston, on his way from the prison into the town, on an errand for one of the warders. Quickly going after him, Breslin is able to get the message to him. The breakout tomorrow has been called off. Everyone must stay with their normal routines. It may be a matter of days, or a matter of weeks, before it is back on.

Cranston nods. He understands. He will tell the others.

Desmond is sent back to Perth to await developments, while John Breslin must pass the worst of nights, going through all possible scenarios, and, if it is as bad as he suspects, trying to work out a way to salvage the whaler and the situation.

The following day, Holy Saturday, in the mid-morning, when again the telegram boy arrives, Breslin is keenly aware that the content of the telegram he hands over, whatever it is, will likely tell their fate for weeks to come.

He rips it open, and reads.

> *I shall certainly sail to-day. Suppose you will leave for York Monday morning.*
> *Good-bye.*
> *G. S. Anthony.*[45]

It is back on!

Breslin heads to the Telegraph Office himself, and sends a reply.

> *Your telegram received. All right. Glad you got off without damage. Au revoir.*
> *J. COLLINS.*[46]

It really *is* happening. Now, everything must be quietly reactivated. Brennan is told that his role will be to go in the vanguard, early in the morning, inform those on the beach that the others are on their way – or race back to inform them if, perchance, the boat is *not* waiting for them. (In which case their best hope is to . . . pray. Beyond that, they will have to hide the best they can, and even have organised a 'safe house' to flee to, with Irish settlers, while organising their next move.)

King is sent to Perth on horseback to make sure that Desmond, with horses and trap, will be back by Sunday evening, ready for Monday morning.

Meantime, Breslin secures his own horses and trap for another two days and then heads out into Fremantle, hoping that, as had happened with Cranston the evening before, he will be able to see one of the prisoners. Miraculously, he does! For here now, on the jetty is none other than James Wilson, the very one whose impassioned letter, 'from the tomb', had really got this whole plot under way. He is on a work detail with a warden and several other prisoners.

Now, in previous conversation, Breslin had established with Wilson a signal – a tapping of the nose – that would mean, 'We start to-morrow morning.'[47]

Momentarily forgetting that he doesn't mean that at all, Breslin indeed makes the signal and is about to turn away when he sees Wilson's puzzled look.

For, locked in their cells on a Sunday morning, there will be no escape for any of them.

Oh. Oh dear.

Gathering himself, Breslin returns to Wilson and, choosing the exact moment when neither the warder or prisoners are looking their way, casually says, as simple as you please, 'Monday morning.'[48]

•

Not surprisingly, the chopping and changing, the sending of telegrams back and forth, the debilitating delays has put even the stoical John Breslin a little on edge . . . until, as he walks away from James Wilson, it suddenly dawns on him that 'Monday morning' is actually so perfect for the breakout, he can barely believe they didn't plan it like that in the first place!

For Monday morning is also when the Royal Perth Regatta will be beginning, set to showcase world-class rowing races on the Swan River, and establish who reigns supreme in the 'great rivalry existing between Perth and Fremantle in all sporting matters',[49] and in the process draw away much of the population of both towns, the Governors of the Colony and The Establishment, the police heads and the prison's highest officials. Oh yes, it is *the* day of the year to see who reigns supreme between the 'Portonians' of Fremantle, and the 'Metropolitans',[50] and everyone who is anyone must be there, putting on their best. For it is not just about seeing who wins the races – with everything from the '4-oared Gig Race, open to all comers, with a prize of £8', to 'a swimming race over 400 yards for a prize of £2'[51] on offer. It is about being seen at the races, in your finest, and ideally with your finest steed.

It is happening. It is *really* happening.

Down in Bunbury, Captain Anthony heads to Customs House once more, for official clearance for his departure. Fortunately, it is not long in coming.

So it is that, at two o'clock on this afternoon of Holy Saturday, Captain Anthony can give the orders.

'Weigh anchor!'

'Make sail!'[52]

A moderate breeze coming from the south-south-west fills the sails, and the *Catalpa* is soon in the open sea, heading to her position off Garden Island. Knowing what is to come, not long after sundown, Captain Anthony heads below for a sleep, only telling First Mate Smith to stick tight to the coast at no more than three knots.

'Wake me at midnight if all is well,' he says, 'but sooner if there is any change in the weather.'[53]

Woken after the twelfth hour, he is soon back on deck and relieved that they are being propelled by a fair and following wind, which stays with them at least until noon the following day, Easter Sunday, when they are some 15 miles south of Fremantle, right off Rockingham Beach.

Mr Smith, to my cabin, please.

Smith arrives to find the newly purchased charts of this part of the Western Australian coast spread across the table, and Captain Anthony eager to give him specific instructions.

Pointing out the lighthouse on Rottnest Island on the charts, Captain Anthony notes that it is 'twelve miles off-shore,' slightly to the north-west of Fremantle and 'one hundred and ninety-seven feet above the level of the sea, with a signal station on top from which the approach of vessels is signalled to the town'.[54]

Now, my dear Samuel, as we are now 15 miles off Rockingham Beach and 30 miles south-west off the lighthouse at Rottnest, here is the point.

The moment is upon us. I am about to head to shore in a whaleboat. I will spend the night on the beach with the men, pick up the Fenian prisoners tomorrow morning, and then we shall row back to you. You must lay off the land and keep a sharp lookout for my return. But when it comes to that lighthouse, meantime, you must stay well south of its range, so as not to signal that you are there. The broad plan is that when I get the prisoners, we will get out beyond the reef and meet you in international waters off Mandurah to the south, which will give us a rendezvous further removed from whatever the Fremantle authorities send at us.[55]

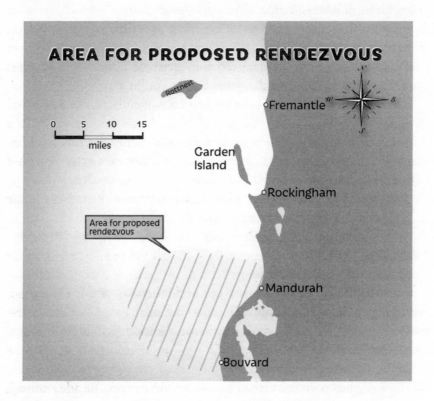

AREA FOR PROPOSED RENDEZVOUS

Rottnest

°Fremantle

0 5 10 15
miles

Garden
Island

°Rockingham

Area for proposed
rendezvous

°Mandurah

°Bouvard

Oh. And one more thing . . .

'If I do not come back,' Captain Anthony says, 'you must use your best judgement. Go whaling or go home, as you like.'[56]

The two rise and clasp hands. Theirs is a friendship that has seen sunny and joyous times, together with storms that both thought might see the end of them. But it has endured and prospered through it all, and that is precious. From this point on, Captain Anthony will be relying on Smith to keep the home fires burning, and he does so with the utmost confidence and gratitude.

The idea of commanding the whaleboat himself is a brave decision by Anthony, and beyond the original plan. By staying on the *Catalpa*, in international waters, he is safe and will not be breaching any British laws. But by actively aiding and abetting escaping prisoners within British jurisdiction, he suddenly risks decades in prison. Nevertheless, he feels he has no choice. It is a difficult and dangerous exercise, and while Sam Smith could do it, it is simply not fair to ask him to take the risk when he is not the one bearing primary responsibility to see the job done. Captain Anthony is, and he must do it alone.

Heading up to the deck, he is quick to assemble the crew he has selected after deep consideration of who on the voyage to date – most particularly including the dangerous exercise of killing whales – has shone through as good men to have beside you in a crisis.

He knows he can rely on his two best crew-members, Mr Sylvia and the sailor everyone knows simply as 'Toby'. As to the rest, he picks a Portuguese sailor by the name of Lewis, and two Malays, known as Mopsy and Lombard. Men, get your coats from below and be back here in two minutes.

'We are going to go ashore, and make our way to Fremantle for an anchor to supply the place of one that was broken in the gale at Bunbury,'[57] he cheerfully lies to them.

It makes a certain amount of sense, and all the men take him at his word.

'None of them,' Captain Anthony would recount, 'knew my errand, nor did anyone on board the ship except my mate . . . I kept it a secret from my boat's crew, for their own good, knowing that there was a great chance of our being caught, and feeling that in such a case their ignorance would clear them.'[58]

Throwing his own coat into one of the whaleboats, he adds enough supplies to get them through the next 24 hours – a couple of small kegs of water, half a boiled ham, and a bag of hardtack.

With all of the men present, the boat is attached first to the ropes swinging from the davits and now lowered to the waters below, before they all climb down on 'grip ropes' and take their place aboard.

It is one o'clock on Sunday afternoon. Yes, they are leaving the ship some 21 hours before they are due to meet with Breslin and the escaped Fenians on the beach the next day, but Captain Anthony is leaving plenty of time for misadventure. Whatever problems might lie ahead; he wants to have enough time to solve them.

And . . . stroke.

And . . . stroke.

And . . . stroke.

They pull away from the *Catalpa*, towards Rockingham Beach, well over the eastern horizon, some 15 miles away – a good distance, made easier when, once clear of the bark, they put up a sail to catch the prevailing onshore wind. Soon enough, as expected, just a couple of hours before dark, Garden Island appears and they steer to pass by on its southern end. Taking his brass spyglass, the skipper begins to earnestly scan the white sand ahead, the sand-hills and gum trees behind, looking for any sign of troopers waiting for them, any clue that their plans had been discovered. Mercifully, there is nothing, not that that means much. They would hardly be in the open. For all that, the American has the sails lowered to make themselves less visible to anyone nearby.

Though they are now close, Captain Anthony does not wish to make landfall until it is fully dark and they will have a better chance of landing unseen.

The problem, as it turns out, is not the danger of being seen, but that they are being overtaken by a danger unforeseen. For they suddenly hear repeated thunderous crashing, coming from just ahead of them. That thunder now engulfs them all as they are borne aloft at least ten feet on a series of raging breakers.[59]

Like men on a bucking horse, they are hurled every which way, as crashing white water bursts all around them.

Are they about to be swamped?

Not if Captain Anthony can help it.

Barking orders, he soon has the men moving their oars in exactly the right way and, just in time, is able to point the stern to the breakers, and their bow to the shore – to at least give them some chance of riding it out.

As if shot from an aquatic cannon, they surge forward. Three times it happens, as three waves hit them, still without carrying them until . . .

Until suddenly all is calm. Miraculously, the waves have carried them towards a gap in the reef and shot them straight through it, into safe waters once more.

They are now in the calm of Cockburn Sound, which lies on the lee side of the reef and Garden Island, protected from the anger of the ocean.

The men continue to pull hard, and Captain Anthony guides them in the last gasp of dusk by the outline of the topography he can dimly see onshore, particularly a magnificent gum tree he had noted the last time he was here, with Mr Breslin. The sound of lapping waves up ahead and the band of sand in the moonlight tell him they are just 50 yards away.

After their bow strikes sand, Captain Anthony wades through the gurgling waters to get his bearings on the beach itself.

No more than 100 yards from where they have landed, the American finds the plank he had pounded into the sand almost a week before, which again gives Captain Anthony pause. If there have been any informers, any leaks, any arrests and confessions in the time since his last contact with Mr Breslin, there is still every chance he and his men will be met with an armed force intent on arresting them, about . . . *now.* Straining his eyes, he looks for any sign . . . but sees nothing and no-one. And there is no-one.

It is 8.30 pm, Easter Sunday. They haul the boat out of the water onto the firm sand and settle down for a rough evening meal of ham and bread – for there can be no fire to cook anything – before the men fall asleep on the sand for the night.

Captain Anthony lies awake, staring up at the night sky wondering how Mr Breslin and his men are getting on, up Fremantle way.

•

Now that's a little odd.

This Easter Sunday evening at the Water Police base at Fremantle, the policeman on duty reads a report that has just come in from the lighthouse keeper on Arthurs Head. That afternoon he had observed, 'a strange sail in a somewhat peculiar position beating about outside Garden Island . . .'.[60]

The report is filed, for possible action tomorrow morning.

•

If it is not one thing, it is another.

Though Thomas Desmond has indeed returned to Fremantle with his trap, it is not with the fine horses of two days earlier, which had no longer been available. The influx of visitors into town for the Perth Regatta has meant the finest beasts are taken.

Mr Breslin himself has faced much the same issue as the fine horses he had selected have now been promised to Mr John F. Stone, the Superintendent of the Water Police, to go to the same event. Breslin knows Superintendent Stone quite well, having met him on many social occasions. With his men, the Superintendent is responsible for good order being kept on all visiting sailing vessels – ensuring they carry no contraband, no stowaways, and no escapees.

If Superintendent Stone wants 'Mr Collins's horse' he will have Mr Collins's horse, and no argument will be entered into by Mr Collins himself.

Ah, but things get grimmer still, for now Breslin's horse dealer, Henry Albert, admits the next best two horses have also been engaged by an important official going to the Regatta.

It means that all four of the fine horses they had been counting on have now been replaced by inferior nags. But things are too far advanced now to brook any further delay, even if it is catch-as-catch-can – and they have to scramble wildly, leaving the British to catch them if they can.

Of John Breslin's many concerns, one of the last remaining is to say goodbye to the buxom maid, his sweet Mary Tondut, who is ever so slightly beginning to pop out around the belly. Without giving her details – for even she must operate on a needs-to-know-basis – he makes clear that he will very shortly be departing, and gives her money to follow him to America, where they can settle, marry and raise their child.

•

Ask not for whom the owl hoots, it hoots in the haunting night for thee . . .

'Neath the Southern Cross on Rockingham Beach, Captain Anthony walks back and forth, worrying, going over everything, again and again. Will the escape party be there on time? What if mid-morning passes, and they go on into the afternoon, and there is still no sign. At what point would his loyalty to his own men, and the needs for their safety, over-ride his commitment to be right here, and 'meet you with my boat if God spares my life'.[61]

And on the subject of the men he has with him, at what point should he tell them what is afoot? Still none of them has asked, but that cannot endure long. It is not fair to them not to tell them. But, when?

Twice during the night, when he must wake his men to haul the boat higher from the rising tide, he considers it, but they are too sleepy, too grumbly, and it is not the moment.

And so he continues to pace, continues to worry.

On and on it goes, as his tracks become ever deeper on the sand in the moonlight, going over and over old ground, until the light in the east and the calls of the magpies, kookaburras and cockatoos taking over from the owls, indicates that dawn is not far away.

•

They are two figures in the night, some 12 miles apart.

It is just before dawn, Easter Monday.

The two Irishmen, John Walsh and Dennis McCarthy, are about to strike the first blow for the coming Republic of Ireland. At first light, they move. Five miles south of Fremantle, by the Bunbury road, Walsh shinnies up a telegraph pole and cuts the wire, which gives way with something between the sound of a whelp and a yelp, before he climbs down, hides the cut wire in nearby bushes, and goes on to the next five telegraph poles.

Six miles north of Fremantle, on the road to Perth, Dennis McCarthy does the same thing.

By sunrise, Fremantle is cut off from the outside world.

The breakout has begun . . .

CHAPTER ELEVEN

MAKING A BREAK FOR IT

It was on Easter Monday, in 'Seventy-six,
In Freemantle the jailers were all in a fix,
From Fauntleroy, down to Amen-timbertoe,
There was racing and chasing and bother, you know,
For the Fenians had 'sliddered' right off in a row.[1]

John Breslin, The Cruise of the Catalpa, 17 April 1876

Early morning, Easter Monday, 17 April 1876, opening the tomb
It is time.

On the dot of 5.30 am, Breslin calls for the Emerald Isle Hotel's ostler.

I wish you to harness Mr Brennan's trap with his horses, and bring it around the back. With Brennan already up and about, the two go down to see that it is done, and within a few minutes all the luggage of Mr Breslin, Mr Brennan, Mr Desmond and Mr King is loaded into the trap, together with some pistols and rifles carefully secreted. Finally they place on board boxes of ammunition and some basic provisions of food and water to keep them all going until they can reach the *Catalpa*.

Breslin goes back into the hotel to wake Desmond and King. He finds them sleeping lightly, if at all.

'We were all in a state of nervousness for fear that something unforeseen would turn up at the last moment,' King will recount. 'We were all awake and stirring.'[2]

By 6 am, Breslin is back outside and ordering Brennan to leave now for Rockingham Beach.

With a flick of his whip, Mr Brennan is on his way south.

An hour later, Mr Breslin leaves his room for what he hopes is the last time, and heads over to Albert's stable. Pausing momentarily in the Emerald Isle's courtyard to note with satisfaction that Thomas Desmond is harnessing his horses, nearly ready to go – a fact confirmed by an all but imperceptible nod from him.

The beaming John King is also there, with his horse saddled and tethered, and confirms that he, too, is ready to follow them hard, a little later, after he has determined whether or not the escape has been discovered. If necessary, he can also fight a rear-guard action to give the prisoners time to get away. And he won't be alone.

For with grim satisfaction, Breslin notes the rest of his rear-guard, Walsh and McCarthy, hovering nearby, having returned from cable-cutting duties. Each man is wearing a heavy great-coat under which, Breslin knows, they are armed to the teeth with pistols and a rifle each, together with plenty of ammunition.

'If there is a fight you are to join in,' Breslin had told them. 'If there is no fight, you are to remain behind.'[3]

Once the breakout occurs, each man is to return to his digs and wait. In case of failure to board the *Catalpa* for any reason, they would provide the safe houses necessary to provide succour to the fugitives, 'whilst awaiting a favourable opportunity to escape from the colony'.[4]

It is the Breslin way. Not only does he have a plan, but also a backup plan. And even that backup plan has a backup plan.

Very well then.

Arriving at Albert's stables, Breslin sees that his two horses are harnessed to the four-wheeled trap and are ready to go, just as he has ordered.

'Let them stand for twenty minutes,'[5] he tells the ostler. He will be back directly.

Breslin hurries back and confirms the plans with Desmond, who is finishing harnessing his steeds.

'Be ready to leave at half past seven.'[6]

Desmond nods. He has been preparing for this moment for months. He will be ready.

Once more heading to the stables of Henry Albert, Breslin jumps into the trap that has been prepared for him, and quickly covers the short distance to the Emerald Isle for the final time, where his men are ready for him. In that evil shadow cast by The Establishment over Fremantle in the early morning sun, the men move quickly and wordlessly, loading both traps with rifles, revolvers and ammunition.

Everything is in order.

There remain just two things left to do.

Now, not to forget . . .

First, they must actually grab the Irish prisoners from the jaws of the British lion.

And then they will have to flee for their lives to the other side of the planet.

•

Inside Fremantle Prison, it is time for the prisoners on duty to fall in. They have been up since 5 am, folded their beds, tidied their cells, been fed their bread and tea for breakfast, and stood outside their cells until the bell rings to summon them to the prison yard.

There they stand, shoulder to shoulder in tight ranks of dreariness, eyes cast down, backs straight, hands by their sides, not saying a word until their numbers are called.

'9702?'

'Here,' says Cranston.

'9707?'

'Here,' says Darragh.

'9915?'

'Here,' says Wilson.

'9757?'

'Here,' says Harrington.

'9758?'

'Here,' says Hassett.

'9767 . . . ?'

'Here,' says Hogan.

All present and accounted for, sir.

What remains now is to be assigned to their warders and marched out to their various work details. Among the six Fenians, there is a barely restrained tension, but restrain it they must – at least the outward expression of it. To a man, they know that today really is the day. After a decade of waiting, of yearning, of praying to God for their liberation, it is possible – pray to Mary – that they have just spent their last night in prison and . . .

And there is a problem.

The inveterate drunk Fenian, Thomas Delaney – in and out on ticket-of-leave – is aware of the plan and now, in the slim, inopportune window between parade and work, he insists he wishes to come too. Wilson delivers the speech of his life in an irate whisper: you are not coming. It is too late. You are NOT coming. You place everything at risk. If you insist, our own insistence to either stop you, or exact revenge for stopping us, will not be pretty. Thomas, you are NOT COMING.

It is done. Delaney, glowering, gets the message.

•

Now in full daylight down on Rockingham Beach, Captain Anthony is appalled to see something that he had not only missed the night before, but which had also entirely escaped his attention when he first visited the beach in the company of John Breslin. For, just half a mile up the beach, towards Fremantle, is a working timber station – a jetty large enough for a steamer to pull in, and load logs, and very likely the origin of that fresh plank he'd found on the beach and stuck in the ground as a marker – and before long a gang of five men appear and begin work, hauling logs down onto the jetty, clearly in preparation for a boat to take them away.

As for Captain Anthony's own men, they too are up and about, brushing the sand from their clothes, wolfing down some more ham and bread for breakfast, and looking expectantly to him for orders.

What now, skipper?

7.30 am, Easter Monday, 17 April 1876, Fremantle, all aboard for Rockingham!

The gentle *clip-clop-clip-clop* of horse hoofs on the stony streets of Fremantle on this sparkling morning attracts no attention. It is no more than a well-heeled-looking fellow in a top-hat, going about his business courtesy of a pair of horses and a four-wheeled trap. He's likely off to the Perth Regatta with the rest of Swan River's finest.

Ah, but if only the good burghers of Fremantle could know what business Thomas Desmond is on, how different their reaction would be.

Leaving the Emerald Isle Hotel along a different route, John Breslin heads towards High Street with his own trap and pair of horses.

Yes, he does give one quick glance to note that the *Georgette* is at her moorings, a lazy trail of smoke coming from her funnel as she prepares for the day's errands, but that is all he gives her. For he has the air of a man meandering, with no cares to speak of, and just a general inclination to head towards the bigger burgh until, on the edges of Fremantle . . . he pulls lightly on the right reins to circle around to the road which runs below Fremantle Prison, and is soon proceeding at a leisurely pace, the horses just *clip-clopping* casually, right past The Establishment just at the time that some of the prisoners are out and about on their work details of the day.

Again, barely glancing their way, Breslin keeps drifting by – *clip* . . . *clop* . . . *clip* . . . *clop* – and can feel that he has been seen by those who count. His rendezvous point beneath the well-known tree is just a mile down this road, on the way to Rockingham. Sure enough, soon coming up beside him, and not even glancing his way, is Thomas Desmond.

As planned, they stop 'neath the shade of the designated gum tree.

Without a word, Desmond hands Breslin three hats and three coats he has brought with him.

All set?

All set.

Very slowly, about 50 yards apart – the minimum distance to show they just happen to be on the same road at the same time, without travelling together – the two traps head back up the road towards Fremantle Prison, their eyes peeled.

It is 7.55 am.

In the dining room of the Emerald Isle Hotel, John King is taking his leave, when, momentarily alone, he notices a large cake on the sideboard . . .

Why not?

At the exact instant when none of the few people in the dining room are looking his way, he reaches out, grabs it, puts it under his coat, and walks out grinning.

•

It is 7.55 am.

James Wilson and Michael Harrington are off to their work detail, down by Fremantle Harbour, while Martin Hogan is heading off with two other convicts to his duties of painting the verandah of the house of the Governor, his stately residence nestled snugly alongside the Gatehouse, on the terrace in front of the prison. Governor Fauntleroy is, of course, off at the Regatta with his family, meaning the convicts and their warders have the place entirely to themselves.

And wouldn't you know it? On this same morning, Thomas Darragh and Thomas Hassett have been assigned to plant potatoes in the back garden of the nearby home of the Clerk of Works of the Convict Department, James Broomhall. Yes, five of the six Fenians have been assigned work duties within coo-ee of the prison walls, while the only one with duties inside, Robert Cranston, takes the opportunity to decamp from his duties at the Stores Room, the cool underground room where food supplies are kept.

Taking from his pocket an enormous key he has previously purloined, he swings it from his finger on a piece of string. *La-de-di, dum-da-da*, Cranston appears to be no more than a trusted lackey, a prisoner going about his business on this bright Easter Monday.

Arriving at the Gatehouse, he tells Francis Lindsey – the Gatekeeper and once-reticent disciplinarian who'd been promoted to Warder after shooting an escapee – that he has an urgent message from the household of the Governor, which requires a couple of the prisoners now on work detail to come with him to move some furniture. He just has to retrieve them.

A little bored, Gatekeeper Lindsey waves the Fenian convict through. Cranston is a frequent bearer of messages and, clearly, any man moving in and out of a prison with a key swinging from his finger – the key to the vice-regal residence, no less – is a man to be trusted.

Who is Lindsey to question him, when the most senior officer of the entire prison so trusts him?

Quickly proceeding down towards the south jetty, Cranston overtakes the party of convicts just before they arrive by the new jetty on the south harbour for today's task of 'quarrying and dressing stone for dock purposes'.[7] They are under the watchful eye of warder Thomas Booler.

Well, hello there.

Showing Warder Booler the key, Cranston says, as easy as you please, 'I have been sent to take Wilson and Harrington to move some furniture at Government House . . .'[8]

Really?

Booler is uncertain.

It seems a little irregular to take the convicts from their assigned role to go to another role. Why hadn't he been told about this before?

And anyway . . .

'I cannot spare both men off the works.'[9]

'They will only be away a short time,'[10] Cranston assures him, before using the same trick as before.

'Here is the key of the gate,' he says, flourishing said key. It is a reminder that he is so trusted he has been given the *gate key*, so who is Booler to question him?

So . . . so be it. The warder, considering that Cranston has received 'a verbal request from "Head Quarters" to perform a bona fide service'[11] before, nods his acquiescence, and says, 'Wilson, Harrington, go with Cranston'.[12]

Grumbling lightly at the imposition, Wilson and Harrington put down their tools, follow Cranston, and are soon out of sight, heading up High Street in the direction of Government House, out on the Mandurah Road – or what the locals tend to call the Rockingham Road – a mile or so down the rise from the prison, the closest building to the gum tree where John Breslin will, hopefully, be waiting.

Alas, for Big Bob, Wilson and Harrington there's a small problem. They cannot get to the rendezvous point by going the shortest route, through Fremantle's commercial streets – as convicts like them are seldom seen there, and would stand out. Instead, they must go the long way, back up towards the prison and right by the yard of the Pensioner Barracks. Hopefully there will be no nosey guards out the front.

Keep your head down, men, hurry.

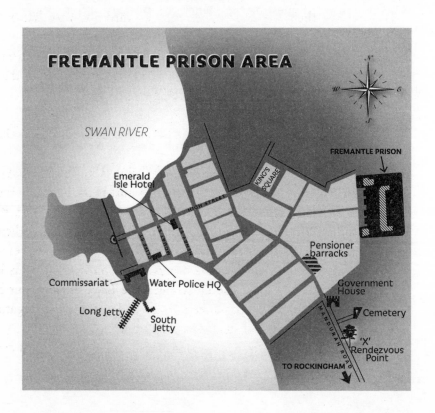

•

What a great day to be alive!

Right on the edge of manhood, at the age of 13, Billy Lynch had never been much one for school in any case, and the wonderful thing is that because this is Easter Monday, there is no school.

Closing the door of his family's barracks, a terraced cottage in the Pensioner Barracks right by Fremantle Prison – where his father, as a Military Pensioner, is engaged as a works supervisor – he quickly joins the sons of other prison warders to decide how they will spend their precious free time.

Very likely they will go 'bird-nesting', pinching eggs from birds' nests and collecting them the way some kids collect stamps.

Yes, let's!

Still, they have only gone along the road as far as Government House when the day is already so hot, they decide to go swimming down by Fremantle Harbour instead.

Yes, let's!

They retrace their steps, past the barracks yard and turn left onto Fremantle's High Street, leading down to the beach, when . . .

Hulloa, who is this? Why it's three convicts hurrying towards them – in full prison garb.[13] But it's all right, young Billy knows one of them well. It's 'Big Bob' Cranston, the prison letter-carrier.

'Hi, Big Bob!'[14] Billy calls cheerily.

'Go away,' Big Bob growls back, as he passes in a rush, the other two tightly behind him.

Billy is stunned, and a little bit hurt. Fancy being talked to like that by Big Bob, and in front of his mates! In fact, so hurt is he, he just stands there for a moment, while his mates go on ahead to the harbour. Big Bob talk to him like that? It's just not right. Billy stays standing there, watching them go, all the way to the Rockingham Road corner, before he turns back, to catch up with the others at the harbour. Idly, as he arrives, Billy notes the huge paddle steamer, the *Lady Stirling*, out by the north jetty, loading up passengers to go to Perth for the Regatta. Perhaps they should try and steal a passage on it?

Forget Big Bob and his strange reaction. This is going to be a great day!

•

You there! Stop!

It's a stern sergeant shouting from the yard of the Pensioner Barracks.

Cranston, Wilson and Harrington look up in unison to see a military guard of 24 soldiers on parade, all of them staring.

What are you doing? Where are you going? What is your business?

The Fenians freeze. This is not a sergeant who will be fooled by familiarity and the swagger of having a big swinging key.

Perhaps they can fool him with unfamiliarity.

Like a card-sharp on the Dublin docks, Big Bob Cranston pulls out the ace from his inside pocket, and casually shows the sergeant. It is a forged written order, beneath official letterhead, with instructions to allow Cranston to get Wilson and Harrington and take them 'to Government House to remove furniture'.[15]

Lindsey and Booler would have recognised the forgery in an instant. But this sergeant is not familiar with this part of the process. Carefully looking at it, he nods, and hands it back.

They move on.

A few minutes later, when they have gone around the corner, Wilson and Harrington even start to breathe again. It is only at this point that they warmly congratulate Big Bob on his ruse, on having a fall-back forged document against the chance of what has occurred. The main thing is, they are still free, still moving to their rendezvous.

•

Excuse me, Warder Liddelow?

Yes, Hogan, what is it?

I just need to nip back and get some kerosene, to make sure my paint brushes don't clag up – I'm afraid I have spilt the last lot. I am very sorry.

Very well, but don't be long in getting back here.

Warder Albert Liddelow decides to take the opportunity to go inside Governor Fauntleroy's residence to check on the three convicts cleaning the chimneys, as the Governor had specifically told him to keep a close eye on these convicts while they were in his home alone. As Liddelow goes inside, it leaves Hogan momentarily alone to do one more thing before he departs.

Surveying his handiwork, he is satisfied.

Putting down his pail of paint and his brushes, he too is soon out of sight, taking his kerosene can with him. Within minutes he is over at Mr Broomhall's place, where he can see Thomas Darragh and Thomas

Built by convicts, the Fremantle Prison – known as The Establishment – was made of limestone quarried on site. The convicted Fenians imprisoned here had a punishing schedule of manual labour which started at 4.30 am and concluded at 6 pm.

(1859 watercolour of the Main Cell Block, by Henry Wray (1824–1900). Courtesy of the National Library of Australia.)

The Pensioner guards were mostly comprised of retired soldiers who acted as security on the *Hougoumont* and then took up roles at The Establishment.

(Enrolled Pensioner Force, Perth, ca. 1868. Courtesy of the State Library of Western Australia.)

Conditional Pardon

Whereas Reg. No 9735. John Flood was convicted of Treason Felony at Dublin in Ireland in the month of April one thousand eight hundred and sixty seven, and sentenced to Fifteen Years Penal Servitude.

And Whereas Her Most Gracious Majesty Queen Victoria issued a Warrant under Her Sign Manual and Signet, given at the Court of St. James's on the Twenty Ninth day of December one thousand eight hundred and seventy in the Thirty fourth Year of Her Reign and directed to the Governor of Her Majesty's Territory of Western Australia, Whereby Her Said Majesty was graciously pleased to grant to the said John Flood a Pardon for the Crime of which he stands convicted, on condition that the said John Flood shall not return to the United Kingdom of Great Britain and Ireland during the remainder of the said above mentioned term of Penal Servitude.

Now I Frederick Aloysius Weld, Governor and Commander in Chief of the Territory of Western Australia aforesaid, Do hereby certify and make known to all whom it may concern that the said John Flood has become entitled to the above mentioned Conditional Pardon of Her Most Gracious Majesty Queen Victoria

Given under my Hand and the Public Seal of the said Territory at Government House Perth this Thirteenth day of March in the Year of our Lord, one thousand eight hundred and seventy one

Fred A. Weld

Governor and Commander in Chief

Conditional Pardons were granted to the civilian Fenians in March 1871, including John Flood – whose original sentence of 15 years ended at just five years.

(Courtesy of the Mitchell Library, State Library of New South Wales.)

At just over 200 tons and 90 feet long, with a depth of just over 12 feet, and three masts, the *Catalpa* was a substantial vessel. ('Bark Catalpa' by Charles Sidney Raleigh. Donated to the New Bedford Whaling Museum in 1961.)

Whaler Captain George S. Anthony agreed to captain the *Catalpa*, which they hoped would take the Fenian prisoners to the safety of the United States.

John Breslin became involved with the Fenian movement in 1865, while working as a medico at Richmond Bridewell Prison. It was from here that he orchestrated the escape of Fenian leader, James Stephens. Ten years' later, in 1875, he set sail to West Australia with Thomas Desmond to implement the daring plan to rescue the Fremantle Six.

ESCAPE OF FENIAN CONVICTS FROM FREMANTLE, WESTERN AUSTRALIA.

Breslin, Desmond and their six runaways stole away from the prison to meet Captain
Anthony at their rendezvous point at Rockingham Beach.

('Escape of Fenian convicts from Fremantle, Western Australia', engraving, paper, ink, published in the *Australasian Sketcher*.)

The missing convicts made their escape on an American whaleboat, but their
abscondment was quickly discovered and a police boat (left) and the *Georgette* (right)
were sent to intercept the prisoners.

Major Charles Finnerty served as the Commanding Officer of the Mounted Troopers in Fremantle and commanded the Pensioner guards aboard the *Georgette* tasked with capturing the escaped Fenians. (Photograph courtesy of Royal Western Australian Historical Society.)

The six Fenians arrived in New York, where thousands of well-wishers awaited to celebrate their escape. ('The grand procession in honor of the Fenian exiles, in New York City, February 9, 1871', Haasis & Lubrecht, publishers.)

John Devoy received an Honour Guard as he arrived to meet William Cosgrave, the President of the Executive of the Irish Free State. (Photograph by W.D. Hogan, 1924. Courtesy of the National Library of Ireland.)

Mrs E. Kilmurry of Naas, née Eliza Kenny of Tipper, County Kildare. (John Devoy Family Photographic Collection. Courtesy of the National Library of Ireland.)

John Devoy, back in Ireland in 1924. (Photograph by W.D. Hogan. John Devoy Family Photographic Collection. Courtesy of the National Library of Ireland.)

Hassett planting their potatoes. With a low whistle, he gets their attention. Both men are so trusted they have no warder at all, and so it is a simple matter to quietly start walking towards Hogan – though Hassett keeps his shovel with him, as if he is going on an errand himself. All three are quickly out on the road, where they can see Wilson and Harrington with Cranston, all of them walking fast, just ahead . . .

•

John Breslin spots them first.

It is a group of three men in convict garb, hurrying down the road towards them.

With a sharp word to Desmond, and two flicks of their whip, both traps are quickly trotting down the road to meet them.

Reaching them first, Breslin recognises Wilson, Cranston and Harrington, and with a nod of his head to the road behind, tells them to get into Desmond's trap.

In anticipation, Mr Desmond is already wheeling his horses around so they are facing Rockingham when the breathless convicts climb aboard.

Quickly, gentlemen. Here are your coats, here are your hats and . . . here is your hurry. We will make day-tripping civilians out of you yet.

With enormous relief and excitement, Breslin now sees the next three convicts, Darragh, Hogan and Hassett, and sends his horses quickly trotting towards them. Hogan is carrying a kerosene can and Darragh a spade. Recognising Mr Breslin – their salvation! – Hogan kicks the kerosene can away as if it were a football, while Hassett breaks into a grin and hurls his spade into the bushes. They would love to jump into the trap, and pause only for Mr Breslin to wheel his horses around, only . . .

Only to find the horses revolt at the prospect. Spooked by the bang of the clattering kerosene can, they become fractious and refuse to turn, whereupon the cursing Darragh grabs one by its halter and tries to *lead* it around. Now the animal is so alarmed it bucks and plunges violently enough that Mr Breslin fears it will break the harness.

'Let him go!'[16] Breslin shouts.

Mercifully, the animal calms, and by trotting a little further up the road to a wider spot, Mr Breslin is indeed able to wheel the horses around, bring them back, and pick up the three infinitely relieved convicts, who are quickly donning their own hats and coats that Mr Breslin has with him.

Home, James, and don't spare the horses!

Mr Breslin certainly does *not* spare them, and they are soon cantering south towards Rockingham Beach, even as the three men beside him grasp the revolvers and rifles proffered them and – *click, click, click* – smoothly load the chambers. After a decade of being prisoners under guard, they are now, suddenly, soldiers once more. Mr Desmond and his three men are already out of sight. There is a momentary panic a few minutes later, when a galloping horseman comes at them from behind – Breslin grips his loaded pistol with intent – but it proves to be the grinning John King who reports that, 'All was quiet when I left.'[17]

As fast as they can, they push on, down the road to freedom that most of these convicts had happened to pave themselves – fate can be a cruel mistress, but perhaps she is a Fenian herself. The thick bush, the towering gums, the pressing wandoo and jarrah trees flash by on either side as they rattle along through the dappled light. The horses grunt and whinny, the wheels creak and protest against the pace, flocks of cocka-toos take flight in screeching riot as these wild geese charge through.

No longer are they convicts, however. Suddenly, they have become experienced tough soldiers, with arms, who are prepared to fight for their freedom. It will be a brave lot who tries to stop them now.

•

Strange. Things are quiet. Maybe a little . . . *too* quiet.

Where has Big Bob Cranston got to?

Back at the prison, it has been noted by Gatekeeper Francis Lindsey that the Fenian prisoner has been gone a rather long time? When one of the warders mentions in passing his absence to the Superintendent, he references the fact that Cranston was last seen with a key going out through the Gatehouse to get some men to help move some of the Governor's furniture, so . . .

So, where is he now?

Gatekeeper Lindsey has no answer for him.

One thing is for sure, once they find him, his punishment will be severe. Quickly now, some prison guards are dispatched to look for him. He most certainly can't be far away.

•

At Governor Fauntleroy's residence, Warder Albert Liddelow, now returned from checking on the chimney-sweepers, is equally troubled. Where has Hogan got to? He had just gone to get more kerosene, and had promised he would not be long. But he should have been back long before now.

Has he perhaps already come back and is working somewhere else around the house?

Walking to the side of the house, Liddelow suddenly sees it – nothing less than Hogan's farewell card. Around the side, Hogan had painted one of the prison governor's windows emerald green. *Erin go Bragh!*

Liddelow starts running towards the gatehouse of The Establishment.

•

Down at Fremantle Harbour, meanwhile, Thomas Booler, the warder who had allowed Wilson and Harrington to leave with Cranston, keeps glancing up High Street in the direction of the prison, expecting them back. It most certainly shouldn't be taking this long?

The seconds tick by, and with every passing minute, Warder Booler feels ever sicker.

They couldn't have, could they . . . ?

Finally, he decides he has no choice and must report their absence. He begins to walk back up the hill, his eyes scanning up and down every street he crosses, hoping to see their familiar forms loping his way.

But there is nothing, and very nearly nobody, as the streets are all but deserted for the Regatta.

•

To this point Superintendent Joseph Doonan has been having a good day, as all is calm and this week he has something to look forward to – on the morrow, His Excellency the Governor will be visiting in the company of the Chief Justice of the Supreme Court of Western Australia, His Honour Sir Archibald Burt, the latter to lay the cornerstone in readiness for the construction of the new Freemasons' building. Doonan's dear wife, Harriet, has already put aside his best uniform for the occasion, and will be wearing her own best dress and . . .

And suddenly, everything caves in.

There are sounds of whistles in the yard, and running feet, and now a warder comes tumbling, stumbling to his door, to give him the news.

Gatekeeper Lindsey begs to inform him that a man is missing.

A *Fenian*.

Who?

Bob Cranston.

Sick of stomach, Gatekeeper Lindsey is explaining how he'd allowed Cranston to leave the prison, swinging a key, because he had said he'd been told to get some men to help to move furniture in the Governor's house . . . when Warder Booler arrives wondering if anyone has seen those perfidious laggard wretches, Wilson and Harrington?

Why, where did you last see them?

They went with Cranston to move furniture at Government House.

But Cranston is missing too.

And now here is Warder Liddelow, who'd been minding Hogan. He begs to report that the prisoner is missing, having gone to get kerosene, he's not been seen since!

That makes four missing, maybe more.

Quickly, where are the other Fenian prisoners?

Thomas Darragh and Thomas Hassett? They're planting potatoes behind Broomhall's house.

Guards are quickly dispatched, and they return with the feared but expected news: they're gone!

Around Fremantle Prison now, gates are being closed, whistles are being blown, orders are being roared, and guards are running in all directions.

We need a roll call!

We need to know if anyone else is gone.

And, most of all, we need to recapture the Fenians.

All eyes are on Superintendent Doonan as an earnest discussion ensues between him and his most senior officers. Clearly the prisoners have gone, but where could they go *to*? How could they possibly make good their escape?

A ship is the only answer. Have there been any suspicious ships around of late? What about that whaler that put into Bunbury a fortnight or so ago, whose Captain has been seen out and about in Fremantle of late, what is that vessel's name?

The *Catalpa*?

That's it. We need to know, first and foremost, if she is still at Bunbury, or has been sighted elsewhere.

Superintendent Doonan has heard enough. Fenian prisoners missing. American whaler suspected. Where would the Fenians go to get on a boat to take them to the whaler? Obviously one of the beaches between here and Bunbury, and probably one of the ones closest to Fremantle.

On the instant, Constable 'Big John' McKenna is put in charge of a trooper and two black-trackers, given the finest steeds available, and dispatched south at all possible speed.[18]

•

All together, Messrs Breslin and Desmond, with their six runaways, proceed quickly, at least over the first ten miles, where the road is good, with Desmond's trap in the lead and Breslin's just far enough back that they are not choked by the dust.

Slowing down to pass through the sorry hamlet of Ten Mile Well – for it simply will not do to attract attention in any manner – the horses are momentarily able to get their breaths back, before Messrs Breslin and Desmond reach for their whips once more and now it is Mr Breslin who, with the better horses, takes the lead.

And yet, for the next six miles, they must slow down anyway as the road is rough and their traps jerk from side to side, the men inside thumping from one rut to the next.

•

At Rockingham Beach, Captain Anthony and his five men continue to wait, their ears straining for the sound of anyone approaching. It has been agreed that they will meet in the mid-morning, and it is already 10 am. If all has gone well, the men from Fremantle will be here soon.

Of course, if things have gone very badly, there is also a chance that those arriving will be troopers.

•

Some 14 miles off Rockingham Beach, the *Catalpa* continues lightly sailing back and forth, essentially holding position off Garden Island. Without Captain Anthony things are quite relaxed, and all Samuel Smith knows is that, if all goes well, he should be seeing the skipper and the rest of the crew sometime in the mid-afternoon. Of course, he can't help but wonder how they are faring.

•

The messenger from The Establishment arrives a'gallop with two urgent telegrams to be sent to Albany and Perth – to, respectively, recall HMS *Conflict*, and to alert His Excellency the Governor of an escape – only to find . . . curious inactivity. Instead of the woman behind the desk pounding away at a key, there is confusion, bewilderment and silence.

What is going on?

The lines to both Albany and Perth are dead. It seems likely that someone has cut them. We have men out there now, looking for the break. We will let you know when we are again able to send telegrams. But it is unlikely to be in the next hour or so.

•

Oh my Lord.

Throughout the mid-morning, growing progressively more anxious to hear the sound of approaching traps – but hearing only the lapping of waves, the cawing of seagulls, and a breeze that slyly whispers that things might be going wrong – George Anthony has kept an eye on the workmen loading timber on to yonder jetty, hoping that they will keep to themselves. But, no . . .

One man detaches himself from the others, and starts to walk on the wet, firm sand towards them. Captain Anthony, in turn, starts to walk towards the stranger, the better to keep him away from the men and the whaleboat.

'What's going on?' the red-headed buck of a man asks, when they meet some 400 yards down the beach, with the air of one who has a right to know. Now red-heads, true, are oft just like that, but the muscles on this man, and his attitude, says he also usually gets an answer.

'I am bound to Fremantle for an anchor, to supply the place of one broken,' Captain Anthony says lightly. 'We've come this far, and have just stopped to rest.'[19]

But the man – a local farmer by the name of James Bell,[20] who had been herding cattle on the common and is not actually a timber worker – is not impressed.

'Lad,' says he, 'you've hooked it from some ship, and I advise you to get out. This is no place to lay.'[21]

'I *am* the master of a ship,'[22] Anthony insists, but the man is not convinced.

Very well then. Let the skipper come to the point.

'What is the best way to get out with my boat?'[23] he asks the local directly.

Very well, then. Let the local be equally frank. Now he leans forward, slightly conspiratorially.

'I *knew* you were after somebody.'[24]

Now, they understand each other.

'Keep close to Garden Island,' the fellow advises. 'There is a dangerous reef further out, and it would be sure destruction to the boat to attempt to go out that way.'[25]

There is more, much more, as this remarkably garrulous chap explains the labyrinth of reefs that lie between them and the open sea and how the best way to thread them is to head south, once you have got through the first gap next to Garden Island, and then head just to the west of Point Peron, before again edging your way to the south-west.

Quietly aghast, Captain Anthony realises that the path of sure destruction pointed out – the white water over yonder coral reef – is *exactly* the way he had come in the previous night. Those blind rollers that had carried them to shore must have taken them right over those very reefs. How close they had come to complete failure, and worse.

Captain Anthony absorbs it all, and shakes the man's hand, who soon heads off whence he came, which is a relief. Anthony is just heading back towards his men when he hears a noise, behind. He turns to see a horse with a trap, galloping towards him, along the beach. In the trap is Brennan, carrying the luggage of Breslin, King and Desmond. Having lost his way in the rough track leading to the beach, he has come out on to the sand at an unexpected place and pace, and is clearly infinitely relieved to see the American mariner. But he has one query . . .

'Who is that man?' Brennan asks, indicating the departing stranger.

'He's working on that jetty,' Captain Anthony replies.

'We must shoot him,' says Brennan flatly.

'There will be no shooting yet. Where are the others?'

'Close behind,' says Brennan, even as he starts to throw down the valises and bags.

At least Brennan hopes they are close behind, having had no contact with them since setting off.

•

Steady now.

Slowly, *slowly*.

Pulling back on the reins in the lead trap, Breslin brings the horses down from a canter to a *clip-clop* as they pass through the small settlement of Rockingham. With his three companions looking intensely casual beside him, their grins fixed in place with determined casualness, Breslin waves with earnest cheer to the proprietor of the Rockingham Hotel, William Summers,[26] who is standing in the doorway and glad to see them. Surely so many men in a couple of traps like theirs, might stop for a drink on this hot morning? But no, Mr Collins shows no sign of slowing down. Never mind. Mr Summers still calls out cheerily to him:

'What time will the *Georgette* be at the timber jetty?'

What?

'The *Georgette* was at the jetty in Fremantle when I left,' Breslin calls back lightly, 'but I do not know when she will be at Rockingham.'[27]

He trots on.

(*Good Lord. It seems there is some chance that the* Georgette *might soon be coming this way? This was not in their plans.*)[28]

The instant they are out of sight of the Rockingham settlement, Breslin thrashes his horses once more.

As they approach the rendezvous point on the beach – just four miles to go, now! – things become slower still on the sandy track, with the wheels of their traps frequently sinking so deep that it is all the horses can do to keep going. Every now and then, the escaped prisoners must leap from their seats and put their shoulders to the wheel to keep the traps moving, but keep moving they do.

And soon they can smell the sea, and feel the breeze off the water, and the heavy, pressing bush starts to give way to seaside scrub.

They are close, very close.

Erin go Bragh!

•

Now here is King, galloping onto the beach on a horse that is nearly as breathless as he is. Racing on ahead, his job is to establish whether or not the whaleboat is indeed there, and he is infinitely relieved to see it and Captain Anthony with his men there.

'We have got away with the prisoners,' he calls to the Yankee skipper, 'and they will be at the beach in a short time.'[29]

With that happy news imparted – for the whaling Captain is equally relieved – King turns and races back to meet the oncoming traps.

Captain Anthony turns his attention back to his crew, still hovering nervously by the whaleboat, some of them taking what shade they can by lying down in its shadow. They have been ashore for 14 hours now, still with no clue what they are doing here, and only a strong presentiment that something climactic is about to happen. They just don't know what it is yet, but whatever it is, it is likely urgent. The skipper has insisted they push the boat down to the water's edge and rig up the detachable mast so they can launch at a moment's notice.

Trying to address their disquiet, Captain Anthony talks calmly to them.

'Obey my orders and no harm will come to you.'[30]

To action, men. Push the boat into the water and stand by – each man next to his rowing position – ready to push off. Our guests will be here shortly.

Guests? What guests?

Captain Anthony goes on.

As soon as they are in the boat, look to me.

'When I give the order, shove the boat off as quickly as possible, to take the oars and pull. Whatever happens, don't be afraid.'[31]

The men look at each other nervously. Just what is happening?

Captain Anthony keeps looking to the bush bordering the beach, hoping, *praying*, for the expected men's speedy arrival.

Fifteen minutes later, he is rewarded with the sound of a clatter of hoofs, and creaking of wheels, coming their way.

•

Here they are!

At least, here come some horses and traps, at roughly the time expected, and Captain Anthony is filled with hope that these are their men arriving for the planned rendezvous, not the troopers come to capture them.

There is Breslin, in the first trap, waving his hat at him, with Desmond wielding the whip in the one behind. And both traps are carrying three disguised convicts apiece!

Quickly now, as the traps pull up, the six Fenians scramble out, all of them notable for their broad grins. More noteworthy still, however, is that visible beneath their long linen coats are both their prison garb of calico smock and grey trousers, and the fact that around those suits they have leather belts from which hang two six-shooters apiece. Still not content with those, the first thing the former soldiers do once they have their boots on the sand is to reach into the carriages for rifles and cartridges, and move towards the whaleboat.

What on *earth* is going on?

Down by the whaleboat the sailors still stand, aghast, and in some ways alarmed at these developments, which appear to be climaxing with six heavily armed men now charging towards them across the sands, just like military men, if a little scrawny.

Surely, these must be government officials, come to arrest Captain Anthony? Instinct takes over. They will fight for his freedom! While one Malay sailor draws his knife, the others reach for whatever weapons come to hand – from oars to wooden buckets – as they prepare to defend themselves! It takes several sharp cries from Captain Anthony, in a handful of languages, to avert disaster.

So, these armed men piling into the whaleboat are our guests? Our friends, not our enemies?

Well, if you say so.

But, given their guns, and haste, it seems clear that whoever their enemies are, they are likely not far behind.

At least Captain Anthony can take heart from one thing in particular, as he gets a close-up look at his guests for the first time. These men handle their weapons like professional soldiers and wear a look of pure determination – they will not be going back to that prison, that's for sure.

While Breslin and Desmond quickly lead the horses and traps back up the track a little, to hopefully block whoever might be coming, the six Fenians, King and Brennan leap into the whaleboat and 'stow themselves in the smallest possible space, so as not to interfere with those at the oars'.[32]

Breslin and Desmond are soon leaping into the boat as well.

'Shove off, men!' Captain Anthony yells. 'Shove off!'[33]

Before they can, the troublesome red-headed farmer, James Bell, has rushed onto the beach. Stunned by everything he sees, he manages to ask the stranger in the top-hat, 'What is to be done with the horses?'[34]

'See that these horses are returned, safely, to Albert's stables at Fremantle,'[35] John Breslin tells him with typical aplomb, flipping him a sovereign for his trouble.

Wading forward, the sailors all grip the boat's gunwales and start hauling, which sees the stern of the whaleboat soon losing contact with the sand, and all of them scrambling aboard. Yes, they are afloat, but precariously. The boat is suddenly so overladen – they are 16 in a boat built for ten – that there are only a few inches of freeboard between the top of the gunwales and the sea.

'Out oars,' Captain Anthony barks again, 'and pull for your lives! Pull as if you were pulling after a whale!'[36]

With all of Breslin, King and Desmond sitting on the stern, while the Skipper stands just before the stern, with the 23-feet steering oar in hand, and the guests huddling at their feet – pull they do, as the whaleboat now surges in successive leaps through the open ocean.

And . . . stroke, and . . . *stroke*, and . . . STROKE.

Standing at the stern, the voice of Captain Anthony directs them further.

'Come down all together. Pull away, my men, pull away!'[37]

It is sluggish going, with a lot of water slopping over the sides, but pull away they do, to the best of their abilities.

Encouraging them to pull even harder is the vision of what is happening on the shore they have left behind.

For look now at that troublesome red-headed fellow, James Bell. Running like a mad thing, he gathers in the one horse with a saddle – King's – leaps atop him, and rides away, hell for leather, firstly down the beach towards the jetty, and then up one of the paths into the bush. He rides like a man with a story to tell, who just can't wait to tell it.

•

At about 11.30 am, an hour after the whaleboat has left the shore, it is struggling against the waves and the tide, some two miles out to sea, well beyond the breakers – those on board see something even more troubling than Bell leaving. From a different path come two mounted troopers, distinctive by their bright white uniforms, thundering up to the spot the whaleboat has departed from and gazing in their direction. Breslin strains his eyes to get a better look. He'd recognise that squat form anywhere. It's Bog John McKenna. And right beside him, jog-trotting along now that they are on the spoor, are two black-trackers.

Their escape has been discovered. Will the mounted troopers fire upon them?

STROKE, and . . . STROKE, and . . . STROKE.

No. The escapees and their enablers are beyond rifle range, and getting further with every pull.

Mercifully, they are pulling so hard that the men on the beach soon get very small indeed, though they can still see the ant-like figures gathering in the horses and, with the gigs, herding the lot towards the jetty.

There remains just one thing to do in this moment, and Breslin does it. Both the tide and wind, blowing onshore, will conspire to do the rest. From his pocket he takes a sealed bottle, and hurls it into the water. Inside the bottle is the note he had penned earlier that morning, in readiness for this very moment.

> ROCKINGHAM, *April 17, 1876.*
> To HIS EXCELLENCY THE BRITISH GOVERNOR OF WESTERN
> AUSTRALIA.
> *This is to certify that I have this day released from the clemency of Her Most Gracious Majesty Victoria, Queen of Great Britain, etc., etc., six Irishmen, condemned to imprisonment for life by the enlightened and magnanimous government of Great Britain for having been guilty of the atrocious and unpardonable crimes known to the unenlightened portion of mankind as 'love of country' and 'hatred of tyranny'; for this act of 'Irish assurance' my birth and blood being my full and sufficient warrant. Allow me to add that in taking my leave now, I've only to say:*
> *A few cells I've emptied (a sell in its way);*
> *I've the honour and pleasure to bid you good-day,*
> *From all future acquaintance, excuse me, I pray.*
> *In the service of my country,*
> JOHN J. BRESLIN.[38]

No more 'Mr Collins'.

Hear me, and hear me well.

I am John Breslin, Irish patriot, the most wanted man in all of the British Empire. I am here. I have done it again.

And if you want me, you'll have to come and get me.

RAH!

CHAPTER TWELVE

THE CHASE

Death to every foe and traitor.
Forward, strike the marching tune
And hurrah, me boys, for Freedom!
'Tis the Rising of the Moon![1]

Popular song in Ireland, from the early 1800s

Easter Monday, 17 April 1876, south of Rockingham, haven't we met?

On Rockingham Beach, Constable 'Big John' McKenna – described as 'a combination of bloodhound and bulldog when on the trail of crime'[2] – is beside himself with rage. Kicking the sand, cursing, throwing down his hat and kicking it, too – how the blazes did such a thing happen right under their very noses? There will be hell to pay for those most responsible. And yet, for all his rage, McKenna is also aware of the colossal opportunity that suddenly presents itself for the trooper who might find a way to capture the Fenian wretches and make them pay. Whatever else, he is intent on doing exactly that.

A quick search of the first of the carriages reveals three prison hats and, more significantly, 60 rifle cartridges. It means the fleeing convicts and their enablers are ready to fight, and perhaps kill if necessary, to preserve their freedom. They are armed and dangerous. But who exactly *are* the men in the traps who have helped the escaped convicts get this far?

McKenna and his men race to the promontory at the southern end of Rockingham Beach, which juts well out into the Indian Ocean, nearly as far out as the southern tip of Garden Island. If they are quick they might be able to get level with the boat, and the way the reefs lie mean that the whaleboat will have to track *towards* them before breaking free.

Ride, men!

Racing along the beach and then to the harder ground of the promontory, they are just in time, and just close enough, to get a good view of the whaleboat and its occupants.

And who is that at the tiller? Why it is Captain Anthony who, only a week or so before, had bought McKenna a drink at the Emerald Isle Hotel! And there, right beside him, is none other than that well-known figure about Fremantle for the last few months, Mr Collins, who McKenna had accompanied on more than one visit to The Establishment!

Big John McKenna is beside himself with rage.

The whaleboat is still out of gunshot but not earshot, for now Mr Collins stands, takes off his hat, and in very friendly fashion calls to him across the waters, 'Goodbye, John McKenna, we are not likely to meet again . . .'³

Now, much as he had liked Mr Collins, McKenna will have none of it. 'We'll see about that!'⁴ he screams back.

Gazing further out, McKenna can see no sign of Captain Anthony's whaler, the *Catalpa*, but suspects it must be hovering just beyond the horizon. Or, perhaps it is waiting for them further south, which is why they are heading in that general direction now.

All he can do for the moment, however, is keep his men together and keep the whaleboat in sight the best they can as they mirror its movement down the coast on the seaward side of the reefs.

Noon, 17 April 1876, Fremantle, an alarm, to arms

Such is life . . .

Billy Lynch and his mates try again. They sneak onto the ferry bound for the Perth Regatta . . . only to be sprung once more and chased off.

But, nothing lost!

It's all a jolly jape, no harm done. They have had a refreshing swim in the harbour, done some fishing, and now decide to pack up their lines and catches – a few whiting and herring – and head into the village.

Heading up Cliff Street, they are walking onto Fremantle's main thoroughfare, High Street, when Billy's attention is drawn by the sound of thundering hoofs – a very rare occurrence in the middle of sleepy Fremantle. He looks up, like everyone does, to see a coatless horseman tearing down the street at full gallop. He is coming from Rockingham way, and seems to have been whipping his horse the whole way, to judge from the way the heaving beast is frothing at the mouth, its flanks soaked with sweat. The horseman's eyeballs are rolling, his red whiskers flare back as he ducks his head into the wind.

'He looked every inch a madman,'⁵ Billy will ever after recount.

Watching closely, Billy sees the fellow pull up in a clatter of hoofs just outside the police station, not 50 yards away. He dismounts and charges inside. The young lad is not sure what is going on beyond the fact that whatever it is, it's very exciting and this is clearly the place to be, so he doesn't move.

Only a few minutes later, there is more excitement as a mounted trooper charges out with his black-tracker and both men jump onto their horses, to gallop down to the headquarters of the Water Police, some 200 yards away, down by the harbour.

Recognising that this is the new centre of action, Billy wanders down there, arriving in time to see the Water Police swing into action, under the command of Senior Petty Officer[6] William Mills in the absence of Superintendent John F. Stone, who is still away at the Perth Regatta. Quickly, the officious officer barks out orders and Billy watches the men, 'in a great excitement running about everywhere'.[7]

Just ten minutes later the police boat – essentially a small open whale-boat with a sail and a small engine – is ready to launch. On board is seemingly every man-jack available, five of them, bolstered by two regular policemen, all armed.

That leaves how many Water Police in Fremantle?

Let's see . . . *none.*

Excellent!

With no Water Police, Fremantle Harbour is at Billy's mercy. Unfortunately, the ferry to the Perth Regatta has now gone, but Billy and his mates take this rare opportunity to fish off the jetty – something normally banned, but what do they care? There is no-one here to stop them.

In the distance, Billy hears a big bell clanging, the sound coming from Fremantle Prison. Residents look up the hill, and quickly affirm the news, as a red flag of alarm scales the flagpole.

There has been an escape!

•

Shots ring out in the distance . . .

Firearms are being discharged *en masse.*

For you see, though most of Fremantle has headed off to the Regatta, a certain number of Military Pensioners, troopers and police have stayed behind – to mind the fort. For their amusement, the powers above have decided to hold a target shooting competition on the rifle range some two miles from the river mouth, in the lee of the sand-hills on the south side of town near Robb's Jetty.

There, the Military Pensioners are in the dappled shade of a magnificent cypress tree, either firing away or waiting their turn, when someone gallops up, yells something before wheeling his horse round and galloping off. Two mounted policemen are suddenly galloping off after him, back towards Fremantle.

'Each of us,' one of the Military Pensioners would recall, 'surmised from experience what it meant was that someone had made a bid for freedom.'[8]

Oh, but it proves to be much more dramatic than that. For only a minute or so later, a civilian horseman who had asked the troopers as they passed what their hurry was now comes to give the rest of them the news: 'All the prisoners are out!'[9]

Instantly, there is a stampede of Military Pensioners and police rushing back towards Fremantle, not at all sure of what they will find.

'As we ran and walked and talked and surmised and predicted and wondered where we should hide, imagination had killed one-half of Fremantle and mournfully buried all the rest, [ourselves] excepted . . .'[10]

•

In his crowded office at Fremantle Prison, Superintendent Joseph Doonan is sick with worry and desperate for news – oh, the *disgrace*, to have nearly all of the Fenian prisoners escape on his watch – when at last it comes. It is a Rockingham resident, a local farmer himself, by the name of James Bell, 'so out of breath as to be almost incoherent'.[11] Heaving and spluttering, he begins his story.

He was on the beach by the landing of the Jarrah Timber Company. Go on, Mr Bell!

More heavy breathing and spluttering. 'I have seen an American whaleboat, manned and armed with rifles, take on board from the beach 10 men,[12] some in prison clothes, and pull off from the shore.'[13]

Good God! It is every bit as bad as he has feared.

Sick at heart – he is nearly on the point of collapse – Doonan fires questions at Bell.

It quickly becomes clear. Firstly, there is no doubt that the whaleboat Bell saw is indeed carrying the missing convicts. The descriptions match exactly, right down to Darragh's red hair, Hogan's black whiskers and Harrington's haggard aspect.

Secondly, it is obvious that the man that Bell had been talking to just before the two traps arrived, the one in charge of the whaleboat, was none other than Captain George Anthony of the *Catalpa*, who had arrived in Bunbury in late March, and been seen in Fremantle several times since. The Telegraph Office has just sent up copies of the telegrams sent and received by Anthony since arrival, and it is clear he has been in coded communication with . . . James Collins, the well-heeled Yankee millionaire!

Good God Almighty above.

Doonan reels at the revelation.

Collins is the very man he had shown round the prison, talking of all their methods of tracking down escaped prisoners! With sickening certainty, Doonan realises how badly this will reflect on him.

Clearly, the most urgent thing now is to establish exactly how many men are missing from the prison, and so he must compose himself to head out into the yard to see it done.

In the prison, the prisoners who've just answered the roll call – to find six names missing – are all agog with the news. Can you believe it? The Fenians! They've done it! They've got away!

QUIET! All of you. And back to your cells.

You are all confined to your cells until further notice.

Joseph Doonan returns to his office, very close to a broken man. Yes, some men have been sent to search the houses of all ticket-of-leave men and known Fenian sympathisers, but he sets little store by that. His best hope, perhaps his only hope at this point, is that the police boat will catch up with them and apprehend them. They must be getting close . . .

•

Arriving in Fremantle *en masse* from the rifle range, the Military Pensioners and troopers have their hands on their loaded weapons, unsure of what they will find. Mercifully, upon reaching the outskirts of town, they are told the true state of affairs.

'Six of the Fenian prisoners have escaped but no further news has been made known . . .'[14]

They rush off to report in. It looks like it is going to be a very busy afternoon.

•

Out on the water, it is a race to the death, so committed are the participants. Their chests heave, their eyeballs roll, they haul on their oars like mad, trying to beat, with everything in them, the vessel right beside them – which is also straining for its last ounce of speed.

And stroke! And stroke! And STROKE!

Oh how the crowd roars just to see it.

The Perth Regatta, pitting the town's most accomplished rowers, scullers and sailors against each other, is one of the most popular days of the year, and everybody who is anybody can judge their own importance by how closely they are seated to His Excellency the Governor of Western Australia, Sir William Cleaver Robinson. One seated very near, as it happens, is Governor William Robert Fauntleroy of Fremantle Prison. But who is this approaching both men, on the official dais? It looks to be a trooper, in somewhat of a lather.

Your Excellency, Mr Fauntleroy, some bad news. It appears there has been an escape from The Establishment . . . the Fenians. Six of them. *Gone.*

Both men are upright and on their way in a flash, each climbing into his carriage, their drivers ready, hoping against hope that by the time they get to Fremantle the Fenians will have been recaptured.

•

In the whaleboat, the sailors keep pulling hard on their oars, making tough headway against a close onshore wind. Thankfully, a little after 1 pm, the wind shifts north. The men hoist a small sail to harness its power.

The pause from rowing allows the sailors and convicts to anxiously scan the horizon for some sign of the *Catalpa*.

There is nothing. Just endless blue all around, with white horses of water galloping hither and thither.

•

At last, they see it!

In the police boat, cruising off Rockingham Beach in the mid-afternoon, Senior Petty Officer Mills is the first to spot a vessel off their starboard quarter. Closing quickly, guns at the ready, alas, it proves to be no more than a local fishing vessel. The fishermen report having seen a heavily manned whaleboat in the distance, which had made its way 'through the South Passage, between Peron Point and the south end of Garden Island' in the late forenoon.

And what direction had it gone?

'South . . .'[15] the fishermen reply, albeit a little vaguely.

Our warm thanks.

The police boat heads off in pursuit.

•

When Billy comes back, after lunch, toting no fewer than a couple of dozen herring, it is to find the Military Pensioner Barracks *abuzz* with excitement. For the first time, Billy realises what it is all about.

Big Bob Cranston! *That* is why he was so gruff this morning. He and the other Fenian prisoners had got clean away, and now all the Military Pensioners, including Billy's father, have been confined to barracks until they are called to action. If the Water Police don't get them, then the Military Pensioners might just have to do it themselves!

Billy can't help but hope that Big Bob and the others might escape the clutches of the law for a bit longer still, so that his dad and the others might have the glory of recapturing them.

•

Finally, at 2.30 pm, the Telegraph Office reports that the lines are fixed and they are in contact with Perth and Albany once more.

The first telegram the operator sends is a request for the *Conflict* to immediately return to Fremantle, looking out for the *Catalpa* along the way, as well as a whaleboat with escaped Fenians. In both cases, they must apprehend immediately.

Alas, the answer comes back almost immediately: *Conflict* left port just 30 minutes ago. They can still see her, steaming away in King George's Sound, but have no way of catching her before she gets to Adelaide.

Very well, then.

Governor Robinson, who has just arrived from Perth in a flurry of hurry and worry to take command, makes the decision.

The 'gunship' sent in pursuit of the fugitives will have to be the *Georgette*. Yes, there is some resistance, but the Governor personally assures the apprehensive owners that they are 'indemnified against the risk of damage or loss'.[16]

Formally, now, His Excellency, in consultation with the Colonial Secretary, commissions the *Georgette* – her old boilers, sails and all – as, *ahem*, a warship of Her Majesty's Navy. It is to go out after the *Catalpa* with all possible haste, and demand the surrender of the escaped prisoners.

But with whom?

The Colony of Western Australia has no active regiment to call on, and while it does have some 40 retired soldiers who've seen action in the Crimea and the like, most of them are so old and decrepit they're more likely to fall over than 'Fall in', even if you could find them all at short notice.

So be it – that'll do. You have to use what you have.

Up in the Military Pensioner Barracks, shortly afterwards, the men get the call: all Military Pensioners to report to Major Charles Finnerty, *immediately*! No more than 20 minutes later, Major Finnerty has 18 former soldiers *marching* down to Long Jetty. Around and about them as they go, bouncing like muted but excited sheep-dogs, are Billy Lynch and his mates, excited to see their fathers marching off to war, 'cos that is what it feels like. Eight of the Water Police have also been commissioned to join the *Georgette*.

His Excellency appoints Superintendent John Stone of the Water Police to command the whole 'force' – which is filled out by the clearly reluctant Captain Michael O'Grady and his ten sailors of the *Georgette* passenger and mail steamer.

The growing crowd down by the wharf watch agog the burst of furious activity around the *Georgette*. She is being crammed with men, arms and ammunition. From the look of the portly Major, this is likely the greatest mission of his life, his nose getting progressively redder as he bustles about shouting orders, exhorting his men to ever more speed. They *must* get away, *must* get after the escaped convicts.

For all that, Billy Lynch knows from experience that it will still take several hours for the ship to get under way – as it takes that long for her boilers to produce the steam – but still, the men are doing everything they can to ready her for action meantime.

It is all so exciting!

•

Very quietly?

Captain Mick O'Grady of the *Georgette* is not happy.

Go out after men who had done no more than fight for the liberty of their country, and are now trying to do no more than liberate themselves?

It does not sit easily with him, but now is not the time to say it. (Nor is it time to confess that he had not only personally told Captain George S. Anthony of the *Catalpa* everything he knew about tides, currents and reefs off Rockingham Beach, but that he had *liked* the Yankee whaler! And still does . . .)

What the Captain can say is that he would like to go with a full load of coal to keep the boilers going, but this is dismissed out of hand by Superintendent Stone. Loading the full 30 tons of coal will take too long. We will just have to catch the *Catalpa* before our coal runs out – and, if not, the sails can make up the difference.

Captain Mick O'Grady knows better. But now is not the time to say so.

•

One minute James Kiely had been out and about in the prison yard, minding his own business, and the next all hell had broken loose as he had been fallen upon by the warders, hand-cuffed, and frog-marched back to his cell.

It was the first he heard that the others had escaped . . . without him. Clearly he had been left out by his one-time comrades, which is devastating enough. Making things worse now, however, is that Superintendent Joseph Doonan is standing over him, two burly warders backing him, *refusing* to believe he knows nothing about it.

'They tried to pump me,' Kiely would later recount, 'promising me my release if I would tell all I knew.'[17]

Of course, he cannot – as he knows nothing.

But it is too humiliating to admit that. Besides, it is simply not in his nature to say . . . *nothing.*

•

Aboard the *Catalpa*, First Mate Samuel Smith has his spyglass to his eye, scanning the waters ahead. If things have gone as planned, it is around about now, in the mid-afternoon, that they should see the whaleboat returning with its precious cargo. But there is nothing.

Under darkening skies – it looks as though a storm is brewing to the west – all he can see are the growing white-caps and the distant hazy outline of the Australian coast. Aloft in the crow's nest, swaying back and forth alarmingly as the wind lifts and the waves start to batter, one of his men shakily calls down with regular updates of his own – there is no sign.

Sam Smith does not like the look of it, he does not like it at all. Has something, perhaps, gone terribly wrong?

There is no way of telling. All he can do, for the moment, is keep the *Catalpa* on its course trawling back and forth in the waters some dozen miles off Garden Island, hoping to pick up some sign of the whaleboat before it gets dark – for if the men are out there, it is unimaginable how they could weather the vicious storm coming their way. And the bigger the swells, the more difficult it will be to see them as they spend more and more time obscured.

Smith buttons his coat tightly against the biting wind, and keeps scanning the waters to the east. He thinks of Amy, waiting for him in Martha's Vineyard.

Where *are* they?

•

Just as 'there is a tide in the affairs of men, which taken at the flood, leads on to fortune',[18] so too, can the tide be flooding the other way, threatening to sweep all before it.

And today has risked being a case in point.

For the strong wind and tide that had been so propitious for pushing Breslin's message in a bottle to the shore, has made rowing against it very hard going. It had been mid-afternoon when the men in the whaleboat found passage through the reef at the southern end of Garden Island. Captain Anthony had been able to see close up the cruel barbs that they had so luckily passed over the evening before, and is infinitely relieved to at last be in the open sea.

They have spent a gruelling afternoon on the open sea pushing south to the agreed rendezvous area, forever looking to the far horizons for the sails of the *Catalpa*, to no avail.

At around four o'clock, when the wind dies down to a baby's breath as the sun begins its long descent to the west – where a menacing storm looks to be brewing out at sea – they decide to follow the sun's lead, take in sail and row directly away from the Australian coast. Captain Anthony is able to cheer both sailors and Fenians alike by saying, 'If we can keep on this course, the ship should be raised in an hour.'[19]

Sure enough . . .

It is half-past five in the late afternoon when the *Catalpa* appears some 15 miles away, a speck on yonder western horizon.

'Sail ho!'[20] the shout goes up from Toby.

Just the sight of it gives the men renewed vigour. Hopes of contact dashed for today, they are eager to at least get as close as possible before dark, so they can be picked up in the dawn. (Unless, of course, the *Catalpa* is able to see them and comes to pick them up.)

They pull towards her, making good headway. Within an hour they are close enough that, although the *Catalpa* is still no more than a small shape on the horizon, they can actually see her topsails from the top of each crest in the swell.

Now, there is enough wind, and they are far enough from the spying eyes onshore that Captain Anthony gives the orders to put up the sails on their own boat again, and it is quickly done. Alas . . . although the newly filled sails help for a while, the wind proves to be a harbinger of hell as the sky turns dark, the wind starts to howl like a banshee, the waves rise, and they are hit by a succession of rain squalls which leave them thoroughly soaked and shivering from the bitter cold.

Captain Anthony orders the 15 motley men to sit on the weather gunwale, which allows them to put more sail up, and sees them surging forward like a hunting hound off the leash, even if with every rolling wave the men get a good drenching. For a while it is manageable, but when the wind lifts and the waves get bigger and the clouds darker, the whaleboat frequently threatens to capsize.

The whole thing is becoming desperate.

Captain Anthony is frankly not sure they will be able to survive a night out here in a storm . . .

•

It has been a long and brutal day for Constable Big John McKenna and his men since they first sighted the whaleboat off Rockingham Beach and pushed south from there, trying to keep it in sight for as long as possible. Just as darkness is falling, they arrive in the tiny fishing village of Mandurah, where they hope to commandeer a boat and crew, to head out a short way from the coast in the hope of intercepting the absconders, 'or at least be able to keep them under surveillance during the night'.[21]

Alas, no suitable boat is found and they must pass an uncomfortable night in what limited accommodation Mandurah has to offer.

•

The whaleboat roars towards the *Catalpa*, the soaked men brace for each wave that crashes over them . . . only for a vicious squall to fill their sail with such force that it breaks their mast off near its base, sending the whole thing crashing into the ocean.

Instantly, expertly, Captain Anthony puts the steering oar hard over so that what remains of the whaleboat's momentum is harnessed to turn it to face the wind, which keeps the boat from being swamped and capsizing – for the moment. They are lucky to be alive, not crushed by the falling mast or cast into the surly sea. All they can do right now is to bail furiously – using containers that had previously held their food and water, which they have now knocked the tops from – and get the broken mast back on board along with the waterlogged sail. All is chaos in the gloom, the men sure in the knowledge that just one big wave could finish them all.

Improvising, Captain Anthony grabs one of the mid-ship oars and with spare rope lashes it upright and secures the jib to it. By extending the other end of the jib aft they soon have a makeshift sail, which at least gets them under way once more, able to steer and not at the total mercy of the waves.

Strangely, amid all the chaos and confusion, all the grunts, groans and moans, Captain Anthony notices in the near pitch darkness the brilliant phosphorescence every time their vessel crests a wave and crashes back down again. The phosphorescent beams of light cascade out in a perfect symmetry that is such a contrast to what is happening *on* the boat.

Those who can, huddle below the gunwales, hugging each other for warmth, while Captain Anthony resolutely stands at the stern for hour after hour, holding the steering oar, shouting orders at his frantic sailors.

Through the night, Anthony is the rock, the immovable object that the wind, the waves, the panic has no effect on. Those who have swapped their prison cells for this watery hell on earth at least draw solace from the image of him standing so resolutely, not so much an immovable force of nature, as an immovable force against whatever nature can throw at them.

Most troubling of all is the time and progress they lose by retrieving the sails and mast. Any hope of reaching the *Catalpa* before dark is lost as she disappears in the gloom, perhaps moving a little further off-shore for her own safety.

The men in the whaleboat continue to bail for their lives through the long, soaking perilous night. When a gigantic wave whisks away their food and water, they are left not only freezing, but desperately hungry and thirsty. The Fenians have not eaten since dawn of the previous day, back at Fremantle Prison, which feels like another world, at another time. They must try to survive long enough to find the *Catalpa* on the morrow.

Bail, men!

•

Excitement in the air!

In the quiet settlement of Fremantle, something is actually happening! Through this late evening and into the night, those in Fremantle who are at liberty to do so remain down at the wharves – all a'twitter at the latest stunning news and speculative gossip – the *Georgette* has been loaded with men and munitions and at least enough coal to get her down and back to the area where it is thought the *Catalpa* might be.

It steams away from Long Jetty in a billow of black smoke in the dusky twilight, and heads north-west, around Rottnest Island, before heading south. The crowd onshore, including Billy Lynch, whose father is on board, watch until the last black puff disappears into the gloom.

Reluctantly, they wander home, knowing they will be back at the crack of dawn, determined not to miss a moment of excitement.

•

That is that then.

Aboard the *Catalpa*, First Mate Smith finally accepts that they won't be finding the whaleboat any time before dawn. There is, nevertheless, some chance the whaleboat could find them.

Smith orders the lanterns to be lit and lashed across the highest yard-arms of the foremast, mainmast and mizzenmast, together with a large one on the bows, and two from the stern.

In shorter order, those on deck in the howling wind are lit in an ethereal glow as the light of the lanterns traces crazy criss-crossing arcs against the black clouds – which are themselves occasionally flicker-ingly illuminated by flashes of lightning. It promises to be a singularly desperate night . . .

•

The worst of it?

It is that in this profound darkness, Captain Anthony can no longer see the waves coming at them, can no longer change the angle of the boat at the last instant to better stabilise the vessel.

Broadly, he tries to *feel* the motion of the waves to keep their boat heading in the direction that the *Catalpa* was last seen, knowing that Samuel Smith will have put up lanterns for them to see. Mostly, though, their energies are devoted to trying to survive.

The freed Fenian convicts – miserable, cold and soaked – must keep bailing as if their lives depend on it – because they do.

Prospects are grim, growing grimmer.

'Captain,' one of the drenched, freezing Fenians occasionally asks above the roar of the wind and crashing waves, 'do you think we will float through the night?'

'Oh, yes,' the Captain cheerily shouts back, 'I've been out on many a worse night.'[22]

Truly, however?

He is all but certain that they are one dreadful wave from destruction and drowning. And yet, just when their demise appears inevitable, the gale starts to subside a little, making room for a little optimism that they will see the dawn.

What shall they do to lift their spirits higher still?

Let's do as we did on the *Hougoumont*.

Sing?

Yes, sing!

First one Fenian, and then another, and then all of them, take up the beloved hymn of their youth.

> *Hail, Queen of Heav'n, the ocean Star,*
> *Guide of the wand'rer here below!*
> *Thrown on life's surge we claim thy care,*
> *Save us from peril and from woe.*
> *O Mother of Christ, Star of the sea,*
> *Pray for the wanderer, pray for me . . .*[23]

And so they keep bailing and singing through the night.

Dawn, 18 April 1876, off the Western Australian coast, no answer to our prayers

The dawn, the dawn, the blessed dawn! It has come and they are still alive. Looking to the east, those in the whaleboat can see the low grey smudge of the Australian continent. It looks to be about six miles away. Alas, to the west, there is no sign of the *Catalpa*.

Never mind. Having made it through the night and now being on a calming sea is miracle enough. Captain Anthony has no doubts about the abilities and loyalty of his First Mate, Samuel Smith, and knows the *Catalpa* must be out there. It is simply a matter of getting far enough out so that Sam will be able to find them.

So row, boys, row. They take up the oars once more, and the whale-boat is soon pushing further out into the Indian Ocean.

•

On the beach at Mandurah, Constable Big John McKenna earnestly scans the western horizon, looking for some sign of the whaleboat, or the whaler it had presumably been heading to. There is no sign of either. Downhearted, deeply disappointed at their lack of success, he leads his men on the long trek back to Fremantle, 40 miles to the north. Where can the escaped convicts be?

•

Still pulling hard on the oars, occasionally they despair, but, wonderfully, at 8 am, they come to believe there *is* a God after all, for . . .

For there she is!

It is the sails of the *Catalpa*, some 15 miles away. And she is closing on them! They have been seen!

But the *Catalpa* is not the *only* vessel to have seen them.

Far to their north, one of the crew points out a plume of smoke rising from the burning boilers of a boat coming out of Fremantle, which they *hope* is just the *Georgette*, heading off on her usual Tuesday routine – taking in and delivering the colonial mail to Albany – and not now coming specifically looking for them. With his heart in his mouth, John Breslin keeps her under close observation, trying to determine whether she is sticking close to the coast to deliver the mail, or heading further out, looking for them.

'A little further observation convinced me that she was too far out of her regular course to be going to Albany,' Breslin will recount, 'and a slight alteration in her bearing answered the question, showing us that she was making for the *Catalpa*, which she must have seen before we did.'[24]

He alerts Captain Anthony who assesses the threat . . .

On the *Georgette*'s current course, he tells the men, she will pass by within less than a mile of them, and it seems impossible that the men aboard will fail to spot us.

To give themselves every chance, Captain Anthony barks his order: 'Douse the sail! Ship the oars! Everyone down!'

To accomplish the last in such a tight space, the grown men lie tightly on top of each other. Within 30 seconds, they are all uncomfortable and squashed but hidden beneath the gunwales. And this time, the fact that there is only a few inches of freeboard works in their favour, because their whole boat makes no more profile on the waters than the top of a long log.

Barely anyone breathes.

Could they be missed?

Perhaps!

Only Captain Anthony allows himself to bring a beady eye above the level of the gunwale, and the *Georgette* – all billowing black smoke, full sails and churning propellers leaving a white wake – passes by so close to them that Anthony can even see, as he will recount, 'an officer on the bridge with glasses, scanning . . .'[25]

Can he *possibly* miss them?

If they are spotted and the *Georgette* alters course toward the whale-boat, long years lie ahead in the cells – likely chained to the wall for the Fenians. Mercifully, however, the steamer passes them by, some few miles to windward of their position. The men sit up and watch for many long minutes as the *Georgette* runs alongside the *Catalpa* in the distance, wondering exactly what is happening . . .

•

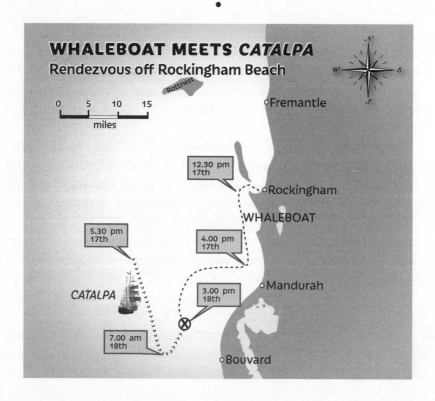

WHALEBOAT MEETS *CATALPA*
Rendezvous off Rockingham Beach

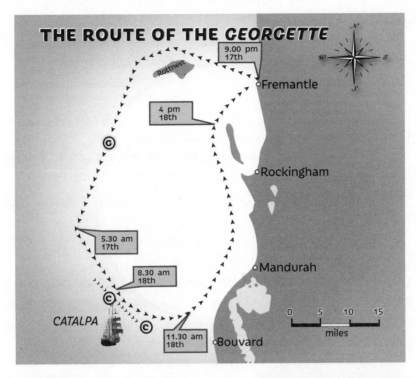

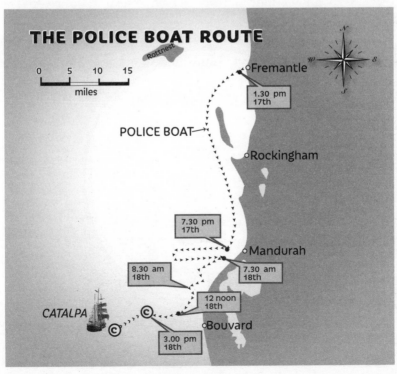

All hands on deck!

Aboard the *Georgette*, Major Finnerty is beside himself as, in the light of dawn, a bark is sighted to their south-east, a sail is spied.

Could it be their quarry?

It is!

Within ten minutes it is reported as a three-masted bark. Twenty minutes after that it is confirmed as the *Catalpa*!

The excitement aboard the steamer is fairly evenly matched by the consternation on the whaler.

Samuel Smith has himself been watching the approach of the *Georgette* for the last two hours, and now is the time for action.

At 8.30 am on this Tuesday, the *Georgette* pulls alongside the *Catalpa*, the steamer about the same tonnage as the bark.

Using a loudhailer – a cone with a hole at the tip – the first man to speak is Captain Michael O'Grady, who calls across the waters in his booming voice:

'Have you seen a boat with a lot of men in it?'[26]

'No,' comes the reply from First Mate Smith.

Good. Captain O'Grady appears pleased to hear it, but clearly, he is not quite the man in charge.

For now, another fellow – Superintendent John Stone of the Water Police, as it happens, though Smith does not know him – takes the loudhailer and asks:

'Have you seen a boat with a lot of men in?'

'No.'

'Is the Captain on board?'[27]

'No.'

'Do you have any strangers on board?'

'No.'[28]

'Where is the whaleboat, missing from the cranes?'[29]

'The captain has gone ashore.'[30]

'What for?'

'I don't know anything about it,'[31] says Mr Smith.

'Can I board your ship and search?'

'Don't know, got no instructions,' Samuel says in his peculiar Yankee way, 'but guess you'd better not, anyhow.'[32]

Well, that's that then.

As the *Catalpa* is in international waters – 13 miles off-shore – and no-one can board her without the permission of her masters, there is no option.

With the *Georgette*'s bunkers soon to be empty of coal, Superintendent Stone decides the best thing is to return to Fremantle, close by the shore of the mainland, and scour the inlets as they go, looking for signs of the whaleboat. The fact that it has not returned to the *Catalpa* is encouragement that the escaped prisoners are somewhere between their current position and the shore. And thanks to the violent gale of the night before, it is not surprising. If she has not sunk, she must be around here somewhere . . .

Yes, that is the plan. They will search as they head back to Fremantle to report the position of the *Catalpa* and stock up on coal.

•

Throughout the whole exchange, the men in the whaleboat must sit there, waiting for something to happen and, at last, it does. With a renewed plume of smoke, the *Georgette* heads back for Fremantle, albeit on a slightly different course, hugging the coast.

Wonderful!

Less pleasing is the *Catalpa*, which to their consternation – and none more so than Captain Anthony's, who for the life of him can't work out why – is also under sail, and moving *away* from them, heading to the sou'-sou'-west. Hauling on the oars they follow the best they can – the sight of her comes and goes and comes again. Frustrated, the freed Fenians recognise that the so-called myth is coming true! The *Catalpa* is like the *Flying Dutchman*, and they start calling her the 'phantom ship'[33] – the vessel that appears close and then fades. The harder they strive to reach her beckoning profile, the more evasive she becomes.

Finally, after hours, she entirely recedes from view.

Perhaps Samuel Smith is trying to divert all attention away from the rendezvous? Or perhaps he has been spooked.

•

Aboard the *Georgette*, as it pushes north, a sudden cry goes up. There they are!

It is their colleagues and friends in the police boat.

Calling to them from the high deck of the steamer, Superintendent Stone is able to give them the news. We have seen the *Catalpa*, and have all but confirmed that it is the whaler intended to take the Fenians away. It also seems certain that the escaped prisoners are not on board. The whaleboat must be somewhere off the coast, waiting to rendezvous with the whaler.

'Cruise along the coast in search of the ship's boat, which is most probably somewhere off [Mandurah],'[34] Superintendent Stone advises, before ordering his men onto the police boat to keep going with the search.

•

Samuel Smith is more than worried.

Though satisfied to have seen off the impertinent questions of the fellows on the *Georgette*, the fact remains, it is now nearly 18 hours since he had been hoping to see Captain Anthony coming out from the shore in the whaleboat, and there has been no sign. His only solace is the fact that if the authorities are looking for them so aggressively, it means they aren't caught. They're around here somewhere.

Still, for caution's sake, he decides to take the *Catalpa* away from the direct search area for the moment. The alternative, to stay hovering here, will near-guarantee increased scrutiny on the spot they least want to be noticed.

And so the *Catalpa* continues sailing sou'-sou'-west, with Smith intending to come back in due course, on course, of course, for Captain Anthony and the men.

He hopes.

•

On board the *Georgette*, a restless figure stands on the bridge earnestly gazing to every horizon with his spyglass. Major Finnerty's chief fear at this point is that the wretched escapees might have drowned in last night's tempest, denying him the great triumph of apprehending the villains and returning them to His Excellency, as all of Fremantle watches. He has already done so much to lay the foundations of justice for Britain's colonial authority in Fremantle, but this? This would be one for the ages, a slap to his critics and incontrovertible proof that he is a man worthy of promotion, at least to the rank of Colonel.

It is nothing less than his destiny to find these dangerous criminals, and if intensity of purpose alone will do it, then he is already halfway there!

•

In the whaleboat, all Captain Anthony and his men can do is to keep hauling on the oars, pursuing their mothership in the direction it has disappea . . .

There it is!

Just after two o'clock the cry goes up. Just this side of the far horizon ahead they see the distant sails of the *Catalpa* steering straight for them.

Hurrah!

But wait . . .

So too is another vessel . . . ?

Thomas Desmond gazes closely, aghast, and is the first to exclaim: 'My God! There's the guard-boat, filled with police. Pass out those rifles.'[35]

•

In the police boat, Senior Petty Officer Mills suddenly sits bolt upright and peers with purpose through his spyglass.

There they are!

There they are!

For some time, they had been watching the *Catalpa*, had watched it turn and tacked themselves accordingly. But now to their north-west, at a distance of about two miles, they can see a whaleboat filled with men. They have found the Fenian criminals!

Barking orders, Mills sets their sails for God, for England and for justice!

•

Good God!

In the whaleboat, they are now close enough to see the seven or eight armed men in the police boat,[36] closing on the *Catalpa* from the other side – white water cascading from its thrusting bow – at much the same distance, and much the same pace as they are, though propelled by two mutton-leg sails.

Upon Captain Anthony's instructions, a sudden burst of furious activity takes place as all the men not rowing take up rifles, and load them, even as they take out the wet cartridges from their revolvers and slot in fresh ones, ready to fire.

'We will fight,' the Fenians tell each other, 'until the last man is killed.'[37]

Meantime the men on the oars continue to give it their all. Captain Anthony roars at them, using the same cadence as when trying to get the last bit of oomph out of them when closing on a whale.

'Come down, Mopsy, come down. You, Big Louis, pull! Toby, pull! Give them stroke, Mr Sylvia. What do you say, men? Come down all together. Pull away, my men, pull away!'[38]

Their chests heave, their eyeballs roll, their tongues flail, they haul on their oars like mad things, trying to beat, with everything in them, the vessel coming from the other direction – which is also straining for its last ounce of speed, in what feels like a life-and-death struggle.

And stroke! And stroke! And STROKE!

A furious race ensues, with both vessels making for the *Catalpa*.

And the *Catalpa* itself?

She is turning!

CHAPTER THIRTEEN

FLAGGING FORTUNES

So come all you screw warders and jailers
Remember Perth Regatta day
Take care of the rest of your Fenians
Or the Yankees will steal them away[1]

Catalpa ballad

18 April 1876, seaward of Cape Bouvard, deliverance!

Whaleboat ho!

Up in the crow's nest the whaleboat has been spotted, and Samuel Smith has barked orders accordingly, and from about two-and-a-half miles away, the *Catalpa* is now making for it with all possible speed.

In the whaleboat, the men continue to make for the *Catalpa* with all possible speed as well – but not impossible speed. When the Fenians try to take up oars of their own, Captain Anthony yells at them to stop immediately. They are more hindrance than help.

It's going to be close, but when it becomes clear that the whaleboat will reach the *Catalpa* ahead of the police boat, Captain Anthony guides them to the seaward side of the *Catalpa*, so as to put the whaler between them and the police boat.

Now, as the whaleboat comes broadside onto the flanks of the *Catalpa* – crashing in with a jolt, and throwing everyone sideways – Mr Smith has everything waiting for them. Instantly, one of the davit's boat tackles is thrown to Mr Sylvia at the bow of the whaleboat, and the other to Captain Anthony at the stern. After Anthony attaches his end he turns around, so as to command the others to quickly board the *Catalpa* at all possible speed, only . . .

Only to find the men have already scrambled up the sides via the grip ropes thrown down to them, taking their rifles and pistols with them, and he is entirely on his own.

Meanwhile, as soon as John Breslin's feet are on the deck, Samuel Smith calls to him:

'What shall I do now? What shall I do?'

'Hoist the flag!' Breslin roars back, 'and stand out to sea.'[2]

Rising to the occasion, much as the Stars and Stripes now rises up the mizzenmast, the First Mate roars the order – 'Make sail! Make sail! Make sail!'

Though this is a bizarre turn of events for the crew – totally stunned by so many unexpected things happening one after the other – following orders and asking no questions, like good sailors should, they turn into crazed monkeys once more, scrambling up the ropes and along the spars, unfurling sails.

'Never,' Breslin would document, 'was a manoeuvre executed in a more prompt and seamanlike manner.'[3]

By the time Captain Anthony, still in the whaleboat, is hauled up on the davits level to the gunwale, and is able to step lightly on to the deck of the *Catalpa*, it is to witness an extraordinary scene. For the police boat has also now pulled abreast at just 50 yards off the *Catalpa*'s starboard quarter, full of Water Police, many of whom the escaped prisoners know from their work around Fremantle. And the Water Police not only know them, but also one of the men who is with them – Mr Collins! What is he doing in the midst of this mayhem? Has he been held hostage?

No, for he is clearly very happy, grinning at them from the deck! And he is not the only one bursting with joy, for now the escaped Fenians, brandishing their rifles and pistols, gleefully call to their former over-seers, 'shouting salutations and farewells, calling the officers by name'.[4]

What can the Water Police do in reply?

As the officer in command, Senior Petty Officer Mills, recognises: not much. The Fenians are not only armed and free, they are on a Yankee whaler in international waters. For the Water Police, trying to board the much larger vessel, bristling with men and guns of all descriptions, is out of the question. It would be nothing less than a massacre.

So Senior Petty Officer Mills offers a word of defeated-for-the-moment farewell, complete with a military salute.

'Good afternoon, Captain,' he calls across the waters.

'Good afternoon,'[5] Captain Anthony calls back.

And there is really not much left to say, for both men accept the reality of the situation. If the police boat had managed to get to the whaleboat before it got to the *Catalpa*, it would have been different – they might conceivably have recaptured them all, and arrested those aiding and abetting an attempted escape. But, now the guard boat simply has insufficient firepower to do anything.

'The men on board the ship appeared to be armed,' one contemporary account will run, 'and it was quite evident from the behaviour of the escaped prisoners while the police boat was within range that they were only restrained from firing upon the boat by the influence of the captain.'[6]

Not that that is quite the end of it.

'We have not done with you yet!'[7] shouts Senior Petty Officer Mills of the Water Police, his words floating back across the waters from the receding police boat.

Turning to Breslin, Captain Anthony asks, 'What now . . . ?'

'Put to sea,' the Irishman replies.

''Bout ship!' Anthony roars, 'Put to sea!'[8]

As the sailors in turn roar into action, the newly liberated Fenians, braced in the first winds of freedom they have felt in nigh on a decade, gaze after the departing police boat in savagely delighted amazement. John Breslin captures the mood by blowing the police a kiss of farewell, sparking a round of riotous jeers and hoots that carry across the water to the Water Police, ringing in their ears, like salt to a wound.

Alas, for the moment, Breslin's kiss is perilously close to the only thing that is blowing, as the wind has now dropped to nearly nothing. The nation of origin of the new arrivals notwithstanding, the luck of the Irish has deserted them.

But they will deal with that problem later. Right now, the wild scenes of exultation aboard the American bark go for well over an hour. Beside themselves with joy, the freed Fenians cheer the captain of the *Catalpa* and his crew three times through, as they do John Breslin, Thomas Desmond, John King and Thomas Brennan, who have been the masterminds and servants of making this happen.

In all the extraordinary hurly-burly of the high-stakes game they have been playing, this really is a precious moment to take pause, and reflect on the glory of the moment.

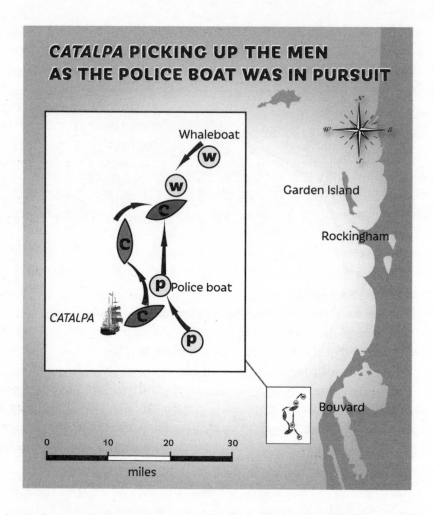

'Twenty-eight hours in an open boat, with a liberal allowance of rain and seawater, cramped for want of room, and cheered with the glorious uncertainty as to whether we should gain freedom or the chain gang – a suit of dry clothes, a glass of New England rum and a mug of hot coffee were just the things to put "where they would do the most good," and were put accordingly.'[9]

In the meantime, after Captain Anthony compliments Samuel Smith on how well things have been handled in his absence, he calls the steward and orders: 'Get up the best dinner the ship can afford. We're hungry.'[10]

As it happens, the entire crew join them, a fitting reward for their extraordinary co-operation. From being told nothing, the likes of Mopsy, Big Louis, Toby, Lombard, Lewis, Mr Sylvia and the whole retinue of maritime men from so many lands had indeed been stunned to suddenly find themselves in the middle of a prison break, but had barely blinked. They had first trusted the skipper, and then become even more enthusiastic once they realised they were giving England one in the eye – as so many of them are from lands that had laboured under the English yoke for too long. Do their bit then, to fight for justice, liberty and freedom from all things English? Yes! They have proved themselves happy to answer the call – and now take their seats at the table of celebration as equals.

As it happens, those on watch can even join in, as the wind has dropped so low that what few sails they have up only occasionally manage a wan flap, and when they bring down the Stars and Stripes for the night, it's in the same limp position it had been when they ran it up the flagstaff.

•

All else being equal, Superintendent John F. Stone would right now be one of the dignitaries presiding at the laying of the cornerstone of Fremantle's new Masonic Hall, as he is one of the key members of the committee that has been organising the whole thing.

But all is not equal.

That ceremony, planned to be grand and well-attended, is going ahead without him, with Chief Justice Sir Archibald Paull Burt laying the stone before not much more than a mere smattering of a scattering of Freemasons – those who have to be there – while everyone else is down by Fremantle docks awaiting developments.

And here is a key development now ...

4 pm, Tuesday, 18 April 1876, their ship comes in

No sooner has the Union Jack been hauled up the flagpole by the lighthouse on Arthur Head than the word spreads.

Come quickly! The *Georgette*! She's approaching Fremantle Harbour, and will soon be docking.

From everywhere – homes, barracks, public bars, the streets themselves – the crowd streams to the docks as the steamer gets closer. Some have come straight from the Masonic Hall ceremony.

Here she is! Eyes scan the deck for some signs of triumph, perhaps even manacled prisoners?

There are none. All they can see is Superintendent Stone, Major Finnerty and Captain O'Grady, all with the hang-dog expressions of men who have gone out on a hunt and returned with stone-cold motherless nothing. With shouts from the deck to those on the wharf, soon everyone hears the news:

They had found the whaler about nine miles off-shore from Cape Bouvard, and actually spoken to those on board. Those on the whaler denied all knowledge of the Fenians, but both the whaleboat and the *Catalpa*'s Captain were indeed missing, so it all fits.

The *Catalpa* is the one.

A telegram is sent to Governor Robinson, informing him of the situation, while the excited crowd mills about, exchanging snippets of news and views.

'The general feeling,' the journalist for the *Fremantle Herald* will note, 'was clearly one of pleasure that the pursuit had been so far unsuccessful. This arose chiefly out of the popular impression that the Fenian convicts are political prisoners, convicted and punished for offences against a system of government, not against society, and from the sympathy that the public everywhere displays towards the weak in a contest against the strong.'[11]

Billy Lynch is there, with his mother, Winifred, both of them relieved that the head of the household has returned safely to them. So, too, is young Harry Passmore, who *now* understands why his friend Thomas Darragh had said goodbye to him, and told him he was 'going away'. Fingering the compass Thomas had given him for his watch chain, young Harry can't help but hope that Thomas has done exactly that, and will stay free so he can find his family once more.

Among the throng, too, is young Elizabeth McCann.

'I can still picture the excitement when it became known that the Fenians had got away,' she would recall, 'and that the police boat and the steamer *Georgette* had failed to intercept them on the *Catalpa*.'[12]

As she watches closely, policemen and warders first gather by the harbour's edge and then seem to start running in all directions, even as the crowd of good burghers come together in knots to share notes on what they know, who has escaped, who has gone after them, what likelihood there is of capture and whose fault the whole thing is. And how wondrous the whole thing is! In their tiny burgh, a military settlement where nothing much changes from one year to the next, least of all underwear, something has actually . . . *happened*. It seems too good to be true, and yet really is true, so what else do you know? With emissaries going from one knot to the next, and the knot with the best news getting bigger and attracting yet more emissaries, the rumours are soon ripping through the town like bushfire out of Bunbury with a southerly buster behind it. The best rumour of the lot is quickly the loudest – it is John Boyle O'Reilly! He has returned, to pluck his brethren from the brink of the clink and just as quickly got them away again. Yes, it seems absolutely certain he 'had a finger in the pie',[13] for *everyone* says so.

Ah well. Elizabeth McCann, of course, knows the truth – that it is dear 'Mr Collins,' the town favourite, who has pulled off this extraordinary coup, and has *all* of his fingers in this pie, but mum's the word.

It's all so thrilling!

And now, more news. And exciting news it is.

A telegram is dispatched to Government House, advising both that the *Georgette* has returned and that she has failed to recapture the prisoners, His Excellency, Governor Robinson, convinced that 'all further pursuit will be futile',[14] reads it solemnly. He has returned to Perth, reluctantly leaving the issue squarely in the lap of the gods.

Governor Fauntleroy, painfully aware that his honour is at stake – not to mention, his job – promptly arrives with Superintendent Doonan, and their leading officers.

It does not take long to decide.

The *Georgette* must go out again. But this time it must be ready for a long pursuit, with its coal hoppers as full as its pantry, and its deck stacked and packed with men with guns.

Yes, but with *which* men? And with *what* guns?

The *Georgette* has a crew of just ten ordinary seamen, not one of whom has ever fired a shot in anger, or been shot at. Even if the former collier could catch the whaler, her own manpower would be no match for the *Catalpa* crew and the six Fenians they have with them. As to guns, the steamer simply does not have any.

Options?

Very few.

In the entire Colony of Western Australia, in terms of artillery and crew, there are just two old 12-pounder Armstrong guns, occasionally rolled out by a company of fairly ratty and tatty, rat-a-tat-tatty volunteers, but neither those guns nor those men could be brought together and got on board within a couple of days at best, so that is out and . . .

And, in the corridor outside, a flurry of footsteps is heard and an urgent knock. 'Big John' McKenna stands in the doorway, bedraggled, exhausted and bursting with news. He begs to report that they had followed the whaleboat down the coast as far as Mandurah. It seems likely that their meeting point was somewhere west of there.

Governor Fauntleroy has decided.

Superintendent Stone, I want your Water Police to refresh themselves and I want eight of them aboard the *Georgette* by ten o'clock this night. Major Finnerty, you will bring 18 fresh Military Pensioners on board, fully armed. And you will mobilise a fatigue party of Military Pensioners to help get coal onto the *Georgette* as quickly as possible, starting immediately. This time you will have a cannon with a makeshift artillery crew, and a full load of coal in your bunkers.

Now everyone, stand back!

A large Water Police whaleboat is also brought aboard, to swing from the *Georgette*'s davits – in case it is needed to board the *Catalpa*.

Outside the Military Pensioner Barracks, the order is given.

On parade!

All of them stand to rigid attention as Major Finnerty – who has had a quick change of fresh uniform for the occasion, and whose red nose is shining more brightly than ever with righteous indignation – gives orders. We are going out after them. We might be in for the fight of our lives. All of you report to the steward and his staff, to be issued with 25 rounds of ball ammunition. Your Martini–Henry rifles are to be cleaned and your bayonets sharpened. Get yourselves ready.

•

On the wharf by the *Georgette*, and on the deck of the steamer itself, some 20 Military Pensioners are now covered in greasy black muck, as their perspiration mixes with the coal dust. From a succession of drays, enormous bags of coal are being hoisted by pulleys up and over the side of the ship, placed in wheelbarrows and hauled across the deck to be poured down chutes into the bunkers below.

It is no less than a *bastard* of a job, but not the worst. No, that would be going out after the escapees like the other blokes who have been called up. The workers in the fatigue party feel for them, fear for them. It is like they are preparing for a war, which is not something you expect on sleepy duty in this backwater of the British Empire.

Keep loading.

Up and over. Up and over. Haul it forward. Haul it forward. Down the chute. Down the chute.

The Military Pensioners are still going hard and the bunkers are half-full – much like their lungs, with coal dust – when, nearing eight o'clock in the evening, another shout goes up.

It is the police boat returning!

Alas, the news from Senior Petty Officer Mills is also grim. Yes, they made contact with both the whaleboat and the *Catalpa*. They had all come together at the one time, earlier in the afternoon. The police can confirm that the *Catalpa* now has the escaped convicts on board. But, of course, there was nothing they could do. When last seen, the *Catalpa* was positioned off Cape Bouvard, with the only saving grace being that 'as the wind had remained light the vessel might be intercepted a short distance off the coast'.[15]

Very well then, there is a lot to do.

One of the most important things is to give the *Georgette* some much needed firepower, and young Billy Lynch, who is among the large crowd soaking it all up, is thrilled to see another party of Military Pensioners hauling towards the harbour an 'Armstrong gun' – essentially two wheels at either end of an axle, upon which rests a six-foot long cannon!

With much heaving and groaning, the Armstrong gun is rolled down the embankment, along the jetty and through the pressing crowd.

Listening carefully to the remarks of the Military Pensioners grunting and groaning and cursing in their thick Irish accents as they push it forward, young Harry Passmore has the distinct impression not a lot of them are happy about going out in pursuit of their countrymen, but toil away they must regardless.

Once aboard, the men use strong ropes to tie the Armstrong gun into a precise position on deck so that it may fire through the gangway portal. Next they lug the bags of powder and shells on board and place them beside the cannon.

Now, stand back once more. Stand back, I say!

That rhythmical sound of men marching comes from the darkness. It is more Military Pensioners from The Establishment.

In formation, by the left, quick marrrrrch, they have come down the hill and are now marching out onto the wharf. At their head is Major Finnerty, a man on a mission, a veteran of the Crimean War who doesn't reel from danger, he embraces it, dominates it, brings it to heel and wins! His expression says this is just such an occasion, and he is just the man for the job.

Grim-faced, the men make their way up the gangplank and are all on board. (Actually, they are *nearly* all on board. The excitement is too much for one man, who collapses, and is taken back to the prison hospital.)

The loading continues, even as the boilers are made ready for full steam ahead.

•

Aboard the *Catalpa*, the steward has outdone himself. The pantry, larder and stores have all been raided and the new arrivals have sat down to a dinner of chicken, lobsters, potatoes and fruit, washed down by tea, coffee and ale.

For the first time in nearly a decade, the escaped Fenian prisoners can enjoy themselves as free men!

What the morrow will bring, they cannot be sure.

If all goes well, a wind will spring up overnight that will allow them to sail away to safety before either the *Georgette* or the police boat can come back with reinforcements.

But for now, as darkness starts to descend, they briefly head back up on deck to take what they hope will be one last look at the shores of Western Australia. To make their honoured guests more comfortable, Captain Anthony insists that John Breslin – who is now in charge of the whole united operation – takes his own Master's Cabin.

Upon Captain Anthony's instructions, meanwhile, they try to work the *Catalpa* westward. However, the wind is listless at best, non-existent at worst. Occasionally, a breath of wind from the shore slaps and flaps the heavy canvas of the sails, which is deeply frustrating. Such is the state of exhaustion of nearly all those on the *Catalpa*, however, that by 9 pm all bar those on watch are asleep. At least, in the wee hours, there is a breath of wind that allows Samuel Smith to get the *Catalpa* gently under way 'working to windward on a light breeze . . .'[16] which will bring them, on a north-west bearing, slowly heading right past Fremantle and Rottnest Island.

Thus blows the wind of fate . . .

•

At Fremantle wharf, at 11 o'clock at night, all is at last in readiness.

With a burst of black smoke from its funnel – or it might be from Major Finnerty in his frustrated eagerness to get going – the *Georgette* signals she is up to steam, the sailors on the wharf detach the heavy ropes and quickly scramble up the gangplank and squeeze past the menacing black blob of the Armstrong gun before the steamer moves off.

Families crowd along the wharf as far as they are allowed, to farewell the brave souls about to head off after the renegades. Aboard the steamer, those brave souls in turn crowd to the stern, waving to their loved ones. They are still none too happy about this, but have no choice in the matter. Duty calls.

'There was intense excitement,' an account in Perth's *Western Mail* will later note. 'A naval battle was expected . . . The jetty was crowded. Wives and children bade tearful farewells to husbands and fathers whom they thought they might never see again.'

Among them are Billy Lynch and his mother, Winifred.

'I will not try to describe the scene among the wives of those old Pensioners who were away on war duty that night,' young Billy will recall, 'except to say that, like my mother, none went to bed . . .'[17]

Within ten minutes, there is nothing left to see.

The *Georgette* has been swallowed by the night.

•

Tossing and turning in his quarters at Fremantle Prison, Superintendent Joseph Doonan cannot sleep. His wife, Harriet, does her best to soothe him, but it is to no avail.

In the history of The Establishment, there has *never* been a breakout like this, and it has happened on his watch. It appears to have been masterminded by a man he has personally shown around the prison; a man he had briefed on security arrangements!

How could this have happened?

How could he have been so *stupid*?

In the Prison Governor's House, William Fauntleroy is also troubled. He had personally authorised the tour of the prison by Collins, and had been warned by Governor Robinson that Lord Carnarvon feared a breakout from The Establishment by the Fenians – and it had still happened!

And at Government House in Perth, Governor Robinson is asking himself much the same question. He had been warned by Lord Carnarvon about a possible Fenian breakout, and to keep his eyes open. But just 15 days ago, he had entertained the two key movers of the breakout, 'Mr Collins' and the Captain of the *Catalpa*, at dinner, right before he had personally assured Lord Carnarvon that his warning about preventing an escape of the Fenians had been heeded, and there was no chance of it happening.

If his men don't recapture the convicts, it will take some exculpatory manoeuvring to retain his position.

They *must* recapture them!

•

Sail ho!

The man high in the crow's nest of the *Georgette*, now well outside Rottnest Island, can see it clearly.

Surely it is the *Catalpa*? It is two miles off the for'ard quarter, to the sou'-sou'-east bearing north, and the steamship starts to close.

There is instant excitement on deck, most of it emanating from Major Charles Finnerty and Superintendent John F. Stone – with a few rather empty echoes in the much more reluctant spirits of Captain O'Grady, the Military Pensioners and the Water Police.

Upon the orders of Superintendent Stone, both the Union Jack and the Vice-Admiral's flag are raised, and the call rings out: 'All hands under arms.'[18]

On the instant, Military Pensioners and Water Police alike bring their weapons to bear.

•

Dawn, 19 April 1876, aboard the *Catalpa*, it's not over till it's over

Captain . . . ?

I say, Captain?

Yes, Mr Smith, what is it?

'The *Georgette* is approaching . . .'[19]

Instantly awake, Captain Anthony throws his boots on in three seconds flat and bounds up the ladder to the deck, where he joins John Breslin, who has been closely watching the approaching vessel for several minutes. At first Breslin had been convinced that it was no more than a small coasting vessel, but Samuel Smith had been sure from the first that it was trouble coming their way. He's right.

Sure enough, with the sun just coming up, here is the *Georgette*, steaming towards them from the direction of Fremantle, coming round the northern end of Rottnest Island and closing on them fast, 'with a man-of-war and vice-admiral's flag flying'.[20]

The significance of those flags does not escape Captain Anthony – the *Georgette* has been commissioned by the Governor as a vessel of Her Majesty's fleet, a vessel of war, acting on behalf of the British Government.

Well, if that is the game, the skipper must play.

Haul up the Stars and Stripes, he tells Smith before heading up to the poop deck to have full command of the situation.

When the 200-ton steamer comes closer still, they can see many more people on board than last time, though they can't make them out individually.

But when the *Georgette* crosses just half a mile in front of their steady nor'-nor'-west course, they can certainly see a large artillery piece mounted on her deck, pointing right at them, with what looks to be nearly a couple of dozen Military Pensioners. It is, of course, all calculated to intimidate the men on *Catalpa*, but the new arrivals are to be disappointed in that regard, as no such wilting is apparent, and *still* the whaler continues on her course, the men on each vessel staring at each other, as the *Georgette* now turns and pursues the whaler.

It is 6 am.

Like a hound hunting a fox – eager but wary – the *Georgette* continues to hunt the *Catalpa*, just off the whaler's stern. As the wind freshens, and the sails on the whaler fill, the gap between the two vessels starts to grow.

Excitement grows on the *Catalpa* at the idea they might simply be able to out-race the steamer and get clean away, only for the wretched wind to start to fall away again.

Aboard the *Georgette*, it is all hands to the shovels. The boilers are fully fired up, and the steamer billows black smoke as it tries to make up the distance. It also has every sail it has to the piffling wind.

It is a long haul, but by a quarter to eight the *Georgette* has indeed closed on the *Catalpa* and now sits close enough to the windward of the whaler that for the first time everyone on the decks of both vessels can see each other clearly.

Those on the *Catalpa* gaze across to the deck of the *Georgette*, lined with Water Police and Military Pensioners, the latter all resplendent in their sombre grey uniforms, frock coats a-flurry, with their polished brass gleaming in the morning sun. All of them are carrying rifles with their fixed bayonets glittering. Those Martini–Henry rifles, the military Fenians on the *Catalpa* know, are breech-loaders, meaning they are capable of firing 12 rounds every minute.

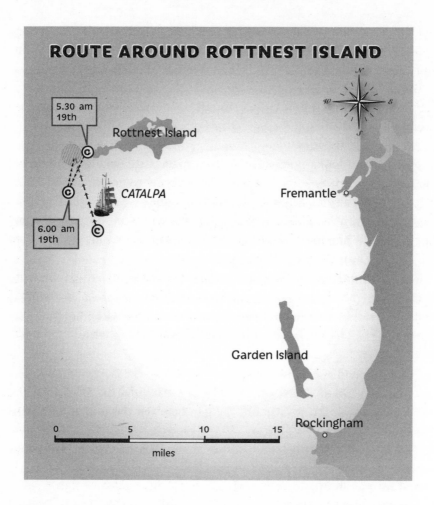

ROUTE AROUND ROTTNEST ISLAND

5.30 am 19th

Rottnest Island

CATALPA

6.00 am 19th

Fremantle

Garden Island

Rockingham

0   5   10   15

miles

Behind and above the armed men on the *Georgette*, a large whaleboat hangs from its davits, indicating they have the capacity to try to board.

So *that* is the way it is going to be.

And here, too, is Major Finnerty, as Breslin will describe him, 'heavily laden in the gorgeous trappings of a British army officer',[21] clearly in charge of the Military Pensioners and their artillery piece. But who is that man Captain Anthony spies over Finnerty's left shoulder, choosing this moment – when Finnerty's attention is fiercely focused on looking for a sign of the escaped convicts – to cheerily wave his hat at him? Of course, it is Captain Mick O'Grady, who had recently been so helpful telling him of reefs, tides and currents around Rockingham Beach. Choosing his own moment to reply, when Finnerty turns to give some orders about the cannon, Captain Anthony waves back.

It is understood. We are maritime men. Circumstance has placed us on opposite sides of this clash, but we still enjoy a rough brotherhood and will to some extent seek to protect each other and our respective men.

Breslin barks orders to his men, and within seconds, as he would delight in recounting, 'the men of our party were all assembled in the cabin with their rifles and revolvers ready'.[22]

Above deck, only the man at the helm and the lookout remain.

John Breslin looks poignantly at the emaciated Fenians standing at the front of the pack – one last push, he is saying to his Irish brethren – before starting a singularly sobering speech to the assembled throng. Yes, *he*, John Breslin, is willing to fight. But *his* will alone is not enough. The men with him must have their own will to fight, or surrender, once fully apprised of the whole situation.

'If the officials on board the *Georgette* are determined to fight for your re-capture,' he addresses the Fenians, 'they will, most probably, succeed, as they have the advantage of us in every way – more men, better armed, cannon, and a steamer with which they could sail round and round us.'

His words are soaked up in complete silence.

'While the rest of us in this party who have not been in prison can only suffer imprisonment, those of you who have been in prison risk being hanged if any life is lost by our resistance. It is simply a matter of dying now or waiting to die in prison, if the officials on the *Georgette* fire into or board us.'[23]

Such are the horns of their acute dilemma. Surrender, or fight?

The response is unanimous.

'We'll do whatever you say.'[24]

Breslin has got them this far, and they are happy to place their entire trust in him.

Very well then. All eyes are on Breslin, for his decision.

'I'll hold out to the last,'[25] he says, turning on his heel, to head back on deck.

The die is cast. If they have to, they will fight for their lives.

Superintendent Stone has decided to bring things to a head. Steaming tightly alongside and then a little further ahead of the *Catalpa*, he gives orders for the ship's cannon to be primed. He'll scare them into submission.

Like a rusty cuckoo clock not used for years, but now called on to tell the time the best it can, the 'artillery crew' do the best they can – not like a smoothly oiled machine, but like men who roughly remember the routine, and move to the memory. And they do pretty well under the circumstances, inserting a shell into the breech, putting a power charge behind it, and closing and locking the breech block.

As they work, the two vessels continue to ride the swells on a parallel course. Everything is nearly ready.

The artillery crew now point the Armstrong gun in the broad direction of the *Catalpa*, which will soon cross the line of fire as the steamer slows on Major Finnerty's command.

'Fire the first shot across her bow,' Finnerty directs the lead gunner in a voice crackling with excitement, 'but do not hit her.'[26]

Major Finnerty now steps forward and rather theatrically raises his sword in the air. It glints in the morning sun.

A few more barked words and now . . . the sword flashes downwards, whereupon the Military Pensioner holding the lanyard – *My God, he is really going to do it! Everyone get down!* – pulls on it. A bare instant later the firing lock snaps down on the cap, sending a spark into the powder bag, igniting it. A puff of black smoke appears from the top of the cannon, followed by a burst of flame from the muzzle, and with a shattering boom, the cannon fires like thunder.

Pfffffeeeeeeeeeeeeeeeeeeeeeeeeeeeeewwwwwwwwwwwww . . .

The cannon ball whistles over the heads of those crouching on the *Catalpa*'s bow.

SPLASH!

They spring up to see a massive spout of water rising, higher than the *Catalpa*'s masthead, just 200 yards to their starboard.

On board the *Georgette*, the rusty artillery men do their best to reload, swabbing out the barrel to douse remaining sparks, inserting a fresh shell through the breech and ramming into the bore, and, finally, inserting a powder cartridge into the chamber.

It is 8 am.

Captain Anthony looks to Breslin for guidance, asking what he wants done.

'Hold on,' Breslin instructs, 'and don't take any notice of the shot yet.'[27]

Three minutes later, the *Georgette* comes alongside, the mouth of the cannon pointed right at the *Catalpa* from such a close range that a conversation between the two boats can be spoken into their loudhailers, not shouted.

'Now,' Breslin whispers to Captain Anthony while subtly motioning his head towards Superintendent Stone on the *Georgette*'s deck, 'ask him what does he want?'[28]

Captain Anthony steps up to the weather rail to do exactly that, raising his speaking trumpet, when Superintendent John F. Stone calls across the waters first, 'Bark ahoy!'[29]

'What do you want?' Captain Anthony bellows.

'Heave to,' comes the reply.

'What for?'[30] Anthony retorts, for all the world as though he is bemused by the question. (An escape from The Establishment. *What* escape from The Establishment, officer?)

After a long pause, comes the reply.

'Have you got any convict prisoners on board?' calls Stone across the water.

'No prisoners here, no prisoners that I know of!'[31] Captain Anthony calls back in his almost casual Yankee lilt.

Both Superintendent Stone and Major Finnerty are ruminating on their next move. On the one hand, it would be madness to fire. But, on the other, the claims of Britannia to rule the seas are so steeped in every fibre of their being, most particularly in the face of thieving Yankee upstarts, that they simply can't resist trying one ploy . . .

Captain Anthony watches the crew of the *Georgette* like a hawk, considering his next move.

But he doesn't consider it long, for, almost as if the boom of the cannon has awoken the weather gods, the breeze starts to stiffen, and even become a little gusty.

The *Catalpa* starts to pick up speed.

Captain Anthony gives the orders, and his crew scramble to get more canvas to the wind.

It helps! At least now they are less a sitting duck than a fast paddling one, and just the fact of movement, of riding the swell with speed, lifts spirits all around.

But what if, instead of blowing the *Catalpa* out of the water – always an extreme option, particularly in international waters – the men of the *Georgette* attempt to board her?

•

There is a pause as Superintendent Stone confers with Major Finnerty.

'I demand,' Stone calls out, 'six escaped convicts now on board your vessel, in the name of the Governor of Western Australia. I know you and your vessel. I know the men I want are on board, they were seen boarding by the police boat yesterday. If you don't give them up you must take the consequences.'[32]

'I have none on board,'[33] Anthony replies.

Oh, really?

'I telegraphed to your government,' Major Finnerty calls, momentarily usurping Superintendent Stone's role. 'Don't you know that you are amenable to British law in this Colony? You have six convict prisoners on board. I see some of them on deck now.'[34]

This time, it is Captain Anthony who pauses, as John Breslin whispers to him: 'This fellow is lying and trying to bluff us.'[35]

It's true. All communications from Perth must first go via ship to the telegraphy hub of Adelaide, then across the country to Darwin, and from there to Java, to England, then across the Atlantic to the United States. Getting a message from Fremantle to the United States then back to Fremantle might take four weeks in all.

Still, taking the silence from the *Catalpa* as wavering, Major Finnerty follows up: 'I give you fifteen minutes to consider, and you must take the consequences; I have the means to do it, and if you don't heave to I'll blow the mast out of you.'[36]

This time, Captain Anthony needs no time to reply.

Standing tall, bristling, a proud and pure Yankee from tip to toes – whose very nation was forged in opposition to bullying Brits – he points to the Stars and Stripes fluttering overhead – 'Old Glory', as the Americans refer to it – and roars . . .

'That's the American flag. I am on the high seas. My flag protects me. If you fire on this ship you fire on the American flag.'[37]

This time the silence that ensues comes from the *Georgette*, as they must reflect on the gravity of the situation.

Aboard the *Catalpa*, however, there is outrage among the Americans, at the very idea of firing on their flag – which somehow makes them even more incensed than the idea of firing on the ship. Fire on our *flag*? Fire on this, our sacred symbol of liberation from the British yoke? Fire on *our* mighty flag, fluttering high on the flagstaff of a vessel hailing from the place the Boston Tea Party was held, the very place where the first moves were made towards freedom forever from the tyranny of monarchs and their self-ordained 'divine' rights, of viceroys and their lamentable lackeys the likes of which Major Finnerty is the very embodiment?

We'll see you in *hell* first!

'Damn him,' says Smith, 'let him sink us. We'll go down with the ship. I'll never start sheet or tack for him.'

Still, turning to Breslin, he asks, 'What will you do if he attempts to board us?'

'Sink his [whaleboat] when it comes alongside,' says the Irishman true. 'You have a couple of good heavy grindstones; let us have them handy to heave over the side.'[38]

Good idea. Just one of those heavy grindstones hurled into the middle of a whaleboat would surely take out a couple of men, *and* put a hole in the hull.

And don't forget the heavy logs in the hold, Captain Anthony reminds the First Mate. Get the crew to bring them up on deck. If it comes to it, we can hurl those, too, down on to those swarming below. Excellent idea.

Now, for good measure, Samuel Smith arms his men with the ship's arsenal of blubber spades – the cruel cutting spades that can not only cut whale flesh like a hot knife through butter, but could do exactly the same to humans.

Any attempt to board will see carnage unleashed.

•

Aboard the *Georgette*, Superintendent Stone has another idea. Forget the gun for now, he does not wish trouble with the United States Government, if he can avoid it.

He instructs Captain O'Grady to keep the steamer tightly on the port side of the whaler as they proceed north up the coast, hemming the whaler in the best they can.

And so the two vessels continue to proceed on roughly parallel courses, the *Georgette*'s black smoke only lazily drifting away on what remains a relatively light wind.

Soon enough, however, it is not the *Georgette* that takes Captain Anthony's attention, it is Rottnest Island. If they get within three miles of it, they will be back within territorial waters. But the Massachusetts mariner will have none of it. And this is not a matter for John Breslin, it is a matter for him as Captain of this ship.

''Bout ship, keep off to sea!'[39] he roars, emitting a further stream of orders that goes fully 30 seconds.

The officers aboard the *Georgette* watch with intrigue . . . as the crew of the *Catalpa* 'unexpectedly hauled up the clew on the mainsail, hauled down the head of the spanker, and let the gaff topsail run down',[40] which sees the *Catalpa* clearly slowing. Beaming, infinitely relieved, if a little surprised, Superintendent Stone orders the *Georgette* to slow. It seems that the Yankees have seen sweet reason, and are turning to surrender and allow themselves to be boarded, and . . .

And Captain Anthony now suddenly pulls his wheel *hard over*. Within moments, instead of having Rottnest Island in the hazy distance in front of them, the *Catalpa* has . . . the *Georgette* . . . dead ahead. The whaler, her sails hard on the wind, is heading right for the British ship!

Rrrrrrammmming speed.

The move takes those aboard the *Georgette* by complete surprise. One second they were proceeding on a parallel course, edging the Yankee whaler to the shore, the next second they were effectively declaring victory and calling the chase to a halt . . . only to have the hard copper-coated bow of the whaler – strong enough to break Arctic ice – coming straight for them!

Captain Mick O'Grady has no interest in testing the *Georgette*'s durability – he never wanted to be here in the first place, did he mention? – and snaps back into his role as commander, Superintendent Stone be damned. He jams *Georgette*'s helm hard over to starboard, meaning the whaler misses them by . . . mere *feet*, as it turns out.

There are shouts of alarm and imprecations of fury coming from the *Georgette*, and cries of exultation coming from the *Catalpa*. But nothing changes the essential result.

For, far from being hedged in towards land, the *Catalpa* is now racing towards the open ocean with the *Georgette* left in her wake. The steamer's crew take to the shovels with renewed fury. Soon, black smoke billows once more as the ship nigh bursts a boiler to catch up, steam madly chasing sail.

Thirty minutes later, the steamer is again off the *Catalpa*'s port side, when it makes a move of its own, suddenly changing direction so it cuts right across the stern of the whaler, giving the artillery men a perfect shot right into their sails . . . if the commander orders it done.

From the point of view of Superintendent Stone, if just one of the riled-up men on the *Catalpa* is ill-disciplined enough to fire at the *Georgette* – provoked by their menacing closeness – then the Stars and Stripes will no longer protect them.

Aware of the danger, Breslin barks to the armed sailors standing guard on deck to lower their guns. No-one is to fall into this trap.

Still, so tense is the situation that Breslin braces himself for the raking shot among the masts, which he knows must come . . .

But to his amazement, no shot is forthcoming.

•

A furious conversation is taking place aboard the *Georgette*.

Now that the ruse of crossing their stern has failed, Major Finnerty is decided.

'I will fire on the ship unless the Fenians are given up,'[41] he says to Superintendent Stone, and proceeds to give orders to his men to do exactly that. They must come around again, train the cannon on the American ship's masts and sails, and fire.

But Superintendent Stone will have none of it. He is the son of the Colony's long-time Advocate-General – the leading legal officer in the land – and is himself trained in the law, so he knows that however much the prisoners and their enablers have broken the laws of the Colony by escaping, the writ of that law simply does not run this far out on the high seas.

It had been one thing to fire a shot across her bows, and another thing to cruise in so closely across her stern to show how easily they could blow her mast and sails away.

But, actually fire into an American vessel on the high seas?

No.

He orders Major Finnerty to desist. They have no legal right to detain the *Catalpa*.

Still the Major persists in ordering his men to prepare to fire.

'Major Finnerty,' Superintendent Stone says sharply, 'I will place you under arrest if you persist in ordering your men to fire.'[42]

Stunned, humiliated, Major Finnerty nevertheless has no choice. His men stand down.

Superintendent Stone has just one more chance to stop the *Catalpa* getting away, and gives Captain O'Grady the orders to bring the *Georgette* within hailing distance once more.

Now, aboard the *Catalpa*, they see Superintendent Stone step up to the gunwale and call out to them:

'Won't you surrender to our government?'[43]

No-one on the *Catalpa* makes reply.

So he calls out once more.

'I see three of those men on board now.'[44]

'You are mistaken, sir,' Captain Anthony replies. 'The men you see are my ship's crew.'[45]

'Can I come on board?' Superintendent Stone[46] calls.

'No, sir,' Captain Anthony says. 'I am bound for sea and can't stop.'[47]

Superintendent Stone tries one *last* time: 'Will you let me board your ship and judge for myself?'[48]

'No! You shan't board my vessel.'[49]

'Then your Government will be communicated with, and you must take the consequences.'[50]

Captain Anthony: 'All right.'[51]

If you say so.

As a matter of fact, you may say *anything* you like, but the central point remains. We will forcibly resist any attempt you make to board us, and there will be bloodshed. And while you have indeed the option of firing your cannon into us, or into our masts, this would be a clear breach of international law, while we are in international waters and beyond your jurisdiction.

It just might be check-mate if this representative of the British Empire is to play by the rules that Britannia insists on. It is she who presumes to rule the waves across the globe, so she cannot waive the rules herself.

And, in fact, as Breslin would delightedly recount, 'the *Georgette* still kept us company as if loath to part, until half-past nine A. M., when she slowly swung off, and without having the courtesy to bid us bon voyage, steamed back to Fremantle'.[52]

They have won!

Wild cheering breaks out aboard the *Catalpa*, none stronger than that coming from the six Fenians.

'Boys,' Captain Anthony calls to the Fenians, 'take a good look at her. Probably you'll never see her again.'[53]

Aboard the *Catalpa* the wild rejoicing continues: cheers and tears as fears abate. They have seen off the most immediate danger.

And if things had not *quite* gone their way to this point, from now things change. As free men, now they clearly have the luck of the Irish with them, the luck of the newly liberated Irish, for within hours the *Catalpa* is helped along by a very strong easterly that sees them roar away from Fremantle and all chance of a belated attempt to stop them, coming from there.

No, they are not yet home free, for there remains an enormous distance to traverse and no doubt British warships will be on the lookout for them, but at least that distance means that any chase coming from Fremantle will be futile.

•

And look there!

By the Roundhouse on Arthur Head at the entrance to Fremantle Harbour, a Union Jack goes up to indicate an approaching vessel, followed by a blue flag being raised on the south yard-arm to indicate it is approaching by the South Passage and . . . sure enough!

Within minutes it is confirmed as the *Georgette*.

The sight of the steamer once more returning to the wharves of Fremantle causes enormous consternation, and speculation as to what can possibly be the cause.

Bets are even taken, with some maintaining that the only reason it could be back so quickly was that 'the *Catalpa*, warned of the steps the governor was taking by the previous visit of the *Georgette*, had attacked her and beaten her off'.[54]

Nonsense! And we'll take that bet.

For my money – and I have cash down, right here – I say the only reason it could be back so quickly is if, 'overawed by the determination of force on board the *Georgette*, the captain of the *Catalpa* had quietly surrendered the runaways'.[55]

With so much money riding on it, nigh on every glass in Fremantle is trained on the *Georgette*'s deck when it comes into range.

But again, there is confusion. The fact that none of the crew appears to be bloodied seems to knock back the first theory. And yet it is equally undeniable that there are no prisoners in chains visible – as would surely be the case if the *Georgette* is returning in triumph.

When finally the truth is revealed – through shouts from the crew to those waiting anxiously on the wharves – both sides of the argument are underwhelmed.

Can it really be that an armed steamer has been sent on its way, as the local *Fremantle Herald* will put it, 'fooled by a Yankee skipper'?[56]

Extraordinary.

The hang-dog expressions of Superintendent Stone and Major Finnerty make it clear that they think so too, while the Military Pensioners and Water Police wear a curious expression of bemusement and relief. On the one hand they feel, as the *Fremantle Herald* will report, 'that they had been taking part in a very silly farce, and had been laughed at by the

Yankees at sea',[57] but so too are they grateful to be safely in the harbour without losing any of their number to a bloody cataclysm.

It is over.

•

Never a particularly athletic man, Major Charles Finnerty can nevertheless move quickly when the occasion warrants, and there will never be a more urgent occasion than now. For no sooner has the *Georgette* come into the wharf than the good Major, 'ropeable',[58] *leaps* from the deck to the walkway, his men close behind. Together, they march – by the *riigggggggght*, quick – up to the Telegraph Office.

Storming to the counter he sends a telegram immediately to Governor Robinson in Perth: 'The flag of old England has this day been defied and disgraced by a handful of blatant Americans.'[59]

Out there, somewhere, the *Catalpa* sails on, laughter and song drifting in its wake . . .

CHAPTER FOURTEEN

THE AFTERMATH

For twenty-five years past – with the exception of the abortive Fenian movement – the Irish people have acted as if green flags, denunciation of England, and poetic sunburstry were enough to establish Ireland's claim to national independence . . .

The rescue of the political prisoners proves that the Irishmen who talk least can do most. It proves also that distrust is not chronic in the Irish people – that they can stake great issues on the faith of single men – when they have selected them for their capacity and intelligence instead of their braggadocio.[1]

John Boyle O'Reilly, writing in the Boston Pilot, June 1876

Here's the good ship Catalpa, and all her ship's crew;
Land of felons and jailers, here's to you adieu,
From your dry, sandy shores we are speeding away.
May your fortune be brighter at no distant day;
Here's the land of the free, may it flourish and grow, –
And God prosper old Ireland wherever we go.[2]

John Breslin, descriptive poem of the rescue of the Fenian prisoners, 1876

Now boys if you will listen to the story I'll relate,
I'll tell you of the noble men who from the foe escaped,
Though bound with Saxon fetters in the dark Australian gaol,
They struck a blow for freedom and for Yankee land did sail.[3]

Irish ballad, unknown origin

Now, while many of the Fremantle folk are quietly thrilled that the Fenians have got away, neither The Establishment itself, nor the establishment of Fremantle and Perth – in the sense of the ruling class – take the escape with anything resembling good humour. Many 'sincerely hoped that instructions would be given to go out again and take the prisoners by force'.[4]

His Excellency, however, is made of more sober stuff. After receiving Major Finnerty's telegram, the red-tape ruler Robinson replies that they are 'not to be led into committing a breach of international law to gratify a feeling of resentment at the cool effrontery of the Yankee'.[5] He orders the armed parties on board the *Georgette* dismissed with His Excellency's thanks.

But there are other measures Governor Robinson can take.

•

A week after the escape, and all is in a state of flux. The first action by the authorities – led by Governor Robinson and his counterpart at The Establishment, Governor Fauntleroy – has been to crack down on all remaining Fenians, and just about anybody and anything starting with 'F', just in case.

Even those few Fenians still in Western Australia on their ticket-of-leave, 'and leading exemplary and, irreproachable lives', are rounded up and marched into The Establishment, 'under unnecessary strong police escort, to be immured in the solitary and suffocating dens of the Fremantle prison until it is his Excellency's pleasure to restore them their limited liberty'.[6]

The *Fremantle Herald* is appalled and says so, calling it, 'a most arbitrary stretch of power on the part of the Governor, unprecedented in the usages of convict discipline'.[7]

For, yes, the actions of the Government and The Establishment do not sit well with much of the population and press, who can see the clear injustice of punishing men who have had nothing whatsoever to do with the breakout and now find themselves back in prison.

Governor Robinson doesn't care. With six Fenians gone on the high seas, for the moment he must be sure that no others get away, and if that means putting entirely innocent men back in prison, so be it.

So to with swarming all over vessels visiting from one nation in particular. The next American vessel that arrives at Fremantle, the *Na Malole*, has no sooner dropped anchor on 1 May than officials are boarding and using prodding bayonets to look into every nook and cranny for anyone that might be secreted there, and they continue to do so until such time as it leaves – without any escapees, the British are sure.

Beyond Governor Robinson's fear of more Fenians getting away, he must deal with the sheer embarrassment of his administration, caused by the stunning escape – as is not so helpfully pointed out by the Perth *Inquirer*:

> It seems humiliating, that a Yankee with a half dozen coloured men should be able to come into our waters and carry off six of the most determined of the Fenian convicts – all of them military prisoners – and then to laugh at us for allowing them to be taken away without an effort to secure them.[8]

For its part, at least Perth's *Western Australian Times* is happy to point the finger further afield.

> The Home Government have themselves to blame for escapes of this description, and as there is now no doubt as to the necessity for a man-of-war cruiser being always on our coast, it may possibly be deemed prudent to station one here to prevent a repetition of this unparalleled piece of Yankee impudence.[9]

But, as Governor Robinson knows only too well, the Home Government is unlikely to come to the conclusion that the cause of the outrage is . . . the Home Government. No, they will need someone in the colony itself, and it is with that in mind that His Excellency writes a telegram to Lord Carnarvon to inform him that, 'without wishing to impute blame prematurely to anyone', *much*, he knows where the starting point should be – Governor Fauntleroy.

> Instead of keeping a close watch on the Fenian prisoners, and of placing them under the charge of his most tried and trusted warders – the only condition on which I would have consented to their continuing to be attached to the outside working parties – he has actually allowed them to be employed as grooms, gardeners, orderlies, thus removing them altogether from the supervision of the warders and positively facilitating their escape . . . It is incomprehensible to me how an officer of Mr. Fauntleroy's experience can have been guilty of such terrible want of judgment.[10]

For his part, Governor Fauntleroy is equally clear who is most responsible for the disaster and it is certainly not him, as he personally writes to Governor Robinson:

I consider Assistant Warder Booler gravely to blame in acting
contrary to all regulations in allowing any prisoner to detach any
men from his party without a regular written order.[11]

The way forward, Governor Robinson decides, is to announce that
an Official Inquiry will be held, and sure enough it is quickly under
way, presided over by the Honourable Colonial Secretary Mr Anthony
Lefroy, together with two senior officials and . . .

And what now?

A popular song is starting to take hold in Fremantle and Perth in a
population that seems to be ever more openly on the side of the escaped
convicts.

> *A noble whale ship and commander,*
> *Called the Catalpa they say,*
> *Came out to Western Australia,*
> *And took six poor Fenians away.*

> *So come all you screw warders and gaolers,*
> *Remember Perth Regatta Day;*
> *Take care of the rest of your Fenians,*
> *Or the Yankees will steal them away.*[12]

Oh, how they sing it with such gusto!

> *Now remember those six Fenian colonials*
> *And sing o'er these few verses with skill.*
> *And remember the Yankee that stole them*
> *And the home that they left on the hill.*
> *For now there in the States of America*
> *When all will be able to cry*
> *'We will hoist the green flag with the*
> *shamrock.'*
> *Saying, 'Hurrah, for Old Ireland we die'.*[13]

That problem, at least, is easy to solve, as His Excellency promptly
has the song banned, punishable by prison for all those heard singing it.

In the meantime, Governor Robinson braces for the reaction from
London and the world when the news finally gets through of the escape
of the Fenians.

A naturally calm man, he soothes himself, as ever, with his music.

For those not blessed with such natural calm – read Major Finnerty – the times are more difficult to navigate. When a rumour spreads that Finnerty had 'purposely left the powder and shot behind at Fremantle',[14] so that he and his men would not have to engage in an actual battle, there proves to be an enormous commotion in the newspaper offices on the morning of publication. The editor is advised that there is an enormous man with a very red nose here to see him, a 'Major Finnerty', and he is not taking no for an answer. Indeed!

Seconds afterwards, Major Finnerty bursts into the offices proper, threatening the editor with, 'solitary, flogging, hulks, bread and water, and penal oakum'.[15]

The editor will have none of it, with another newspaper later gleefully reporting that Finnerty had been 'ejected at the point of a strong boot, the printer called in to assist, being of herculean build and athletic manners'.[16]

•

Aboard the *Catalpa*, the festive atmosphere endures even as everyone is put to work bringing timber up from the hold and, supervised by Denis Duggan, building new berths on deck for the new arrivals. Captain Anthony has two new suits of clothes handed out to each Fenian, so they may look the part of free men as well as being so.

By keeping the vessel broadly around the latitude of 33° South, they are able to benefit from the south-east trade-winds, and push as much as 200 miles a day towards the Cape of Good Hope. Rounding it, they must continue to push north-west across the oft stormy seas of the Atlantic Ocean, hopefully all the way to New York and then New Bedford!

A song written by John Breslin, and regularly sung by them all on evening get-togethers, captures much of the spirit of the moment.

All together sing, starting with . . .

> . . . *Six Irish soldiers brave, rescued from the living grave,*
> *In which the cursed spite of England bound them.*
> *Life and liberty to save, came flying o'er the wave.*
> *And along with our bold skipper there we found them.*
> *Then the British lion roared for his captives; and, on board*
> *A steamer, sent out soldiery to find them . . .*

And finishing with . . .

Streaming gaily in the breeze, our peak adorning . . .
So they left us in despair, and skulked off to their lair,
Whilst our starry flag with joyful hearts we hail her,
For the lion dropped his tail, and his growl became a wail,
When bearded by a simple Yankee whaler.[17]

However, it is not as if the trip back is without tension. Most of it is generated by the American shoemaker Thomas Brennan, who, at last in the mix with the freed Fenian prisoners, agitates – staggeringly, with the help of the ever-drunken Denis Duggan – against the authority of John Breslin. The key issue is whether or not they should head straight back to America or, as Breslin and Captain Anthony are inclined, do some more whaling to defray costs. With Brennan representing himself as high up in the *Clan-na-Gael*, and practically implying that Breslin is not the real power on ship, it is a difficult situation. At one point things get so ugly and heated – from men incarcerated so long that they can barely think straight in their desire to be back on land and free as soon as humanly possible, all of it whipped up by Brennan – things even teeter on the edge of mutiny. Nevertheless, Breslin, capable of spiriting James Stephens out of Richmond Bridewell Prison, and the Fenians out of Fremantle, is more than capable of dealing with the uppity Brennan. For all that, the view of the Fenians themselves – not surprisingly, they are eager to get to America as quickly as possible – is acceded to.

22 May 1876, House of Commons, Westminster, too little, too late!

If it please the House!

The question has been put to Prime Minister Benjamin Disraeli, in response to the petition recently presented, signed by 138 Members of Parliament: Will he offer a final amnesty to those few Fenians still in prison both in England and on the other side of the world in Western Australia?

In response, Disraeli notes his satisfaction that the Fenians in prison in England remain there, while he confesses his frustration at, after receiving the petition, not being able to quickly find out the state of the prisoners in Western Australia, given the difficulty of sending and receiving telegrams from that remote outpost. But in any case, he is confident that his government has pursued the right course to this point.

'I am bound to say,' the Prime Minister says firmly, 'that I am not prepared to advise Her Majesty to release the prisoners . . .'[18]

And so it is done. For John Devoy and all the organisers of the Fenian breakout it is . . . *their* lucky escape. How ludicrous would they appear, to have gone to such effort when the British have proven happy to grant them amnesty anyway. But it is not to be.

Prime Minister Disraeli dismisses all chance of amnesty, while blithely unaware that it is all beside the point anyway, for the prisoners are out and gone.

22 May 1876, Perth, herewith the findings of the Inquiry

Today is the day. The three members of the Western Australian establishment who have been interviewing most of the available players in the drama – six key players had been unavailable – hand down their findings.

They are pleased to announce that Governor Robinson is blameless, as is Governor Fauntleroy, or very nearly. The same, however, cannot be said of Francis Lindsey, the Gatekeeper, who had allowed, 'Cranston, Hassett and Darragh all to pass out without any special authority, and no special note had been taken of their comings and goings'.[19] The Inquiry is particularly critical of Lindsey having allowed Bob Cranston to pass simply by saying he was on an errand for the Governor. He is immediately suspended.

Thomas Booler, however, could be absolved from 'any special blame', as, though he released his prisoners on oral messages only, it was established that this was part of normal practice. Albert Liddelow, the warder in charge of two parties working at the Governor's residence, is absolved because, 'he was left without the possibility of effectually guarding those who composed it'.[20]

Generally, the Commissioners find fault with the fact that 'a lax system has gradually obtained in some matters of prison discipline that messages have been transmitted by prisoner constables with far too much freedom, and that too much has been left to the discretion of warders'.[21]

While there is in that finding implicit criticism of Superintendent Joseph Doonan, there is no specific rebuke.

(Doonan is relieved, but still emotionally scorched, having been mortified by testimony made and affidavits tabled during the Inquiry which, as he had written in a letter of protest, 'appear to have been made this day for the purpose of damaging my character'. The result of all of this?

'I have incurred not only the hostility of the prisoners, but also of many of the warders.'[22])

So, yes, it is something not to have been condemned by the findings of the Inquiry, but he remains mortified by the finger of blame he still feels is being pointed at him by everyone from the shadows. They are talking about me, I tell you, saying it was all my fault!

For their parts, Governors Robinson and Fauntleroy are infinitely relieved not to have been criticised at all. The major outcome of the Inquiry is that, after serving his suspension, Gatekeeper Francis Lindsey is summarily sacked.

•

Getting out a weekly newspaper is a little like standing under a Dutch windmill. You have no sooner hurled yourself forward with every ounce of energy you have in you to escape one crushing deadline . . . and regained your equilibrium . . . than the next deadline looms over you, closing fast and you must do it again.

It means John Boyle O'Reilly, as editor and, since recently, part-owner of the paper, is always busy – writing stories, commissioning stories, doing lay-outs, having meetings – with barely a moment to himself. It takes a lot for something to make him stop stock-still, and stare . . . and there it is. For one of the *Pilot*'s copy-boys has just blithely laid a cablegram on his desk. A single word leaps out at him – 'Catalpa' – and he quickly devours the rest: 'London, June 6. A dispatch from Melbourne, Australia, states that all the political prisoners confined in Western Australia have escaped on the American whaleship *Catalpa* . . .'[23]

O'Reilly reads it again. And again. And again!

They're out! They're free! The whole extraordinary scheme has *worked*!

John Devoy is a hero. John Breslin is a hero. Captain Anthony is a hero. And his Fenian friends, now on their way to America, who have borne a decade of imprisonment for fighting for the cause of Ireland, are the greatest heroes of all!

And England in all this?

Here, friends, is the real significance. After clearing the front page of the next edition of the Boston *Pilot* to expand upon the good tidings, he settles to the wonderful task of writing the nub of this staggering news, for Ireland, for England, for the struggle for liberty of his homeland:

There has never been an enterprise so large and so terribly dangerous carried out more admirably. It will be remembered of Irish patriots that they never forget their suffering brothers. The prisoners who have escaped are humble men, most of them private soldiers. But the PRINCIPLE was at stake and for this they have been released. England will now realize that she has made a mistake that will follow her to her deathbed in making Ireland so implacable and daring an enemy ... The men who sent the *Catalpa* to Australia are just the men to send a hundred *Catalpas* to wipe British commerce from the face of the sea![24]

To John Devoy, he writes an exultant letter:

This is the most memorable and honourable affair, and will do more good for Ireland than a whole unsuccessful attempt at rebellion. It will put vim and confidence into men and make them ...[25]

•

And John Devoy himself? In the offices of the New York *Herald*, he has seen the same cablegram and simply slumps with relief – the *work* they put in, the *risks* they took, the obstacles they have overcome, to reach this TRIUMPH – before his office is stormed by fellow Irish–Americans, overcome with the emotion of it all.

•

There are similarly joyous reactions around the world as the news breaks, with explosions of joy heard everywhere from Liverpool, with its huge Irish population, to San Francisco, from New York to Dublin, where, on the following Saturday night, a torchlight procession down the principal boulevard, O'Connell Street, is held.

Oh, and when it comes to Disraeli, John Boyle O'Reilly also has a few words reserved for him in his endless stream of editorials in the Boston *Pilot*.

Two weeks ago the English Prime Minister scornfully refused to release those prisoners at the earnest request of Ireland. It was in his hands then to render this escape meaningless, and to make Irishmen believe that they had better wait for the slow course of English justice. But the old spirit of domineering insolence was too strong in the British House of Commons. To show mercy to Ireland would be a confession of weakness; they determined to refuse the Irish petition . . .[26]

More fool them!

Also in New York at the time – for he has just arrived in America, having come by way of London and brief sojourns in Dublin and Tipperary – is none other than . . . William Foley, the ailing Fenian who had put Breslin in touch with James Wilson in Fremantle.

Though struggling badly, with 'very little of that soldier's strut so characteristic of British cavalrymen',[27] these wonderful tidings invigorate him to the point that, when interviewed by one of John Devoy's journalists from the New York *Herald,* Foley is almost peppy!

'The news,' Foley exults, 'seems too good to be true; it is so short a time since I saw them within the prison walls, and all I can say is, God speed them on their way, and may God bless the Yankee captain who took them aboard.'[28]

That Yankee Captain, having just guided the *Catalpa* around the Cape of Good Hope days before, sets sail for the North Atlantic Ocean . . .

Now, under normal circumstances they would have pulled in at a port to clean the barnacles off the hull of the *Catalpa* – but these are not normal circumstances. Every port, and certainly every port of the British Empire, presents danger of capture. It is for the same reason that Captain Anthony has no desire to meet with other ships while on the high seas. Yes, their American flag will offer the same protection in the international waters of the Indian and Atlantic oceans as it did off the coast of Western Australia, but why take that chance? The fact that those on the *Georgette* ceded to international law does not mean that others will, and Captain Anthony's primary concern is to just keep moving.

Certainly the barnacles and seaweed growth slow the *Catalpa* sometimes to as little as 50 miles a day, but still on 10 July 1876 they cross the Equator and are closing fast on the east coast of America.

'You're almost American citizens now,'[29] Captain Anthony tells the Fenians as they cross the line.

What are the lines from the Wild Geese poem, again?

Ah yes.

The Wild Geese fly where others walk;
The Wild Geese do what others talk –

The way is long from France, you know –
He'll come at last when South winds blow.[30]

Well, it's blowing now, and they roar to the north.

Entering the whaling grounds once more in the North Atlantic, Captain Anthony is tempted to stop briefly and try their chances getting some more whales on the way – which had been part of his original instructions.

'Now is just the season for whaling on the Western Grounds,' he tells John Breslin.[31]

Initially, John Breslin agrees, but the desires of the Fenians to get to America with all possible speed once again sway the final decision. They chart a direct course to New York, which has been decided as the best destination – in no small part because it boasts the country's greatest concentration of Irish–Americans.

June 1876, Williamstown, unfair cop

'Allo, 'allo, 'allo.

Who's this, then?

On their way back to Sydney, 'Alfred Dixon' and 'Henry Hopkins' – in fact, the two Fenians from Ireland, Dennis F. McCarthy of Cork and John Walsh, who had cut the telegraph wires on the morning of the escape – are on the P & O Company's mail steamship *Sumatra* from Fremantle, and have just walked down the gangplank on a brief stopover at Williamstown, when they are fallen upon by Victorian detectives!

What on *earth* is going on?

Well, it seems that the two men they take in for questioning, Messrs Dixon and Hopkins, are suspected of being 'accredited agents of the Chief Head Centre in America, and that they were implicated in the conspiracy which resulted in the escape of six convicts who were spirited away by an American whaler'.[32]

Well, Messrs Dixon and Hopkins are appalled, nay *appalled*. Law-abiding men like them, hauled in for questioning, over an atrocity like the one described? Why, they know nothing at all about it! It is true they are just returning from the city where it all took place, and the papers were full of it, but that is all. And yes, you police might have a tip-off, but what *else* do you have?

The short answer is, not much. Dixon and Hopkins seem to be exactly what they say they are – businessmen investors who are travelling the country looking for land, and who have just rejected Western Australia because of its poor climate – and it is not long before the police are apologising for having troubled them so.

'It is sufficient to state,' the *Gippsland Times* reports, 'that the persons referred to appear to be quiet inoffensive individuals, and they state that they are desirous of attending strictly to their own business, which is to either select land or to purchase farms upon which to settle with their families, who intend following them at an early period.'[33]

Within days, Messrs Dixon and Hopkins are on their way once more, never to be heard from again – at least not by those names.

Sunday, 16 July 1876, Fremantle Prison, the unkindest cut of all

Harriet Doonan has been sick with worry about Joseph of late. Shattered by the escape of the Fenians, he had been further decimated by the subsequent Inquiry; enough to see him committed to the lunatic asylum for a couple of weeks.

And yes, at least last Friday he had resumed his duties at the prison, which had been a relief, but what now?

All through last night he had been tossing and turning, moaning and groaning, and this morning his blood-shot eyes reveal a deeply troubled soul.

It is time for Joseph to go. But he intends to go to an entirely different place to the one his wife thinks.

Standing up, Joseph tenderly shakes hands with dear Harriet and says 'Goodbye', before turning away.

After just one step, he takes a razor from his pocket, and viciously slashes his own throat, before falling to the ground with buckets of blood pouring from the frightful gash.

'The haemorrhage was excessive,' the local paper takes up the story, 'and although suppressed at length by the medical gentleman who at once attended him, the patient is so exhausted that there remains but little hope of his recovery. It is rumoured that since the escape of the gang of Fenians per Catalpa, Mr Doonan has entertained gloomy forebodings as to how this affair would be regarded by the authorities in England – perhaps involving his position – and hence the sad stroke . . .'[34]

Early August 1876, New Bedford, some correspondence

A very formal-looking letter comes across the desk of the City Marshal of New Bedford, and he is immediately absorbed by its contents:

POLICE DEPARTMENT.
CHIEF OFFICE, PERTH, WESTERN AUSTRALIA,
April 18, 1876.

SIR,—*I beg to inform you that on the 17th instant the imperial
convicts named in the margin absconded from the convict settlement at
Freemantle, in this colony, and escaped from the colony in the American
whaling bark Catalpa, G. Anthony master. This bark is from New
Bedford, Massachusetts, U. S. A. The convicts were taken from the
shore in a whaleboat belonging to the Catalpa, manned by Captain
Anthony and six of the crew. The abettors were Collins, Jones, and
Johnson.*

*I attach the description of each of the absconders, and have to request
that you will be good enough to furnish me with any particulars you may
be able to gather concerning them.*
I have the honor to be, sir,
Your obedient servant,
M. A. SMITH, Supt. of Police[35]

Detailed descriptions of all the Fenians are included. As it happens,
the City Marshal of New Bedford, Captain Henry Hathaway, is most
interested to read it.

'In view of the fact that he had been rather intimately connected with
the enterprise,' John Devoy would drily note, 'it may be believed that he
was not unduly zealous in assisting the Australian authorities.'[36]

For both Henry Hathaway and John Devoy, the exciting thing is that
the *Catalpa* must surely be getting close to the American coast.

•

At 6 pm on 18 August 1876, the First Mate of an ocean tug throws
them a line and for the agreed fee of $90 tows them to a safe berth in
New York Harbor proper.

At one o'clock on the young morning of Saturday, 19 August 1876,[37]
they hear that joyful cry. High in the crow's nest, the sailor has spotted
the distinct form of the sky-scratching pylons of the new Brooklyn
Bridge on the horizon.

Shortly thereafter they are brought to quarantine, where they have no
sooner tied the ship fast than swarms of reporters are storming aboard.

For the first time, the men on the *Catalpa* realise just how enormous their story has become, how much America in general and Irish–Americans in particular have rejoiced in this grand humiliation of the British Empire.

With formalities completed, the *Catalpa* is able to proceed with many of those press men still on board and at 2 am drops anchor off Castle Garden in Lower Manhattan.

By dawn, Captain Anthony and John Breslin have been rowed ashore and they take a horse and buggy to the hotel of none other than Jeremiah O'Donovan Rossa, which is the stronghold, the HQ, of the *Clan-na-Gael* in America.

And who should be the first person they meet upon entering the premises, furiously shaking their hands, patting their backs and offering his warmest congratulations?

Why it is William Foley!

Yes, he is ailing more than ever but given that most of them thought he would likely be dead by now, his very appearance is greeted as a miracle. In fact, as they will learn, it is less a miracle than the fact that John Devoy has ensured Foley is receiving the best medical care from their large network of Fenian doctors.

Those who have served the coming Republic of Ireland will be looked after by Ireland's sons and daughters, wherever they may be found.

And what of John Devoy?

Breslin and Captain Anthony learn he is ill with the flu – laid up in bed at the Philadelphia home of one of the *Clan-na-Gael*'s leaders, Dr William Carroll. But the moment he is advised by Rossa's son that the *Catalpa* has arrived 'unexpectedly',[38] he is up and on his way.

The delighted O'Donovan Rossa himself is on site from the first and makes clear to Captain Anthony and John Breslin that once the Fenian convicts are ashore they may have the run of his hotel for as long as they like. Whatever they need: rooms, meals, money – they only have to ask.

By the time Breslin and Anthony return to the whaler in the late morning, they find her surrounded by a flotilla of boats, bearing more press – and sightseers.

As reported by the New York *Herald*, 'The excitement in this city was something astonishing, and thousands, nay tens of thousands kept visiting the ship whilst she remained in harbour.'[39]

It is no easy matter for Captain Anthony to make his way through such a mass of maritime formalities, but finally it is done, and – stand by for the Captain! – he is once more on deck.

'Men,' he says to the six overwhelmed Fenians, 'I have a permit for you to go ashore, and you are at liberty to go when you please.'[40]

'God bless you, captain, you've saved our lives,'[41] Darragh says, speaking on behalf of them all.

Captain Anthony nods graciously and shakes them all by the hand. They all recognise the moment. They have come a long way. They have experienced the adventure of their lives. They have accomplished much. And if this moment is not finally the end of the story, it is certainly the end of the most significant chapter. The former Fenian convicts have been delivered to salvation. They are here safely at New York, and can begin the rest of their lives as free men.

The six Fenians make their way to the shore, New York beckoning its welcome, as they are soon engulfed by thousands of ecstatic Irish–Americans who have been waiting dockside, eager to see them in the flesh.

So warm is the reception it all threatens to get out of hand.

The official Reception Committee of the *Clan-na-Gael* has two carriages waiting for the Fenians, under the command of none other than Patrick Lennon, who had been in command of the Dublin men during Stepaside and Glencullen in 1867. Just as the Fenians are gratefully climbing in, however, another two carriages arrive under the command of a rich Irishman who has nothing to do with the *Clan-na-Gael*, but is well-known to Thomas Brennan, who encourages the men to go with the new arrivals.

The situation is only resolved when Lennon walks over to the rich Irishman, leans in close and says, with force and clear intent, 'If you don't get out of here . . . I'll put a hole in you.'[42]

. . .

On second thoughts the rich Irishman decides he has business else-where and rushes off with his empty carriages, leaving the Fenians to Lennon after all, who takes them to O'Donovan Rossa's hotel – where John Devoy arrives to find them a short time later.

He is shocked by their appearance.

'I have known them as soldiers full of enthusiasm and spirit and I was not prepared for the change which ten years of the iron discipline of the British prison system had wrought in some of them,'[43] he would chronicle.

But they are alive, and free! He hustles them into the two carriages he has on hand, and takes them straight to the tailor used by himself and the senior staff of the New York *Herald* – a tailor who is an Irishman himself, who will clothe them on credit, with the Clan to pay later.

For his part, Captain Anthony has already made his own arrangements, via a series of telegrams to his father-in-law, John Richardson, who is also of course part-owner of the *Catalpa*. Having left the vessel and the crew under the command of his worthy First Mate, Samuel Smith, Captain Anthony is soon following the instructions of Richardson, and boards a train in down-town New York, bound for home.

The following morning, Sunday, 20 August 1876, Captain Anthony steps from the train onto the platform of New Bedford Station to be engulfed by thousands of well-wishers – the local branch of the *Clan-na-Gael* has outdone itself to honour him – and the two people he most wants to see in the world.

For there, in the front rank is sweet Emma holding up wee Sophie, except she is not so wee anymore!

Captain Anthony falls into their arms and, once they can extricate themselves from the roaring crowd, he and his family make their way home.

And no, of course Emma says nothing, but quietly she is shocked by his appearance – as are many of the crowd that know George Anthony well. Though he has only been away for 18 months he has aged by *years*. No more jet-black hair – it is now heavily sprinkled with grey, particularly around his temples, while his hairline is now in full retreat and his once sturdy frame has shed nearly three stone!

But the main thing is, he is safely home.

As to the *Catalpa*, it will be for Samuel Smith and the crew to sail her out of New York, and up the coast to New Bedford.

Of course First Mate Smith and most of the crew have returned to the harbour at New Bedford, many, many times. And they have been harbourside when many whalers have returned from far afield, to receive warm welcomes from all who spy them.

But never in all their born days have they seen anything remotely approaching this . . .

Look there by the shore!

The crowds! There are thousands upon thousands of well-wishers – far more than the 25,000 who actually live in New Bedford. Once the *Catalpa* had been spotted coming into the bay, the word had spread and people had come from everywhere, including nearby settlements.

And look now as a whole flotilla of smaller vessels sail and steam out to greet them. And hark . . . as from Battery Park, they are given an artillery salute. Exactly 70 shots are fired in total, 'one gun for every State in the Union, and one for every county in Ireland'.[44]

At the helm of the *Catalpa*, Samuel Smith stands there, stunned, taking it all in, scarcely able to credit that all this is for them, while also scanning the crowd for the ones he truly wants to see.

And there is Amy Chase, the young woman who he has been sweet on all this time, the one he is hoping to marry. From the looks of it, there is a fair chance she will say yes. For although she has beamed upon him many times, never has she beamed like this, and Amy looks as if she is fair bursting with pride.

And there, too, of course, are those two firmest of friends, John Boyle O'Reilly, the esteemed editor of the Boston *Pilot*, right by Captain Henry Hathaway, both beaming at them in turn. And Captain Anthony, with Emma, and their wee bairn.

Home is the sailor, home from the sea, and the hunter from the hill . . .

The *Catalpa* glides into its berth at the dock, and is tied fast, as the merry madness begins.

•

Strike up the band!

On the 25th of August, New Bedford's Liberty Hall is adorned with red-white-and-blue bunting, together with great Irish and American flags, hanging above the stage, for a sold-out public dinner of celebration. And now, as Captain Anthony appears on stage, the band strikes up 'See the Conqu'ring Hero Comes', as the crowd roars.

'On a close observation,' one of the many journalists attending notes, 'the rescuer of the prisoners seems just the man for a desperate undertaking. Short and slight in stature, with brown hair and eyes, straight, handsome features, a square forehead, eyes deep-sunken and dark, modest and retiring in demeanour, about thirty years of age; this was the outline of the brave fellow who was the centre of attraction.'[45] Sitting right next to the celebrated Captain Anthony is, of course, John Boyle O'Reilly, who is the keynote speaker for the night, and he is in turn sitting next to his dear friend City Marshal Henry Hathaway. Also on stage with them are Samuel Smith and Thomas Hassett, the only freed Fenian not so overwhelmed with all that America has to offer that he can happily attend the event, while in the next row behind them sits, 'the entire crew of the *Catalpa*, brawny and bronzed whalemen of varied nationalities . . .'.[46]

(Missing from the gathering is John Breslin, who had received bad news on his return – his father had died in New York during his absence. He at least takes comfort in the fact that his father knew that his son John had been instrumental in freeing the six Fenians in Fremantle, and his dying words had been to pass congratulations to him, and his regret that he could not be there to greet him upon his return. Breslin wept to hear it.)

But to the business at hand.

For there are, of course, many speeches, but the highlight of the night is given by the beaming John Boyle O'Reilly. Hush now. The great man steps to the podium. His rich, resonant voice rings out over everyone privileged enough to be here.

'It is with no ordinary feelings that I am here,' he begins, his strong Irish accent overlaid with that slight American twang which says he is now the product of both nations. 'I owe to New Bedford no ordinary debt, and would gladly have come a thousand miles to do honour to the New Bedford whalemen. Seven years of liberty and a happy home in a free country are my debt of gratitude . . .

'We are here to do honour and to show our gratitude to the man who has done a brave and wonderful deed. The self-sacrifice and unfailing devotion of him who had taken his life in his hand and beached his whaleboat on the penal colony, defying its fearful laws, defying the gallows and the chain gang, in order to keep faith with the men who had placed their trust in him – this is almost beyond belief in our selfish and commonplace time.'

(Loud applause.)

'England says that the rescue was a lawless and disgraceful raid. Not so. If these men were criminals the rescue would be criminal, but they were *political* offenders against England, not against law, or order, or religion.'

(Applause.)

'They had lain in prison for ten years, with millions of their coun-trymen asking their release, imploring England, against their will to beg, to set these men at liberty. Had England done so it would have partially disarmed Ireland. A generous act by England would be reciprocated instantly by millions of the warmest hearts in the world. But she is blind as of old; blind, and arrogant, and cruel. She would not release the men;

she scorned to give Ireland an answer. She called the prisoners cowardly criminals, not political offenders . . .'

A stirring moves through the room, some nodding their heads in strong agreement, while others shake their heads ruefully – not in disagreement, but in wonder that England could, yet again, sink so low.

O'Reilly goes on.

'When the ship sailed and was a long time at sea, doubts and fears for the safety of the enterprise were sure to come, but Captain Hathaway said once and always, "the man who engaged to do this will keep that engagement, or he won't come out of the penal colony".'[47]

And, of course, he was right. For, as good as his word, Captain Anthony risked his life to do the seeming impossible, and rescued these men, some of whom are also here with us tonight.

Spreading his praise, O'Reilly goes on to laud John Devoy, who is also here for the grand occasion. At the very mention of his name, the audience give repeated rounds of applause.

With particular warmth, O'Reilly pays tribute to the greatest friend he has, Captain Henry Hathaway, who he personally owes so much to, who had first rescued him, then saved his life twice more thereafter.

Ah, but now it is another man that O'Reilly wishes to draw their attention to.

'Look at that man sitting there,' the great poet and journalist says, pointing to Thomas Hassett, sitting at the top table. 'Six years ago he escaped from his prison in the penal colony and fled into the bush, and lived there like a wild beast for a whole year, hunted from district to district, in a blind, but manful attempt to win his liberty. When England said the rescue was illegal, America could answer, as the Anti-Slavery men answered when they attacked the Constitution, as England herself answered in the cause of Poland: "We have acted from a higher law than your written constitution and treaties – the law of God and humanity."'

(Applause.)

'It was in obedience to this supreme law that Captain Anthony rescued the prisoners, and pointed his finger at the Stars and Stripes when the English vessel threatened to fire on his ship.'

(Applause.)

There is more, much more from the gifted orator, but his theme is consistent. Most of us in this room owe many great debts: to Captain Anthony and his crew. To the men of the Irish Republican Brotherhood among us who placed their lives on the line for liberty. To Ireland which had borne so many of us. And to the United States of America, which has taken us in, nurtured us, and been so generous as to provide the means by which we soldiers of the Irish Republican Brotherhood could be successfully rescued from the other side of the earth.

'The Irishman,' Mr O'Reilly says then, 'who could forget what the Stars and Stripes have done for his countrymen, deserves that in the time of need that flag shall forget him.'[48]

Thank you and good night. Since the roof of the Liberty Hall had first been placed there, 20 years before, it had never been lifted off. But this night is as close as it comes, so thunderous and enduring is the tumultuous applause.

1 September 1876, Boston, the final scene

A week later, there is another, even grander evening held – a fund-raiser for the freed Fenians in Boston's Music Hall. Again there is standing room only. An Irish drama by the great Robert Emmet is performed, followed by Irish poetry and music.

And, of course, there are speeches, none better than the one by the first Irish Fire Commissioner, John E. Fitzgerald, who notes that, while Ireland was one of many countries that had been occupied for centuries, there was a difference.

'While Poland and other struggling nationalities have been wiped from the map, the intense individualism of the Irish as a nation has preserved them. The movement for which these gallant fellows has suffered is the embodiment of the national idea.'[49]

(Cheers.)

But there are some people the crowd would really like to see.

The first calls go up for 'Captain Anthony!' 'Captain Anthony!' 'Captain Anthony!' but that good man, sitting in the front row beside his friend Henry Hathaway, graciously declines. This night is not about him, it is about the freed Fenians who are with them.

And so the cries go up to get the freed prisoners on stage. Initially there is resistance – that had never been part of the plan – but the roar of the crowd is so strong, it cannot be denied.

One by one, they make their way up from the front row and stand there, blinking in the lights – wiry, bronzed men who can seem barely to gather that this is real – as the people rise.

'The greeting they received,' the Boston *Pilot* chronicles, 'will never be forgotten. It was plain how deep a chord their suffering and escape has struck in the Irish heart. They numbered six, though Mr Wilson, one of the rescued men, was not present; his place was filled by Mr William Foley, the ex-prisoner who arrived in this country about two months ago.'[50]

And still they roar.

William Shakespeare was right:

All the world's a stage, And all the men and women merely players; They have their exits and their entrances, And one man in his time plays many parts, His acts being seven ages . . .[51]

They had started as simple Irish kids, become proud Irish men, soldiers, raging revolutionaries, prisoners, escapees and now they are heroes – free men, who've fought the good fight, paid the price, made extraordinary sacrifices, but ultimately triumphed against all odds. And in the process, they have achieved their original goal. They have weakened England's hold over Ireland.

It will be for other, younger men, to continue that fight . . .

> *Once more unto the breach, dear friends, once more;*
> *Or close the wall up with our English dead.*[52]

But these old convicts, these proud Fenians have done their bit. The crowd knows it, and loves them for it.

Exit, to wild applause.

THE END

EPILOGUE

Here's to the ship Catalpa, *and the boys of Uncle Sam,*
And to all the Irishmen afloat, and the Fenians to a man.
Here's to Captain Anthony, bold Breslin and his crew,
When challenged by the Empire's might, the 'Stars and Stripes'
  she flew.

Here's luck to Captain Anthony, who well these men did free,
He dared the British man-of-war to fight him on the sea.
And here's to that dear emblem which, in triumph shall be seen,
The flag, for which our heroes fought, old Ireland's flag of green.[1]

Irish ballad, unknown origin

In Fremantle Prison, **James Kiely** endured the immediate retribution of his comrades' escape. 'From that hour, and for years after, I suffered persistent persecution from the prison authorities.'[2] After he refused to pick oakum and darn stockings he was placed in solitary and fed on bread and water. This went on until – at least by his account – he 'got hold of a little bit of information' concerning what he would describe as 'the arrears of the goods sent out for the convicts of West Australia',[3] which he is sure the authorities of The Establishment would prefer never saw the light of day.

When he threatens Principal Warder Johnson that he intends to reveal it, things move quickly. Governor Fauntleroy personally comes to see Kiely in his cell.

'You wanted to see me?'

'I will see you in due time,' Kiely replies evenly. 'There is a button off your coat and I will take your coat off you.'[4]

In short, I know about the arrears, and am going to expose the whole administration of this colony.

Again, by Kiely's account at least, within hours, Fauntleroy brings an important-looking visitor to his cell.

'You wanted to see me,' the visitor asks.

Kiely is mystified, having never seen the fellow before.

'I don't know who you are.'

Fauntleroy explodes: 'The Governor, sir! Speak properly to him.'

'Oh, well,' says Kiely, 'if you are the Governor, you've got a very good billet.'

'What can I do for you?' Governor Robinson asks.

'I don't know. I never asked for you, but as you are here now I'd like to know what class of prisoner I am. State prisoner, political prisoner, or felon? What have I done, that I should be punished in this manner?'

'Well,' said Governor Robinson, 'I will communicate with the Colonial Secretary, and see if it would be safe to let you out on ticket-of-leave.'[5]

Two days later, on 6 March 1877, Kiely is let out.

Twelve months after that, he receives a free pardon from Queen Victoria. In October 1883, James Kiely married Mary Ann Roach. They settled in Guildford, Western Australia and of their seven children only two daughters survived.[6]

For his part, the drunkard **Thomas Delaney**, and three other Fenians out on ticket-of-leave who had been thrown back into prison on principle, are released on 28 March 1878, after ongoing agitation from Ireland had seen them given a conditional pardon.

Not that things go easily for them thereafter, as police continue to keep a close eye on them. In the case of Kiely, the surveillance is so strong that he constantly feels harassed. Still, over time it dissipates and he is able to settle down to his life as a ploughman. In 1905 Kiely receives a Royal Pardon as a belated act of clemency,[7] and is, thus, a free citizen for the first time in 40 years.[8]

When the news breaks, a reporter from the *West Australian* tracks him down, living in Mary Street, North Perth, and asks if he is the same James Kiely of Fenian fame?

'The old soldier agreed, not without a touch of pride, that he was Private James Kiely of Her Majesty's 53rd Foot Regiment.'[9]

It seems, despite all the years of suffering, Kiely never lost his gift for the gab, as the journalist notes: 'Despite his distressing infirmity of exceeding deafness, Mr James Kiely . . . is a distinctly interesting man to chat with or, to be more accurate, to listen to. Duly elated at the unexpected receipt of a Royal Pardon for an offence committed 40 years ago, he reflects aloud that he now has the liberty of speech.'[10]

I suppose nobody ever told him the true reason he was left behind. As for Kiely's thoughts on the matter, it is perhaps understandable that Kiely did not confess to the truth, that the others had simply left him behind.

'My luck was out,' he lies flatly to the journalist, 'and I had no opportunity of eluding the warder and making my way across to where a horse was ready saddled for me.'[11]

Such a disaster however – in either way of telling the story – had diminished in no way his passion for the cause which had banished him from his homeland for the better part of a lifetime.

'Yes, I'm mighty glad to be in every way free again,' Kiely says softly, 'but I'd rather have heard of Home Rule for Ireland than of my pardon. Now you make a note of that, young man. I would much rather hear that there was between England and Ireland that unity, tranquillity and general contentment that there is in the relations between England and Australia – and there would be if they would only give Home Rule to the dear old land.'[12]

Kiely died in 1918 at the age of 84, after more than 50 years in exile, and is buried at Karrakatta Cemetery, Perth, Western Australia.

•

In the early hours of 1 November 1876, **William Foley** – having lived long enough to see the liberation of his comrades but only by a few weeks – finally shuffles off this mortal coil, in St Vincent's Hospital, New York.

In the morning, a hearse takes his body to O'Donovan Rossa's Northern Hotel in the Bowery, where, as reported in John Devoy's New York *Herald*, it effectively lies in state, 'encased in a beautiful casket resting on a catafalque draped in velvet', in one of the parlours. 'The room was appropriately draped, and floral tributes to the deceased were placed around the casket. At its head was a harp of beautiful white flowers, while on the top, partly covering a sword and belt, was a large cross of white flowers, with the word "Emerald" spelled out on it in violets.'[13]

Thousands of Irish–Americans file through and pay their respects.

The *Herald* reports that the funeral's 'cortege was the largest ever gathered at the obsequies of an Irishman in America . . . It was after two o'clock when the procession was ready to start; and by this time Chatham Square was one solid mass of humanity, and the Bowery, farther than the eye could see, was lined with crowds on both sides.'[14]

So does this faithful servant of Ireland go to his rest. In Fremantle, less than a year earlier, he could barely feed himself. In New York, he leaves the stage a hero.

•

Captain George S. Anthony never did return to sea, and for good reason.

'It must not be forgotten,' the Boston *Pilot* pointed out shortly after the return of the *Catalpa*, 'that by this achievement Captain Anthony has destroyed his career as a whaleman. He has placed himself beyond the pale of every British harbour in the world. He can no more follow his profession in the South Sea or in the Indian Ocean, for nearly every port at which the whaleships get supplies are possessions of the British Crown.'[15]

One of the first things Anthony did was ensure that his **crew** would not be penalised financially for the fact they had done little whaling. After months of delays, in February 1877, John Devoy and James Reynolds, the *Clan-Na-Gael* member who mortgaged his house to become the official owner of the *Catalpa*, travelled to New Bedford to make a final settlement with that crew. Owing to the expedition's poor catch, an agreement was reached to calculate payment on the average catch of several other vessels whaling out of New Bedford that season, also taking into account current oil prices. The crew was paid off on that basis.

As to the *Catalpa*, its moment in the sun was short-lived. It was handed over by James Reynolds to John T. Richardson, George Anthony and Henry Hathaway, 'for and in consideration of the sum of one dollar and other valuable considerations, lawful money of the United States of America to me in hand paid before the sealing and delivery of these presents . . .'.[16]

It was theirs to sell as reward for their contribution.

The bark subsequently had several American owners and captains, until 1884 when it was recorded as being 'sold foreign'[17], soon after being turned into a mere coal barge, before being condemned and burned while at Belize in the British Honduras.

After his great adventure, Captain Anthony settled down to a relatively quiet life with his wife and daughters – he and Emma having been blessed with another daughter in the years after his return. Initially, Anthony became a policeman before, in 1886, he became the boarding officer for the New Bedford Customs House, giving him the role he once feared in others, most particularly when the *Catalpa* arrived at

Bunbury – checking incoming and outgoing vessels for contraband and stowaways. Even 20 years after the event, the '*Catalpa* Rescue' – as it was now all but universally known – was still fiercely celebrated, and never more than 5 August 1895, when some 10,000 members of the *Clan-na-Gael* gathered in Philadelphia's Rising Sun Park beneath Irish and American flags for a special occasion.

And now, quell the bands and crowd in close to the high platform that has been banged together in recent days, and festooned in bunting that is red, white and blue – *and* green!

For here he is on stage, the man himself, Captain George S. Anthony. The years have treated him well. He is thicker in the waist and face, and his hair now fully grey, but his vitality remains. If you had to wrestle with a man in his early fifties, the Cap'n would not be your man. Not quite the same might be said of Martin Hogan, Thomas Darragh and Big Bob Cranston, who are seated beside him on the podium with other dignitaries – sapped as they were by so many years spent in the British penal establishment – but just the fact that they are here is a triumph in itself. John Devoy, too, would have been there, bar for the fact that, just in recent days, he has taken severely ill.

And hush now, as Luke Dillon, the President of the Irish American Club, makes his way to the lectern even as the band strikes up the American National Anthem and everyone sings it in full voice: '. . . *Oh, say does that star-spangled banner yet wave . . . O'er the land of the free and the home of the brave . . .*'

Yes, it does.

And, as a matter of fact, it is a very specific star-spangled banner that has brought us here today!

As two volleys of shots ring out – a salute by the *Clan-na-Gael* Guards – Captain Anthony rises to thunderous applause and steps to the podium to speak:

'Twenty years ago,' he begins in his soft New England lilt, 'you came to me with a request to aid you in restoring to freedom some soldiers of liberty confined in England's penal colony of Western Australia. Your story of their sufferings touched my heart, and I pledged my word as an American sailor, to aid in the good work to the best of my ability.[18]

Captain Anthony proceeds to tell much of the story of what had happened, building to the climactic moment.

'I brought the party safely in the ship's boat to the *Catalpa* and placed them on board under the shelter of the American flag. Upon sailing forth in international waters, the commander of an armed British steamer accosted us and demanded the surrender of the rescued men. When I refused, he fired a solid shot across the *Catalpa*'s bows. I held our course while the steamer pranced alongside for a time, its excitable commander bellowing a further threat to blow out the masts of my vessel if I failed to comply. I refused, and told him that if he fired on the American flag on the high seas he must take the consequences.'[19]

That flag, of course, is the one he has, carefully folded, in his hand right now.

'The flag which floated over the *Catalpa* on that April day in 1876 – the Stars and Stripes which protected the liberated men and their rescuers – I have preserved and cherished for twenty years as a sacred relic. I would fain keep it and hand it down to my children as a family heirloom, but I am confident it will be safe in the keeping of those who were associated with me in an enterprise of which we have all reason to be proud. Your countrymen have ever been loyal to the flag of the United States and ever ready to shed their blood in its defense.'[20]

Lifting up his right hand, for all to see the sacred folded bundle, he draws to a conclusion.

'I, therefore, present you with this flag of the *Catalpa* as a memento of our common share in a good work well done and a token of the sympathy of all true Americans with the cause of liberty in Ireland. I know you will cherish it as I do, and that if the interests of that flag should ever again demand it your countrymen will be among the first to rally to its defense.'[21]

On behalf of the ill John Devoy, the Clan's leading representative, Michael J. Ryan, steps forward to receive this most gracious and sacred of gifts, and the applause becomes more thunderous still as he takes it in hand.

Only when there is silence once more does Ryan speak, reading from the prepared speech that John Devoy had given him:

> Captain Anthony, old friend and comrade, I accept this flag on behalf of the organisation which fitted out the *Catalpa*, selected you as her commander, and which shared with you the credit for the work of humanity. I accept it with pride as a memento of a noble deed and I promise you it shall be cherished by us while life is left us. It is the flag of our adopted country under which Irishmen have fought side by side with native Americans on every battlefield

where the interests and the honour of that flag were at stake, from Bunker Hill to Appomattox. It is the flag which symbolizes the highest development of human liberty on this earth . . .

Captain Anthony, in the name of the *Clan-na-Gael*, I thank you for the *Catalpa*'s flag and wish you a long and happy life.[22]

George S. Anthony achieved exactly that, and could only quibble with his maker for the missing three months and one day of his allotted 'three score years and ten' when he died of pneumonia, at home in New Bedford, on 22 May 1913.

The local newspaper carried an obituary for the ages.

George S. Anthony

This gently spoken, smiling, unassuming man, quietly going his ways in this town for a generation, occupied with a prosaic work, who has just gone out from what we describe as life – how could he be a hero of thrilling and romantic adventure? Yet he was the living demonstration of Emerson's declaration that the world is a proud place, peopled with men of positive quality, with heroes and demigods standing around us . . . The episode of which Captain Anthony was the central notable figure was the great opportunity of his life, and that he acquitted himself splendidly was due to what he was. Had this experience never come to him, his outward life might have been greatly different – but the man would have been the same man, high-minded, courageous, modest.[23]

George's blessed wife, Emma, survived him by over two decades, dying on 5 November 1935, aged 80, and is buried beside him in the Rural Cemetery, New Bedford.

For the record, that very **American flag** has indeed been cherished thereafter and can now be found in Rothe House, Kilkenny, Ireland. Yes, a triumphant fate for that most triumphant of flags. The fate of other people and things involved in the saga was many and varied.

A quick look . . .

•

John Joseph Breslin returned to New York as no less than the toast of the town and wider – and was soon delivering lectures all across the United States, giving a blow-by-blow account of the *Catalpa* affair. When that quietened, he began working for John Devoy's newly established Boston/New York newspaper, *Irish Nation*.

Second only to John Devoy in terms of his prestige among the Irish community in America, Breslin became ever more heavily involved in the bid to liberate Ireland by force, not just politics. His work included helping a famed Irish–American engineer, John Holland, to push Holland's grand vision of building submarines capable of wreaking devastation on foreign navies. Convinced that the Royal Navy would be the ideal place to start, the submarine project was partly funded by the *Clan-na-Gael*, and two of the trustees of the initial fund to develop the project were none other than John Breslin and John Devoy. Holland was successful, and in 1881 the first submarine to be formally commissioned by the US Navy was designed by him.

Rumour has it that Breslin was also involved in personally sending small bombs filled with dynamite, known as 'love apples',[24] to Irish rebels in England, with the backing of Ireland's Irish Republican Brotherhood and Jeremiah O'Donovan Rossa – who openly ran the 'Brooklyn Dynamite School' teaching Irish rebels how to cause devastating explosions from common materials.

In 1880, John Breslin married Theresa Brosnan, with the couple going on to have two children, Madeline and Hugh. His time to enjoy family life was short-lived, however, as Breslin died on 18 November 1887, of liver disease when he was just 54. His death – announced in the *New York Times* with a quote from John Boyle O'Reilly that he was one 'whom Irishmen respected as one of the bravest and most devoted of all Irish patriots'[25] – would see leaders and members of the *Clan-na-Gael* journey from all over the United States to New York for his funeral. Due to get under way at 1 pm on 20 November it had to be delayed for an hour and a half as so many thousands tried to attend and order had to be restored. As the hearse finally started off from his home at 451 Canal Street in Lower Manhattan it was followed by thousands of Irishmen, and made its way to Calvary Cemetery – where, wisely, the service was held graveside in open ground to accommodate the crowd.

'It was,' the *New York Times* reported, 'one of the largest funerals ever held in New York, and, in many respects, was a public demonstration.'[26]

Of course, as the funeral was held 'under the auspices of the Irish National League and the Clan-na-Gael',[27] due honours were paid to what Breslin had achieved for the cause.

The *Catholic News* wrote of the man: 'There was no more romantic figure in the stormy history of Ireland than Breslin, whose unselfish life, burning love of country, wild, mad, chivalry and unparalleled bravery are written in the hearts of Erin's sons and daughters.'[28]

Typically, the most eloquent words on Breslin were written long before, by John Boyle O'Reilly in the Boston *Pilot*:

> Out of all the incidents of the so-called 'Fenian Movement,' the most brilliantly daring have been two rescues of prisoners – namely, that of the Chief Organizer, James Stephens, from Richmond Prison, Dublin, in 1865, and of the six military prisoners from Western Australia [in 1876] . . . They have a resemblance, these two rescues, and so they ought to have – for the same mind planned and the same hands carried both to a conclusion.
>
> In both these desperate undertakings, John Breslin was 'the man in the gap.' In both, John Devoy was his careful, patient, forethoughtful fellow-worker.[29]

As for John Devoy's thoughts on the man in the gap, they are clear in the speech he wrote for the occasion of receiving the *Catalpa*'s flag from Captain Anthony. He said of his good friend and co-conspirator: 'Our chief regret today is that the man most closely associated with you in the rescue, John J. Breslin, the man who commanded the land force of the expedition, and to whose skill and courage its success was wholly due, is not here to receive this flag from your hands. As he has gone to his last account, the honour of taking his place has been assigned to me, although I was only concerned in the American end of the enterprise.'[30]

Devoy's support of Breslin did not stop with the latter's death.

As Breslin's passing left his wife, Theresa, destitute with two young children, she wrote to Devoy seeking help from the Irish community, which was extended to the family of one of the cause's most honoured sons.

As for the 23-year-old maid, **Mary Tondut**,[31] less than a month after the *Catalpa*'s escape, she left Fremantle for Sydney – and was perhaps just in time . . .

In his report for the Western Australian Police, Inspector Thomas Rowe wrote: 'Mary Tondut, a Roman Catholic girl of this colony, late servant at the Emerald Isle Hotel, where Collins lodged, was seduced by Collins and is now [pregnant]. She left this colony in the schooner *Northern Light*. Her expenses were paid by Collins through Moloney.

She is to be accouched at Sydney where further arrangements are promised to be made to take her to Collins.'[32]

At the end of the year Mary and John Breslin's son was born, John Joseph Tondut. His baptism certificate records his father as, 'John Joseph Brislan' – a sure sign Mary knew Mr Collins's real name and likely his purpose all along! For whatever reason, however, she did not go to America to join the father of her child, instead staying in Sydney, where she married a Sydney watchmaker, Harry James Thomas, in 1880. They went on to have seven children of their own, before Mary died of pneumonia in St Vincent's Hospital on 2 January 1896, aged just 43.

And John Breslin's Australian son? He took his step-father's last name and settled in the rural NSW town of Nyngan, becoming a horse-breaker, grocer, and leader of the Nyngan Town Band before returning to Sydney for his later years, dying in 1951, aged 74 – it is believed without ever knowing the story of his biological father.

•

John Boyle O'Reilly's career as a journalist, editor, poet and author continued to grow, and he counted among his friends and admirers such contemporary American greats as Oliver Wendell Holmes and Mark Twain. His first book of poetry, *Songs from the Southern Seas*, was published in 1873. This collection mainly comprised poems inspired by O'Reilly's experiences in Western Australia, in which the dedication at the front of the book was deeply considered.

TO
CAPTAIN DAVID R. GIFFORD,
Of the whaling bark *Gazelle*, of New Bedford,
I DEDICATE THIS BOOK

On the subject of O'Reilly's escape aboard the *Gazelle*, more in hope than expectation, even long after O'Reilly's disappearance, the *Western Australian Police Gazette* continued to publish notices, as late as 1876:

> ABSCONDERS.
> 2. John O'Reilly, Reg. No. 9843, Imperial convict; arrived in the colony per convict ship Hougoumont, in 1868; sentenced to 20 years, 9th July, 1866. Description—Healthy appearance, present age 30; 5ft. 6 in. high, black hair, brown eyes, oval visage, dark

complexion; an Irishman. Absconded from Convict Road Party, Bunbury, on the 18th February, 1869.[33]

When O'Reilly reads it, he makes a quick reply:

Mr. M. S. Smith. Supt of Police,
Dear Sir,
I have just seen a copy of the Police Gazette *of West Australia in which under the head 'Absconders' I found my name and description. Should you desire any information regarding my affair I shall be happy to give it you. Do not perpetuate the stupid folly of printing my name among your criminals. I am far beyond the reach of your petty colony land; and I really wish to preserve something of a kindly and respectful memory of your country in which I have some dear friends. Should you ever visit this Republic, I shall be happy to see you. As your Gazette is published for Police information only; please tell your officers . . . that I send them my respects.*
Yours very truly
John Boyle O'Reilly[34]

His first novel, *Moondyne* – concerning a convict of The Establishment who successfully escaped – was published in 1879.

He was already an established poet, journalist, editor and publisher, and the novel helped establish him as a writer, too, and his combined income from all activities allowed his wife, Mary, and their four daughters to continue to live comfortably in Boston.

So, too, did his newspaper, the *Pilot* – which exists to this day – prosper. Among other things, it was the first American journal to publish the works of Ireland's future Nobel Laureate for Literature, W.B. Yeats – when he was but little published in Ireland itself – and also the first to publish that greatest of all Irish literary figures, Oscar Wilde.

In the course of the years, O'Reilly received many visitors to his newspaper offices, none more surprising, in the mid-1870s, than **Patrick Foley**, the very snake who had spied on him then testified against him in the subsequent court-martial.

'This fellow, after O'Reilly's conviction,' the poet's biographer would note, 'found himself so despised and shunned by his fellow-soldiers, both English and Irish, that his life became unendurable. He deserted the army and fled to America, where the story of his treachery had preceded him. He was starving in the streets of Boston when he went to see his former victim, and threw himself upon his mercy. Almost any other man would have enjoyed the spectacle of the traitor's misery. O'Reilly saw only the pity of it all, and gave the wretch enough money to supply his immediate wants, and pay his way to some more propitious spot.'[35]

Such was the generosity of spirit of this extraordinary man. In the bloom of his life he boasted everything a man could desire for a long, happy and fruitful existence . . . bar good health.

In 1890, at the age of just 46, John Boyle O'Reilly died of heart failure – possibly worsened by long years of insomnia and having, on the fateful night, taken too much of his wife's sleeping medicine. His funeral was an extravaganza, a celebration of his extraordinary life, and grief at his death. After lying in state at St Mary's Church, Charlestown, a Requiem High Mass took place for 1000 people inside in the pews, and many times that number outside.

'At the close of the services, the crowd outside was allowed to pass through the church and view the remains. Eight employees of the Boston *Pilot* then bore the coffin to the hearse, and the funeral procession, one of the largest ever seen in Boston, started for Mount Calvary Cemetery,'[36] where his body lay in the receiving tomb until 7 November before being taken to Holyhood Cemetery for final interment.

But he would be far from forgotten.

One of the many memorials to O'Reilly in Boston would be designed by none other than Daniel Chester French, who had previously designed the iconic Lincoln Memorial in Washington, DC. It was unveiled in 1896 with warm words from none other than the incumbent American President, Grover Cleveland. O'Reilly's Irish home town, Dowth, also has a statue of their favourite son standing proudly in the main square. (Alas, the greatest *living* monument to the spirit of John Boyle O'Reilly – the enormous gum tree that he saved in 1868 – did not, ultimately, survive. In a joint decision by the State Energy Commission, the Main Roads Department and Bunbury Council, it was cut down in 1951 as a menace to heavy traffic on the highway.)

O'Reilly's first poem of major renown, 'The Old School Clock', became a beloved Irish staple, courtesy of having been 'printed on the backs of millions of National School copy books'.[37]

Beyond that, Rose Fitzgerald, later the matriarch of the famed Irish–American Kennedy family of Boston, grew up on John Boyle O'Reilly's poetry and passed on the love to her son, John F. Kennedy.

On St Patrick's Day 1962, President Kennedy observed how the day is not just one of celebration, but

> a day of dedication as well, as purely American as it is Irish, recalling for all that ours is a nation founded, sustained, and now preserved in the cause of liberty. None more than the Irish can attest the power of that cause once it has gripped a nation's soul.
>
> It is well to love liberty, for it demands much of those who would live by it. Liberty is not content to share mankind. John Boyle O'Reilly, who came to Boston by way of a penal colony in Western Australia, understood this as few men have. 'Freedom,' he wrote, 'is more than a resolution – he is not free who is free alone.'
>
> To those who in our time have lost their freedom, or who through the ages have never won it, there is a converse to this message. No one – in the darkest cell, the remotest prison, under the most unyielding tyranny – is ever entirely lost in bondage while there are yet free men in the world. As this be our faith, let it also be our pride – and to all who share it, I send the greetings of this day.[38]

In more recent times, no less than the world's most popular rock band, U2, has taken an interest, led by their lead guitarist and lyricist, The Edge. 'I was interested in the history of this character, John Boyle O'Reilly,' The Edge recounted to the magazine *New Musical Express* in 1988, telling how while out walking one day with wife Aislinn in County Meath, they came across a monument to John Boyle O'Reilly which told something of his life and inspired The Edge to pen 'Van Diemen's Land'.

'He was, to me, a prisoner of conscience in a way,' The Edge recounted. 'He was not a man of violence and he was sent away for 20 years, so I wrote a song about that.'[39]

Vale, John Boyle O'Reilly, you were one of the greats.

•

Henry Hathaway, who went on to become a US Shipping Commissioner in New Bedford, mourned the death of 'Boylo' for the rest of his days and journeyed from New Bedford to Boston every Memorial Day – 30 May, to remember those who served in the armed forces – for the next 20 years to lay a wreath on his grave at Holyhood Cemetery in Boston.[40] Hathaway himself died in 1931, aged 89.

•

James Stephens, the mysterious Wandering Hawk, flew into relative obscurity, at least in comparison to his glory days as a young revolutionary when he was more responsible than anyone for building the Irish Republican Brotherhood and Fenianism into an actual force to be reckoned with. He spent most of the decades afterwards in Paris, living quietly with his wife – that lovely Tipperary lass who had nursed him back in '48, Jane Hopper – doing translation work. But in the latter part of the 1890s, when he was an old man, discredited within the Irish revolutionary ranks, the British authorities decided that he no longer presented a danger and he and his wife were allowed to return to Ireland. Again, he lived quietly, largely forgotten – and grieving for his wife, who died shortly after their return – until on 29 March 1901, while living with family in Blackrock just south of Dublin, he collapsed and died.

It was only with the announcement of his death that it was realised by all but a very tight, yes, circle, that Stephens had returned to Ireland to live.

Still, there was warmth extended him in death that had been denied him in life for decades.

> He was beyond doubt the most prominent personality in the Fenian movement, and the greatest of its leaders. He made mistakes of course. What leader of a revolutionary or political movement has not? These, however, weigh as nothing against the record of a whole life's constant and consistent devotion to the great ideal of an independent Ireland, and it can also be said of him that he went nearer to the achievement of that ideal, at one period of the movement which he did more than any other to create, than any Irish leader since Wolfe Tone. He also knew how to surround with respect a movement that has failed, and it was this part of his career we see the fine and exceptional qualities of James Stephens . . . his passing has vindicated him from the attacks of his enemies. He had not a shilling to leave to relative or friend, but he has left to Ireland the rich legacy of a name and a record which will always be an incentive to young Nationalists to cherish this great ideal for which he lived and fought. Irish men everywhere will be pleased to know that he lived in his retirement in contentment and happiness, attended by loving friends, and that his death was untroubled by either want, suffering or pain.[41]

At least enough of the Irish remember the 'Old Captain's' contribution, however, that he is buried with some fanfare – with some 30 mourning carriages behind the hearse – in Dublin's Glasnevin Cemetery, his coffin borne to its resting place right beside Mrs Stephens by six elderly men who had been part of The Rising of '67.

•

After farewelling his great friend O'Reilly, heading south to Bunbury that day in 1868, **John Flood** never did see the poet again, and remained in Australia for the rest of his long life. His period as editor of the *Wild Geese* would hold him in good stead for his subsequent career. For, after his release from Fremantle Prison in 1871, he made his way to Sydney where he established a paper called *The Irish Citizen* before heading to Brisbane to join the *Courier* and then to Gympie, where in 1888 he took over the *Gympie Miner*. He became such a leading citizen of the Queensland town – with a Tasmanian wife and six children – that when he died in 1909, Gympie extended to him its largest funeral to that point, and two years after his death a 14-foot high monument to his memory was built over his grave, with 3000 people attending its unveiling.

> Sacred to the memory of John Flood (a true Irish patriot), born 21st May, 1841, at Sutton, Dublin, Ireland, died 22nd August, 1909, aged 68 years. Erected in 1911 by friends and admirers to commemorate his life's work in the cause of Irish nationality. R.I.P.[42]

•

There were no retributions against **Governor Sir William Cleaver Robinson** for his men having observed international law. They had been right and proper to do so, and that was that. His career continued entirely untroubled, as, after Western Australia, he became Governor of South Australia and then temporary governor of Victoria, before returning to Western Australia for another two terms. He died in 1897, aged 63.[43]

•

Governor William Fauntleroy retired from his position at The Establishment in January 1878, after control of convicts and prisons was transferred to the Colonial Government. After visiting the Eastern Colonies, he returned to England, where he lived for some years. At length, finding the climate too wet, he settled on the Continent and died in France in 1887, aged 56.[44]

•

Major Charles Finnerty, despite his rather emotional nature, short fuse and propensity for dashing off troublesome cables and letters, was promoted to the rank of Lieutenant Colonel on 1 January 1881, meaning he must now be addressed by all and sundry as *Colonel*, if you please. He could now die a happy man, and promptly did so, suddenly dying on 18 December 1881, aged 66, of an apoplexy – a stroke.

•

Although the press held little hope for his survival, **Superintendent Joseph Doonan** left the prison service shortly after his failed suicide attempt, still embittered at his treatment.

'The ill health which led to my retirement,' he will write to the Secretary of State for the Colonies, 'was entirely due to the persecution of [Governor Fauntleroy] and his friends, and to an apprehension of the grossest foul play used against me by those persons . . . I was daily subjected to every kind of persecution and annoyance until at last from want of sleep was completely driven out of my senses . . .'[45]

Well, he was now glad to be well out of it, and entered the drapery and grocery business, where with the help of his wife, Harriet, and family, he prospered, as together they built Joseph Doonan & Sons into a remarkably successful enterprise. He died in 1888, aged 57.

•

Warden Thomas Booler, who had been in charge of the convicts heading towards the south jetty and allowed Wilson and Harrington to join Big Bob Cranston, was initially found blameless by the Board of Inquiry, but, as reported by *The Inquirer and Commercial News*, 'the Home authorities on a perusal of the papers did not concur'.[46]

And that was the end of his time at Fremantle Prison, as he was dismissed upon the direction of the Secretary of State.

Not everyone agreed. 'Booler has been in the public service 29 years, and his dismissal is considered an excessively severe punishment.'[47]

Booler sold everything he had, and re-settled in the Sydney harbourside suburb of Glebe. Ah, what an ace he had to play, whenever perchance the local fishermen might boast of 'the ones that got away . . .' and his mind turned back to Easter Monday 1876 . . . Booler died in Sydney in 1906, aged 81.

•

Whether or not flame-haired **Thomas Darragh** was ever able to reunite with his wife and two children in America is uncertain, though he initially settled in a boarding house in Philadelphia, and worked for the Clan. He died in 1912, aged 78, and his resting place is the Most Holy Redeemer Cemetery, Philadelphia.

•

Shortly after arriving in New York, **Robert 'Big Bob' Cranston** married and settled down in Philadelphia. He worked for a time as assistant to O'Donovan Rossa with the *Clan-na-Gael* and embarked on a cotton and woollen waste business with a lifelong friend, which did not go well. By 1910, he was employed as a police night-watchman. Big Bob Cranston died in 1914, aged 72. Like Thomas Darragh, he is buried at the Holy Redeemer Cemetery, Philadelphia.

•

Master swordsman **Martin Hogan** moved to Chicago, also remaining active in Fenian affairs. He married and had one daughter, though he had trouble adjusting to his new life after so many years in prison and reportedly may have developed a drinking problem. Hogan, who had been in straitened circumstances for some time, died in Cook County Hospital, Chicago, in 1901, aged 63.

•

The hard man's hard man **Michael Harrington** married two months after arriving in America. He became the father of two children, and served in the Central Park police force. A heavy drinker, he died in 1886, aged 60, and was laid to rest in Calvary Cemetery, New York.

•

Thomas Hassett settled in New York, where he married an Irish–American woman and ran a saloon, heavily frequented by followers of the Clan. He died in 1893, aged 52, and was also buried in Calvary Cemetery.

•

As to the last of the Fenians left standing, therein lies a tale which needs a little lead-up . . .

For, courtesy of men such as **Jeremiah O'Donovan Rossa**, forces were building that would provide an interesting twist to the tale of the tail of his life. Ever the luminary, Rossa established a newspaper called *The United Irishman* and was a key leader of the 'Skirmishing Campaign' – the use of dynamite to overthrow British occupation. Rossa died in New York in 1915, aged 83, and, as with Terence Bellew MacManus, his body was returned to Ireland with much fanfare, as the cortege passed by 50,000 people on its way to Glasnevin Cemetery.[48] Within the procession, the Irish *Times* would report, 'It is estimated that at least five thousand rifles were carried in the procession, and that at least seven thousand of the processionists were healthy young men of military age.'[49]

In a famous oration over his grave, the rising leader of the Irish Nationalists in favour of Home Rule, Padraig Pearse – teacher, barrister, poet, and passionate orator to beat them all – referred to the armed men, and the recent resurgence of fervour for liberating Ireland.

'The seeds sown by the young men of '65 and '67 are coming to their miraculous ripening today.'[50]

Yes, because of the men like Rossa, we are on our way to liberation at last, no matter what the British try to do to stop us.

'The Defenders of this Realm have worked well in secret and in the open. They think that they have pacified Ireland. They think that they have purchased half of us and intimidated the other half. They think that they have foreseen everything, think that they have provided against everything.'[51]

Rising to a climax, his final words not only ring out over the cemetery, but through the ages.

'But the fools, the fools, the fools! – they have left us our Fenian dead, and while Ireland holds these graves, Ireland unfree shall never be at peace.'[52]

As Ireland built to yet another Rising in the months after the burial of Rossa, the *Clan-na-Gael* and **John Devoy** were more involved than ever. In the wake of the *Catalpa* Rescue, the authority and popularity of both were enormously enhanced. John Devoy continued to be the Clan's driving force. Nevertheless, the years had been tough on him spiritually, giving him a more forbidding feel, a grimmer countenance, than ever. Through all the decades, John Devoy had never married. Yes, he had been betrothed to sweet Eliza Kenny from County Kildare, nigh on 60 years ago, but then he had been arrested and imprisoned, and the rest of his life had been devoted all but exclusively to liberating Ireland. For her part, Eliza had waited for him for *17 years* before – thinking John Devoy had forgotten her and everything they'd meant to each other – going on to marry another man. Devoy had been devastated threefold by news he'd heard about Eliza over the years. Firstly when he heard of his mistake, and that Eliza had been waiting for nearly two decades after all! Secondly, that she'd married one of his acquaintances from back in the day in Ireland, that fellow Thomas Kilmurry. (She'd deserved so much better – she deserved *him*!) And finally, the worst news of all, which had come to him in 1904: his fair and fine Eliza had died. From missing her for decades, he now mourned her.

All he can do, as ever, is to throw himself into his work – liberating Ireland.

When World War I broke out, he knew it was time. For the slogan of the Irish nationalists – 'England's difficulty is Ireland's opportunity'[53] – was clearly irrefutable. He led a delegation to meet the German Ambassador to the United States to discuss ways in which Germany and Ireland could help each other. This included Germany sending munitions to Ireland, which would have occurred had the Royal Navy not sunk the German ship bearing those munitions. Nevertheless, the *Clan-na-Gael* was the key financier of what became known as the **Easter Rising**, which relied on German munitions.

For that Easter of 1916, Irish republicans still frustrated at English refusal to grant Home Rule to Ireland – legislation in 1914 to that effect had been passed, only to be withdrawn because of the war – staged the biggest Rising since 1798, starting on Easter Monday, a neat 40 years after the great Fenian escape from Fremantle Prison.

Just a little after noon, Padraig Pearse – fashioned for the occasion as the President of the Provisional Government of the Irish Republic – stands on the steps of Dublin's General Post Office and reads a proclamation verbally asserting the establishment of the Irish Republic. As he speaks, some 1000 armed men and 200 armed women storm strategic locations in Ireland and proclaim it physically. One revolutionary, Commandant Éamon de Valera, is particularly outstanding, leading his men to storm and occupy the huge Boland's Mill on Grand Canal Street, which will allow them to fire on any British forces that try to enter the city by its main south-eastern artery. The General Post Office is strongly held by Pearse and his worthiest lieutenants, including one Michael Collins, and a large band of well-armed rebels. The whole affair is co-ordinated by the Irish Republican Brotherhood Military Council, which has representatives from its constituent paramilitary bodies – the Irish Volunteers, the Irish Citizen Army and the League of Women.

In response, the British Army can put just 400 soldiers against them on the first day, but five days later has no fewer than 20,000 heavily armed soldiers in the field firing their guns and heavy artillery at all buildings held by the rebels, finally restoring order by the Sunday when Pearse sues for peace. No fewer than 450 people were killed in all and 2600 wounded.

The British retributions are swift and brutal.

In short order 3430 men and 79 women are arrested on grounds that they are thought to be 'Sinn Féiners', activists in favour of Home Rule, and – with shades of 1865 – the first courts martial are started within days.

Three of the leaders, including the 36-year-old Padraig Pearse, are found guilty and sentenced within *a* day, and the following morning at dawn are put up against the wall at the disused Kilmainham Gaol and shot by firing squad. No fewer than 90 death sentences are quickly handed down, but so great is the Irish outcry, so real is the risk that all of Ireland will rise once more if those sentences are carried out, that the British authorities commute all but 15 of them.

Great Irish leaders like William Cosgrave and Éamon de Valera – the latter of whom was the last commander to surrender – survive, *in extremis*. Presently, things settle down – sort of. For while this Easter Rising of 1916 did not succeed militarily, it did politically, as public opinion swung heavily behind the rebels.

As Ireland moved towards Home Rule it looked, as ever, to Irish–Americans for help, for inspiration, and to pay its dues. In June 1919, Éamon de Valera went to America, looking for funds, and support so that Irish leader Michael Collins and other rebels could be properly armed as they took the fight to Britain. And there were a couple of people de Valera specifically insisted on seeing, to pay his respects. The first was **James Wilson**, now ailing, 84 years old – the last man left standing of the Wild Geese. He is living in the town of Pawtucket, Rhode Island. It is the place he had gone to after landing in the United States, where he had married and raised a family.

The old man with the glittering blue eyes has been forewarned and answers the knock on the door with warmth. And they have much to talk about. For de Valera, too, had fought the good fight, as a soldier for Ireland not Britain, and, just like Wilson, had been court-martialled, and sentenced to die, only to have that sentence commuted – before, he, too, had made a miraculous escape from Lincoln Prison in England!

Oh, how they talk.

Their lives have essentially run in parallel, half a century apart.

Shortly thereafter, de Valera journeys to New Bedford, where he goes to visit a very old lady in her home on Seaview Terrace. Emma Anthony has been ill, but rises to the occasion and accepts his compliments to her late, great husband, and presents to him as a gift the as-told-to biography written about her love.

As chronicled by a journalist attending, de Valera 'handled [the book] with a certain reverence [and] gazed curiously and closely at the autograph on the first page, written in the shaky [hand-writing] of age . . . the name known to all friends of Irish freedom – Captain George Smith Anthony'.[54]

As much as he is honoured by her gift, this future President of the Republic of Ireland declines to take it from her and instead, with her blessing, adds his own signature below that of his hero, saying to her, 'Having been a prisoner myself, I can appreciate what that expedition meant then and now . . . We are only carrying on in our generation what they set out to further in theirs – the cause of Irish Freedom.'[55]

Thereafter flanked by Captain Henry Hathaway – and with a large crowd gathering for the occasion – de Valera goes to lay a wreath and Irish flag on the brave Captain's grave.

'Standing bareheaded at the grave mantled in a white covering and with the snow softly falling upon the crowd which came to do honour to Captain Anthony . . .' a local paper chronicles, 'De Valera addressed the gathering.'

'I am glad to have this opportunity to pay tribute to the memory of Captain Anthony,'[56] he says, noting that his own fight for Irish freedom should be an inspiration for Americans of the present generation.

James Wilson dies just months after de Valera's visit, and is laid to rest in Old St Mary's Graveyard in Pawtucket – surprisingly, without a gravestone to tell where he lay.

In fact, it is a strange circumstance that four of the six Fenians were buried without gravestones, with only the graves of Hassett and Harrington in New York properly marked. In the case of Hogan and Wilson that was at least rectified in October 2017 when the Fenian

Memorial Committee raised money to place handsome stones atop their graves.

And in May 2018, two new headstones were unveiled at the head of the graves of Tommy Darragh and Big Bob Cranston in Philadelphia's Most Holy Redeemer Cemetery.

But I digress . . .

Now, as to the long-yearned-for Rising to beat them all, the one to tip the balance, it finally came in the form of all-out warfare, when from 1919 onwards the Irish Republican Army fought a War of Independence against British forces in Ireland. Never was it more bloody than on 'Bloody Sunday', 21 November 1920, when in the autumnal sunshine of that fateful Sabbath in Dublin, 15 British intelligence operatives, heirs to the likes of Patrick Foley and Thomas Talbot, were executed by the IRA.[57] In the afternoon, Dublin's Royal Irish Constabulary struck back, firing upon a crowd at a Gaelic football match, killing 14 civilians and wounding 65.

Tragically, there was much more to come as the violence escalated over the next seven months – 1000 people were killed and 4500 republicans were locked up – until finally a ceasefire was agreed to on 11 July 1921, which led to the signing of the Anglo-Irish Treaty on 6 December 1921.

The Treaty sees the island of Ireland partitioned: Northern Ireland, made up of six counties of Ulster, remains under British rule, while Southern Ireland, with its capital of Dublin, is declared the **Irish Free State**, a self-governing Dominion of Britain.

Alas, far from quelling the violent unrest, this declaration exacerbates it.

Bitter disagreements break out between the Nationalists, the ruling republicans of the Irish Free State who are naturally enough pro-treaty, and the republicans who are against the treaty – and still fighting under the auspices of the IRA – break out. The clashes build into nothing less than the Irish Civil War, which rages for 11 months until the pro-treaty Nationalists, well provided with weapons by none other than the British – strange bedfellows indeed – declare victory against the much-weakened IRA on 24 May 1923.

•

Just 15 months after the cessation of Civil War hostilities in Ireland, in the summer of 1924, an old Irishman leaves American shores and heads towards Ireland, at the invitation of the great Irish poet W.B. Yeats, with whom he has enjoyed a warm correspondence. Frail at 82 years old, **John Devoy** has worked towards Irish independence for a period spanning eight decades . . . and Ireland knows it.

As his ship, *The President Harding*, approaches the Irish coast, the ancient revolutionary is just having his breakfast when he is handed a wireless message that has just been received from the Irish Head of State, President of the Executive Council William T. Cosgrave, welcoming him home and hoping he will regard himself a guest of Ireland.[58]

John Devoy quickly replies: 'I thank you for your kind and cordial message of welcome, and reciprocate good wishes. Will land at Cobh and proceed immediately to relatives in Dublin. As my visit is entirely personal . . . I wish to avoid public demonstrations . . . and avoid other public appearances.'[59]

He simply wishes to spend a few quiet weeks with his niece and nephews at their home in Fairview, just two miles from Dublin Castle.

Which is fine.

But Ireland will not let such a servant of the nation as John Devoy go unrecognised while here.

When his ship – proudly bearing the flags of both Ireland and the United States of America in honour of its famous passenger – docks in Cork's Cobh Harbour on Saturday, 26 July 1924, Ireland is ready. As the tender bearing John Devoy comes to the wharf and he steps off, he is greeted by a full military honour guard standing to rigid attention as he walks down the gangplank, with the Minister for External Affairs, Mr Desmond FitzGerald, waiting with outstretched hand.

When he steps off a train at Dublin's Kingsbridge Station the next day, Devoy is again met by a military guard of honour – who *preeeeeee-sent* arms! – all while buglers sound the salute. Nodding graciously, while surely reflecting on the extraordinary change the span of his life has both witnessed and helped to cause, the old revolutionary, 'a venerable figure wrapt in the dignity of honourable years',[60] according to a journalist from the *Irish Independent*, makes his way through the guard, to be engulfed by the embrace of his niece and three nephews who he is meeting for the first time.

While in Dublin, he is overwhelmed with invitations to appear and speak at public celebrations of his return, but accepts very few. One he accepts from the Aonach Tailteann Committee to speak briefly at their Irish cultural festival, and the second . . . to in fact visit Cosgrave in his office, where he is again saluted by a military guard of honour, before going inside to meet the Irish Head of State for an hour.

Afterwards, Cosgrave escorts the old revolutionary to Glasnevin Cemetery, where they visit the graves of, among others, O'Donovan Rossa and James Stephens.

The old man stands there, hat off, head bowed, saying his prayers. It had all been so long ago. They had fought mightily, risked much, and devoted their entire lives to the cause. Somehow, he is still here, all these years on.

And the fact that he is standing here beside an Irish Head of State, with most of Ireland now in charge of its own affairs, is a testament to the fact that they had won in the end, whatever the cost to their own lives.

Honouring both the sacrifices Devoy has made, and the achievement he has wrought, Cosgrave will later say at the final invitation Devoy accepts, a banquet held in his honour: 'No man deserves greater thanks from the nation.'[61]

For John Devoy so many memories come flooding back, and never more than when he takes his niece and nephews back to where his old family home had stood in the village of Greenhills in County Kildare. The house is long gone now, and all that is left are its foundations, but still he walks around, showing them where all the rooms had been, the spot where his father had played the fiddle, the place where his mother had sung her Irish lullabies to send them to sleep.

Is it too late to retrieve some of the joy lost from his youth? For the most part it won't come from finding old friends, now that he is back in Ireland. After all, most of them are dead, disappeared or departed. Everywhere he goes, everything he does, reminds him of them. He inwardly weeps for friends and loves long gone . . .

But now a letter comes to him at his niece's place, in hand-writing that is . . . strangely . . . familiar.

It couldn't possibly be, could it?

Could it?

With trembling hand he opens it.

It is *another* voice from the tomb.

But this one is his love.

Eliza!

She *lives*!

And she is widowed!

And she is living near the place he used to visit her in Naas, and wants to see him!

'It has been the work of my life to meet you once more,'[62] she writes simply.

The old man reels.

'It was like a voice from the grave,' Devoy would recount, 'when I learned that she still lived.'[63]

Like a young man trapped in an old man's body – for when it comes to his love for Eliza that precisely describes him – John Devoy goes to see her in the company of his niece and three nephews, and with his old bony hand, softly knocks on her door just as he had all those decades ago, when he had come in the dead of night.

And, just as it had then, the door opens near instantly to reveal . . . sweet Eliza!

The two embrace. Not with vigour as in days of yore, tumbling into each other's arms, but with delicacy, as befitting two very old people for whom tumbling of any kind can be dangerous.

'I have mourned you as dead, for twenty years,'[64] Devoy tells her with no little emotion, still incredulous that she is here before him, *alive*.

Gently, delicately, John Devoy gets a good look at this woman, the love of his life, who he has not seen for 58 years. He remembers her, of course, as 'a fine, strong, healthy girl of twenty-one'.[65]

That health, it would appear, has long gone and he realises with great sadness that it is very likely 'that she could not last long'.[66]

Oh, yes.

'I had not seen her for 58 years,' he would recount, 'and the contrast between the splendid girl of 20 and the old woman of 79 crippled with rheumatism, was very saddening. The bitterest reflection for me was my misfortune in failing (through a series of mishaps) to get her for my wife.'[67]

Against that, as he will later chronicle, 'I found her as warm as ever and it made me very sad to think of the life of happiness I had missed through my misfortunes.'[68]

In her salon and then over lunch, the two talk, as the years fall away and he is stunned by her 'vivid recollection of the old days when her family sheltered me while "on the run" a hunted outlaw'.[69]

They work out how there had been a mix-up, first that she had been married while he was in prison in England, which she hadn't. In fact, she had very *faithfully* waited for him for 12 years after his release in 1871, but, thinking Devoy had forgotten her, eventually married a Mr Kilmurry who has since passed away. (It was a young fellow by the name of Rathmore who was responsible for the mix-up. It was him who had told John Devoy, and he had believed him, without checking . . . he had believed him . . . without *checking*.) As to the report of her death, it was her sister who had succumbed to an illness, and not her. But he hadn't checked. He hadn't . . . *checked*.

'It was all my fault,' Devoy will recount, lashing himself, 'that I did not investigate and find out the facts.'[70]

And yet it still all goes so wonderfully well that, as he will later note, despite his sadness, 'it was a great consolation for me to find that she had the same feeling for me as of old'.[71]

And he has, as God is his witness, the same feeling for her.

They meet many times over the next few weeks, recalling old times, visiting the old places where the whimsies of youth had taken them, catching up on their lives and lamenting their long ago loss of each other – most particularly how tragic that he should have heard she had married while he was in prison, instead of the *truth*, that she was waiting for him patiently.

And it is undeniable that as he has never married, and she is now a widow, they are legally free to right the historic wrong and marry now. But there is also a tragic truth. Her life, what's left of it, is in Ireland. His life is in America. At this stage of their lives, relocating for either of them could only lead to unhappiness.

For the moment, all he can do is promise to keep in touch, as, even now, he must prepare to return to America.

After attending one last banquet in his honour, this'un at Dublin's Dolphin Hotel, hosted by Cosgrave, he returns to New York, with another guard of honour there to see him off.

Oh, the contrast to when he had been expelled from Ireland in 1867, dragged aboard a prison ship by burly guards. This time the guards form two lines either side of the path leading to the gangplank and they salute as the mighty John Devoy walks past, the soldiers counting it as one of the great honours of their lives just to be in his presence.

Upon returning to America, Devoy is sure to keep in touch with Eliza. When she falls ill early in 1925, her devoted niece, Mary, writes to Devoy with the news. He replies with concern and good wishes for Eliza's speedy recovery, adding: 'I always forget her married name. I can only remember her as Eliza Kenny, when she was a fine young girl, always ready to welcome me and to help me when I was on the run.'[72]

Later that year he sends her a photograph, on the back of which he writes in his elegant long-hand:

> To Mrs. E. Kilmurry (nee Eliza Kenny) in loving memory of our engagement when she was a fine girl of 20 (1866) and with deep regret at the misfortunes which separated us.
> From John Devoy
>
> New York, July 2 [1925][73]

Several weeks later, he receives her reply, with a letter and photo of herself, which he cherishes. On the back of the letter he inscribes the words: 'Mrs E Kilmurry of Naas, nee Eliza Kenny of Tipper, County Kildare, engaged to John Devoy at the time of his arrest . . . waiting for him for 12 years after his release in 1871.'[74]

Yes, John Devoy might be permitted for shifting uncomfortably in his seat as he writes those words.

Nevertheless, in 1927 Devoy decides to go and see her again – the two have kept in close touch, 'I often think of the good days we had when we were young . . . they didn't last long, but I never forgot them.'[75] – and is on the point of returning to Ireland when he hears the news, from her niece. She has taken ill. He quickly writes back.

> Dear Miss Curley,
> I am greatly grieved at the news of your aunt's illness . . .
> I hope that she will still be alive when you get this letter, so that you can tell her that I consider it the greatest misfortune of my life that bad luck prevented me from having her as my wife when we both were young and had the world before us.[76]

John Devoy weeps.

The letter arrives the day before her death, and is read to Eliza by her niece. Upon receiving the sad tidings, Devoy writes in sympathy to Mary Curley, lamenting:

> What a splendid devoted wife she would have been. I have had many misfortunes living my life but missing Eliza Kenny was the worst of all. Both our lives would have been happier.[77]

Though he had been right on the point of returning to Ireland again specifically to see her, he cancels his trip and throws himself into his current project – writing his memoirs, *Recollections of an Irish Rebel*.

The next year, on the morning of 29 September 1928, while in a hotel room in Atlantic City, John Devoy himself dies, aged 86. After a funeral Mass at New York's Church of the Ascension, his body is returned to Ireland. There, his body lies in state in Dublin's City Hall, before a State Funeral – with at least 100,000 mourners estimated to have turned out on the day – and he is interred in Glasnevin Cemetery, an honoured son of Ireland, returned to her green bosom.

Erin go Bragh.

An enormous monument is shortly afterwards erected on his final resting place, bearing a fitting epitaph.

> *His life was a ceaseless protest*
> *And his voice was a prophet's cry*
> *To be true to the Truth and faithful*
> *Though the world were arrayed for the Lie.*[78]

Bravo, John Devoy. You were an extraordinary man who masterminded an extraordinary operation. And nudging 100 years since your death, Sir, Ireland and we of the Irish diaspora talk about you still.

We dips our lids to a great man.

BIBLIOGRAPHY

NLI   National Library of Ireland

ML   Mitchell Library (State Library of New South Wales)

SLNSW   State Library of New South Wales

Books, eBooks or Audio Books

Author unknown, *James Stephens: Chief Organizer of the Irish Republic (Embracing an Account of the Origin and Progress of the Fenian Brotherhood. Being a Semi-Biographical Sketch of James Stephens, with the Story of his Arrest and Imprisonment; also his Escape from the British Authorities)*, Carleton, New York, 1866 (online access: https://babel.hathitrust.org/cgi/pt?id=hvd.32044019338284;view=1up;seq=1)

Barry, Liam, *Voices from the Tomb: A Biographical Dictionary of the 62 Fenians transported to Western Australia*, National Gaelic Publications, Australind (WA), 2006

Barry, Liam, *Western Australia's Great Escape: The Dramatic Escape of Fenian John Boyle O'Reilly*, C.F.N. Publications, Australind (WA), 1992

Breslin, John J., *The Cruise of the Catalpa*, Press of Rockwell & Churchill, Boston, 1876

Burke, Thomas F. and Chamney, William Graves, *'The Fenian Conspiracy': Report of the Trials of Thomas F. Burke and Others, for High Treason, and Treason-Felony, &c., at the Special Commission, Dublin, held at the Court-house, Green-street, Dublin, commencing 8th April, 1867, Ireland. Courts of Oyer and Terminer and Geneal Gaol Delivery*, Alexander Thom, Dublin, 1869

Burnett, Graham, *Trying Leviathan: The Nineteenth-Century New York Court Case that Put the Whale on Trial and Challenged the Order of Nature*, Princeton University Press, Princeton, 2010

Campbell, Malcolm, *Ireland's New Worlds: Immigrants, Politics, and Society in the United States and Australia, 1815-1922*, University of Wisconsin Press, Wisconsin, 2008

Colwell, Max, *Whaling Around Australia*, Rigby, Adelaide, 1969

Coogan, Tim Pat, *The Famine Plot: England's Role in Ireland's Greatest Tragedy*, Palgrave Macmillan, New York, 2012

Cowan, Richard, *Mary Tondut: The Woman in the Catalpa's Story*, Richard Cowan, Sydney, 2008

Dakin, William John, *Whalemen Adventures in Southern Waters*, Angus and Robertson, Sydney, 1963

Darby, Andrew, *Harpoon: Into the Heart of Whaling*, Allen & Unwin, Sydney, 2007

Davidson, Ron, *Fremantle Impressions*, Fremantle Press, Fremantle (WA), 2008

Davis, Thomas Osborne, *The Poems of Thomas Davis*, James Duffy, Dublin, 1846 (online access: https://archive.org/details/poemsofthomasdav00davi/page/n5)

Denieffe, Joseph, *A Personal Narrative of the Irish Revolutionary Brotherhood, Giving a Faithful Report of the Principal Events from 1855 to 1867, Written, at the Request of Friends*, The Gael Publishing Co., New York, 1906 (online access: https://archive.org/stream/personalnarrativ00deni?ref=ol#page/n5/mode/2up)

Devoy, John, *Recollections of an Irish Rebel: A Personal Narrative*, [Place of publication not identified], [publisher not identified], [date of publication not identified]/[New York?] : [s.n.], 1929 [info from World Cat]; ca. 1929 (online access: https://archive.org/stream/reollectionsofir00john)

Doheny, Michael, *The Felon's Track: A Narrative of '48 Embracing the Leading events in the Irish Struggle from the Year 1843 to the Close of 1848*, Farrell & Son, New York, 1867 (online access: https://archive.org/stream/felonstracknarra00doheuoft?ref=ol#page/n5/mode/2up)

Downie, Alan, *Jonathon Swift: Political Writer*, Routledge, New York, 1984

Durney, James; Corrigan, Mario; and Curran, Seamus (eds), *A Forgotten Hero, John Devoy*, John Devoy Memorial Committee, 2009 (online access: http://www.kildare2016.ie/wp-content/uploads/2016/03/John_Devoy_Book.pdf)

Ellison, Robin, *Red Tape: Managing Excess in Law, Regulation and the Courts*, Cambridge University Press, Cambridge (UK), 2018

Evans, A. G., *Fanatic Heart: A Life of John Boyle O'Reilly*, University of Western Australia Press, Nedlands (WA), 1997

Fennell, Philip and King, Marie (eds), *John Devoy's Catalpa Expedition*, NYU Press, New York, 2006

Fennell, Thomas McCarthy, *Voyage of the Hougoumont and Life at Fremantle: The Story of an Irish Rebel*, Xlibris Corporation, New York, 2000

Fitzpatrick, David, *Descendancy: Irish Protestant Histories since 1795*, Cambridge University Press, Cambridge (UK), 2016

Foster, Robert Fitzroy (ed.), *The Oxford History of Ireland*, Oxford University Press, Oxford (UK), 2001

Gibbs, Martin, 'The Convict Places of Western Australia', in: Sherriff, Jacqui and Brake, Anne (eds.), *Building a Colony: The Convict Legacy*, Centre for Western Australian History, University of Western Australia, Perth, 2006

Golway, Terry, *Irish Rebel: John Devoy and America's Fight for Ireland's Freedom*, Merrion Press, Kildare (Ireland), 2015 (Kindle edition)

Great Britain, House of Lords, *Parliamentary Debates: Forming a Continuation of 'The Parliamentary history of England, from the earliest period to the year 1803'*, Vol. IX, T. C. Hansard, London, 1832 (online access: https://api.parliament.uk/historic-hansard/lords/1831/dec/15/tithes-in-ireland)

Great Britain, Parliament, House of Commons, *The Parliamentary Debates (Hansard): Official Report*, H. M. Stationary Office, London, Vol. 199, February 1870 (online access: https://api.parliament.uk/historic-hansard/commons/1870/feb/10/tipperary-election-jeremiah-odonovan)

Great Britain, Parliament, House of Commons, *The Parliamentary Debates (Hansard): Official Report*, H. M. Stationary Office, London, Vol. 229, May 1876 (online access: https://api.parliament.uk/historic-hansard/commons/1876/may/22/ireland-the-upper-shannon-ballyconnell)

Hughes, Kyle and MacRaild, Donald M., *Crime, Violence and the Irish in the Nineteenth Century*, Liverpool University Press, Oxford (UK), 2018

Keneally, Thomas, *The Great Shame: A Story of the Irish in the Old World and the New*, Random House, Sydney, 1998

Keneally, Thomas, *Three Famines: Starvation and Politics*, PublicAffairs, New York, 2011

Kenna, Shane, *Jeremiah O'Donovan Rossa: Unrepentant Fenian*, Merrion Press, Sallins (Ireland), 2015

Kimberly, Warren Bert, *History of West Australia: A Narrative of her Past together with Biographies of her Leading Men*, F. W. Niven & Co., Melbourne, 1897 (online access: https://en.wikisource.org/wiki/History_of_West_Australia)

Lalor, J. F., 'Clearing Decks', *The Irish Felon*, No. 5, 22 July 1848, in: Fogarty, L., *James Fintan Lalor: Patriot and Political Essayist*, The Talbot Press Ltd, Dublin, 1919

Lalor, J. F., 'The First Step – The Felon Club', *The Irish Felon*, No. 2, 1 July 1848, in: Fogarty, L., *James Fintan Lalor: Patriot and Political Essayist*, The Talbot Press Ltd, Dublin, 1919

Lalor, J. F, 'To the editor of The Felon', *The Irish Felon*, 24 June 1848, in *James Fintan Lalor: Patriot and Political Essayist*, Fogarty, L., The Talbot Press Ltd, Dublin, 1919

Lalor, J. F, *The Irish Felon*, 24 June 1848, in: Fogarty, L., *James Fintan Lalor: Patriot and Political Essayist*, The Talbot Press Ltd, Dublin, 1919

MacManus, Seumas, *The Story of the Irish Race: A Popular History of Ireland*, Irish Publishing Company, New York, 1921

McDonnell, Vincent, *The Catalpa Adventure: Escape to Freedom*, The Collins Press, Cork (Ireland), 2010

Meagher, Thomas Francis (Griffith, Arthur (ed.)), *Meagher of the Sword, Speeches of Thomas Francis Meagher in Ireland, 1846–1848: His Narrative of Events in Ireland in July 1848, Personal Reminiscences of Waterford, Galway, and his Schooldays*, M. H. Gill, Dublin, 1916 (online access: https://archive.org/details/cu31924028141665/page/n5)

Mitchel, John, *The Last Conquest of Ireland (Perhaps)*, R. & T. Washbourne, London, 1882 (online access: https://archive.org/details/lastconquestofir00mitc/page/n7)

Murphy, James H., *Abject Loyalty, Nationalism and Monarchy in Ireland during the Reign of Queen Victoria*, Catholic University of America Press, Washington, DC, 2001

O'Brien, Connor Cruise, *The Great Melody: A Thematic Biography and Commented Anthology of Edmund Burke*, Sinclair-Stevenson, London, 1992

O'Donovan Rossa, Jeremiah, *Irish Rebels in English Prisons: A Record of Prison Life*, P. J. Kenedy, New York, 1899 (online access: https://archive.org/stream/irishrebelsineng00odon?ref=ol#page/n5/mode/2up)

O'Donovan Rossa, Jeremiah, *Prison Life: Six Years in Six English Prisons*, P. J. Kenedy, New York, 1874

O Luing, Sean, *Fremantle Mission*, Anvil Books, County Kerry, 1965

O'Reilly, John Boyle, *Moondyne: A Story from the Underworld*, Sydney University Press, Sydney, 2003

O'Reilly, John Boyle, *Moondyne: A Story from the Underworld*, Roberts Brothers, Boston, 1883

O'Reilly, John Boyle, *Songs From The Southern Seas, and other Poems*, Roberts Brothers, Boston, 1873

Pease, Zephaniah Walter, *The Catalpa Expedition*, George S. Anthony, New Bedford (Mass.), 1897 (online access: https://archive.org/details/catalpaexpeditio01peas/page/n0)

Philbrick, Nathaniel, *In the Heart of the Sea*, Penguin, USA, 2001

Ramon, Marta, *A Provisional Dictator: James Stephens and the Fenian Movement*, University College Dublin Press, Dublin, 2007

Regan, Stephen, *Irish Writing: An Anthology of Irish Literature in English 1789–1939*, Oxford University Press, Oxford, 2008

Roche, James Jeffrey, *Life of John Boyle O'Reilly*, Cassell Publishing Company, New York, 1891 (online access: https://archive.org/details/lifejohnboyleor00rochgoog/page/n0)

Rossa, Jeremiah O'Donovan, *Rossa's Recollections: 1838 to 1898*, Mariner's Harbor, New York, 1898

Ryan, Desmond, *The Fenian Chief: A Biography of James Stephens*, Gill & Son, Dublin and Sydney, 1967

Ryan, Desmond, *The Phoenix Flame: A Study of Fenianism and John Devoy*, Arthur Barker, London, 1937

Ryan, Mark, *Fenian Memories*, M.H. Gill & Son, Dublin, 1946

Shakespeare, William, *As You Like It*, The Copp Clark Company, Toronto, 1919

Shakespeare, William, *Julius Caesar*, H. Altemus, Philadelphia, 1890

Shakespeare, William, *Hamlet*, John Cawthorn, London, 1806

Shakespeare, William, *Henry V*, University Society, New York

Smith, Jeremy, *Britain and Ireland: From Home Rule to Independence*, Routledge, New York, 2013

Sullivan, Timothy Daniel; Sullivan, Alexander Martin; and Sullivan, Denis Baylor, *Speeches from the Dock, or, Protests of Irish Patriotism*, Excelsior Catholic Publishing House, New York, 1904 (online access: https://archive.org/details/speechesfromdock00sull/page/n9)

Swift, Jonathan, *The Works of Dr. Jonathan Swift: Dean of St. Patrick's*, Vol. III, G. Hamilton, J. Balfour, L. Hunter, Edinburgh, 1757

Tone, William Theobald Wolfe (Ed.), *Life of Theobald Wolfe Tone*, Vol. II, Gales and Seaton, Washington, 1826

Traubel, Horace, *Intimate with Walt: Selections from Walt Whitman's Conversations with Horace Traubel, 1888–1892*, University of Iowa Press, Iowa City, 2001

Williams, Heathcote, *Whale Nation*, Harmony, New York, 1988

Wordsworth, William, *The Poems of William Wordsworth*, Edward Moxon, London, 1858

Yeats, William Butler, Finneran (Ed.), *The Collected Works of W.B. Yeats, Volume I: The Poems*, Simon and Schuster, New York, 2010

Newspapers and gazettes

Adelaide Express (SA)

Adelaide Observer (SA)

Advocate (Melbourne)

Australasian (Melbourne)

Ballarat Star (VIC)

Bendigo Advertiser (VIC)

Bunbury Herald (WA)

Burrangong Argus (NSW)

Catholic Press (Sydney)

Dalby Herald and Western Queensland Advertiser (QLD)

Darling Downs Gazette and General Advertiser (QLD)

Empire (Sydney)

Freeman's Journal (Sydney)

Gippsland Times (VIC)

Goulburn Herald and Chronicle (NSW)

Gympie Times and Mary River Mining Gazette (QLD)

Inquirer and Commercial News (Perth)

Irish Canadian

Irish Examiner

Leader (Melbourne)

Macleay Chronicle (NSW)

Morning Advertiser

New York Times

Perth Gazette and West Australian Times (WA)

Pilot (Boston)

Police Gazette (WA)

Queensland Times, Ipswich Herald and General Advertiser (QLD)

Queenslander (Brisbane)

Smith's Weekly (Sydney)

South Australian Chronicle and Weekly Mail (Adelaide)

South Western Advertiser (Perth)

Southern Cross (Adelaide)

Sydney Morning Herald

Sunday Times (Perth)

The Herald (Fremantle)

The Horsham Times (VIC)

The Irish Times (Dublin)

The Irishman

The Mercury (Hobart)

The Nation (Ireland)

Victorian Express (WA)

W.A. Record (Perth)

West Australian (Perth)

Western Australian Times (Perth)

Western Mail (Perth)

Magazines

Co. Kildare Online Electronic History Journal, *The Rescue of the Military Fenians from Australia*, 2016, http://www.kildare.ie/ehistory/index.php/the-rescue-of-the-military-fenians-from-australia/

Cobbett, William, *Cobbett's Weekly Register*, Vol. 43, 1822, p. 57

Fennell, Philip, 'History into Myth: The "Catalpa's" Long Voyage', *New Hibernia Review*, Vol. 9, No. 1, 2005

Irish-American Weekly, Lincoln, Nebraska, USA, 20 March 1892

Kelly, John Edward, *The Wild Goose*, Vol. 1 Number 4, 1867, p. 3

McCord, Norman, 'The Fenians and Public Opinion in Great Britain,' *University Review*, Vol. 4, No. 3, Special Fenian Issue (Winter, 1967), p. 229

McDermott, Eamon, 'Martin Hogan and the Catalpa Rescue', 1988, *The Old Limerick Journal*, Vol. 23, Australian edition, pp. 112–124 (online access: http://www.limerickcity.ie/media/martin%20hogan%20 and%20the%20catalpa.pdf)

Morley, Mike, 'Hogan's Heroes', 2014, *Irish American News*, July Issue (online access: https://issuu.com/ irishamericannews/docs/0714)

Punch, 8 April 1848, p. 147

Waters, Ormonde, 'John Boyle O'Reilly,' *Seanchas Ardmhacha: Journal of the Armagh Diocesan Historical Society*, 1988, Vol. 13, No. 1

Waters, Ormonde, 'The Escape of the Fenians, Western Australia, 17 April 1876', 1996–97, *Seanchas Ardmhacha: Journal of the Armagh Diocesan Historical Society*, Vol. 17, No. 1

Whelan, Fergus, 'Fenians in the Foothills: Patrick Doran and the Rising of 1867,' *History Ireland*, Vol. 25, No. 4, July–August 2017, p. 30

Online Newspapers or Magazines

The Bulletin, 16 December 1882, p. 5, http://nla.gov.au/nla.obj-237816958/

Fremantle Shipping News: An Online Magazine all about Freo, 9 January 2018, Sir William Heseltine, 'The Escape of the Military Fenians from Fremantle Prison: The Warders' Perspective', https://fremantleshippingnews.com.au/2018/01/09/escape-military-fenians-fremantle-prison-warders-perspective/

History Ireland: Ireland's History Magazine, [no date for online article], Lar Joye, 'Flags of the Fenians', https://www.historyireland.com/volume-24/flags-of-the-fenians/ (mentions: Published in Artefacts, Issue 1 (January/February 2016), Vol. 24)

Humanities: The Magazine of the National Endowment for the Humanities, March/April 2010, Vol. 31, Nr. 2, James Williford, 'Whaling the Old Way', https://www.neh.gov/humanities/2010/marchapril/feature/whaling-the-old-way (web page mentions: James Williford, *Humanities*, March/April 2010, Vol. 31, Nr. 2)

The Irish Times (Online), 5 March 2017, Ronan McGreevy, 'How "The Irish Times" reported the Fenian rising 150 years ago', https://www.irishtimes.com/news/ireland/irish-news/how-the-irish-times-reported-the-fenian-rising-150-years-ago-1.2998474

Manuscripts

'Denieffe's Story', O'Leary Papers, National Library of Ireland, Ms. 8002(1), in Ramon, p. 69

'The Wild Goose: A Collection of Ocean Waifs', Vol. 1, No. 1, 9 November 1867, p. 6 in John Flood Papers, SLNSW, MLMSS 1542 (Safe 1/409), http://archival.sl.nsw.gov.au/Details/archive/110319433

'The Wild Goose: A Collection of Ocean Waifs', Vol. 1, No. 4, 30 November 1867, p. 3 in John Flood Papers, SLNSW, MLMSS 1542 (Safe 1/409), http://archival.sl.nsw.gov.au/Details/archive/110319433

'The Wild Goose: A Collection of Ocean Waifs', Vol. 1, No. 1, 21 December 1867, p. 1 in John Flood Papers, SLNSW, MLMSS 1542 (Safe 1/409), http://archival.sl.nsw.gov.au/Details/archive/110319433

Anthony, George S., Letter to John Devoy, 27 March 1893, MS 18,000/4/1, John Devoy Papers Collection, NLI

Casey, John, 'Journal of a Voyage from Portland to Freemantle on board the convict ship *Hougoumont*, 7 October 1867–9 January 1868,' 9 January 1868, SLNSW, MLDOC 1447, p. 46, http://archival.sl.nsw.gov.au/Details/archive/110359301

Cashman, Denis B., Diary, 13 December 1867, p. 20, in Denis B. Cashman Papers, 458.1.b, East Carolina Manuscript Collection, J. Y. Joyner Library, East Carolina University, https://digital.lib.ecu.edu/957#details

Cashman, Denis B., *Fenian Diary*, Edited by Charles Sullivan III, 2001, p. 20

Doheny, Michael, to William Smith O'Brien, Letter, 20 August 1858, in: Ural, Susannah, *The Harp and the Eagle: Irish-American Volunteers and the Union Army, 1861–1865*, NYU Press, NY, 2006, p. 39

Donegan, Luke, 'Convict Daily Life,' Government of Western Australia, Fremantle Prison, Fremantle, 2009, http://fremantleprison.com.au/media/1150/fp-convict-daily-life.pdf

Irish Prison Service, Booklet, *40th Anniversary of Arbor Hill Prison as a Civilian Prison*, Peter Murphy personal collection

Kelly, Thomas, Letter to General Halpin, 12 March 1867, Joseph Denieffe, *A Personal Narrative of the Irish Revolutionary Brotherhood*, 1906, p. 278

O'Reilly, John Boyle, Letter to John Devoy, 28 January 1871, MS 18,010/12/1, John Devoy Papers Collection, NLI

O'Reilly, John Boyle, Letter to John Devoy, 13 February 1871, MS 18,010/12/2, John Devoy Papers Collection, NLI

O'Reilly, John Boyle, Letter to John Devoy, 4 December 1874, MS 18,010/13/1, John Devoy Papers Collection, NLI

O'Reilly, John Boyle, Letter to John Devoy, 10 June 1876, MS 18,010/13/6, John Devoy Papers Collection, NLI

O'Reilly, John Boyle, Letter to Matthew Skinner Smith (Superintendent of Police), 11 September 1876, Peter Murphy's family collection

Roantree, William F., Letter to John Devoy, 17 September 1874, MS 18,011/14/3, John Devoy Papers Collection, NLI

Stephens, James, Letter on his removal as head of the Brotherhood, John Devoy Papers Collection, NLI

Wilson, James, Letter to John Devoy, 4 September 1873, MS 18,013/13/1, John Devoy Papers Collection, NLI

Wilson, James, Letter to John Devoy, 15 June 1874, MS 18,013/13/2, John Devoy Papers Collection, NLI

Wilson, James, Letter to John Devoy, 4 December 1874, MS 18,010/13/1, John Devoy Papers Collection, NLI

Other

Robinson, William C. F., 'Remember Me No More', Wickins & Co, London, 19—(year unknown), https://nla.gov.au/nla.obj-179773646/view?partId=nla.obj-179774310#page/n6/mode/1up

The Real McKenzies, 'The Catalpa', song lyrics seen at: ABC, Radio National, Hindsight, 'The *Catalpa* escape', broadcast 28 July 2013, http://www.abc.net.au/radionational/programs/archived/hindsight/the-catalpa/4806338

Widescreen Studio, 'The Catalpa Rescue: Hidden History' (Documentary), YouTube, https://www.youtube.com/watch?v=1Fm8dQZXzdA

Websites

Birman, Wendy, 'O'Reilly, John Boyle (1844–1890)', *Australian Dictionary of Biography*, National Centre of Biography, Australian National University, http://adb.anu.edu.au/biography/oreilly-john-boyle-4338/text7043, published first in hardcopy 1974

Crowley, F. K., 'Sir William Cleaver Francis Robinson,' *Australian Dictionary of Biography*, National Centre of Biography, Australian National University, Vol. 6, 1976, http://adb.anu.edu.au/biography/robinson-sir-william-cleaver-francis-4494

East Wall for All: A site for all things to do with East Wall in Dublin, 'John Flood: Fenian Leader, Australian Citizen and East Wall Smuggler', 1 August 2018, http://eastwallforall.ie/?p=2930

National Centre of Biography, Australian National University (ANU), *Australian Dictionary of Biography*, F. K. Crowley, 'Robinson, William Cleaver Francis (1834–1897)', http://adb.anu.edu.au/biography/robinson-sir-william-cleaver-francis-4494 (web page mentions: 'This article was published in *Australian Dictionary of Biography*, Volume 6, (MUP), 1976')

National Museum of Australia (NMA), Richard Reid, '"A Noble Whale Ship and Commander": The *Catalpa* Rescue, April 1876' (Part of the Exhibition 'Not Just Ned: A True History of the Irish in Australia', 17 March – 31 July 2011), http://www.nma.gov.au/__data/assets/pdf_file/0015/2553/NMA_Catalpa.pdf

Quigley's Cartoons, Catalpa Log, Part 5 (18 April 1876), http://www.quigleycartoon.com/?page_id=5471

Quigley's Cartoons, Catalpa Log, Part 5 (19 April 1876), http://www.quigleycartoon.com/?page_id=5471

The American Presidency Project, John F. Kennedy, Statement of the President on St. Patrick's Day (17 March 1962), https://www.presidency.ucsb.edu/documents/statement-the-president-st-patricks-day

U2, 'The Edge' about their song 'Van Diemen's Land' (*New Musical Express*, 1988), https://www.atu2.com/lyrics/songinfo.src?SID=454

U2, 'Van Diemen's Land', YouTube, https://www.youtube.com/watch?v=8yQk5HQtQ4Q

http://cms.slwa.wa.gov.au/dead_reckoning/government_archival_records/t-z/volunteers

http://guardiansofthecity.org/sheriff/sheriffs/desmond.html

http://members.iinet.net.au/~perthdps/convicts/con-wa42.html

http://museum.wa.gov.au/sites/default/files/MILITARY%20FIREARMS%20IN%20COLONIAL%20WESTERN%20AUSTRALIA%20THEIR%20ISSUE%20AND%20MARKING.pdf

http://mysite.du.edu/~ttyler/ploughboy/Ashley%20whaling%20glossary.htm

http://onesearch.slq.qld.gov.au/primo-explore/fulldisplay?docid=slq_alma21111693640002061&context=L&vid=SLQ&lang=en_US&search_scope=FHCOMBINED&adaptor=Local%20Search%20Engine&tab=fhcombined&query=any,contains,Robert%20Cranston&sortby=rank&offset=0

http://onesearch.slq.qld.gov.au/primo-explore/fulldisplay?docid=slq_alma21108947820002061&context=L&vid=SLQ&lang=en_US&search_scope=FHCOMBINED&adaptor=Local%20Search%20Engine&tab=fhcombined&query=any,contains,Martin%20hogan&sortby=rank

http://researchrepository.murdoch.edu.au/id/eprint/16505/1/who_were_the_pensioners.pdf

http://www.bostoncatholic.org/ThePilot.aspx

http://www.museum.wa.gov.au/maritime-archaeology-db/wrecks/georgette

http://www.sfsdhistory.com/eras/sheriff-tom-desmond-irish-republican-hero

https://de.wikipedia.org/wiki/James_Stephens_(Fenier)

https://en.wikipedia.org/wiki/Boston_Evening_Transcript

https://en.wikipedia.org/wiki/George_Jenkinson#Political_career

https://en.wikipedia.org/wiki/Grace_Bussell

https://en.wikipedia.org/wiki/James_Stephens_(Fenian)

https://en.wikisource.org/wiki/Catholic_Hymns_(1860)/Hail,_Queen_of_Heaven

https://en.wikisource.org/wiki/Life_of_John_Boyle_O%27Reilly/Chapter_6

https://en.wikisource.org/wiki/The_Wild_Goose/Number_4

https://fremantlestuff.info/arthurhead/lighthouses.html

https://fremantlestuff.info/jetties/index.html

https://fremantlestuff.info/organisations/pensioners.html

https://www.findagrave.com/memorial/98784980/john-f.-hathaway

https://www.history.com/topics/inventions/telegraph

https://www.historyireland.com/volume-24/flags-of-the-fenians/

https://www.whalingmuseum.org/learn/research-topics/overview-of-north-american-whaling/whales-hunting

ENDNOTES

Introduction

1 Devoy, *Recollections of an Irish Rebel*, Peter Devoy, Dublin, 1929, p.iii.
2 Keneally, *The Great Shame: A Story of the Irish in the Old World and the New*, Random House, Sydney, 1998, p. 417.
3 Author's note: At the time it was sometimes spelt Freemantle, but to avoid confusion, I have used Fremantle throughout.
4 Letter, George S. Anthony to John Devoy, 27 March 1893, MS 18,000/4/1, John Devoy Papers Collection, NLI.
5 Pease, *The Catalpa Expedition*, George S. Anthony, New Bedford, 1897, p. iv.

Dramatis Personae

1 Pease, *The Catalpa Expedition*, p. 110.
2 County Kildare Online Electronic History Journal, *The Rescue of the Military Fenians from Australia*, 2016, http://www.kildare.ie/ehistory/index.php/the-rescue-of-the-military-fenians-from-australia/
3 Heseltine, *The Escape of the Military Fenians from Fremantle Prison: The Warders' Perspective*, Fremantle History Society, 9 January 2018, https://fremantleshippingnews.com.au/2018/01/09/escape-military-fenians-fremantle-prison-warders-perspective/
4 Heseltine, *The Escape of the Military Fenians from Fremantle Prison: The Warders' Perspective*.

Prologue

1 Pease, *The Catalpa Expedition*, pp. 5–6.
2 Downie, *Jonathan Swift: Political Writer*, Routledge, New York, 1984, p. 298.
3 Great Britain, House of Lords, *Parliamentary Debates: Forming a Continuation of 'The Parliamentary history of England, form the earliest period to the year 1803'*, Vol. 9, T.C. Hansard, London, 1832, p. 235.
4 Author's note: With thanks to W. B. Yeats' famous line: 'There are no strangers here; only friends you haven't yet met.'
5 Author unknown, *James Stephens: Chief Organizer of the Irish Republic*, Carleton, New York, 1866, pp. 7–8. Author's note: Although the source says 'William of Nassau', I assume it means King William III, otherwise known as William of Orange, under whom the Treaty of Limerick was signed in October, 1691.
6 Author unknown, *James Stephens: Chief Organizer of the Irish Republic*, pp. 8–9.
7 Regan, *Irish Writing*, Oxford University Press, Oxford, 2008, p. 178.
8 Author unknown, *James Stephens: Chief Organizer of the Irish Republic*, p. 25.
9 MacManus, *The Story of the Irish Race*, Irish Publishing Company, New York, 1921, p. 521.
10 Tone (ed.), *Life of Theobald Wolfe Tone*, Vol. II, Gales and Seaton, Washington, 1826, p. 529.
11 Cobbett, *Cobbett's Weekly Register*, Volume 43, 1822, p. 57.
12 Swift, *The Works of Dr Jonathan Swift*, Vol. III, G. Hamilton, J. Balfour, L. Hunter, Edinburgh, 1757, p. 314.
13 Swift, *The Works of Dr Jonathan Swift*, Vol. III, p. 314.

14 Devoy, *Recollections of an Irish Rebel*, p. 8.

15 Author's note: With apologies, and due acknowledgement, to the famous line by my literary hero, Charles Dickens: 'It was the best of times, it was the worst of times.'

16 Coogan, *The Famine Plot*, Palgrave Macmillan, New York, 2012, p. 121.

17 Fennell and King (eds), *John Devoy's Catalpa Expedition*, NYU Press, New York, 2006, p. 4.

18 Durney, Corrigan, and Curran (eds), *A Forgotten Hero, John Devoy*, John Devoy Memorial Committee, 2009, p. 11, http://www.kildare2016.ie/wp-content/uploads/2016/03/John_Devoy_Book.pdf

19 Rossa, *Rossa's Recollections: 1838 to 1898*, Mariner's Harbor, New York, 1898, p. 142.

20 Author's note: In the longer term, the famine was a demographic disaster. In 1844, Ireland's population was 8.5 million, but by 1921, it was half that.

21 Devoy, *Recollections of an Irish Rebel*, p. 4.

22 Devoy, *Recollections of an Irish Rebel*, p. 4.

23 Keneally, *Three Famines: Starvation and Politics*, PublicAffairs, New York, 2011, p. 65.

24 Mitchel, *The Last Conquest of Ireland (Perhaps)*, R. & T. Washbourne, London, 1882, p. 219.

25 Mitchel, *The Last Conquest of Ireland (Perhaps)*, p. 148.

26 Lalor, 'The First Step – The Felon Club', *The Irish Felon*, No. 2, 1 July 1848, in Fogarty, L., *James Fintan Lalor: Patriot and Political Essayist*, The Talbot Press Ltd, Dublin, 1919, p. 85.

27 *Punch*, 8 April 1848, p. 147. Author's note: Punch has misspelt Mitchel's name. Yes, I am the masked avenger of errant sub-editors, 150 years later!

28 Author unknown, *James Stephens: Chief Organizer of the Irish Republic*, p. 19.

29 Lalor, 'The First Step – The Felon Club', p. 85.

30 Lalor, 'To the editor of The Felon', *The Irish Felon*, 24 June 1848, in *James Fintan Lalor: Patriot and Political Essayist*, Fogarty, L., The Talbot Press Ltd, Dublin, 1919, p. 57.

31 Lalor, 'Clearing Decks', *The Irish Felon*, No. 5, 22 July 1848, in *James Fintan Lalor: Patriot and Political Essayist*, Fogarty, L., The Talbot Press Ltd, Dublin, 1919, p. 111.

32 Lalor, 'Clearing Decks', p. 115.

33 Meagher (Griffith (ed.)), *Meagher of the Sword*, M. H. Gill, Dublin, 1916, p. 212.

34 Shakespeare, *Hamlet*, John Cawthorn, London, 1806, p. 67.

35 Ryan, *The Fenian Chief*, Gill & Son, Dublin and Sydney, 1967, p. 11.

36 Author unknown, *James Stephens: Chief Organizer of the Irish Republic*, p. 32.

37 Wordsworth, *The Poems of William Wordsworth*, Edward Moxon, London, 1858, p. 162.

38 *Advocate* (Melbourne), 15 February 1896, p. 17, https://trove.nla.gov.au/newspaper/article/170313326

39 Ramon, *A Provisional Dictator*, University College Dublin Press, Dublin, 2007, p. 65.

40 MacManus, *The Story of the Irish Race*, p. 612.

41 Denieffe, *A Personal Narrative of the Irish Revolutionary Brotherhood*, The Gael Publishing Co., New York, 1906, p. 29.

42 County Kildare, *The Rescue of the Military Fenians from Australia*, http://www.kildare.ie/ehistory/index.php/the-rescue-of-the-military-fenians-from-australia/

43 Devoy, *Recollections of an Irish Rebel*, p. 56.

44 Ramon, *A Provisional Dictator*, p. 171.

Chapter One

1 McCord, 'The Fenians and Public Opinion in Great Britain', University Review, Vol. 4, No. 3, Special Fenian Issue (Winter, 1967), p. 231.

2 Fitzpatrick, *Descendancy*, Cambridge University Press, Cambridge (UK), 2016, p. 69.

3 Regan, *Irish Writing*, p. 178.

4 Ramon, *A Provisional Dictator*, p. 176.

5 *The Horsham Times* (VIC), 13 May 1884, p. 3, https://trove.nla.gov.au/newspaper/article/72951502

6 *The Horsham Times*, 13 May 1884, p. 3.

7 Ramon, *A Provisional Dictator*, p. 175.

8 Author unknown, *James Stephens: Chief Organizer of the Irish Republic*, p. 67.

9 *Empire* (Sydney), 23 January 1872, p. 3, https://trove.nla.gov.au/newspaper/article/60880332

10 *Adelaide Observer* (SA), 29 January 1881, p. 34, https://trove.nla.gov.au/newspaper/article/160140665

11 *Goulburn Herald and Chronicle* (NSW), 27 January 1872, p. 8, https://trove.nla.gov.au/newspaper/article/101095056

12 *Queensland Times, Ipswich Herald and General Advertiser* (QLD), 25 August 1866, p. 4, https://trove.nla.gov.au/newspaper/article/123333265 [Reported Speech].

13 *Queensland Times, Ipswich Herald and General Advertiser* (QLD), 25 August 1866, p. 4.

14 Ramon, *A Provisional Dictator*, p. 177.

15 Ramon, *A Provisional Dictator*, p. 178 [Reported Speech].

16 Ramon, *A Provisional Dictator*, p. 178 [Reported Speech].

17 Ramon, *A Provisional Dictator*, p. 179.

18 *Darling Downs Gazette and General Advertiser* (QLD), 27 January 1866, p. 1, https://trove.nla.gov.au/newspaper/article/75515510

19 McCord, 'The Fenians and Public Opinion in Great Britain', p. 230.

20 Hughes and MacRaild, *Crime, Violence and the Irish in the Nineteenth Century*, Liverpool University Press, Oxford (UK), 2018, p. 136.

21 Devoy, *Recollections of an Irish Rebel*, p. 144.

22 *Western Mail* (Perth), 23 December 1937, p. 12, https://trove.nla.gov.au/newspaper/article/37845115

23 Fennell and King (eds), *John Devoy's Catalpa Expedition* (2006), p. 76.

24 Devoy, *Recollections of an Irish Rebel*, p. 153.

25 Devoy, *Recollections of an Irish Rebel*, p. 153.

26 Devoy, *Recollections of an Irish Rebel*, p. 153.

27 Devoy, *Recollections of an Irish Rebel*, p. 153.

28 Pease, *The Catalpa Expedition*, p. 10.

29 Devoy, *Recollections of an Irish Rebel*, p. 155.

30 Devoy, *Recollections of an Irish Rebel*, p. 155.

31 Ramon, *A Provisional Dictator*, p. 181 [Reported Speech].

32 Ramon, *A Provisional Dictator*, p. 181 [Reported Speech].

33 Author's note: These are generic commands, consistent with the terminology of the time.

34 Ramon, *A Provisional Dictator*, p. 181 [Reported Speech].

35 Author unknown, *James Stephens: Chief Organizer of the Irish Republic*, p. 72.

36 *Freeman's Journal* (Sydney), 27 January 1866, p. 4, https://trove.nla.gov.au/newspaper/article/115451875/12661580

37 *Freeman's Journal* (Sydney), 27 January 1866, p. 4.

38 *Freeman's Journal* (Sydney), 27 January 1866, p. 4.

39 Author unknown, *James Stephens: Chief Organizer of the Irish Republic*, p. 73.

40 *Freeman's Journal* (Sydney), 27 January 1866, p. 4.

41 *Freeman's Journal* (Sydney), 27 January 1866, p. 4.

42 *Freeman's Journal* (Sydney), 27 January 1866, p. 4.

43 *Freeman's Journal* (Sydney), 27 January 1866, p. 5, https://trove.nla.gov.au/newspaper/article/115451875/12661581

44 *Freeman's Journal* (Sydney), 27 January 1866, p. 5 [Reported Speech].

Chapter Two

1 Fennell, King (eds), *John Devoy's Catalpa Expedition* (2006), p. 37.

2 *Southern Cross* (Adelaide), 28 October 1892, p. 5, https://trove.nla.gov.au/newspaper/article/166345687

3 *Southern Cross* (Adelaide), 28 October 1892, p. 5.

4 *Southern Cross* (Adelaide), 28 October 1892, p. 5.

5 *Southern Cross* (Adelaide), 28 October 1892, p. 5.

6 *Freeman's Journal* (Sydney), 18 June 1892, p. 6, https://trove.nla.gov.au/newspaper/article/111324298

7 *Freeman's Journal* (Sydney), 18 June 1892, p. 6.

8 *Freeman's Journal* (Sydney), 18 June 1892, p. 6.

9 *Freeman's Journal* (Sydney), 27 January 1866, p. 4.

10 *Leader* (Melbourne), 24 March 1866, p. 8, https://trove.nla.gov.au/newspaper/article/196561994

11 Hughes and MacRaild, *Crime, Violence and the Irish in the Nineteenth Century*, p. 140.

12 Hughes and MacRaild, *Crime, Violence and the Irish in the Nineteenth Century*, p. 140.

13 Ryan, *Fenian Memories,* M.H. Gill & Son, Dublin, 1946, pp. 82–83.

14 Denieffe, *A Personal Narrative of the Irish Revolutionary Brotherhood,* p. 126.

15 Denieffe, *A Personal Narrative of the Irish Revolutionary Brotherhood,* p. 126 [Reported Speech].

16 Denieffe, *A Personal Narrative of the Irish Revolutionary Brotherhood,* pp. 126–127.

17 Denieffe, *A Personal Narrative of the Irish Revolutionary Brotherhood,* pp. 127–8.

18 Devoy, *Recollections of an Irish Rebel,* p. 59.

19 *Freeman's Journal* (Sydney), 11 February 1871, p. 5, https://trove.nla.gov.au/newspaper/article/120722287 [Reported Speech].

20 *Freeman's Journal* (Sydney), 11 February 1871, p. 5.

21 Roche, *Life of John Boyle O'Reilly,* Cassell Publishing Company, New York, 1891, p. 124.

22 Roche, *Life of John Boyle O'Reilly,* p. 124.

23 Burke and Chamney, *The Fenian Conspiracy,* Alexander Thom, Dublin, 1869, p. 933.

24 Devoy, *Recollections of an Irish Rebel,* p. 65.

25 *The Irish Times* (Dublin), 14 August 1866, p. 4, https://www.newspapers.com/newspage/61100204

26 *Police Gazette* (WA), 7 June 1876, p. 60.

27 Roche, *Life of John Boyle O'Reilly,* p. 18.

28 Devoy, *Recollections of an Irish Rebel,* p. 156.

29 Golway, *Irish Rebel: John Devoy and America's Fight for Irish Freedom,* Merrion Press, Kildare, 2015, p. 61 [Reported Speech].

30 Golway, *Irish Rebel,* p. 61

31 Author's note: Details for this, come from *The Adelaide Express* (SA), 12 April 1866, p.3 (https://trove.nla.gov.au/newspaper/article/207607696). Though Devoy is not named in this article as being one of those arrested on this day, Corporal Chambers is mentioned. Given that Devoy notes in his memoir that he was arrested with Chambers, I have concluded Devoy was among those arrested on this day.

32 Author's note: For the record, there has been considerable confusion by authors over the years between William Foley and Patrick Foley, in large part because in this account in the Boston *Pilot,* which appeared in *Freeman's Journal* on 11 February 1871 (https://trove.nla.gov.au/newspaper/article/120722287), John Boyle O'Reilly mistakenly names the informer as William Foley, when it was Patrick Foley. In fact, William Foley was a loyal Fenian, and something of the hero of the piece when, once released with a Certificate of Freedom in Fremantle, he was instrumental in helping John Breslin in his communications with the Fenian prisoners.

33 Denieffe, *A Personal Narrative of the Irish Revolutionary Brotherhood,* p. 208.

34 *Catholic Press* (Sydney), 11 November 1899, p. 6, https://trove.nla.gov.au/newspaper/article/104662233

35 *Catholic Press* (Sydney), 11 November 1899, p. 6.

36 *Catholic Press* (Sydney), 11 November 1899, p. 6.

37 Devoy, *Recollections of an Irish Rebel,* p. 156 [Reported Speech].

38 Devoy, *Recollections of an Irish Rebel,* p. 156 [Reported Speech].

39 Devoy, *Recollections of an Irish Rebel,* p. 156.

Chapter Three

1 *The Herald* (Melbourne), 14 May 1866, p. 3, https://trove.nla.gov.au/newspaper/article/244423668

2 Finneran (ed.), *The Collected Works of W.B. Yeats, Volume I: The Poems,* Simon and Schuster, New York, 2010, p. 187.

3 Roche, *Life of John Boyle O'Reilly,* p. 22.

4 Pease, *The Catalpa Expedition,* p. 17.

5 *The Herald* (Melbourne), 14 May 1866, p. 3 [Reported Speech].

6 *The Herald* (Melbourne), 14 May 1866, p. 3.

7 *Dalby Herald and Western Queensland Advertiser,* 28 June 1866, p. 4, https://trove.nla.gov.au/newspaper/article/215449307

8 *Dalby Herald and Western Queensland Advertiser,* 28 June 1866, p. 4 [Reported Speech].

9 *Empire* (Sydney), 21 August 1866, p. 2, https://trove.nla.gov.au/newspaper/article/60598587

10 *Empire* (Sydney), 21 August 1866, p. 2.

11 *Empire* (Sydney), 21 August 1866, p. 2.

12 Roche, *Life of John Boyle O'Reilly,* p. 23.

13 Roche, *Life of John Boyle O'Reilly*, p. 23.
14 Roche, *Life of John Boyle O'Reilly*, p. 23.
15 Roche, *Life of John Boyle O'Reilly*, p. 23.
16 Roche, *Life of John Boyle O'Reilly*, p. 24.
17 Roche, *Life of John Boyle O'Reilly*, p. 28.
18 Roche, *Life of John Boyle O'Reilly*, p. 28.
19 Devoy, *Recollections of an Irish Rebel*, p. 156.
20 Roche, *Life of John Boyle O'Reilly*, p. 35.
21 Roche, *Life of John Boyle O'Reilly*, p. 35.
22 Roche, *Life of John Boyle O'Reilly*, p. 35 [Tense changed].
23 Roche, *Life of John Boyle O'Reilly*, p. 39.
24 Roche, *Life of John Boyle O'Reilly*, p. 39.
25 Roche, *Life of John Boyle O'Reilly*, p. 40.
26 Roche, *Life of John Boyle O'Reilly*, p. 40.
27 Roche, *Life of John Boyle O'Reilly*, p. 40.
28 *Goulburn Herald and Chronicle* (NSW), 27 January 1872, p. 8, https://trove.nla.gov.au/newspaper/article/101095056
29 Roche, *Life of John Boyle O'Reilly* 1891 p. 48.
30 Irish Prison Service, Booklet, *40th Anniversary of Arbor Hill Prison as a Civilian Prison,* Peter Murphy personal collection.
31 Roche, *Life of John Boyle O'Reilly*, p. 22.
32 Roche, *Life of John Boyle O'Reilly*, p. 20.
33 *The Horsham Times*, 13 May 1884, p. 3.
34 Letter from Colonel Thomas Kelly to General Halpin, 12 March 1867, in: Denieffe, *A Personal Narrative of the Irish Revolutionary Brotherhood*, p. 278.
35 Golway, *Irish Rebel*, p. 70.
36 *The Mercury* (Hobart), 17 April 1867, p. 3, https://trove.nla.gov.au/newspaper/article/8845310/777029
37 *The Mercury* (Hobart), 17 April 1867, p. 3.
38 Denieffe, *A Personal Narrative the Irish Revolutionary Brotherhood*, p.137.
39 Devoy, *Recollections of an Irish Rebel*, p. 230.
40 Whelan, 'Fenians in the Foothills: Patrick Doran and the Rising of 1867', *History Ireland*, Vol. 25, No. 4, July–August 2017, p. 30.
41 Whelan, 'Fenians in the Foothills,' p. 30.
42 Whelan, 'Fenians in the Foothills,' p. 31 [Reported Speech].
43 Whelan, 'Fenians in the Foothills,' p. 32.
44 Whelan, 'Fenians in the Foothills,' p. 32.
45 Golway, *Irish Rebel*, p. 71.
46 Golway, *Irish Rebel*, p. 71.
47 Devoy, *Recollections of an Irish Rebel*, p. 213.
48 *Freeman's Journal* (Sydney), 29 March 1884, p. 8, https://trove.nla.gov.au/newspaper/article/110064763/12539857
49 Denieffe, *A Personal Narrative of the Irish Revolutionary Brotherhood*, p. 93.
50 *The Irish Times* (Online), McGreevy, 'How 'The Irish Times' reported the Fenian rising 150 years ago', published: 5 March 2017, https://www.irishtimes.com/news/ireland/irish-news/how-the-irish-times-reported-the-fenian-rising-150-years-ago-1.2998474
51 Pease, *The Catalpa Expedition*, p. 4.
52 Burke and Chamney, *The Fenian Conspiracy*, p.1064.
53 *Queenslander* (Brisbane), 20 July 1867, p. 9, https://trove.nla.gov.au/newspaper/article/20314253 [Reported Speech].
54 Devoy, *Recollections of an Irish Rebel*, pp. 55–6.
55 Pease, *The Catalpa Expedition*, p. 62 [Reported Speech].
56 Cashman, *Fenian Diary*, Edited by C. W. Sullivan III, 2001, p. 55.
57 Cashman, *Fenian Diary*, p. 56 [Reported Speech].
58 Cashman, *Fenian Diary*, p. 56.
59 Cashman, *Fenian Diary*, p. 56.

Chapter Four

1 Cashman, *Fenian Diary*, p. 20.

2 Fennell, *Voyage of the Hougoumont*, Xlibris Corporation, New York, 2000, p. 61.

3 Fennell, *Voyage of the Hougoumont*, pp. 218–19.

4 Roche, *Life of John Boyle O'Reilly*, p. 66.

5 Roche, *Life of John Boyle O'Reilly*, p. 66.

6 Roche, *Life of John Boyle O'Reilly*, p. 66.

7 Roche, *Life of John Boyle O'Reilly*, p. 66.

8 Fennell, *Voyage of the Hougoumont*, p. 68.

9 O'Reilly, *Moondyne*, Sydney University Press, Sydney, 2003, p. 162.

10 Roche, *Life of John Boyle O'Reilly*, p. 66.

11 Fennell, *Voyage of the Hougoumont*, p. 65.

12 Fennell, *Voyage of the Hougoumont*, p. 67 [Reported Speech].
   Author's note: Fennell uses the word 'excrement', to describe their sneering words. Loyal to what was most likely said, rather than what was delicately reported, I strongly suspect the word was 'shit'.

13 Roche, *Life of John Boyle O'Reilly*, p. 66.

14 Pease, *The Catalpa Expedition*, p. 52.

15 Fennell, *Voyage of the Hougoumont*, pp. 61–2.

16 Roche, *Life of John Boyle O'Reilly*, p. 66.

17 Roche, *Life of John Boyle O'Reilly*, pp. 66–7.

18 Roche, *Life of John Boyle O'Reilly* p. 65.

19 Fennell, *Voyage of the Hougoumont*, p. 75.

20 Fennell, *Voyage of the Hougoumont*, p. 75.

21 Fennell, *Voyage of the Hougoumont*, p. 75.

22 Fennell, *Voyage of the Hougoumont*, p. 75.

23 *Morning Advertiser*, 16 October 1867, p. 3.

24 *Morning Advertiser*, 16 October 1867, p. 3.

25 Fennell, *Voyage of the Hougoumont*, p. 69.

26 Fennell, *Voyage of the Hougoumont*, p. 69.

27 Fennell, *Voyage of the Hougoumont*, p. 175.

28 Fennell, *Voyage of the Hougoumont*, p. 76.

29 Fennell, *Voyage of the Hougoumont*, p. 78.

30 O'Reilly, *Moondyne*, p. 184.

31 Roche, *Life of John Boyle O'Reilly*, p. 66.

32 Fennell, *Voyage of the Hougoumont*, p. 79.

33 Roche, *Life of John Boyle O'Reilly*, p. 67.

34 Fennell, *Voyage of the Hougoumont*, p. 78.

35 'The Wild Goose: A Collection of Ocean Waifs" Vol. 1, no. 1, 9 November 1867, p. 6 in John Flood Papers, SLNSW, MLMSS 1542 (Safe 1/409), http://archival.sl.nsw.gov.au/Details/archive/110319433

36 Author's note: This is inspired by the old Irish blessing: 'May love and laughter light your days, and warm your heart and home. May good and faithful friends be yours, wherever you may roam.'

37 Cashman, Diary, 24 October 1867, p. 7, in Denis B. Cashman Papers, 458.1.b, East Carolina Manuscript Collection, J. Y. Joyner Library, East Carolina University, https://digital.lib.ecu.edu/957#details

38 Foster, *The Oxford History of Ireland*, Oxford University Press, Oxford (UK), 2001, p. 160.

39 Cashman, Diary, 26 October 1867, p. 8.

40 Roche, *Life of John Boyle O'Reilly*, pp. 528–9.

41 *Freeman's Journal* (Sydney), Saturday 1 August 1868, p. 11.

42 Cashman, Diary, 26 October 1867, p. 8.

43 Cashman, Diary, 26 October 1867, p. 8 [Reported Speech].

44 Cashman, Diary, 26 October 1867, p. 8.

45 Cashman, Diary, 5 November 1867, p. 11.

46 Davis, *The Poems of Thomas Davis*, J. Duffy, Dublin, 1846, p. 145.

47 'The Wild Goose: A Collection of Ocean Waifs,' Vol. 1, No. 1, 9 November 1867, p. 1.

48 'The Wild Goose: A Collection of Ocean Waifs,' Vol. 1, No. 1, 9 November 1867, p. 3.

49 'The Wild Goose: A Collection of Ocean Waifs,' Vol. 1, No. 1, 9 November 1867, p. 3.

50 'The Wild Goose: A Collection of Ocean Waifs,' Vol. 1, No. 1, 9 November 1867, p. 4.

51 'The Wild Goose: A Collection of Ocean Waifs" Vol. 1, no. 1, 9 November 1867, p. 6.

52 'The Wild Goose: A Collection of Ocean Waifs,' Vol. 1, no. 1, 9 November 1867, p. 8.

53 'The Wild Goose: A Collection of Ocean Waifs,' Vol. 1, no. 4, 30 November 1867, p. 3.

54 Letter from James Wilson to John Devoy, 4 September 1873, MS 18.013/13/1, John Devoy Papers Collection, NLI.

55 Letter from James Wilson to John Devoy, 15 June 1874, MS 18.013/13/2, John Devoy Papers Collection, NLI.

56 Cashman, Diary, 13 December 1867, p. 20.

57 *Advocate* (Melbourne), 4 October 1890, p. 16, https://trove.nla.gov.au/newspaper/article/168053387

58 'The Wild Goose: A Collection of Ocean Waifs,' Vol. 1, no. 1, 21 December 1867, p. 1.

59 'The Wild Goose: A Collection of Ocean Waifs,' Vol. 1, no. 1, 21 December 1867, pp. 10-12.

60 'The Wild Goose: A Collection of Ocean Waifs" Vol. 1, no. 1, 21 December 1867, p. 16.

61 Casey, 'Journal of a Voyage from Portland to Freemantle on board the convict ship Hougoumont, 7 October 1867 - 9 January 1868,' 9 January 1868, SLNSW, MLDOC 1447, p. 46, http://archival.sl.nsw. gov.au/Details/archive/110359301

62 Casey, 'Journal of a Voyage from Portland to Freemantle,' p. 46.

Chapter Five

1 O'Reilly, *Moondyne*, Roberts Brothers, Boston, 1883, p. 251.

2 Casey, 'Journal of a Voyage from Portland to Freemantle,' p. 46.

3 Fennell, *Voyage of the Hougoumont*, p. 198.

4 O'Reilly, *Songs from the Southern Seas*, Roberts Brothers, Boston, 1873, p. 7.

5 Pease, *The Catalpa Expedition*, p. 53.

6 Fennell, *Voyage of the Hougoumont*, p. 184.

7 Fennell, *Voyage of the Hougoumont*, p. 184.

8 Fennell, *Voyage of the Hougoumont*, p. 170.

9 Fennell, *Voyage of the Hougoumont*, p. 184.

10 Fennell, *Voyage of the Hougoumont*, p. 184.

11 Fennell, *Voyage of the Hougoumont*, p. 184 [Reported Speech].

12 McDermott, 'Martin Hogan and the Catalpa Rescue', *The Old Limerick Journal*, Vol. 23, 1988, p. 116.

13 Donegan, 'Convict Daily Life,' Government of Western Australia, Fremantle Prison, Fremantle, 2009, p. 1, http://fremantleprison.com.au/media/1150/fp-convict-daily-life.pdf

14 Roche, *Life of John Boyle O'Reilly*, p. 69.

15 McDermott, 'Martin Hogan and the Catalpa Rescue', p. 116.

16 McDermott, 'Martin Hogan and the Catalpa Rescue', p. 116.

17 McDermott, 'Martin Hogan and the Catalpa Rescue', p. 116.

18 *Police Gazette* (WA), 3 May 1876, p. 39, https://slwa.wa.gov.au/sites/default/files/187605_m.pdf

19 *Police Gazette* (WA), 3 May 1876, p. 40.

20 *Police Gazette* (WA), 7 June 1876, p. 60, https://slwa.wa.gov.au/sites/default/files/187606_m.pdf

21 Fennell, *Voyage of the Hougoumont*, p. 185.

22 Fennell, *Voyage of the Hougoumont*, p. 188.

23 Fennell, *Voyage of the Hougoumont*, p. 188.

24 Fennell, *Voyage of the Hougoumont*, p. 192 [Reported Speech].

25 Fennell, *Voyage of the Hougoumont*, p. 195.

26 Fennell, *Voyage of the Hougoumont*, p. 194.

27 Fennell, *Voyage of the Hougoumont*, p. 194.

28 Fennell, *Voyage of the Hougoumont*, p. 194.

29 Heseltine, *The Escape of the Military Fenians from Fremantle Prison*.

30 Fennell, *Voyage of the Hougoumont*, p. 210.

31 Donegan, 'Convict Daily Life,' p. 3.

32 Fennell, *Voyage of the Hougoumont*, p. 211.

33 Fennell, *Voyage of the Hougoumont*, p. 204.

34 Breslin, *The Cruise of the Catalpa*, Press of Rockwell & Churchill, Boston, 1876, p. 5.

35 *Western Mail* (Perth), 30 December 1937, p. 12, https://trove.nla.gov.au/newspaper/article/37845536

36 O'Reilly, *Moondyne*, p. 5.

37 O'Reilly, *Moondyne*, p. 8.

38 Kimberly, *History of West Australia*, F. W. Niven & Co., Melbourne, 1897, p. 171.

39 Kimberly, *History of West Australia*, p. 171.

40 Campbell, *Ireland's New Worlds: Immigrants, Politics, and Society in the United States and Australia, 1815-1922*, University of Wisconsin Press, Wisconsin, 2008, p. 113.

41 *Sydney Morning Herald*, 14 March 1868, p. 5, https://trove.nla.gov.au/newspaper/article/13154858

42 Roche, *Life of John Boyle O'Reilly*, p. 107.

43 Evans, *Fanatic Heart*, University of Western Australia Press, Nedlands (WA), 1997, p. 103.

44 Author's note: This quote comes from Oscar Wilde's *The Importance of Being Earnest*. 'Bunbury +⬚ -ing, was coined by Wilde after Bunbury, the fictitious invalid friend of the character Algernon whose supposed illness is used as an excuse to avoid social engagements.' Wilde, an Irishman, who was first published in America by John Boyle O'Reilly, likely knew of John Boyle O'Reilly's story.

45 *Western Mail* (Perth), 23 December 1937, p. 12, https://trove.nla.gov.au/newspaper/article/37845115

46 Gibbs, *Convict Places of Western Australia*, in: Sherriff and Brake (eds), *Building a Colony: The Convict Legacy*, Centre for Western Australian History, University of New England, 2006, p. 89, https://www.researchgate.net/publication/264496094_Convict_Places_of_Western_Australia

47 Roche, *Life of John Boyle O'Reilly*, p. 72.

48 Roche, *Life of John Boyle O'Reilly*, p. 72.

49 O'Reilly, *Moondyne*, p. 5.

50 *Inquirer and Commercial News* (Perth), 13 January 1869, p. 2, https://trove.nla.gov.au/newspaper/article/66033268

51 Words from the song 'A Dreamer Forever', composed by Shane Thomas for Peter Murphy's short film, *In Search of the Vigilant*, about O'Reilly's time on the peninsula. https://goo.gl/vEWfGo

52 *Advocate* (Melbourne), 11 November 1882, p. 4, https://trove.nla.gov.au/newspaper/article/170027882

53 *Advocate* (Melbourne), 11 November 1882, p. 4.

54 *Advocate* (Melbourne), 11 November 1882, p. 4.

55 *Advocate* (Melbourne), 11 November 1882, p. 4.

56 O Luing, *Fremantle Mission*, Anvil Books, County Kerry, 1965, p. 38.

57 O Luing, *Fremantle Mission*, pp. 39-40.

58 *The Irishman*, 11 April 1868, p. 9.

59 *The Irishman*, 1 August 1868, p. 9.

60 *Advocate* (Melbourne), 11 November 1882, p. 4, https://trove.nla.gov.au/newspaper/article/170027882

61 *Advocate* (Melbourne), 11 November 1882, p. 4.

62 *Advocate* (Melbourne), 11 November 1882, p. 4 [Reported Speech].

63 *Advocate* (Melbourne), 11 November 1882, p. 4.

64 Waters, 'John Boyle O'Reilly,' *Seanchas Ardmhacha: Journal of the Armagh Diocesan Historical Society*, Vol. 13, No. 1, 1988, p. 179.

65 *Advocate* (Melbourne), 11 November 1882, p. 4.

66 *Advocate* (Melbourne), 11 November 1882, p. 4.

67 *Advocate* (Melbourne), 11 November 1882, p. 4 [Reported Speech].

68 *Advocate* (Melbourne), 11 November 1882, p. 4 [Reported Speech].

Chapter Six

1 Waters, 'The Escape of the Fenians, Western Australia, 17 April 1876,' pp. 98–99.

2 *Advocate* (Melbourne), 11 November 1882, p. 4.

3 *Advocate* (Melbourne), 11 November 1882, p. 4.

4 Author's note: Though in O'Reilly's account he only lists his name as 'M----', Bunbury historian Peter Murphy strongly believes it is William Moriarty as he was a close friend of both McCabe and Maguire. The Catholic church owned land next to Moriarty's farm at Ludlow, and Maguire (Roads Board)

worked in Ludlow area assisting Moriarty to drain the Koagalup wetland. Peter suspects that the horses to pick up O'Reilly came from Moriarty's farm.

5   *Advocate* (Melbourne), 11 November 1882, p. 4 [Reported Speech].

6   *Advocate* (Melbourne), 11 November 1882, p. 4.

7   *Advocate* (Melbourne), 11 November 1882, p. 4.

8   McDermott, 'Martin Hogan and the Catalpa Rescue', p. 116.

9   *Advocate* (Melbourne), 11 November 1882, p. 4.

10 *Advocate* (Melbourne), 11 November 1882, p. 5, https://trove.nla.gov.au/newspaper/article/170027882/20261909

11 *Advocate* (Melbourne), 11 November 1882, p. 5 [Reported Speech].

12 *Advocate* (Melbourne), 11 November 1882, p. 5 [Reported Speech].

13 Author's note: Thomas Jackson and his son, Matthew, aided O'Reilly when he was marooned on the peninsula awaiting a second chance to escape. O'Reilly wrote an account of his escape many years later when he felt it was safe to reveal most of the names of the people who had helped him. In it he referred to Jackson as 'Johnson' – probably as an extra precaution. 'Johnson's' actual name was Thomas Jackson.

14 *Advocate* (Melbourne), 11 November 1882, p. 5.

15 *Inquirer and Commercial News* (Perth), 27 February 1867, p. 2, https://trove.nla.gov.au/newspaper/article/69386934

16 *Catholic Press* (Sydney), 8 September 1910, p. 7, https://trove.nla.gov.au/newspaper/article/104993701

17 *Catholic Press* (Sydney), 8 September 1910, p. 7 [Reported Speech].

18 *Catholic Press* (Sydney), 8 September 1910, p. 7.

19 *Catholic Press* (Sydney), 8 September 1910, p. 7.

20 *Catholic Press* (Sydney), 8 September 1910, p. 7.

21 *Advocate* (Melbourne), 11 November 1882, p. 5 [Reported Speech].

22 Author's note: Though this is the name used by John Boyle O'Reilly in his account, his actual name was Thomas Henderson.

23 *Catholic Press* (Sydney), 8 September 1910, p. 7.

24 *Catholic Press* (Sydney), 8 September 1910, p. 7.

25 O'Reilly, *Moondyne: A Story from the Underworld*, Roberts Brothers, Boston, 1883, p. 11

26 *Advocate* (Melbourne), 4 August 1894, p. 5.

27 Pease, *The Catalpa Expedition*, p. 57.

28 *Freeman's Journal* (Sydney), 2 July 1870, p. 13, https://trove.nla.gov.au/newspaper/article/115292458

29 *Perth Gazette and West Australian Times* (WA), 25 June 1869, p. 2, https://trove.nla.gov.au/newspaper/article/3750400

30 *Freeman's Journal* (Sydney), 31 July 1869, p. 6, https://trove.nla.gov.au/newspaper/article/115430202

31 Letter from James Wilson to John Devoy, 4 September 1873, MS 18,013/13/1, John Devoy Papers Collection, NLI.

32 *Advocate* (Melbourne), 28 February 1891, p. 9, https://trove.nla.gov.au/newspaper/article/169273879

33 https://www.findagrave.com/memorial/98784980/john-f.-hathaway

34 *Freeman's Journal* (Sydney), 24 February 1877, p. 7, https://trove.nla.gov.au/newspaper/article/115375160/12712435 [Reported Speech. Tenses changed.]

35 *Inquirer and Commercial News* (Perth), 2 November 1870, p. 3, https://trove.nla.gov.au/newspaper/article/66032537

36 *Inquirer and Commercial News* (Perth), 2 November 1870, p. 3.

37 *Inquirer and Commercial News* (Perth), 2 November 1870, p. 3.

38 Author's note: Although O'Reilly's biographer, James Roche, says the *Gazelle* stopped at the island of Roderique, I have concluded he meant Rodrigues, where Barkly was Governor.

39 Pease, *The Catalpa Expedition*, p. 77.

40 *Catholic Press* (Sydney), 8 September 1910, p. 7, https://trove.nla.gov.au/newspaper/article/104993701

41 *Catholic Press* (Sydney), 8 September 1910, p. 7.

42 *Catholic Press* (Sydney), 8 September 1910, p. 7.

43 *Catholic Press* (Sydney), 8 September 1910, p. 7 [Reported Speech].

44 *Catholic Press* (Sydney), 8 September 1910, p. 7 [Reported Speech].

45 *Catholic Press* (Sydney), 8 September 1910, p. 7 [Reported Speech].

46 Roche, *Life of John Boyle O'Reilly*, p. 87.

47 *Western Mail* (Perth), 30 December 1937, p. 12, https://trove.nla.gov.au/newspaper/article/37845536

48 Roche, *Life of John Boyle O'Reilly*, p. 88.

49 Roche, *Life of John Boyle O'Reilly*, p. 88 [Reported Speech].

50 Roche, *Life of John Boyle O'Reilly*, p. 88.

51 Roche, *Life of John Boyle O'Reilly*, p. 88.

52 Roche, *Life of John Boyle O'Reilly*, p. 88.

53 Roche, *Life of John Boyle O'Reilly*, pp. 84–5.

54 Roche, *Life of John Boyle O'Reilly*, p. 85.

55 Roche, *Life of John Boyle O'Reilly*, p. 85.

56 *Catholic Press* (Sydney), 8 September 1910, p. 7 [Reported Speech].

57 Roche, *Life of John Boyle O'Reilly*, p. 91.

58 Roche, *Life of John Boyle O'Reilly*, p. 100.

Chapter Seven

1 Traubel, *Intimate with Walt*, University of Iowa Press, Iowa City, 2001, p. 226.

2 Roche, *Life of John Boyle O'Reilly*, p. 72.

3 *W.A. Record* (Perth), 30 January 1915, p. 16, https://trove.nla.gov.au/newspaper/article/212354620

4 *W.A. Record* (Perth), 30 January 1915, p. 16.

5 *W.A. Record* (Perth), 30 January 1915, p. 16.

6 Fennell, 'History into Myth: The "Catalpa's" Long Voyage', *New Hibernia Review*, Vol. 9, No. 1, 2005, p. 82.

7 Roche, *Life of John Boyle O'Reilly*, p. 109.

8 *Australasian* (Melbourne), 30 July 1870, p. 23, https://trove.nla.gov.au/newspaper/article/138066054

9 Roche, *Life of John Boyle O'Reilly*, p. 110.

10 Roche, *Life of John Boyle O'Reilly*, p. 110.

11 *Australasian* (Melbourne), 30 July 1870, p. 23.

12 *Australasian* (Melbourne), 30 July 1870, p. 23.

13 *Australasian* (Melbourne), 30 July 1870, p. 23.

14 *W.A. Record* (Perth), 30 January 1915, p. 16.

15 Letter from James Wilson to John Devoy, 4 September 1873, MS 18,013/13/1 John Devoy Papers Collection, NLI.

16 O'Donovan Rossa, *Prison Life: Six Years in Six English Prisons*, P. J. Kenedy, New York, 1874, p. 416.

17 Murphy, *Abject Loyalty*, Catholic University of America Press, Washington, DC, 2001, p. 167.

18 *The Irish Canadian*, 1 February 1871, p. 2.

19 *The Irish Canadian*, 1 February 1871, p. 2.

20 *The Irish Canadian*, 1 February 1871, p. 2.

21 *Advocate* (Melbourne), 22 April 1871 p. 5, https://trove.nla.gov.au/newspaper/article/170153250

22 *Advocate* (Melbourne), 22 April 1871 p. 5.

23 *W.A. Record* (Perth), 30 January 1915, p. 16.

24 Roche, *Life of John Boyle O'Reilly*, p. 116.

25 Roche, *Life of John Boyle O'Reilly*, p. 117.

26 Fennell and King (eds), *John Devoy's Catalpa Expedition*, p. 187.

27 Letter from John Boyle O'Reilly to John Devoy, 28 January 1871, MS 18,010/12/1, John Devoy Papers Collection, NLI

28 Letter from John Boyle O'Reilly to John Devoy, 13 February 1871, MS 18,010/12/2, John Devoy Papers Collection, NLI

29 Durney, Corrigan and Curran (eds), *A Forgotten Hero, John Devoy*, p. 14.

30 Devoy, *Recollections of an Irish Rebel*, p. 252.

31 Fennell and King (eds), *John Devoy's Catalpa Expedition* (2006), p. 37.

Chapter Eight

1 Yeats, *The Collected Poems of W. B. Yeats*, Wordsworth Editions, UK, 2000, p. 216.

2 Letter from James Wilson to John Devoy, 4 September 1873.

3   Fennell and King (eds), *John Devoy's Catalpa Expedition* (2006), p. 43.

4   Fennell and King (eds), *John Devoy's Catalpa Expedition* (2006), p. 37.

5   Great Britain, Parliament, *Hansard's Parliamentary Debates*, Third Series, p. 707, https://api.parliament.uk/historic-hansard/commons/1870/feb/10/tipperary-election-jeremiah-odonovan

6   Great Britain, Parliament, *Hansard's Parliamentary Debates*, Third Series, p. 707.

7   Letter from James Wilson to John Devoy, 4 September 1873.

8   Letter from James Wilson to John Devoy, 15 June 1874.

9   Letter from James Wilson to John Devoy, 15 June 1874.

10 Fennell and King (eds), *John Devoy's Catalpa Expedition* (2006), p. 35.

11 McDermott, 'Martin Hogan and the Catalpa Rescue', p. 119.

12 Letter from John Boyle O'Reilly to John Devoy, 4 December 1874, MS 18,010/13/1, John Devoy Papers Collection, NLI.

13 Fennell and King (eds), *John Devoy's Catalpa Expedition* (2006), pp. 41–7.

14 Letter from William F. Roantree to John Devoy, 17 September 1874, MS 18,011/14/3, John Devoy Papers Collection, NLI.

15 Fennell and King (eds), *John Devoy's Catalpa Expedition* (2006), p. 48.

16 Letter from James Wilson to John Devoy, 4 September 1873.

17 McDermott, 'Martin Hogan and the Catalpa Rescue', p. 118.

18 McDermott, 'Martin Hogan and the Catalpa Rescue', p. 119.

19 Fennell and King (eds), *John Devoy's Catalpa Expedition* (2006), p. 47.

20 Fennell and King (eds), *John Devoy's Catalpa Expedition* (2006), p. 41.

21 Devoy, *Recollections of an Irish Rebel*, p. 153.

22 Devoy, *Recollections of an Irish Rebel*, p. 45 [Reported Speech].

23 Fennell and King (eds), *John Devoy's Catalpa Expedition* (2006), p. 45.

24 Fennell and King (eds), *John Devoy's Catalpa Expedition* (2006), p. 45.

25 Fennell and King (eds), *John Devoy's Catalpa Expedition* (2006), p. 45.

26 Pease, *The Catalpa Expedition*, p. 73.

27 Pease, *The Catalpa Expedition*, p. 73.

28 Pease, *The Catalpa Expedition*, p. 75 [Reported Speech].

29 Pease, *The Catalpa Expedition*, p. 75 [Reported Speech].

30 Pease, *The Catalpa Expedition*, p. 76 [Reported Speech].

31 Devoy, *Recollections of an Irish Rebel*, pp. 253–4.

32 *Irish-American Weekly*, Lincoln, Nebraska, USA, 20 March 1892.

33 Devoy, *Recollections of an Irish Rebel*, p. 254.

34 Fennell and King (eds), *John Devoy's Catalpa Expedition* (2006), p. 63.

35 *The Herald* (Fremantle), 18 November 1876, p. 4, https://trove.nla.gov.au/newspaper/article/106307720/10126525

36 Pease, *The Catalpa Expedition*, p. 80.

37 Pease, *The Catalpa Expedition*, p. 80.

Chapter Nine

1   *The Western Australian*, 9 October 1895, p. 6, https://trove.nla.gov.au/newspaper/article/4542968

2   Author's note: These are generic commands, consistent with the terminology of the time.

3   Pease, *The Catalpa Expedition*, p. 80.

4   Pease, *The Catalpa Expedition*, p. 80 [Tenses changed].

5   Pease, *The Catalpa Expedition*, p. 80.

6   Fennell and King (eds), *John Devoy's Catalpa Expedition* (2006), p. 73.

7   Devoy, *Recollections of an Irish Rebel*, p. 255.

8   Fennell and King (eds), *John Devoy's Catalpa Expedition* (2006), p. 73.

9   Fennell and King (eds), *John Devoy's Catalpa Expedition* (2006), p. 72 [Reported Speech].

10 Fennell and King (eds), *John Devoy's Catalpa Expedition* (2006), p. 72 [Reported Speech].

11 Pease, *The Catalpa Expedition*, p. 82.

12 Pease, *The Catalpa Expedition*, p. 140. Author's note: This is the same phraseology used later in the story, as they escape Rockingham beach, with George S. Anthony's biographer Zephaniah Pease noting it was the kind of thing the whaling captain would say when they were closing on a whale kill.

13 Author's note: These are generic commands, consistent with the terminology of the time.

14 Burnett, *Trying Leviathan*, Princeton University Press, Princeton, 2010, p. 119.

15 Pease, *The Catalpa Expedition*, p. 84.

16 Williford, 'Whaling the Old Way', *Humanities*, Vol. 31, No. 2, March/April 2010, https://www.neh.gov/humanities/2010/marchapril/feature/whaling-the-old-way

17 Roche, *Life of John Boyle O'Reilly*, p. 173.

18 Pease, *The Catalpa Expedition*, p. 87.

19 Fennell and King (eds), *John Devoy's Catalpa Expedition* (2006), p. 145.

20 Pease, *The Catalpa Expedition*, p. 92.

21 Pease, *The Catalpa Expedition*, p. 94.

22 Pease, *The Catalpa Expedition*, p. 94.

23 Pease, *The Catalpa Expedition*, p. 95.

24 Pease, *The Catalpa Expedition*, p. 95.

25 Author's note: Thomas Desmond adopted the alias of 'Thomas Johnson' for his sojourn in Western Australia. Other narratives give his alias variously as 'Johnston' or 'Jones'. However, the name 'Johnson' can clearly be ascertained from the ship's passenger lists that accompany his and Breslin's arrivals and departures in the colony.

26 Devoy, *Recollections of an Irish Rebel*, p. 255.

27 *Freeman's Journal* (Sydney), 24 February 1877, p. 7, https://trove.nla.gov.au/newspaper/article/115375160/12712435

28 *Sunday Times* (Perth), 7 August 1921 p. 17, https://trove.nla.gov.au/newspaper/article/57975318

29 *Sunday Times* (Perth), 7 August 1921 p. 17.

30 *Sunday Times* (Perth), 7 August 1921 p. 17.

31 Pease, *The Catalpa Expedition*, p. 190.

32 *The Herald* (Fremantle), 18 November 1876, p. 3, https://trove.nla.gov.au/newspaper/article/106307720/10126524

33 *The Herald* (Fremantle), 18 November 1876, p. 3.

34 Pease, *The Catalpa Expedition*, p. 99 [Reported Speech].

35 Pease, *The Catalpa Expedition*, p. 99.

36 Pease, *The Catalpa Expedition*, p. 101.

37 Pease, *The Catalpa Expedition*, p. 101.

38 Pease, *The Catalpa Expedition*, p. 102.

39 Fennell and King (eds), *John Devoy's Catalpa Expedition* (2006), p. 116 [Reported Speech].

40 Fennell and King (eds), *John Devoy's Catalpa Expedition* (2006), p. 116 [Reported Speech].

41 Author's note: Over the years there have been many versions of why Kiely was left behind. The most prevalent has been that the others regarded him as informer who had tried to betray them all, during their courts martial back in Ireland. That does not fit, in my view. If that was the case, why, in his 1874 letter to John Devoy, did James Wilson include him as one who should be saved? And why would the British have cast an informer to the outer darkness for what turned out to be the rest of his natural life? Despite Kiely's later assertion that on the day in question he was unable to elude his warder, the most credible reason, I believe, is the one sourced to Elizabeth McCann, stated later, 60 years after the event with no reason to lie.

42 *Sunday Times* (Perth), 8 March 1936, p. 33, https://trove.nla.gov.au/newspaper/article/58764425

43 Fennell and King (eds), *John Devoy's Catalpa Expedition* (2006), p. 116.

44 Fennell and King (eds), *John Devoy's Catalpa Expedition* (2006), p. 86 [Reported Speech].

45 Fennell and King (eds), *John Devoy's Catalpa Expedition* (2006), p. 86.

46 Keneally, *The Great Shame*, p. 563.

47 Pease, *The Catalpa Expedition*, p. 190.

48 Pease, *The Catalpa Expedition*, p. 190.

49 *Sunday Times* (Perth), 8 March 1936, p. 33, https://trove.nla.gov.au/newspaper/article/58764425

50 *Sunday Times* (Perth), 8 March 1936, p. 33.

51 *The Herald* (Fremantle), 18 November 1876, p. 3, https://trove.nla.gov.au/newspaper/article/106307720/10126524

52 Crowley, 'Sir William Cleaver Francis Robinson,' *Australian Dictionary of Biography*, Vol. 6, 1976, http://adb.anu.edu.au/biography/robinson-sir-william-cleaver-francis-4494

53 Robinson, 'Remember Me No More', Wickins & Co, London, https://nla.gov.au/nla.obj-179773646/view?partId=nla.obj-179774310#page/n6/mode/1up

54 *The Bulletin*, 16 December 1882, p. 5, http://nla.gov.au/nla.obj-237816958/

55 *The Bulletin*, 16 December 1882, p. 5.

56 Author's note: There is an anomaly as to the captain of the *Ocean Beauty* during this encounter with the *Catalpa*. The captain of the *Hougoumont* on the final convict voyage to Australia in 1867–68 was a Captain William Cozens. Pease, in *The Catalpa Expedition*, tells of an encounter George Anthony had in the Indian Ocean with the captain of the bark, the *Ocean Beauty*. This captain claimed to have been the master of the *Hougoumont* on the 1867–68 voyage to Fremantle. Philip Fennell, in *John Devoy's Catalpa Expedition*, claims Lloyd's Register lists a 'Pearce' as captain of the *Ocean Beauty* during that encounter. However, in 1876, the *Ocean Beauty* was captained by a James Newman Seagrove. Captain Seagrove had once been master of the convict vessel *Palmerston* which transported convicts to Fremantle in 1861. How the story was skewed to represent this captain as master of the *Hougoumont* during the 1867–68 voyage rests with either Seagrove, Anthony and/or Pease. Shipping reports in later years often spelled Seagrove as 'Seagrave'. Here is the link, to show who was the Master of the *Ocean Beauty* at the time: https://trove.nla.gov.au/newspaper/article/136854579

57 Pease, *The Catalpa Expedition*, p. 103.

58 Pease, *The Catalpa Expedition*, p. 104.

59 Pease, *The Catalpa Expedition*, p. 105.

60 Pease, *The Catalpa Expedition*, p. 106.

Chapter Ten

1 *Freeman's Journal* (Sydney), 24 July 1897, p. 6, https://trove.nla.gov.au/newspaper/article/115471670

2 Fennell and King (eds), *John Devoy's Catalpa Expedition* (2008), pp. 150–1 [Reported Speech].

3 Fennell and King (eds), *John Devoy's Catalpa Expedition* (2008), p. 151.

4 Fennell and King (eds), *John Devoy's Catalpa Expedition* (2008), p. 151 [Reported Speech].

5 Fennell and King (eds), *John Devoy's Catalpa Expedition* (2008), p. 151 [Reported Speech].

6 Fennell and King (eds), *John Devoy's Catalpa Expedition* (2008), p. 151 [Reported Speech].

7 Fennell and King (eds), *John Devoy's Catalpa Expedition* (2008), p. 151 [Reported Speech].

8 Fennell and King (eds), *John Devoy's Catalpa Expedition* (2008), p. 151 [Reported Speech].

9 Fennell and King (eds), *John Devoy's Catalpa Expedition* (2008), p. 151 [Reported Speech].

10 Fennell and King (eds), *John Devoy's Catalpa Expedition* (2008), p. 152 [Reported Speech].

11 Fennell and King (eds), *John Devoy's Catalpa Expedition* (2008), p. 152 [Reported Speech].

12 Cowan, *Mary Tondut: The Woman in the Catalpa's Story*, Richard Cowan, Sydney, 2008, p. 42.

13 *The Herald* (Fremantle), 18 November 1876, p. 3, https://trove.nla.gov.au/newspaper/article/106307720/10126524 [Reported Speech].

14 Barry, *Voices from the Tomb*, National Gaelic Publications, Australind (WA), 2006, p. 118.

15 *The Herald* (Fremantle), 1 April 1876, p. 2, https://trove.nla.gov.au/newspaper/article/109902879

16 Pease, *The Catalpa Expedition*, p. 117 [Reported Speech].

17 Pease, *The Catalpa Expedition*, p. 117.

18 Pease, *The Catalpa Expedition*, p. 117.

19 Pease, *The Catalpa Expedition*, p. 117.

20 Pease, *The Catalpa Expedition*, p. 117.

21 Pease, *The Catalpa Expedition*, p. 117.

22 *The Herald* (Fremantle), 18 November 1876, p. 3, https://trove.nla.gov.au/newspaper/article/106307720/10126524

23 *The Herald* (Fremantle), 18 November 1876, p. 3.

24 *Inquirer and Commercial News* (Perth), 12 April 1876, p. 3, https://trove.nla.gov.au/newspaper/article/66301591

25 *Inquirer and Commercial News* (Perth), 12 April 1876, p. 3.

26 Author's Note: With thanks to William Shakespeare.

27 *The Herald* (Fremantle), 18 November 1876, p. 3, https://trove.nla.gov.au/newspaper/article/106307720/10126524

28 *Inquirer and Commercial News* (Perth), 26 April 1876, p. 3, https://trove.nla.gov.au/newspaper/article/66301659

29 *Western Mail* (Perth), 19 January 1950, p. 14, https://trove.nla.gov.au/newspaper/article/39100163

30 Pease, *The Catalpa Expedition*, p. 123.

31 Pease, *The Catalpa Expedition*, p. 123.

32 Pease, *The Catalpa Expedition*, p. 123.

33 *The Herald* (Fremantle), 18 November 1876, p. 3, https://trove.nla.gov.au/newspaper/article/106307720/10126524 [Reported Speech].

34 *Freeman's Journal* (Sydney), 24 July 1897, p. 6, https://trove.nla.gov.au/newspaper/article/115471670 [Reported Speech].

35 *Freeman's Journal* (Sydney), 24 July 1897, p. 6.

36 Pease, *The Catalpa Expedition*, p. 128.

37 Pease, *The Catalpa Expedition*, p. 129.

38 Pease, *The Catalpa Expedition*, p. 129.

39 Fennell and King (eds), *John Devoy's Catalpa Expedition* (2006), p. 155 [Reported Speech].

40 Pease, *The Catalpa Expedition*, p. 130.

41 Pease, *The Catalpa Expedition*, p. 130.

42 Devoy, *Recollections of an Irish Rebel*, p. 256.

43 Pease, *The Catalpa Expedition*, p. 130.

44 Pease, *The Catalpa Expedition*, p. 130.

45 Pease, *The Catalpa Expedition*, p. 131.

46 Pease, *The Catalpa Expedition*, p. 131.

47 *The Herald* (Fremantle), 18 November 1876, p. 3, https://trove.nla.gov.au/newspaper/article/106307720/10126524

48 *The Herald* (Fremantle), 18 November 1876, p. 3.

49 *Sunday Times* (Perth), 7 August 1921, p. 17, https://trove.nla.gov.au/newspaper/article/57975318 [Tense changed].

50 *Western Australian Times* (Perth), 13 June 1876, p. 2, https://trove.nla.gov.au/newspaper/article/2976137

51 *Western Australian Times* (Perth), 11 April 1876, p. 1, https://trove.nla.gov.au/newspaper/article/2975827

52 Author's note: These are generic commands, consistent with the terminology of the time.

53 Pease, *The Catalpa Expedition*, p. 132.

54 Pease, *The Catalpa Expedition*, p. 133 [Reported Speech. Tenses changed.]

55 Author's note: Given that this is the direction that the whaleboat headed after leaving Rockingham Beach, I can only presume these were the instructions, and this was the reasoning.

56 Pease, *The Catalpa Expedition*, p. 133.

57 Roche, *Life of John Boyle O'Reilly*, p. 162 [Reported Speech].

58 Roche, *Life of John Boyle O'Reilly*, p. 162.

59 Pease, *The Catalpa Expedition*, p. 134.

60 *Sunday Times* (Perth), 7 August 1921 p. 17, https://trove.nla.gov.au/newspaper/article/57975318 [Reported Speech].

61 Pease, *The Catalpa Expedition*, p. 134.

Chapter Eleven

1 Breslin, *The Cruise of the Catalpa*, p. 5.

2 Fennell and King (eds), *John Devoy's Catalpa Expedition* (2006), p. 156.

3 *Western Mail* (Perth), 30 December 1937, p. 13, https://trove.nla.gov.au/newspaper/article/37845539 [Reported Speech].

4 *Western Mail* (Perth), 30 December 1937, p. 13, https://trove.nla.gov.au/newspaper/article/37845539

5 Fennell and King (eds), *John Devoy's Catalpa Expedition* (2006), p. 92.

6 Fennell and King (eds), *John Devoy's Catalpa Expedition* (2006), p. 92.

7 *Western Australian Times* (Perth), 21 April 1876, p. 2, https://trove.nla.gov.au/newspaper/article/2975872 [Reported Speech].

8 Devoy, *Recollections of an Irish Rebel*, p. 256 [Reported Speech].

9 Heseltine, 'The Escape of the Military Fenians from Fremantle Prison' [Reported Speech].

10 *Western Australian Times* (Perth), 21 April 1876, p. 2, https://trove.nla.gov.au/newspaper/article/2975872

11 *Western Australian Times* (Perth), 21 April 1876, p. 2.

12 Devoy, *Recollections of an Irish Rebel*, p. 256 [Reported Speech].

13 Author's note: His recollection, sixty years later, would be four men, but we know it was in fact three men.

14 *West Australian* (Perth), 11 September 1937, p. 7, https://trove.nla.gov.au/newspaper/article/41429151 [Reported Speech].

15 The *Nation* (Ireland), 9 September 1876, p.10.

16 *The Herald* (Fremantle), 18 November 1876, p. 4, https://trove.nla.gov.au/newspaper/article/106307720/10126525

17 *The Herald* (Fremantle), 18 November 1876, p. 4.

18 Author's note: Here I diverge from the narrative in *The Catalpa Expedition* by Pease which tells of a squad of eight troopers arriving on the beach as the whaleboat was heading off-shore. John Breslin's account, written the year of the escape, mentions these troopers, but does not number them. The writer and historian Henrietta Drake-Brockman interviewed Inspector John McKenna in his later years. He gave her a stirring account of the chase, first to Rockingham beach, over the promontory and onto Mandurah. McKenna's account mentions only one trooper accompanying him during that pursuit and that two native trackers were with them on the journey. https://trove.nla.gov.au/newspaper/article/48185450

19 Roche, *Life of John Boyle O'Reilly*, p. 163.

20 Author's note: Despite some contemporary reports listing Bell's Christian name as William, it has been ascertained that the man who rode to Fremantle to raise the alarm of the escape was James Bell, a farmer from Rockingham. Nor was he a former prisoner, but a local farmer.

21 Pease, *The Catalpa Expedition*, p. 143.

22 Pease, *The Catalpa Expedition*, p. 143.

23 Pease, *The Catalpa Expedition*, p. 143.

24 Pease, *The Catalpa Expedition*, p. 143.

25 Pease, *The Catalpa Expedition*, p. 143.

26 Pease, *The Catalpa Expedition*, p. 144. Author's note: John J. Breslin, in his account, names the man to whom he spoke while passing the Rockingham Hotel as 'Somers'. However, it is documented that the proprietor of the Rockingham Arms Hotel in 1876 was a William Summers.

27 *The Herald* (Fremantle), 18 November 1876, p. 4, https://trove.nla.gov.au/newspaper/article/106307720/10126525 [Reported Speech].

28 Author's note: Some contemporary accounts at this point, have the *Georgette* approaching from the north. But, as this article in *The Inquirer and Commerical News* (Perth) pn 26 April 1876 proves, that is not possible, as on 17 April, the *Georgette* was returning from its run to Champion Bay, well to the north of Fremantle: 'PORT OF FREMANTLE. ARRIVED— April. 17. GEORGETTE as., 212 tons, Michael O'Grady, from Champion Bay.' https://trove.nla.gov.au/newspaper/article/66301674 In sum, the *Georgette*, having just returned from Champion Bay, was docked in Fremantle that day, and could not possibly have been south, as reported.

29 Fennell and King (eds), *John Devoy's Catalpa Expedition* (2006), p. 158.

30 Roche, *Life of John Boyle O'Reilly*, p. 163.

31 Pease, *The Catalpa Expedition*, p. 145.

32 Pease, *The Catalpa Expedition*, p. 146.

33 Devoy, *Recollections of an Irish Rebel*, p. 256.

34 *Inquirer and Commercial News* (Perth), 26 April 1876, p. 3, https://trove.nla.gov.au/newspaper/article/66301659 [Reported Speech].

35 *Sunday Times* (Perth), 8 March 1936, p. 33, https://trove.nla.gov.au/newspaper/article/58764425 [Reported Speech].

36 *The Herald* (Fremantle), 18 November 1876, p. 3, https://trove.nla.gov.au/newspaper/article/106307720/10126524

37 *The Herald* (Fremantle), 18 November 1876, p. 4, https://trove.nla.gov.au/newspaper/article/106307720/10126525

38 *The Herald* (Fremantle), 18 November 1876, p. 4.

Chapter Twelve

1 Regan, *Irish Writing*, p. 178.

2 *Smith's Weekly* (Sydney), 28 April 1923, p. 2, https://trove.nla.gov.au/newspaper/article/234287194

3 *West Australian* (Perth), 24 February 1951, p. 17, https://trove.nla.gov.au/newspaper/article/48185450

4 *West Australian* (Perth), 24 February 1951, p. 17.

5 *West Australian* (Perth), 11 September 1937, p. 7, https://trove.nla.gov.au/newspaper/article/41429151

6 Author's note: Contemporary accounts refer to him as Coxswain, which I have altered here, as in modern times that term usually refers to the cox in a rowing boat. Then, it meant the equivalent of a Senior Petty Officer.

7 *West Australian* (Perth), 11 September 1937, p. 7, https://trove.nla.gov.au/newspaper/article/41429151

8 *Sunday Times* (Perth), 7 August 1921 p. 17, https://trove.nla.gov.au/newspaper/article/57975318

9 *Sunday Times* (Perth), 7 August 1921 p. 17 [Reported Speech].

10 *Sunday Times* (Perth), 7 August 1921 p. 17.

11 *Western Mail* (Perth), 6 January 1938, p. 12, https://trove.nla.gov.au/newspaper/article/37845818

12 Author's note: Although Bell reports nine men getting on board, there were in fact ten.

13 *Western Australian Times* (Perth), 21 April 1876, p. 2, https://trove.nla.gov.au/newspaper/article/2975872

14 *Sunday Times* (Perth), 7 August 1921, p. 17, https://trove.nla.gov.au/newspaper/article/57975318

15 *Inquirer and Commercial News* (Perth), 26 April 1876, p. 3, https://trove.nla.gov.au/newspaper/article/66301659 [Reported Speech].

16 *Western Mail* (Perth), 6 January 1938, p. 12, https://trove.nla.gov.au/newspaper/article/37845818

17 *West Australian* (Perth), 29 November 1905 p. 2, https://trove.nla.gov.au/newspaper/article/25529414

18 William Shakespeare, Julius Caesar, Act IV, Scene 3, H. Altemus, Philadelphia, 1890, p. 136.

19 Pease, *The Catalpa Expedition*, p. 148 [Reported Speech].

20 Author's note: These are generic commands, consistent with the terminology of the time.

21 *West Australian* (Perth), 24 February 1951, p. 17, https://trove.nla.gov.au/newspaper/article/48185450

22 Pease, *The Catalpa Expedition*, p. 150 and https://fremantlestuff.info/jetties/index.html

23 *Macleay Chronicle* (NSW), 11 May 1938, p. 7, https://trove.nla.gov.au/newspaper/article/173117640

24 Fennell and King (eds), *John Devoy's Catalpa Expedition* (2006), p. 98.

25 Pease, *The Catalpa Expedition*, p. 152.

26 Quigley's Cartoons, *Catalpa Log*, Part 5 (Tuesday, 18 April 1876), http://www.quigleycartoon.com/?page_id=5471 [Reported Speech].

27 Quigley's Cartoons, *Catalpa Log*, Part 5, [Reported Speech].

28 Quigley's Cartoons, *Catalpa Log*, Part 5, [Reported Speech].

29 Pease, *The Catalpa Expedition*, p. 155.

30 Pease, *The Catalpa Expedition*, p. 155.

31 Pease, *The Catalpa Expedition*, p. 155.

32 *Inquirer and Commercial News* (Perth), 26 April 1876, p. 3, https://trove.nla.gov.au/newspaper/article/66301659

33 *The Herald* (Fremantle), 18 November 1876, p. 4.

34 *Inquirer and Commercial News* (Perth), 26 April 1876, p. 3, [Reported Speech].

35 Pease, *The Catalpa Expedition*, p. 153.

36 Author's note: In this instance, I disagree with the account of Pease, who insisted that there were 'thirty or forty men aboard.' (p. 153) By First Mate Samuel Smith's count, as recorded in the *Catalpa* log, there were no more than ten police on board.

37 Pease, *The Catalpa Expedition*, p. 153 [Tenses changed].

38 Pease, *The Catalpa Expedition*, p. 146.

Chapter Thirteen

1 First published in *Three Street Ballads* in 1957, this version was collected by Russell Ward from Victor Courtney, a journalist for the *Sunday Times*, Perth, Western Australia, who commented, 'I remember in my early days as a cadet hearing a band of old boys in a pub in Fremantle singing this song. It is said that the song became so popular that it was banned by the authority of the day and jail was threatened to anyone caught singing it. It was suggested, too, that the escape was made easy because there was plenty of American gold and some of it was placed in the hands of unscrupulous warders. The incident took place in April 1876.'

2 *The Herald* (Fremantle), 18 November 1876, p. 3, https://trove.nla.gov.au/newspaper/article/106307720/10126524

3 Pease, *The Catalpa Expedition*, p. 154.

4 Pease, *The Catalpa Expedition*, p. 154.

5 Pease, *The Catalpa Expedition*, p. 154. Pease's source was Captain Anthony, and this is clearly the way the good captain remembered the exchange. And yet, equally clearly, the exchange did not take place in the morning. I have, therefore, taken the liberty of altering the quote to reflect what – on the basis of the evidence presented – was actually said.

6 *The Herald* (Fremantle), 22 April 1876, p. 3, https://trove.nla.gov.au/newspaper/article/109902454

7 Roche, *Life of John Boyle O'Reilly*, p. 166.

8 Roche, *Life of John Boyle O'Reilly*, p. 167 [Reported Speech].

9 *The Herald* (Fremantle), 18 November 1876, p. 3.

10 Pease, *The Catalpa Expedition*, p. 155.

11 *Western Mail* (Perth), 6 January 1938, p. 13, https://trove.nla.gov.au/newspaper/article/37845818/4084888

12 *Sunday Times* (Perth), 8 March 1936, p. 33, https://trove.nla.gov.au/newspaper/article/58764425

13 *Sunday Times* (Perth), 8 March 1936, p. 33.

14 Heseltine, 'The Escape of the Military Fenians from Fremantle Prison'.

15 *Inquirer and Commercial News* (Perth), 19 April 1876, p. 3, https://trove.nla.gov.au/newspaper/article/66301843

16 *The Herald* (Fremantle), 18 November 1876, p. 4, https://trove.nla.gov.au/newspaper/article/106307720/10126525

17 *West Australian* (Perth), 11 September 1937, p. 7, https://trove.nla.gov.au/newspaper/article/41429151

18 Author's note: These are generic commands, consistent with the terminology of the time.

19 Pease, *The Catalpa Expedition*, p. 157.

20 *The Herald* (Fremantle), 18 November 1876, p. 4, https://trove.nla.gov.au/newspaper/article/106307720/10126525

21 Pease, *The Catalpa Expedition*, (1897) p. 157.

22 *The Herald* (Fremantle), 18 November 1876, p. 3, https://trove.nla.gov.au/newspaper/article/106307720/10126524

23 *The Herald* (Fremantle), 18 November 1876, p. 3, [Reported Speech].

24 Devoy, *Recollections of an Irish Rebel*, p. 259.

25 Devoy, *Recollections of an Irish Rebel*, p. 259.

26 *West Australian* (Perth), 11 September 1937, p. 7, https://trove.nla.gov.au/newspaper/article/41429151 [Reported Speech].

27 *The Herald* (Fremantle), 18 November 1876, p. 3, https://trove.nla.gov.au/newspaper/article/106307720/10126524

28 Pease, *The Catalpa Expedition*, p. 157.

29 Pease, *The Catalpa Expedition*, p. 157.

30 Pease, *The Catalpa Expedition*, p. 157.

31 *The Herald* (Fremantle), 18 November 1876, p. 4, https://trove.nla.gov.au/newspaper/article/106307720/10126525

32 *Inquirer and Commercial News* (Perth), 26 April 1876, p. 3, https://trove.nla.gov.au/newspaper/article/66301659

33 *Inquirer and Commercial News* (Perth), 26 April 1876, p. 3 [Reported Speech].

34 *The Herald* (Fremantle), 18 November 1876, p. 4.

35 *The Herald* (Fremantle), 18 November 1876, p. 4.

36 *The Herald* (Fremantle), 18 November 1876, p. 3.

37 *The Herald* (Fremantle), 18 November 1876, p. 3.

38 *The Herald* (Fremantle), 18 November 1876, p. 3.

39 *The Herald* (Fremantle), 18 November 1876, p. 4.

40 Pease, *The Catalpa Expedition*, (1897) p. 160.

41 *West Australian* (Perth), 4 October 1909, p. 3, https://trove.nla.gov.au/newspaper/article/26238939 [Reported Speech].

42 *West Australian* (Perth), 4 October 1909, p. 3 [Reported Speech].

43 *The Herald* (Fremantle), 18 November 1876, p. 4.

44 *The Herald* (Fremantle), 18 November 1876, p. 4.

45 *The Herald* (Fremantle), 18 November 1876, p. 4.

46 Author's note: The accounts of John Breslin, James Jeffrey Roche and Zephaniah Pease all name this person as Colonel Edward D. Harvest. Harvest at that time was in command of the Enrolled Pensioner Guard, but he was not on the vessel. The man on board the *Georgette* that day and in command of the Military Pensioner detachment was Major Charles Finnerty. Breslin, having noted Finnerty's uniform, assumed it was Harvest who was communicating.

47 Roche, *Life of John Boyle O'Reilly*, p. 167.

48 *Inquirer and Commercial News* (Perth), 26 April 1876, p. 3, https://trove.nla.gov.au/newspaper/article/66301659

49 *Inquirer and Commercial News* (Perth), 26 April 1876, p. 3.

50 *Inquirer and Commercial News* (Perth), 26 April 1876, p. 3.

51 *Inquirer and Commercial News* (Perth), 26 April 1876, p. 3.

52 *The Herald* (Fremantle), 18 November 1876, p. 4.

53 *The Herald* (Fremantle), 18 November 1876, p. 4.

54 *The Herald* (Fremantle), 22 April 1876, p. 3, https://trove.nla.gov.au/newspaper/article/109902454

55 *The Herald* (Fremantle), 22 April 1876, p. 3.

56 *The Herald* (Fremantle), 22 April 1876, p. 3.

57 *The Herald* (Fremantle), 22 April 1876, p. 3.

58 *Bunbury Herald* (WA), 16 March 1903, p. 3, https://trove.nla.gov.au/newspaper/article/87144094

59 *Bunbury Herald* (WA), 16 March 1903, p. 3, [Reported Speech].

Chapter Fourteen

1 Pease, *The Catalpa Expedition*, p. 204.

2 Breslin, *The Cruise of the Catalpa*, p. 9.

3 Waters, 'The Escape of the Fenians', p. 95.

4 *The Herald* (Fremantle), 22 April 1876, p. 3, https://trove.nla.gov.au/newspaper/article/109902454

5 *The Herald* (Fremantle), 22 April 1876, p. 3.

6 *The Herald* (Fremantle), 7 October 1876, p. 3, https://trove.nla.gov.au/newspaper/article/109902318

7 *The Herald* (Fremantle), 7 October 1876, p. 3.

8 *Inquirer and Commercial News* (Perth), 26 April 1876, p. 3, https://trove.nla.gov.au/newspaper/article/66301659

9 *Western Australian Times* (Perth), 21 April 1876, p. 2, https://trove.nla.gov.au/newspaper/article/2975872

10 Heseltine, 'The Escape of the Military Fenians from Fremantle Prison'.

11 Heseltine, 'The Escape of the Military Fenians from Fremantle Prison'.

12 *South Western Advertiser* (Perth), 20 March 1936, p. 1, https://trove.nla.gov.au/newspaper/article/149594415 and Reid, '"A Noble Whale Ship and Commander" – The *Catalpa* Rescue, April 1876', National Museum of Australia, http://www.nma.gov.au/__data/assets/pdf_file/0015/2553/NMA_Catalpa.pdf

13 *West Australian* (Perth), 11 September 1937, p. 7, https://trove.nla.gov.au/newspaper/article/41429151

14 Sunday Times (Perth), 23 July 1911, p. 21, https://trove.nla.gov.au/newspaper/article/57716688

15 *Sunday Times* (Perth), 23 July 1911, p. 21.

16 *Sunday Times* (Perth), 23 July 1911, p. 21.

17 Breslin, *The Cruise of the Catalpa*, pp. 14–15.
18 Great Britain, Parliament, House of Commons, *The Parliamentary Debates (Hansard): Official Report*, H. M. Stationary Office, London, Vol. 229, cc 1040-52: 1043 (22 May 1876).
19 Heseltine, 'The Escape of the Military Fenians from Fremantle Prison'.
20 Heseltine, 'The Escape of the Military Fenians from Fremantle Prison'.
21 Heseltine, 'The Escape of the Military Fenians from Fremantle Prison'.
22 Heseltine, 'The Escape of the Military Fenians from Fremantle Prison'.
23 Roche, *Life of John Boyle O'Reilly*, p. 159.
24 Pease, *The Catalpa Expedition*, p. 203.
25 Letter from John Boyle O'Reilly to John Devoy, 10 June 1876, MS 18,010/13/6, John Devoy Papers Collection, NLI.
26 Pease, *The Catalpa Expedition*, p. 201.
27 Pease, *The Catalpa Expedition*, p. 192.
28 Pease, *The Catalpa Expedition*, p. 186.
29 Pease, *The Catalpa Expedition*, p. 168.
30 Davis, *The Poems of Thomas Davis*, p. 145.
31 Pease, *The Catalpa Expedition*, p. 165.
32 *Gippsland Times* (VIC), 15 June 1876, p. 3, https://trove.nla.gov.au/newspaper/article/61826083
33 *Gippsland Times* (VIC), 15 June 1876, p. 3.
34 *Inquirer and Commercial News* (Perth), 19 July 1876, p. 3, https://trove.nla.gov.au/newspaper/article/66303243
35 *Advocate* (Melbourne), 21 October 1876, p. 13, https://trove.nla.gov.au/newspaper/article/170433683/20246716
36 Pease, *The Catalpa Expedition*, p. 170.
37 *Western Mail* (Perth), 6 January 1938, p. 13, https://trove.nla.gov.au/newspaper/article/37845818/4084888
    Author's note: According to Pease, it was at 2 am: 'At two o'clock on the morning of August 19, 1876, the Catalpa anchored off Castle Garden.' (Pease, *The Catalpa Expedition*, p. 167).
38 Fennell and King (eds), *John Devoy's Catalpa Expedition* (2006), p. 124.
39 *Freeman's Journal* (Sydney), 21 October 1876, p. 18, https://trove.nla.gov.au/newspaper/article/115302485
40 Pease, *The Catalpa Expedition*, p. 168.
41 Pease, *The Catalpa Expedition*, p. 168.
42 Fennell and King (eds), *John Devoy's Catalpa Expedition* (2006), pp. 125–6.
43 Fennell and King (eds), *John Devoy's Catalpa Expedition* (2006), p. 125.
44 *Freeman's Journal* (Sydney), 21 October 1876, p. 18.
45 *The Nation* (Ireland), 16 September 1876, p. 3.
46 *The Nation* (Ireland), 16 September 1876, p. 3.
47 *The Nation* (Ireland), 16 September 1876, p. 3.
48 *Freeman's Journal* (Sydney), 21 October 1876, p. 18.
49 Pease, *The Catalpa Expedition*, p. 206.
50 Pease, *The Catalpa Expedition*, p. 207.
51 Shakespeare, *As You Like It*, Act II, Scene 7, The Copp Clark Company, Toronto, 1919, pp. 37–38.
52 William Shakespeare, Henry V, Act III, Scene 1, University Society, New York, p. 59.

Epilogue

1 Waters, 'The Escape of the Fenians', 1996–97, *Seanchas Ardmhacha*, pp. 95–6.
2 *West Australian* (Perth), 29 November 1905 p. 2, https://trove.nla.gov.au/newspaper/article/25529414
3 *West Australian* (Perth), 29 November 1905 p. 2.
4 *West Australian* (Perth), 29 November 1905, p. 2.
5 *West Australian* (Perth), 29 November 1905, p. 2.
6 Barry, *Voices from the Tomb*, p. 143.
7 *Catholic Press* (Sydney), 30 November 1905, p. 4.
8 Barry, *Voices from the Tomb*, p. 47.

9 *West Australian* (Perth), 29 November 1905, p. 2.

10 *West Australian* (Perth), 29 November 1905, p. 2.

11 *West Australian* (Perth), 29 November 1905, p. 2.

12 *West Australian* (Perth), 29 November 1905, p. 2.

13 *Advocate* (Melbourne), 20 January 1877, p. 5, https://trove.nla.gov.au/newspaper/article/170434621/20240280

14 *Advocate* (Melbourne), 20 January 1877, p. 5.

15 Pease, *The Catalpa Expedition*, p. 194.

16 Deed of gift. James Ryan family collection. New Bedford Massachusetts.

17 Joy Lefroy and Mike Lefroy, *Catalpa Escape*, Freemantle Press, WA, 2016

18 *West Australian* (Perth), 9 October 1895, p. 6, https://trove.nla.gov.au/newspaper/article/4542968

19 *West Australian* (Perth), 9 October 1895, p. 6.

20 *West Australian* (Perth), 9 October 1895, p. 6.

21 *West Australian* (Perth), 9 October 1895, p. 6.

22 *Freeman's Journal* (Sydney), 19 October 1895, p. 7, https://trove.nla.gov.au/newspaper/article/111111352

23 James Ryan family collection.

24 The *Telegraph* (Brisbane) Friday 10 February 1888, p. 3, https://trove.nla.gov.au/newspaper/article/176700123

25 *New York Times*, 21 November 1887, timesmachine.nytimes.com/timesmachine/1887/11/21/106187987.pdf

26 *New York Times*, 21 November 1887.

27 New York Times, 19 November 1887, https://timesmachine.nytimes.com/timesmachine/1887/11/19/106187675.pdf

28 Cowan, *Mary Tondut: The Woman in the Catalpa Story*, p. 2.

29 Roche, *Life of John Boyle O'Reilly*, pp. 172–3.

30 *West Australian* (Perth), 9 October 1895, p. 6.

31 Author's Note: Much of this information about John Breslin and Mary Tondut comes from research by one of Mary's descendants, Richard Cowan, in his book: *Mary Tondut: The Woman in the Catalpa Story*, Richard Cowan, Sydney, 2008.

32 Cowan, *Mary Tondut: The Woman in the Catalpa Story*, pp. 11–12.

33 *Police Gazette* (WA), No. 10, 3 May 1876, p. 39, https://slwa.wa.gov.au/sites/default/files/187605_m.pdf

34 Letter from John Boyle O'Reilly to Matthew Skinner Smith (Superintendent of Police), 11 September 1876, Peter Murphy's family collection.

35 Roche, *Life of John Boyle O'Reilly*, p. 47

36 *New York Times*, 14 August 1890, https://timesmachine.nytimes.com/timesmachine/1890/08/14/103258823.pdf

37 *Western Mail* (Perth), 6 January 1938, p. 13, https://trove.nla.gov.au/newspaper/article/37845818/4084888

38 The American Presidency Project, John F. Kennedy, Statement of the President on St. Patrick's Day, 17 March 1962, https://www.presidency.ucsb.edu/documents/statement-the-president-st-patricks-day

39 U2, 'The Edge' about their song 'Van Diemen's Land' (*New Musical Express*, 1988), https://www.atu2.com/lyrics/songinfo.src?SID=454

40 The Catholic Press (Sydney), 8 September 1910, p. 7, https://trove.nla.gov.au/newspaper/article/104993701

41 *Freeman's Journal* (Dublin), 30 March 1901, p. 5.

42 *Gympie Times and Mary River Mining Gazette* (QLD), 26 September 1911, p. 3, https://trove.nla.gov.au/newspaper/article/190883527

43 Crawley, *Australian Dictionary of Biography*, Vol 6, 1976, 'Sir William Cleaver Francis Robinson (1834–1897)', http://adb.anu.edu.au/biography/robinson-sir-william-cleaver-francis-4494

44 *West Australian* (Perth), 13 September 1887, p. 3, https://trove.nla.gov.au/newspaper/article/3758089

45 Heseltine, 'The Escape of the Military Fenians from Fremantle Prison', [Reported Speech].

46 *The Inquirer and Commercial News* (Perth) Wednesday 16 May 1877 p. 2.

47 *Leader* (Melbourne), 2 June 1877, p. 2, https://trove.nla.gov.au/newspaper/article/197414673

48 *The Irish Times*, 1 August 2015, https://www.irishtimes.com/culture/heritage/o-donovan-rossa-remembered-100-years-after-funeral-1.2304698

49 *The Irish Times*, 31 July 2015, https://www.irishtimes.com/news/ireland/irish-news/the-irish-times-report-on-o-donovan-rossa-s-funeral-in-1915-1.2303691

50 Smith, *Britain and Ireland: From Home Rule to Independence*, Routledge, New York, 2013, p. 117.

51 Smith, *Britain and Ireland*, p. 117.

52 Smith, *Britain and Ireland*, p. 117.

53 Author unknown, *James Stephens: Chief Organizer of the Irish Republic*, p. 10.

54 *Boston Irish Reporter*, 1 March 2016, https://www.bostonirish.com/history/%E2%80%98-name-known-all-friends-irish-freedom%E2%80%99-day-when-de-valera-hailed-new-bedford-sea-

55 *Boston Irish Reporter*, 1 March 2016.

56 *Boston Irish Reporter*, 1 March 2016.

57 Leonard, '"English dogs" or "poor devils"?: the dead of Bloody Sunday morning' in Fitzpatrick, David (Ed.) *Terror in Ireland 1916-1923*, Lilliput Press, Dublin, 2012, p. 135.

58 *Catholic Press* (Sydney), 11 September 1924, p. 5, https://trove.nla.gov.au/newspaper/article/121868562 [Reported Speech].

59 *Catholic Press* (Sydney), 11 September 1924, p. 5.

60 Durney, Corrigan, Curran (eds), *A Forgotten Hero, John Devoy*, John Devoy Memorial Committee, 2009, p. 22 http://www.kildare2016.ie/wp-content/uploads/2016/03/John_Devoy_Book.pdf

61 Durney, Corrigan, Curran (eds), *A Forgotten Hero, John Devoy*, p. 22.

62 Letter from John Devoy to Mary Curley, 4 February 1927, Seamus Curran family collection, County Kildare. [Reported speech].

63 Durney, Corrigan, Curran (eds), *A Forgotten Hero, John Devoy*, p. 30, [Reported Speech].

64 Durney, Corrigan, Curran (eds), *A Forgotten Hero, John Devoy*, p. 30. [Reported Speech].

65 Letter from John Devoy to Mary Curley, 1 January 1926, Seamus Curran family collection, County Kildare.

66 Letter from John Devoy to Mary Curley, 1927, Seamus Curran family collection, County Kildare. [Exact date unknown].

67 Letter from John Devoy to Mary Curley, 1927 [Exact date unknown].

68 Letter from John Devoy to Mary Curley, 1 January 1926.

69 Letter from John Devoy to Mary Curley, 4 February 1927, Seamus Curran family collection, County Kildare.

70 Letter from John Devoy to Mary Curley, 4 February 1927.

71 Letter from John Devoy to Mary Curley, 1927. [Exact date unknown].

72 Letter from John Devoy to Mary Curley, 8 January 1925, Seamus Curran family collection, County Kildare.

73 Golway, *Irish Rebel: John Devoy and America's Fight for Irish Freedom*, Merrion Press, Kildare, 2015, p. 301.

74 Golway, *Irish Rebel: John Devoy and America's Fight for Irish Freedom*, p. 301.

75 Golway, *Irish Rebel: John Devoy and America's Fight for Irish Freedom*, 2015, p. 301.

76 Letter from John Devoy to Mary Curley, 4 February 1927.

77 Letter from John Devoy to Mary Curley, 1927. [Exact date unknown].

78 Durney, Corrigan, Curran (eds), *A Forgotten Hero, John Devoy*.

INDEX

Aboriginal people 102, 119
Abraham, Patrick 90
Aher, Jeremiah 90
Albert, Henry 250, 252, 253, 270
Allison, David 90
American Fenians xxxviii, xli, 3, 8, 43–4,
    141–4, 148–50, 153, 157
  attempted invasion of Canada 141–4
  O'Reilly's view 153–4
Anthony, Captain George xiii, xix, 168–250,
    295–316, 323, 328–9, 344–7
  arrival back in America 332–5, 338
  biography 361
  Catalpa captain 174–250, 295–8, 304–16,
    323, 328–9
  death 347
  Fremantle 228–34
  Fremantle breakout 265, 266–71, 282–93,
    326
  O'Reilly praising 337
  subsequent career 344–7
Anthony, Emma 171, 176, 177, 179, 182,
    234, 334, 344, 347, 361
Anthony, Sophie 171, 176, 177, 182, 234,
    334
Australian Fenians 193, 194

Baker, Captain Anthony 109, 115, 116,
    119–21, 125
Baker, Colonel Valentine 35, 46
Barkly, Sir Henry 132, 133, 134
Barry, Charles QC 17
Bates, Major-General John 42
Bell, James 266–7, 270, 271, 274–6
Beranger, Pierre-Jean de xxxv
Big Louis (sailor) 294, 298
'Bloody Sunday' 362

Bolles, George 178
Bombay 139
Booler, Thomas xxi, 257, 260, 263, 264,
    322, 325, 356
Boston Music Hall fundraiser 338
Boston *Pilot* 141, 144, 152, 165, 319, 326,
    338, 349, 351
Bowman, Martin 124–6, 133–5
Brennan, Thomas 178–9, 185, 195, 228–9,
    243, 252, 267, 297, 324, 333
Breslin, John xvii, 22–5, 27, 52–3, 59,
    347–50
  arrival back in America 332, 336, 347
  Australian son 350
  background xvii
  Catalpa 296, 297, 304, 306–16, 319,
    323–4, 329
  death and funeral 348
  escape to America 53
  Fremantle (as Collins) 197–211, 216,
    224–50
  Fremantle breakout 255, 261–72, 286,
    297, 326
  Fremantle breakout plan 183–6, 189–211,
    224–50
  Irish Nation newspaper 348
  O'Reilly praising 348, 349
  poems/songs 319, 323
  Stephens' escape 22–5, 183, 189, 193,
    241, 324, 349
  subsequent career 347–9
  travelling to WA 191–4
Breslin, Pat 59
Broomhall, James 256, 260
Brosnan, Theresa 348, 349
Bunbury 99–106
Burt, Sir Archibald 263, 299

Byrne, Daniel 22, 23, 25, 27
Byrne, James 36
Byrne, Miles xxxv

Carnarvon, Lord 209–10, 213, 235, 240,
    305, 321
Carraher, Francis 142
Carroll, Dr William 332
Casey, John 79, 85
Cashman, Denis 62–3, 65, 75–9, 82, 83, 106,
    130, 166
Castlereagh, Lord xxvi
Catalpa 174–90, 194–6, 201–6, 213–16,
    220, 221–7, 344–6
    arrival in America 332–8
    Bunbury 221–7, 235–7, 264
    crew deserting 194–5
    escapees rowing to 273–94
    purchase and fitting out 174–6
    pursuit by Georgette 295–318
    sale of 344
    voyage back to US 323–4, 328–9
    whaling 186–90, 204
Chase, Amy 178, 282, 335
Clan-na-Gael 150, 154, 159, 161–5, 173,
    178, 183–5, 190, 194, 229, 324, 332–4,
    345, 348, 358
Cleveland, Grover 352
Cobbett, William xxvii
Cody, Michael 76, 79, 194
Collins, Michael 359, 360
Conflict, HMS 230, 237, 265, 279
Cosgrave, William 360, 363, 366
Cozens, Captain William 72, 79, 86
Craggs, Elizabeth 207
Craggs, Fred 201, 207
Cranston, Robert 'Big Bob' xviii, 36, 48, 66,
    357
    America 345, 357
    background xviii
    death 357
    Fremantle breakout 257–64, 279, 325,
        356
    Fremantle Prison 91, 131, 151, 164, 198,
        204, 208, 243, 254
    grave 362
Cromien, Denis 29
Cromwell, Oliver xxiv, xxv
Crowley, Peter 59, 60
Cuban Five 149, 150

Curley, Mary 366, 367
Curran, Peter 31, 33, 150, 154–5

Darragh, Thomas xviii, xl, xlii, 66, 357
    America 333, 345, 357
    background xviii
    court martial 42–3
    death 357
    Fremantle breakout 256, 260, 261, 264,
        276, 300, 325
    Fremantle Prison 91, 93, 95, 107, 131,
        151, 164, 191, 198, 208, 232, 254
    grave 362
Davis, Thomas 201
De Valera, Éamon 359–61
Deasy, Captain Timothy 62
Delaney, Father Bernard 71, 79, 81
Delaney, Thomas xix, 32, 52, 161, 209,
    254–5, 342
Denieffe, Joseph xxxvii, 29
Desmond, Thomas xvii, 189, 190, 192, 193,
    197–9, 230–3, 240, 249, 252, 253, 255
    background xvii
    Fremantle, 197–9, 230–3, 240, 249, 252,
        253
    Fremantle breakout 255, 261–71, 293,
        297
Devoy, John 9–14, 21, 25, 30–6, 45, 47, 55,
    59, 61 358, 362–8
    America 148–86, 325–7, 331, 332, 333,
        344, 346, 348
    arrest 35–6
    background xvii, xxix, xxxix
    Chatham Prison 105–6, 127–9, 147
    Clan-na-Gael 154, 159, 161–5, 173, 183,
        346, 358
    death and funeral 368
    Fremantle breakout plan 157–86, 192,
        325, 337
    IRB xxxix–xlii, 1–2, 9–14
    memoirs 367
    New York Herald 153, 156, 179, 327, 334
    O'Reilly praising 337, 349
    pardon 147–8, 154
    return to Ireland 362–8
    subsequent career 358–9
    trial 55–6
Dillon, John Blake xxxii
Dillon, Luke 345
Disraeli, Benjamin 324–5, 327

Doheny, Michael xxxiv, xxxv, xxxviii
Donnelly, General John 143
Doonan, Harriet 263, 305, 330, 356
Doonan, Joseph xx, 88–9, 92, 93, 96, 114, 117, 203
    aftermath of breakout 325, 330
    Fremantle breakout 263, 264, 276–7, 281, 301, 305
    subsequent career 356
    suicide attempt 330, 356
Downing, McCarthy 103
Duggan, Denis xviii, 25, 36, 57–8, 79
    background xviii
    Catalpa 178–9, 185, 194–6, 202, 323, 324
    Hougoumont, on 79
Dumas, Alexander xxxv
Dunne, Thomas 67

Easter Rising 359–60
The Edge 353
Emmet, Robert 338
The Establishment *see* Fremantle Prison

Farnham, Antoine 178, 221
Fauntleroy, William xx, 191, 199, 208, 210, 213, 235, 240
    aftermath of breakout 320, 321, 325, 326, 341–2
    Fremantle breakout, 256, 260, 278, 301, 302, 305
    subsequent career 355
Fenians
    American xxxviii, xli, 3, 8, 43–4, 141–4, 148–50, 153, 157
    amnesty for 103, 130, 146–7, 159, 324
    anthem 1
    arrests 6–8
    Australian 193, 194
    British press view 8
    convicts xviii, 63–84, 130
    courts martial 41–64
    emissaries in Fremantle xvii
    Fenian Cavalry Unit 32
    Fenianism xli
    Flood as leader 38, 60, 75
    leaders xvii, xxiii
    petition for amnesty 103
    recruiting members xxxvii–xl, 45
    shooting Prince Alfred 98–9, 204
    Special Commission 9, 27–8

Stephens as leader xvii, xxxvi–xli, 4, 6–9, 15–27, 37
The Irish People newspaper xxxix, xli, 3, 6, 7, 15, 193
The Rising xxvi, xxxiv, xxxviii, xli, 3–17, 28, 44, 54–62, 129
transportation of convicts 63–84
Fennell, Thomas 57, 61, 65–74, 85
    America 157–86
    Fremantle breakout plan 157–86, 192, 325
    Fremantle Prison 85, 87, 88, 91, 94, 107
    Hougoumont, on 65, 66, 68–70, 72, 74
    release from prison 151
Fernicough, Isaac 90
Finnerty, Major Charles xx, 87, 227, 280, 290, 292, 299, 302–20, 323, 356
5th Dragoon Guards xl, 1, 11, 12, 31–4
    deserters from xviii, xix, 31–2, 34, 47, 54, 71
FitzGerald, Desmond 363
Fitzgerald, John David 9, 27
Fitzgerald, John E. 338
FitzGerald, Michael 45
Fitzgerald, Rose 352
Flood, John xix, 29–30, 37–8, 60, 61, 355
    background xix
    death 355
    Hougoumont, on 75–81, 83
    leader of Fenians 38, 60, 75
    release from prison 151
    subsequent career 355
    trial 61
Foley, Patrick 32, 33, 36, 47–9, 54, 351, 362
Foley, William xviii, 11, 30, 32, 33, 36, 40, 52, 82, 131–2, 145–6
    America 328, 332, 339
    arrest 36
    background xviii
    death and funeral 343–4
    Fremantle breakout plan 200–3, 207, 328
    Hougoumont, on 82
    leaving for America 211
    release from prison 131–2, 145
    trial 40
Foster, General George 142, 143
Fremantle 86, 95–6, 198
Fremantle Prison 86–99, 130, 150–1, 198
    aftermath of breakout 319–20
    breakout 252–72

Fremantle Prison (continued)
  civilian Fenians released from 130, 151
  Fenians at 86–99
  Inquiry into breakout 325–6
  planning breakout 157–250
  warders sympathetic to Fenians 201
Fremantle Water Police xxi, 127, 249, 275,
    279
  pursuing *Catalpa* 279–80, 290, 293–8,
    302, 306–17
French, Daniel Chester 352
Fulham, Lawrence and Luke 67, 130, 145

Gazelle 122–7, 132–8, 350
Georgette 197–8, 227–30, 255, 268, 320
  pursuing *Catalpa* 279–80, 287–92,
    299–318
Gifford, Captain David 123, 124, 125, 135,
    138, 350
Giles, Ernest 199
Gladstone, Sir William 106, 130, 146, 159
Goff, John 162, 169, 184, 185

Hampton, Dr John 96, 212
Harrington, Michael xviii, 36, 55, 66, 357
  background xviii
  death 357
  Fremantle breakout 256–64, 276, 356
  Fremantle Prison 93, 131, 151, 164, 198,
    204, 208, 254
  grave 361
Hassett, Thomas xix, xl, 14–15, 30–1, 34,
    66, 357
  America 335, 337, 357
  arrest 34
  background xix
  branding 54
  court martial 48, 52
  death 357
  desertion from Dragoon Guards xix, 30–1,
    34
  Fremantle breakout 256, 260–1, 264, 325
  Fremantle Prison 131, 153, 164, 198, 208,
    209, 254
  grave 361
  solo escape from prison 144–5, 151–3,
    337
Hathaway, Henry xx, 122–38, 166–9,
    173–6, 335, 337, 338, 344, 353, 361
  background xx

City Marshal of New Bedford 331, 335
  Fremantle breakout plan 166–9, 173–6,
    331
  Gazelle 122–38, 176
Hill, Cyrus 189, 206, 237
Hogan, Martin xix, xl, xlii, 10, 12, 31–5, 40,
    47, 66, 82, 128, 357
  America 345, 357
  arrest 34–5
  background xix
  branding 53–4
  court martial 48–9, 52
  death 357
  desertion from Dragoon Guards xix, 31,
    34, 47
  Fremantle breakout 256, 260–3, 276
  Fremantle Prison 91, 93, 107, 128, 131,
    151, 154–6, 164, 165, 198, 208,
    220–1, 254
  grave 361
  letter to Curran 155–6, 159, 165
Holland, John 348
Homes, Oliver Wendell 350
Hope, Lieutenant Edward 142
Hopper, Jane xxxiv, xxxix, 16, 354
Hougoumont convict ship 68–86, 194, 214
  concerts 75–8
  conditions 72–5
  Wild Goose newspaper 79–81, 83, 100
Howell, Nathaniel 231
Howland, Captain Walter 205, 206
Hussey, Frederick 136

Irish Civil War 362
Irish diaspora xxx, xxxviii, 154
The Irish People newspaper xxxix, xli, 3, 6,
    7, 15, 193
Irish Potato Famine xxix–xxxi
Irish Republican Army 362
Irish Republican Brotherhood *see also*
    Fenians
  formation xxxvi
  Military Council 360
  recruiting members xxxvii–xl, 45
  Stephens as leader xvii, xxxvi–xli, 4, 6–9,
    15–27, 37
  The Rising xxvi, xxxiv, xxxviii, xli, 3–17,
    28, 44, 54–62

Jackson, Thomas 114, 117–19, 125

Jenkinson, Sir George 159
Jordan, Captain 139
Joyce, Dr Robert 60

Keating, Patrick xix, 32, 33, 52, 71, 76, 82, 151, 160–1
Kelly, Edward 59, 60, 61, 79–81, 151, 192–4
Kelly, John see Talbot, Thomas
Kelly, Thomas 9, 19, 21, 25, 29, 37, 55, 56, 62
Kenneally, John 76, 157
Kennedy, John F. 352–3
Kenny, Eliza 12–13, 21, 34, 56, 61, 147, 150, 181–2, 358–9, 364–7
Keogh, William 9, 27
Kiely, James xix, 5, 48, 66, 151, 164, 198
  aftermath of breakout 341–3
  left out of escape plot 208–9, 212, 281
  Royal Pardon 342, 343
Kilmurry, Thomas 359, 365
King, John 8, 193, 194, 217–19, 230, 233, 244, 252, 253, 256, 262, 268, 270, 297
Knockadoon 60, 79, 192

Lake, Colonel Henry 15, 16
Lalor, Fintan xxxi–xxxiii
Lefroy, Anthony 322
Lennon, Captain Patrick 57–9, 333
Lewis (sailor) 247, 298
Liddelow, Albert xxi, 260, 262–4, 325
Lindsey, Francis xx, 94, 150–1, 257, 260, 262–4, 325, 326
Lombard, Eugene 107
Lombard (sailor) 247, 298
Luby, Thomas Clarke xix, xxxvi, xli, 6, 7, 27, 32
Lynch, Billy 259, 274–5, 279, 280, 285, 300, 303, 305
Lynch, Winifred 300, 305

MacManus, Terence Bellew xxxiv, xxxviii, 358
Maguire, Big Jim 107–9, 112, 115, 117, 118, 121, 124–6
Mahon, Patrick 162
Mahony, Con 79
Manning, Sir William 98
McCabe, Father Patrick xx, 105, 107–8, 112, 123, 124, 126, 154–6, 159, 191, 200
McCafferty, Captain John 32–3, 49, 60, 155

McCann, Elizabeth 211–12, 241, 242, 300, 301
McCann, Michael Joseph 1
McCarthy, Dennis 219, 251, 253, 329–30
McCarty, Joseph 237
McClure, Captain John 59, 60
McKenna, 'Big John' 204, 231, 265, 271, 273–4, 283, 286, 301
McMahon, James 201
McNally, Séamus see Wilson, James
Meagher, Thomas Francis xxxii
Meehan, Patrick 3, 4
Military Pensioners 275–80, 302–10, 317
Mills, William 275, 278, 293, 296, 297, 303
Mitchel, John xxxi, xxxii, 32, 163
Mopsy (sailor) 247, 294, 298
Moriarty, William 112, 113, 124–6
Murphy (prisoner) 50, 52

Nagle, Pierce 3–4, 7, 18, 27–8, 54, 160
New York 140–1, 152
New York Herald 153, 156, 166, 327, 334
Noonan 79

Ocean Beauty 213–14
O'Connor, Daniel xxviii
O'Curry, Eugene xxxix
O'Donnell, Red Hugh 1
O'Grady, Captain Michael 229, 280–1, 290, 299, 306, 308, 313–15
O'Leary, John 6
O'Mahony, John xxxiv, xxxv, xxxviii, xl, xli, 3, 55
O'Neill, General John 142, 143
O'Reilly, Eliza 19, 49, 78, 104
O'Reilly, John Boyle xviii, 10–14, 19–20, 32–52, 63–144, 151, 301, 350–3
  Aboriginal people and 102, 119
  America 140–4, 153, 157–9, 335
  arrest 35
  Boston Pilot 141–4, 152, 165, 319, 326, 349, 351
  Bunbury 99–109
  court martial 44–51
  death and funeral 352
  escape from Bunbury 107–27, 236
  Fremantle breakout plan 157–8, 163, 166, 189, 191
  Fremantle Prison 85, 89, 90, 97, 99
  Gazelle, on 125–7, 132–8

O'Reilly, John Boyle (continued)
  Hougoumont, on 65–84
  memorials to 352
  Moondyne (novel) 351
  New Bedford speech 335–8
  poetry 50, 52, 71, 75, 76, 78, 80, 83, 99,
    101, 350, 352–3
  prison 39, 49–50, 65
  Rodrigues Island escape 132–6
  saving tree 101, 352
  subsequent career 350–2
O'Reilly, Mary 158
O'Reilly, William 19, 49, 78, 101
Orridge, John 98

Passmore, Harry 191, 232, 300, 303
Pearse, Padraig 359, 360
Pease, Zephaniah xiii
Perry, Catherine 129
Philpots, Henry 25
Platina 205
Potato Famine xxix–xxxi
Prince Alfred 98–9, 204
Purton, Edward 103

Reynolds, James xxx, 162, 169, 173, 175,
  344
Richards, Alvah 142
Richardson, John 169, 173, 174, 178, 181,
  334, 344
Richmond Bridewell Prison 19, 21
  Stephens' escape from 21–7, 37
The Rising xxvi, xxxiv, xxxviii, xli, 3–17, 28,
  44, 54–62, 129
Roach, Mary Ann 342
Robinson, Sir William xx, 212–13, 227, 230,
  234, 235, 240
  aftermath of breakout 320–2, 325, 326,
    342
  Fremantle breakout 278, 279, 300, 301,
    305, 318
  subsequent career 355
Rodrigues Island 132–6
Rose, General Sir Hugh 9, 11, 30, 36, 82,
  146
Rossa, Jeremiah O'Donovan xxxviii, 106,
  148, 155, 332, 333, 348
Rowe, Private John 142
Ryan, Daniel 4, 6, 15, 16
Ryan, Michael 346

Sapphire 138, 139
Sawyer, Colonel 44, 46
Seagrove, Captain James 213
Seiders, Captain 138
Sheehan (Fenian) 76
Smith, Samuel xx, 177–8
  Catalpa first mate 177–8, 181, 187, 190,
    196–7, 215, 227, 228, 236, 237,
    245–7, 334–5
  Fremantle breakout 265, 281–98, 304,
    306, 313
Smith O'Brien, William xxxii, xxxiv, 1
Soule, John 133, 138
Stephens, James xvii, xxxiii–xli, 4–9, 15–27,
  37, 43–4, 54, 354–5
  arrest 15–16
  background xvii, xxxiii–xxxvii
  death and funeral 354–5
  escape from Ireland 37
  escape from prison 21–7
  failure of Rising, blamed for 62
  IRB leader xvii, xxxvi–xli, 4, 6–9, 15–27,
    354
  reception in America 43–4
  subsequent career 354
  trial 17–19
Stone, John xxi, 127, 249–50, 275, 290–2,
  299, 302, 306, 309–17
Stronge, Magistrate John 17, 18
Summers, William 268
Swift, Jonathan xxiii, xxvii, xxviii
Sylvia, Mr 247, 294, 295, 298

Talbot, John 162
Talbot, Thomas 5, 6, 47–9, 54, 156, 208,
  362
10th Hussars 10–11, 32, 35, 45, 46
Thomas, Harry 350
Timperley, William 116
Toby (sailor) 247, 282, 294, 298
Tondut, John Joseph 350
Tondut, Mary 199, 211, 219–20, 250,
  349–50
Tone, Wolfe xxvi, xxvii, 354
traitors 27, 34–6, 47–9, 54
transportation of Fenian convicts 63–84
Trevelyan, Charles xxx, xxxi
Twain, Mark 350

United Irish Brotherhood 185

Vigilant 109, 113–16, 119–21, 127
Vinegar Hill, Battle of xxvi, 64

Wakeford, Governor Henry 92, 96
Wall, Patrick 106–7
Walsh, John 219, 251, 253, 329–30
Weldon, Captain Nicholas 37
Whelan, Captain Fergus 39, 44, 47
Whitman, Walt 140
Wild Goose 79–81, 83, 100
Wilde, Oscar 351
Wilmott, John 57
Wilson, James xviii, xxx, xl, xlii, 12, 31,
    33–5, 40, 47, 152, 360–1
  America 339, 360–1
  arrest 34–5
  background xviii
  branding 54

court martial 48–9, 52
de Valera's visit 360–1
death 361
desertion from Dragoon Guards xviii, 31,
    34, 47
Fremantle breakout 256–64, 356
Fremantle Prison 91, 107, 126, 128, 131,
    146, 151, 157–65, 198, 201–3,
    207–11, 226, 232, 242, 244, 254
grave 361
Hougoumont, on 66, 82
letters to Devoy 159–60, 164–5
looking after Keating 160–1
Woodman, Henry 102

Yeats, W.B. 41, 157, 351, 362
Young Ireland movement xxxi, xxxiii, xxxiv

PETER FITZSIMONS is Australia's bestselling non-fiction writer, and for the past 30 years has also been a journalist and columnist with the *Sydney Morning Herald* and the *Sun-Herald*. He is the author of a number of highly successful books, including *Mutiny on the Bounty, Burke and Wills, Monash's Masterpiece, Kokoda, Ned Kelly* and *Gallipoli*, as well as biographies of such notable Australians as Sir Douglas Mawson, Nancy Wake and Nick Farr-Jones. His passion is to tell Australian stories, our own stories: of great men and women, of stirring events in our history.

Peter grew up on a farm north of Sydney, went to boarding school in Sydney and attended Sydney University. An ex-Wallaby, he also lived for several years in rural France and Italy, playing rugby for regional clubs. He and his wife Lisa Wilkinson – journalist, magazine editor and television presenter – have three children; they live in Sydney. Peter is Chair of the Australian Republic Movement.